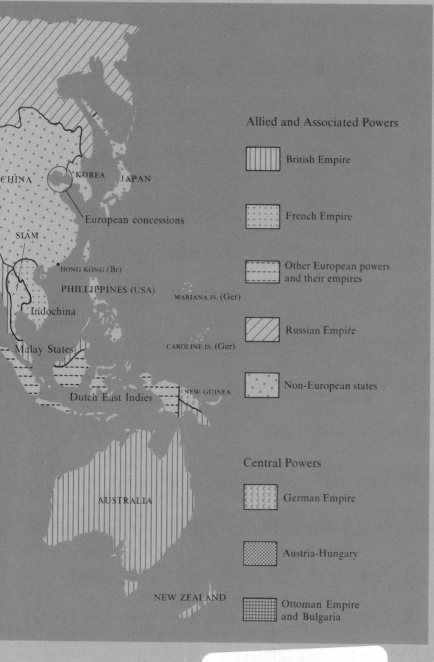

CHINA KOREA JAPAN

European concessions

SIAM

HONG KONG (Br)

PHILLIPPINES (USA)

MARIANA IS. (Ger)

Indochina

CAROLINE IS. (Ger)

Malay States

Dutch East Indies NEW GUINEA

AUSTRALIA

NEW ZEALAND

Allied and Associated Powers

British Empire

French Empire

Other European powers
and their empires

Russian Empire

Non-European states

Central Powers

German Empire

Austria-Hungary

Ottoman Empire
and Bulgaria

D0915913

Nations in Conflict

NATIONS IN CONFLICT

NATIONAL GROWTH
AND INTERNATIONAL VIOLENCE

Nazli Choucri

Massachusetts Institute of Technology

Robert C. North

Stanford University

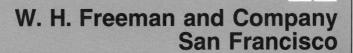

W. H. Freeman and Company
San Francisco

Maps drawn by Judi McCarty, 1974

Library of Congress Cataloging in Publication Data

Choucri, Nazli.
 Nations in conflict.

 Bibliography: p. 339
 Includes index.
 1. International relations—Research.   2. Peace—Research.
I. North, Robert Carver, joint author.   II. Title
JX1291.C48   327   74-23453
ISBN 0-7167-0773-X

Printed in the United States of America

10 9 8 7 6 5 4 2 1

To Hayward R. Alker, Jr.

Contents

Epilog

Appendix

Bibliography

Index

Maps

Tables

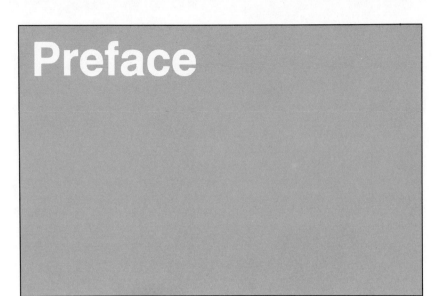
Preface

The investigation reported in this book began as a study of the roots of World War I, particularly the long-range considerations that made war in 1914 highly probable. As we examined the historical material in greater depth and detail it became increasingly apparent that the international dynamics leading to WWI were not unique, but that they were illustrative of interaction among all major powers and the struggle for domination and control. It became apparent also that the "causes" of war in 1914 were not historically unique, that there were many analogies and similarities with other wars in other times and places.

These realizations gradually forced us to shift the focus of our study from the specifics of WWI to the broader framework of nations in conflict. World War I is thus one particular illustration of the dynamics of conflict and warfare, and of the role of national growth and expansion in predisposing nations toward violence. We believe that the long-range tendencies toward war are of a generic nature, and that it is possible through careful systematic analysis to identify them and determine the extent to which they condition and constrain short-term, day-to-day behavior, particularly in crisis situations.

We are indebted to many colleagues, students, and research assistants at Stanford University, Massachusetts Institute of Technology, and elsewhere. Without their ideas, assistance, and helpful criticism this volume and the research behind it would not have been completed or even begun. The works of the late Ludwig von Bertalanffy, Erwin Schrödinger, and Quincy Wright provided us with crucial ideas and perspectives about human beings and their planet that largely inspired this whole undertaking.

Beginning with the earliest stages of our investigation we received invaluable suggestions and criticisms from Edward Azar, Richard Lagerstrom, Raymond Tanter, and J. David Singer. Richard Snyder read the initial draft of our manuscript and gave us many pages of precise, carefully reasoned criticisms and suggestions. The writers are also indebted in fundamental ways to Davis Bobrow, Kenneth Boulding, Richard Brody, John Burton, Karl Deutsch, Heinz Eulau, Harold Fisher, Johan Galtung, Harold Guetzkow, Morton Kaplan, Charles McClelland, Ronald McKinnon, Thomas Milburn, David Munford, A. F. K. Organski, Charles Osgood, Raymond Platig, Volker Rittberger, Richard Rosecrance, James Rosenau, Easton Rothwell, Rudolph Rummell, Bruce Russett, Wilbur Schramm, Melvin Small, Paul Smoker, Peter Temin, Clarence Thurber, Richard Ullman, and Dina Zinnes.

Data-gathering tends to be a slow, painstaking, often frustrating task. Jean Heflin, David Corey, and John Brooks compiled the initial time-series data that was the basis for our early experimentations with quantitative historical analysis. For their willingness, persistence, and dedication we are particularly grateful to Clydia Cuykendall, Randall Fields, Orlene Fingar, Kathleen Foote, Jonathan Medalia, Michael Milburn, Peter Milburn, Woesha Hampson, David Lebling, Susan Newcomer, Elizabeth North, John Shippee, Brenda Williamson, and Denise Wilson. We are indebted also to Ajaj Jarrouge and Michael Mihalka for testing and retesting some of our basic propositions.

The entire data set was subsequently revised, recompiled, rechecked and re-rechecked by Raisa Deber at M.I.T. Her hard work and precision have been essential to the development of the second series of historical data that is the basis for the analysis reported here. In addition to computer assistance and methodological collaboration, Mrs. Deber's skillful editing greatly enhanced the text.

Douglas Hibbs, Jay Kadane, and William C. Mitchell gave priceless assistance and advice on methodological problems. Linda Fields supervised the manuscript through several drafts — revising, organizing, and tightening. And, finally, Howard Beckman, of W. H. Freeman and Company, a most sensitive, talented, and relentless taskmaster, inspired, guided, drove, and gently coerced us through three more revisions — and a kind of transformation.

But it is to the scholar and friend to whom this book is dedicated that we owe the greatest debt of all. At every stage of our investigation Hayward Alker has challenged our assumptions and procedures and has forced us to confront difficult, sometimes insurmountable, methodological and theoretical problems. Like a stern conscience, whenever we thought that what we had done was "good enough," he pressed us to "try one more run." However, much as we would like him to share accountability for errors of omission or commission, we alone are wholly responsible for both the quantitative and historical investigations.

Early phases of our study were supported by the Ford Foundation, the Office of Naval Research, and the Advanced Research Projects Agency; later aspects were undertaken with grants from the National Science Foundation. We are also indebted to the Stern Family Fund for seminal funding in the development of computer applications to problems of conflict and integration. It goes without saying that none of these sources of support is in any way responsible for our concepts, methods, or conclusions.

All quantitative analyses were undertaken on TROLL/1, an interactive computer system for econometric analysis, model-building, and simulation. We are grateful to Edwin Kuh, the TROLL Project director, for allowing us access to the system during early phases of its implementation on IBM 360/67. The staff of the TROLL Project has been particularly helpful in assisting us with data analysis and in supervising our work at various stages. We would like to thank Walt Maling, Jonathan Shane, Alexis Sarris, and Mark Eisner for their patience and perseverance in the face of continuous calls for assistance.

Finally, we would like to thank Mrs. Helen Grace for typing many drafts of this manuscript and for her infinite patience and good nature.

This book is in four parts. Parts I and the Epilog were the joint efforts of the authors. Robert North wrote the historical narrative in Part II, and Nazli Choucri the quantitative analysis in Part III. We both have revised the entire manuscript and, needless to say, share responsibility for the book as a whole.

October, 1974

Nazli Choucri
Cambridge, Massachusetts

Robert C. North
Stanford, California

Nations in Conflict

Introduction

Some of the more important causes of war are rooted in the processes of national growth: a substantially growing state is thus likely to generate expansion, competition, rivalry, conflict, and violence. Growth can be a lethal process. Despite proclamations of nonintervention or even genuinely peaceful intentions, a growing state tends to expand its activities and interests outward—colliding with the spheres of interest of other states—and find itself embroiled in international conflicts, crises, and wars that, at least initially, may not have been sought or even contemplated. The more a state grows, and thus the greater its capabilities, the more likely it is to follow such a tendency. These are serious charges to make, especially in view of the fact that most countries today seem committed to policies of accelerated growth. If war is to be avoided, however, protestations of peaceful intentions are not enough. This book presents the reasoning behind these assertions, together with supporting or qualifying evidence from the period, 1870–1914.

International conflict and war have been accounted for in many ways—in terms of aggressive "instincts," territoriality, population expansion, defense of trade routes, plunder, profit, and imperialism, among others. Some theorists have defined the causes of war in terms of the perceptions, expectations, anxieties, fears or psychopathological deviation of national leaders. Others have emphasized power struggles, arms races, competition for strategic advantage, and struggles for colonial dominance. Although we may admit that all of these factors are relevant, they do not amount to a theory of war—all factors need to be pulled together in some systematic way. The causes of war are highly interrelated; the problem is to find out which factors at any given time in history have contributed most to international violence, how, and in what proportion. The task is to present a conceptual framework within which many more factors may be placed and others linked systematically.

The purpose of our study is to examine some of the factors and processes leading to wars between great powers. We have used World War I as a test case. We do not deal here with conflict in general, but only with those conflicts that themselves involve several great powers and yield very high casualties. Nor are we concerned with the specific events triggering war, but with the long-range processes leading to conflict and violence. Although colonial wars have a place in our theory, we are not directly concerned with them here. In other words, we do not deal directly with hostilities resulting from the attempt of a stronger country to establish or maintain control over a colonial territory, or, similarly, to establish or protect its interests in a vastly weaker country or region.

The evidence presented in this and two other books suggests to us that many ordinary social activities may combine to create the conditions for war, and that states and empires in pursuit of seemingly legitimate interests often lock themselves into escalating competition, rivalry, and antagonism—disentanglement from which may be exceedingly difficult short of war. We do not see in this conclusion a justification for armed conflict. We do conclude, however, that the probability of war will not be significantly lowered by good will alone, by deterrence strategy, by balance-of-terror diplomacy, or by minor adjustments in the international system, such as detente, partial limitation of armaments, or the removal of troops from "sensitive" areas.

We have used three main sources in our study: monographs and other standard historical studies; demographic, economic, political, and military data from statistical series; and data on interactions between countries from published chronologies. The hypotheses presented in Chapter 1 are derived from a broad review of history and a survey of the causes of war put forward by scholars of different disciplines and in a variety of sources.

Our idea of *historical process* derives from the observation that there are patterns, repetitions, and close analogies in the record of human affairs. We proceed from the assumption that most countries resort to war in certain broadly similar situations. Our study focuses on the historical process that helped destroy the European major-power system of the nineteenth and early twentieth centuries. That is, we have attempted to identify those elements and forces that precipitated WWI. To accomplish such a difficult undertaking we have identified long-range trends over a 45-year period (1870–1914) by applying econometric techniques over time and across countries to a variety of aggregate data and to interactions among major powers. Our investigation has uncovered an extensive interdependency among certain variables: growth, expansion, competition, conflict of national interests, alliance, and violence. Moreover, we found that several combinations of these variables and different "paths of causalty" led to similar outcomes.

Computer simulations predicted broad social and political trends up to 1914, using coefficient estimates of the variables. The difference between these predictions and actual history was then measured (Chapter 17 reports the successes and failures of these simulations). Finally, we arbitrarily altered the coefficients of the variables—as if different values and goals had prevailed before 1914—to find out how different policies would have affected subsequent events. This exercise also provided a partial check on the theory being tested. Later in this book (Chapter 18) we shall summarize our findings and discuss their implications for policy analysis. We shall consider how projections can be made into the real future and how sensitivity analysis (the systematic alteration of coefficients for the variables) can be developed into an instrument for policy-makers.

In Part I we identify some important theoretical problems, present the conceptual background and theory, and offer a number of general propositions for testing, analysis, possible modification, or even rejection. In Parts II and III we seek to uncover—in different ways—how countries expanded their national interests, what happened when these interests collided with the interests of other states, to what degree nations compared their military and other capabilities with those of countries they viewed as rivals, and to what extent national leaders were influenced by differences between the resources and capabilities of their own country and those of other countries.

Part II draws from the writings of historians, the memoirs of national leaders, and archives. There we interpret the historical developments during this period in accordance with our conceptual framework. We show that the major elements of our theory of international violence have already been identified but not linked together systematically. We relate this theory to other, more conventional, explanations, and demonstrate some of the ways in which national attributes and actions relate to political decisions.

In Part III we analyze the complex processes that led to WWI, investigating the interdependency of national attributes, capabilities, and actions. Although specific findings in Part III may challenge some of our hypotheses, they will certainly shed light on the historical narrative in Part II. In Part IV we provide a critical assessment of our findings and identify some paradoxes associated with national growth and international violence.

A companion volume to this book, *International Crisis: The Outbreak of World War I,*[1] presents a day-by-day (even hour-by-hour)

---

[1]Nomikos and North, 1975.

narrative of events between the assassination of the Archduke Francis Ferdinand and the outbreak of war. Another companion volume, *Crisis, Escalation and War*,[2] quantitatively analyzes the perceptions and interaction of the great powers during the summer of 1914.

Yet our interests go beyond the summer of 1914, or even the forty-odd years before then—our concerns are more fundamental, more universal, probably more controversial. We believe that WWI was not an isolated conflict, but part of a continued struggle and competition among world powers. We also believe that although the details are different, the same dynamics of growth and competition operate today. It is our hope that the model presented here will be refined and tested for a great many other historical situations.

Among the causes of WWI, historians have cited "the Russian or the German mobilization; the Austrian ultimatum; the Sarajevo assassination; the aims and ambitions of the Kaiser, Poincaré, Izvolsky, Berchtold, and others; the desire of France to recover Alsace-Lorraine or of Austria to dominate the Balkans; the European system of alliance; the activities of the munition-makers, the international bankers or diplomats; the lack of an adequate political order; armament rivalries; colonial rivalries; commercial policies, the sentiment of nationality; the concept of sovereignty; the struggle for existence; the tendency of nations to expand; the unequal distribution of population, of resources, or of planes of living; the law of diminishing returns; the value of wars as an instrument of national solidarity or as an instrument of national policy; ethnocentricism or group egotism; the failure of the human spirit; and many others."[3]

Which is the "true" cause? Where does the truth lie?

The difference of opinion is due not so much to the use of different historical documents by one or another scholar, nor to the events chosen for emphasis, but to the quite different assumptions that investigators bring to the problem—to conflicting views of how people interact, how the behavior of one person affects that of another, how individuals affect their societies and vice versa, and to what extent human affairs are affected by conditions of the physical environment.

Historians, philosophers, and social scientists have used a variety of approaches in seeking to explain warfare. To date, however, none of these has proved wholly satisfactory. The difficulties include the severe problem of establishing final causes—especially in human affairs. Can we ever finally know why human beings act as they do? Is it possible to discover final causes in history? Many otherwise careful scholars will deny the possibility of a single cause, and then go on to

---

[2]Ole Holsti, 1971.
[3]Wright, 1965, pp. 727–728.

find evidence in support of what they call a "motive," and finally infer causality from the motive.

Some social scientists accept the premise that ". . . since war represents aggressive behavior on the part of nation-states, one can understand its causes by examining the determinants of behavior in individuals."[4] Although there is undoubtedly much evidence to recommend this assumption, those who hold to such a belief tend to overlook or at least oversimplify the fact that the behavior of nation-states is an outcome of the behavior of many individuals in different roles, pursuing different ends, representing different interests, bringing quite different amounts of influence to bear on final decisions, and "contributing in very different ways to the complex social processes" that lead to war.[5]

Other social scientists treat war as "a form of [national] deviation comparable to psychotic behavior in individuals."[6] Yet throughout much of history war has been viewed as perfectly normal and justifiable; societies that have not made frequent use of armed force have been considered "deviant."

The idea of a "mad leader" or "sick society" is closely related to the idea of "national psychotic deviation." George III, Jefferson Davis, Wilhelm II, Hitler, Tojo, and, more recently, Franklin Roosevelt, Lyndon Johnson, Richard Nixon, and Ho Chi-minh have all been regarded by one observer or another as "mad." How, in a more or less democratic society, does a "mad" leader succeed in achieving power and attracting support for his "insane" schemes?

Many people have the naive belief that if the people of the world could only come to "know" and "understand" each other, through travel and cultural exchanges for example, they would no longer be predisposed to fight among themselves. This view overlooks the frequency (and often sanguine nature) of family feuds, revolutions, civil wars, and dynastic quarrels. There is ample evidence to support the conclusion that familiarity may invite warfare as well as contempt.[7]

Some observers believe that international trade "damps down" antagonisms; Anglo-German trade, however, had reached a peak just prior to the outbreak of WWI. Some writers, distinguishing between political systems and their "potential" for war, consider democracies peaceful and authoritarian states warlike. Yet both types of state become involved in wars. Marxist-Leninists hold that war will disappear with the eradication of capitalism and imperialism — yet the USSR and

---

[4]Kelman, 1965, p. 5.

[5]*Ibid.*, pp. 5–6.

[6]*Ibid.*, p. 6.

[7]It is worth noting that in 1914 four monarchs — Nicholas II of Russia, Wilhelm II of Germany, George V of England, and Leopold II of Belgium — were kinsmen. Moreover, there had been "cultural exchange" among some of these nations for centuries.

the People's Republic of China have been on the verge of violent conflict a number of times. The opposite view is that Communism is the major obstacle to world peace.

War is often traced to nationalism. The difficulty is, however, that the word "nationalism" has different meanings in different contexts — the ambiguities are extensive. Religion is often offered as an antidote to war — despite the record of bitter struggles between Christianity and Islam, between Protestants and Catholics, the Crusades, and other "holy wars."

These are only a few views on the causes of war. Indeed, there have been so many that we cannot list all of them here, let alone discuss them. Although no one view is sufficient, none is entirely irrelevant.

We believe that recent developments in social-science theory and, more generally, in the research tools available to all scholars, make it possible for investigators to identify interactions among large numbers of variables and thus to clarify some of the dimensions of the problem of causality.

We have not sought to improve on the historical accounts of a period that has been ably investigated by such distinguished historians as Sidney B. Fay and Luigi Albertini. Instead, our purpose has been to examine the history of this period to see the extent to which international violence can be explained in terms of processes involving national growth and competition between nations. Our investigation has not proceeded from newly available documents, but has used readily available materials in new ways; ours is a novel approach to the study of war.

Some controversy has broken out in recent years over the writings of Fritz Fischer and other scholars. Much of this controversy centers on the old issue of responsibility — of culpability — specifically, the degree to which German leaders may have deliberately triggered WWI. In his introduction to Fischer's book, *Germany's Aims in the First World War*, Hajo Holborn takes note of Fischer's belief that highly placed civilians in the German government were "in deep sympathy with the general intent to fight the war" in order to make their country a world power equal to Britain and Russia.[8] Undoubtedly, German leaders were acutely self-conscious of the world status of their country, compared with that of Britain, Russia, and France. Indeed, they seemed determined to make Germany a first-rank power, says Fischer.

Fischer goes considerably further, however. According to James Joll, Fischer "links the development of German war aims during the war with the general climate of opinion among Germany's rulers in the years before the war and shows how the hopes of annexing territory on both Germany's western and eastern frontiers were the logical

---

[8]Fischer, 1967, p. xi.

results of ideas which had been widely discussed for some years before 1914. . . ."[9] In a later work Fischer further documents his thesis that between 1911 and 1914 German leaders decided that a war was necessary, undertook preparations for it, and chose the summer of 1914 because they thought that the situation would then be favorable for them.[10]

Is this view legitimate? Was the war the planned outcome of prewar German ambitions, or were the Germans merely reacting to world events? To Immanuel Geiss it is obvious that "all evils in recent German history were of German making, and that we cannot blame others for it."[11] At the same time, Geiss introduces other factors into the calculus of events: the preceding decades of imperialism, the principle of self-determination, Germany's self-proclaimed role as the great bulwark against revolution and democracy, and the German ambition to attain the status of a world power.[12] In sum, according to Geiss, war became "inevitable" as a result of German *Weltpolitik*, the containment policy of the Entente, and Germany's refusal to be contained.[13] Yet if this combination brought about the war, how can we conclude that "all evils in recent German history were of German making?"

Other scholars have taken sharp issue with Fischer's thesis. In the view of Laurence Lafore, statesmen and soldiers can "reasonably enough" be held responsible for WWI, but this responsibility was not due to any single man or nation. Rather, it "inhered in the offices and institutions, in the system of European states and its shortcomings."[14] Thus, in all the nations involved in WWI "statesmen, like soldiers, obeyed the imperatives of their offices in a system of competing and frightened national states."[15]

According to Joachim Remak, what is wrong with Fischer's thesis (and, in general, with allegations of German responsibility for the war) is that this view "involves a certain amount of confusion between Germany's aims as they developed during the war and Germany's intentions in July 1914."[16] An even more fundamental difficulty is that "it depends for its effect on Germany's actions in isolation." Remak concludes that "Germany indeed wished to be a great power, and why not? The concept of a German Samoa was no more absurd than that of a British Bahamas or a Belgian Congo."[17]

---

[9]Introduction, Fischer, 1967, pp. xviii.
[10]Fischer, 1969, Chapters 18 and 19.
[11]Geiss, 1967, p. 375.
[12]*Ibid.*, pp. 15–17.
[13]*Ibid.*, p. 35.
[14]Lafore, 1965, p. 23.
[15]*Ibid.*
[16]Remak, 1967, p. 138.
[17]*Ibid.*, p. 138.

Lafore concludes that anyone reading Fischer's *Germany's Aims in the First World War* "must admit that the Germans were, at least, frivolously willing to contemplate the possibility of a 'preventive war' and were exploiting the occasion for a 'grab at world power.'" Yet they "were by no means the only people who were prepared to risk a war and who had expansionist programs on their minds."[18] And Remak notes that "in the mountain of documents on the origin of World War I we search in vain for any that will show us that the statesmen of Germany or of any other nation (with the possible exception of Servia) went to war in 1914 for the sake of their later war aims."[19]

It has been widely recognized that the roots of any modern war can be traced far back in time. "Though it is now possible, in a single volume, to treat in detail and somewhat definitively the immediate cause of [World War I]," writes Sidney B. Fay, "this is by no means true in the case of the underlying causes. These are so complex and reach so far back into the past that any attempt to describe them adequately would involve nothing less than the writing of the whole diplomatic history of Europe since 1870, or rather since 1789; since questions go back to the age of Louis XIV, and even to that of Charlemagne."[20] Indeed, almost any prior event can be said to have a bearing, in which case a vast array of events are possible as major or minor causes. But in this study we are concerned with processes — especially the interaction effects of population growth and advances in technology, the development of military and other capabilities that affect a country's power, and patterns of international behavior. We do not focus on discrete events.

The objection can be raised, of course, that to accept *processes* as causes assumes an element of determinism in history; wars are then considered "inevitable." However, processes (when viewed retrospectively) include large numbers of decisions that, had they been made differently, might have altered the course of events in important ways. Thus, our investigation has proceeded from the premise that, like all events, war is best understood as an outcome of an immense number of "small" decisions and their consequences. Our concern is with the "traces" of these decisions: population levels, technological development, military spending levels, national alliances, and so forth.

We are impressed by the perseverance of individual and social habit structures, institutions, and by the tendency of these to resist change. We believe that persistent behavior patterns — for example, many of those associated with cooperation, organization, conflict, and violence — make certain outcomes *highly probable*. The possibility re-

---

[18]Lafore, 1965, p. 22.
[19]Remak, 1967, p. 139.
[20]Fay, 1966, pp. 32–33.

mains, however, that human beings may learn to alter their behavior and thus bring about quite different social outcomes.

The evidence is strong that large populations, and comparatively high levels of technology, high rates of population growth, and high rates of technological development (in various combinations) dispose countries to behave in certain ways and not in others. Warfare may be the most powerful instance of perseverent human behavior. In many (if not most) societies of any considerable size warfare seems to have functioned as a "normal" activity, indeed, as an important institution for the resolution of certain conflicts. It appears that war is extremely difficult for man to renounce.

We are interested in finding out whether fluctuation in the level of violence among the great powers in the period 1870–1914 can be accounted for by changes in specific variables, such as population, technology, trade, military expenditures, colonial territory, and alliances. Depending on the question to be answered, any one of these may be treated as an independent or dependent variable. Do population and technology affect international violence directly? If not, do they affect the level of military expenditures or colonial territory; if they do, then do either military expenditures or colonial territory affect the level of violence?

Our goal is to be able to identify certain trends within a great-power system, not to predict discrete events, such as the outbreak of war. We are concerned, rather, with *changes in the system*, changes that are conducive to crisis and war.

Therefore, we have not tried to link the long-range trends *directly* with such events as the assassination of Francis Ferdinand, the Russian mobilization, or the outbreak of WWI itself. The dynamics on which our study has focused—the dynamics of national growth and expansion, the conflict of national interests, patterns of growth in military expenditures, alliance-formation, and violence-behavior—were not the immediate cause of WWI. These processes set the stage, armed the players, and deployed the forces, but they did not join the antagonists in combat. They created the conditions of an armed camp within which the assassination of the Austrian archduke was sufficient to trigger an international crisis and a major war.

The objection might be raised that we have paid insufficient attention to individual leaders, the exercise of conscious political will, and the national values and goals that shape a country's policies. Many of the assumptions, expectations, predilections, anxieties, and fears of particular national leaders are touched on in Part II. We shall see in Chapter 6 how Lloyd George insisted that Britain retain unassailable supremacy of her navy and how the Kaiser, rationalizing German military and naval strength, thought that the struggle between Germans and Slavs could not be avoided, only delayed. (In view of the relative weakness of reactive factors in arms races in our statistical analysis, the extent to which national leaders prior to WWI spoke of the fear of "falling behind" or failing to "catch up" is remarkable.)

In Part I we draw a distinction between *professed* and *operational* values and goals. We consider our data (the traces left by discrete human decisions) to be indicators of operational values and goals — those values and goals that were acted on in contrast with those that may have been professed but not acted on. We also discuss some of the ways in which the behavior of a nation is the outcome of diverse motivations and decisions.

We are not minimizing the usefulness of analyzing professed political values and goals or the decision-making process. On the contrary, elsewhere we have reported on our own study of official papers for the weeks immediately preceding war in 1914.[21] However, our analysis of aggregate data and interactions among major powers allows us to draw numerous inferences about operational values and goals. Although our general conclusions in this study accord with those drawn by scholars using different methods of study, nevertheless there may be important inferences to be drawn from statistical analysis that cannot be drawn from traditional scholarship.

This work is certain to be controversial, if only because it cuts to the heart of a sensitive issue: the relative merits, defects, respectability, and usefulness of the "traditional" and the "social-scientific" approaches to international relations. To a large extent, these two approaches may be viewed as alternate, or even better, mutually supportive efforts at comprehending reality. Quantitative analysis of historical dynamics is a complex undertaking. This was evident from the start, but after more than a decade of painful trial-and-error learning and qualified successes, the pitfalls and challenges are more evident than ever. One objective of this book is to help reconcile the traditional and social-scientific approaches on the assumption that progress lies ". . . not in rejecting one . . . and . . . favoring the other, but in rendering each the servant of the other."[22]

We are aware of the limitations of this study. To begin with, the dangers of generalizing from a single case are unmistakable. However persuasive limited findings may be, one must continually remind oneself that these might be modified or even eventually rejected. Moreover, this investigation has been constrained by time, resources, and our own skills and ingenuity. Almost certainly, if we had known at the beginning certain of the things we now know, we would have proceeded somewhat differently. Nevertheless, we are optimistic and

---

[21]Nomikos and North, 1975; and Ole Holsti, 1971.
[22]Knorr and Rosenau, 1969, p. 3.

expect that our initial investigations will be vastly improved on in the future.

One further caveat. In examining the processes of national growth and international violence, we are not advocating any particular political or economic position. Although we allow ourselves to make a few speculative suggestions in the epilog to this volume, this book as a whole is not concerned with what *ought* to be.

Part I

1

Conceptual Framework

The purpose of this chapter is to present the conceptual framework within which we have analyzed the policies and actions contributing to war. In general there seem to be at least three major processes that generate conflict and warfare among nations: domestic growth and the external expansion of interests; competition for resources, markets, superiority in arms, and strategic advantage; and the dynamics of crisis.[1]

One of our problems has been to avoid essentially linear causal assumptions—we are interested in dynamic relationships, in which feedback mechanisms are continuously in play. We believe that among great powers the fundamental processes, even allowing for variations in detail, mode, and style of behavior, are universal enough not to be affected themselves by modes, styles, or most events.

By themselves, some of the propositions put forward in this chapter may seem self-evident; it is only when they are considered together that the implications for international conflict and war become fully apparent. We do not believe that war is in any sense inevitable, but our findings do suggest that the tap roots of large-scale violence reach far down into the basic structure of societies and are shaped by human population, technology, and access to resources.

Because individuals are the ultimate source of all increases in population, all advances in knowledge and skills, all social, political, and economic change, and therefore of the behavior of nations, the individual is our basic unit of analysis. All the variables in this study are aggregations of what individual humans have done. (Nevertheless, individuals and the society of which they are a part are intensely inter-

---

[1]Nomikos and North, 1975; Ole Holsti, 1971; Hermann, 1963, p. 64; and Hermann, 1969; see also C. McClelland, 1965, p. 60, for an extensive analysis of the dynamics of crisis.

active. What the individual does or does not do affects the conditions and dispositions of the state, and the conditions and dispositions of the state affect the attitudes and behavior of individuals.)

Man is critically dependent on his physical environment. As biological organisms, humans have certain basic needs, namely, air, food, water, and territory. *In a growing population there will be an increasing demand for basic resources.* In addition to plants and animals required for food, human beings acquire other, harder-to-get resources; the technology of this acquisition brings about both environmental and social changes. A society that can produce electronic computers is likely to be organized quite differently than a society in which steam engines represent the highest level of technology, and even more differently than societies with only crude hand tools. Advances in technology tend not only to increase the range and amount of resources available to a society, but to influence individual and social behavior as well.[2]

Advances in technology often lead to a greater concentration of population.[3] Moreover, historically, the denser the population and the higher the level of technology, the greater is the division and institutionalization of labor.[4] Bureaucratization seems to develop with increases in both the levels and density of population and the advancement of technology.[5]

The more advanced the level of technology in a society, the greater will be the kinds and quantity of resources needed by society to sustain that technology and advance it further. At the same time, demands are likely to increase as technology alters a society's perception of its "needs." Each new level of technology influences manufacturing, transportation, and communication, creating social change and thus new economic and political institutions. Advances in technology, when combined with increases in population, often contribute to the dilemma of rising demands and insufficient domestic resources.[6]

A society (especially one with a growing population) with insufficient resources within its own territory will be seriously constrained in its activities unless it finds some way of acquiring the resources it demands. Whether and how a society reaches for resources beyond its sovereignty is conditioned by location, level of population, level of technology, and the resources, technology, needs, power, and friendliness of neighboring states.[7]

---

[2]However, technology does not substitute for resources. Sprout and Sprout, 1968b, p. 21.

[3]See MacIver, 1947, p. 300, for some of the ways population may be related to social values and practices.

[4]Durkheim, 1933, p. 195.

[5]See Weber, 1968, III: 987.

[6]Sprout and Sprout, 1968a, p. 661; Service, 1962; Farb, 1968; and Campbell, 1969.

[7]See Hawley, 1965, p. 39 for a discussion of the crowding of living forms upon limited resources.

Overall, the entire history of man has been characterized by growth — that is, by larger populations, more advanced technologies, the ability to employ larger amounts of energy for human purposes, and the tendency to demand larger amounts and a wider range of resources and finished products — all requiring more complex modes of governance.

One function of governments is to articulate priorities and to establish these by influencing the allocation of technology, resources, and labor and thus shape national capabilities. Examples of capabilities are agriculture, the skills and implements of trade, the techniques and capital for sophisticated finance, light industry, heavy industry, specific enterprises such as the manufacture of chemicals or textiles, and naval and military establishments. Governments directly influence these allocations through the spending of public monies and through tax policy, and indirectly through, for example, wage and price controls, rationing of commodities, and restrictions on imports and exports.[8]

Ordinarily, natural resources, capital, labor, and technology are limited, so that choices have to be made with respect to the development of national capabilities. These choices reveal the actual or operational, in contrast to the professed, values of a society. Often, the choices become institutionalized and difficult to alter in any significant way. Moreover, they are reinforced insofar as existing capabilities determine what other capabilities can be developed to meet growing demands.

When demands are unmet and existing capabilities are insufficient to satisfy them, new capabilities may have to be developed. But a society can develop particular capabilities (including resources) *only if it has the necessary existing capabilities to do so.* Moreover, if national capabilities cannot be attained at a reasonable cost within national boundaries, they may be sought beyond. Any activity — selling wheat, buying oil, investing capital, increasing the labor force, or moving troops — takes on new meaning once it is extended into foreign territory. We use the term *lateral pressure* to refer to the process of foreign expansion of any activity.

There are three aspects of this process that must be distinguished: (1) the *disposition* to extend activities beyond national boundaries; (2) the particular *activities* that result from the disposition to act; and (3) the *impact* that these activities have on the people of another country and their environment. When we discuss lateral pressure in this study we shall be explicitly concerned with the *measurable ac-*

---

[8]See Sprout and Sprout, 1968a, p. 687.

tivities of this process — although the other two aspects should be kept in mind.

Lateral pressure can be manifested in many different types of activity, depending on the nature of the demands that are not being satisfied domestically and on the capabilities that are available. Lateral pressure is not likely to be expressed unless both demands and capabilities are above some threshold. A society may demand particular commodities that are unavailable domestically, but be wholly lacking in the capabilities — the capital, the credit, the commercial institutions, the shipping facilities, and so forth — required to obtain those commodities. In such a case the demand for those commodities will not generate lateral pressure. On the other hand, a society may demand certain commodities (cotton and rubber, for example) that are unavailable domestically *and* have the capabilities for acquiring them. In this case the combination of demand and capabilities will create the *predisposition* to reach beyond national boundaries to satisfy demands. Now there are two major possibilities. The predisposition may be acted on — the desired resources are acquired — or the country may be prevented from doing so by another state. Thus, if a country demanding resources also lacks the naval or military capabilities necessary to overcome resistance by another country, the *predisposition* for lateral pressure will not be acted on.

Virtually any mode in which lateral pressure is expressed — commercial activities, dispatch of troops into foreign territory, establishment of naval or military bases, acquisition of colonial territory, even missionary activities — may contribute to international conflict and violence. Obviously, however, some activities are more likely than others to lead to violence. Moreover, international differences in the extent and intensity of lateral pressure contribute substantially to international conflict.

Conceivably, a country generating many demands and possessing capabilities appropriate for pursuing activities abroad may "turn inward." It may not require any great amount of resources from beyond its borders; it may use new techniques to uncover hitherto inaccessible resources or find new uses for its resources; it may locate sufficient capital investment fields at home; it may not require foreign markets for its goods; or it may eschew international competition for power, prestige, and status. It would be difficult, however, to identify modern, industrialized countries that do not manifest strong, extensive lateral pressure in some form.

Lateral pressure may be expressed in many types of activities other than those associated with the search for raw materials, markets, or living space. During the great period of world exploration in the sixteenth century, some Europeans were as interested in finding Christians as spices; others wanted military or naval bases, or simply adventure. Nevertheless, Christianization was ordinarily undertaken by societies that were equally interested in spices (or some other product) and, more importantly, were able to build ships and mount large expeditions. Today, as well as during the nineteenth century, business has often "gone abroad" for cheaper labor and resources, new markets and fresh opportunities for investment. As in the sixteenth century, today's foreign commerce may also be connected with a desire for national security, status, prestige, or military advantage. Lateral pressure can therefore be the outcome of both public (or national) and private aims.

For some supporters of colonial policies in nineteenth-century Europe the "policy of colonial expansion was undoubtedly good business."[9] For others, a strong colonial policy was a patriotic ideal, the "pride of standing in the front rank of the nations which were shaping the world of the future, the delight in ruling and the excitement of competing with foreign rivals. . . ."[10] In either case, a policy of growth and expansion was difficult to reverse, once undertaken. National growth can generate a strong demand for greater growth and thus create ever higher demands for resources. Surpluses of such resources as labor and capital generate demands for further research and development, exploration, investment and other enterprise and growth.

The disposition toward foreign activity is not always sound economically. A nation's foreign policy may encourage foreign activities solely for national prestige. Foreign activities may be profitable only so long as the government, often at a huge cost to the taxpayer, protects trade routes and maintains a secure environment for overseas enterprises.

An industrialized country with strong military capabilities may extend its activities into (and even establish domination over) a country with a much larger population that generates comparatively higher demands, but which has a less advanced technology and lower level of industrialization. For example, although the population of India was larger than that of Britain, England enjoyed a considerable advantage over India by virtue of a difference in technological efficiency.

After the Renaissance a relatively few European countries (and, more recently, the United States and Japan) were able to extend their interests throughout the world. This expansion of interests was so widespread and long-lasting that it became institutionalized through

---

[9]Brunschwig, 1966, p. 104.
[10]*Ibid.*

colonies, protectorates, lease-holds, unequal alliances, client-state arrangements, and exploitative trade. Many white men thus inferred that they were innately superior, and were preordained to preside over and exploit societies with lower capability.

Although lateral pressure encompasses some of the propositions about imperialism put forward by J. A. Hobson, V. I. Lenin, and others, the two concepts are not synonymous. The demands of a capitalist economy may contribute to lateral pressure in important ways, but capitalism is not a necessary condition for lateral pressure; both pre-capitalist and socialist societies may generate lateral pressure. Similarly, although class conflict may contribute to lateral pressure, it is not a necessary condition.

As a nation or empire extends its activities, and hence its interests, the feeling may develop among the leaders of such a state or the citizenry or both, that these "national interests" ought to be protected. National interests tend to be intensely subjective among those who define and proclaim them, so that it is often extremely difficult to predict which interests are likely to be defended by arms. The critical factor in determining the importance to a nation of an interest is not the kind of interest, but the existence of the feeling that the interest must be defended (and then the intensity of this feeling, measured by the social costs that a nation is willing to incur in the defense of this interest).

The protection of national interests in far off places may lead to war between colonial powers and their subject populations, or to attempts at attracting, equipping, and financing local power elites benefiting from foreign control. During the late nineteenth and early twentieth centuries, Britain, France, and Germany engaged in such activities throughout much of Africa and Asia. For example, the Afghan Wars were to a large extent a manifestation of British and Russian expansionism in Central Asia. The history of French control in Indochina and British domination in Burma and Siam offer other examples.

Large differences in capabilities between countries mean grossly unequal political and economic relations between them. In most cases of intensive interaction between societies, the nation with vastly greater capabilities tends to dominate the other, even when domination is not a deliberate policy. Such relations invite the domination and exploitation of the weaker country by the stronger. Differences in capabilities between major powers are likely to have a different meaning. *When two or more major powers extend their respective interests outward, there is a strong probability that these interests will be opposing, and the activities of these nations may collide.* These activities may be diplomatic, commercial, military, or so forth, and thus involve quite different levels of intensity. Depending upon the intensity, such conflicts of interests and activities may contribute to the outbreak of war between strong countries, or between their client states, or both. The Fashoda Incident, the Moroccan Crisis, and the Bosnian Crisis of 1908–1909 are examples of military confrontations resulting from conflicts of interests between major powers before WWI.

Collisions can lead to the withdrawal of one (or both) of the parties, an agreement between them, or continuing conflict. In general the stronger the lateral pressure manifested by rival countries, the greater is the likelihood of the intensification of competition or conflict over territory, resources, markets, political or diplomatic influence, military or naval power, status, or prestige. Such behavior tends to be characteristic of the international relations of powerful states and empires.

The more intense the competition becomes, the greater is the likelihood that it will lead to arms competition, crisis, or possibly armed conflict. Major wars often emerge from a two-fold process: internally generated pressures, and mutual comparison, competition, rivalry, and conflict on a number of salient dimensions. Each of these processes is closely related to the other, and each can be accounted for to a remarkable degree by the interaction among three variables: population, technology, and access to resources.

Thus, international competition and conflict are closely linked to domestic growth, with the result that a country's domestic and foreign activities are likely to be intensely interdependent. Just as domestic growth may contribute to a country's foreign activities, so its foreign activities, in conflict with those of other countries, may generate further domestic demands and growth.

Although any activity by one country in or near the boundary of another country, or within the sphere of interest of another, may generate conflict and even violence, some activities are likely to have a stronger influence on international affairs than others. During the years between 1870 and 1914 we would expect that colonial expansion would be especially important for its effect on relations among the major powers. In another era, other manifestations of lateral pressure might be more important — troops overseas, military bases on foreign territory, outside investment in former colonial areas, military aid, technical assistance. In the late nineteenth and early twentieth centuries competition for colonial territory and spheres of control was the principal international concern. A major factor in Bismarck's turn to imperialism and colonialism may have been the fear that "if he failed to authorize the hoisting of the German flag, the flag of another

---

[11]Turner, 1967, p. 51.

European power would quickly go up."[11]The British, leaders of the world's largest empire, felt threatened on many occasions when it appeared that some other power might secure a territorial advantage in some part of the world.

States and empires do not stand still relative to one another in population, technology, territory, resources, military capability, or strategic advantage. Compared with each other, some are growing while others are declining, and thus the condition of the international system is perpetual change. A nation may find itself at a relative disadvantage in the world competition for resources, markets, prestige, or strategic superiority. In this eventuality, such a nation's leaders will look for means of improving the nation's relative position. This may involve increases in military or naval capabilities, or improvements in heavy industry. One method of increasing capabilities is to secure favorable alliances. Such bonds normally imply the pooling of some capabilities for the maintenance of shared interests. In defense alliances, the partners are able to complement one another's military capabilities.

Alliances are not always formed only to enhance national capabilities. Alliances, treaties and other international compacts are often concluded to end or moderate conflicts of interests.[12] But although these arrangements may ameliorate conflict, they may also create conflict. Whenever some compact is achieved between two nations not previously allied, it is likely to damage relations between at least one of the parties and any rivals, unless comparable compacts are made with these. Under such circumstances, the alignment of one group of nations may encourage other nations to create a competing bloc. Although relationships improved between Britain and France after 1904 and between Britain and Russia after 1907 as a result of alliances, none of these three powers achieved alliance with Germany. In such a case the amelioration of conflict among only some powers may be suspected of contributing in the long run to conflict among all the powers.

Broad alliance patterns (including distribution of capabilities within and across alliance boundaries) may define the structure of the international system. From the viewpoint of a nation's leaders, a strong or strategically placed ally may be viewed as organic to their own national power. A leading power may seek an alliance to prevent a growing power from overtaking it in some area, or a growing power may seek an alliance in order to overtake a stronger power. There is usually a price for alliances, however, since international compacts impose some constraints upon a nation's activities.

---

[12]In the quantative analyses of this book we do not distinguish among alliances, ententes, coalitions, blocs, and the like. For a recent survey of work on alliances, see Friedman *et al.*, 1970.

Competition may give rise to "antagonizing," the term given by Arthur Gladstone to "the process by which each side forms an increasingly unfavorable picture of the other as evil, hostile, and dangerous."[13] No matter which side initiates the process, antagonizing tends to become mutual. "When one side criticizes, distrusts, ridicules, or denounces the other, the other side is likely to reply in kind."[14] The more intense the competition and antagonizing, the greater is the probability of interaction being transformed from insult to injury. Thereafter, "when one side takes actions which are or threaten to be harmful to the other side, the other side is even more likely to reply in kind."[15]

With respect to the interactions between two rival countries, the difference between them on any salient dimension — territorial acquisition, trade, armaments, prestige, etc. — can be a powerful factor in motivating further competition or conflict. *An increase in the political, economic or military strength and effectiveness of one nation will tend to generate new demands in the rival nation and a disposition among its leaders to increase appropriate capabilities.* For example, if Nation A with a higher naval budget than Nation B adds further increments, Nation B is likely to increase its naval budget. Also, if Nation B with a lower budget tries to catch up with A, then the latter is likely to add increments in an effort to maintain its advantage. Nevertheless, we show in Part III that arms increases are sometimes better-explained by domestic growth factors than by international competition.

A nation may respond to an increase in the strength and effectiveness of another nation, e.g., trade, by increasing its own strength and effectiveness in a wholly different area, e.g., colonial territory, military strength, or naval power. This possibility tends to complicate the Richardson-type model of arms races in that increases in the military budgets (or shipping tonnage, etc.) of nations may be attributable to increases by a rival nation in some area *other than* military capability.

The interdependency between a country's domestic growth and military expenditures, on the one hand, and the interdependency between military budgets of rival countries are of considerable importance in the great-power system prior to WWI. Most of the major powers were growing or expanding on a number of dimensions — in colonial territory, military expenditures, trade, and so forth. The stronger these tendencies were after 1900 — the more the European countries absorbed available territory for colonialization, the higher

---

[13]Gladstone, 1962, p. 4
[14]*Ibid.*, p. 5.
[15]See Richardson, 1960, p. 15; also Howard and Scott, 1965; Bertalanffy, 1968, p. 79; and Miller, 1954, p. 231.

their military and naval budgets grew, and the stiffer the competition for the world's resources became—the more some leaders saw the possibilities for further growth threatened and their own policy options narrowing, rather than expanding along with the increased power of their nations. The larger the colonial commitments and spheres of interest of Britain and France, for example, the greater was the dissatisfaction of German leaders, who saw the area of unclaimed territories rapidly diminishing. The greater the armaments expenditures of one major power, the stronger the feeling of commitment was likely to be on the part of its rivals to increase their own military expenditures. Finally, as the powers began to adhere to one or another alliance, the more limited appeared to be the possibilities for negotiation and peaceful diplomacy between alliances.

National decisions are frequently thought of as being made in direct response to some perceived threat by another nation, or as steps directed toward certain widely shared and explicit goals, such as "survival of country." But the processes involved in policy formation and action are often exceedingly complex. National decisions, even in an authoritarian state, are usually the outcome of communications—often indirect, subtle, and difficult to trace—among the head of state, his advisers and agents, and the citizenry. Such data as levels and rates of change in population, technology, trade, investment, and colonial expansion are in every case the accumulation and aggregation of the effects of decisions made by individual human beings acting singly, in partnership, or in small groups.

The size of a nation's population at any given time is an outcome of millions of private decisions ("conscious" or "unconscious") to have or not have children. So, too, a country's general level of technology is the outcome of large numbers of research and production enterprises undertaken by individuals working singly, in private firms, and in agencies of government. The decision of ten million Germans to have a second cup of coffee could affect their country's relations with Brazil.[16] In a modern state problems of national security are analyzed by hundreds and perhaps thousands of different institutions. Furthermore, different approaches to national defense are taken simultaneously by dozens or hundreds of research and planning centers in and out of government, and in imperfect communication with one another.[17] Thus, a nation's military budget can be as much the outcome of the personal ambition and interests of bureaucrats in war and navy departments as it is of interactions with rival powers.[18] Often, the accumulation of countless individual decisions creates tendencies that

---

[16]See Boulding, 1969, p. 497; Braybrooke and Lindbloom, 1963, pp. 81–110.
[17]Braybrooke and Lindbloom, 1963, pp. 105–106.
[18]Allison, 1969; see also Halperin, 1974.

were not planned or foreseen.[19] Despite these complexities, since this study focuses on the interaction of certain macrolevel events — growth, expansion, and competition of nations — we shall be concerned only with the *outcomes* of decision-making processes and not with decision-making itself.

National attributes (the levels and rates of change of certain variables) can provide valuable data for studying the processes that lead to war. Chapter 2 presents profiles of the national attributes of the six major European powers during the 45 years prior to WWI. These profiles are an important consideration in the history of the interaction of these powers (presented in Part II) and are the data base for our quantitative analysis (reported in Part III).

Despite our best efforts, the propositions put forward here are crude, and greater precision is required before we can approach a true theory. Our thoughts, observations, assumptions, and propositions constitute at best a "proto-theory." The specific components (variables) of the processes we are studying are presented in Table 1-1. In Part III we introduce an operational model (a system of simultaneous equations) designed to capture some of the complexities of the interdependency and interaction of these components. Even then, we assume that our tentative theory will be only a first cut into the problem, and that the propositions will have to be subjected to much more testing than that reported in this book.

---

[19]Braybrooke and Lindbloom, 1963, p. 93.

Table 1-1. The conceptual model.

Components of the Model	Description-rationale	Measure[a]
Expansion	Demands resulting from the interactive effects of population and technological growth give rise to activities beyond national borders.	Colonial area.
Conflict of interest	Expanding nations are likely to collide in their activities outside national boundaries; such collisions have some potential for violence.	Metricized measure of violence in *intersections* (conflicts specifically over colonial issues) between major powers.
Military capability	States, by definition, have military establishments; these grow as a result of domestic growth and competition with military establishments of other nations.	Military budgets.
Alliance	Nations assess their power, resources, and capabilities in comparison with other nations and attempt to enhance themselves through international alliances.	Total alliances.
Violence-behavior	Nations engage in international violence as a consequence of expansion, military capability, and alliances.	Metricized measure of violence in actions directed toward all other nations.[b]

[a]Data are established for *each* nation and aggregated *annually* for the years 1870–1914. See Appendix A for details on measurement and sources of data.
[b]Target nations include not only the six major powers in the study, but all states.

2 The Major Powers: National Capabilities and Expansion

During the late nineteenth and early twentieth centuries the system of great powers was in flux. Commercial competition, the forging of alliances and counter-alliances, and conflicts over the acquisition and control of overseas territories were accompanied by feelings of profound uneasiness, insecurity, and antagonism. A. J. P. Taylor draws an analogy to the state of nature, where "violence was the only law, and life was 'nasty, brutish and short.' Though individuals never lived in this state of nature, the great powers of Europe have always done so."[1] But Taylor also sees much of the nineteenth century as a time of relative peace — an "astonishingly stable" period in international affairs as compared with twentieth century chaos and with the centuries that preceded it.[2]

To a large extent this appearance of stability and peace can be explained by the fact that much of the attention of the great powers was focused less on European affairs than on activities overseas, including the acquisition and administration of colonies, colonial wars, the maintenance of civil order in colonies, and the defense of expanding national (or imperial) interests. Thus, although Europe itself may have been peaceful, the frequency of armed conflict in overseas colonies casts serious doubt on Taylor's assessment of the stability of European relations in the nineteenth century.

In this chapter we shall identify certain basic attributes of the major powers and relate them, however tentatively, to some of the behavior patterns that seem to have led toward the Great War. We shall be interested primarily in, for example, population, national territory, aspects of technology and production, and trade — those attributes

---

[1]Taylor, 1954, p. xix.
[2]*Ibid.*, p. xxii.

that we see as contributing to the tendency of nations to extend their activities, spheres of influence, and territorial possessions outward from the boundaries of their home territory.[3] We shall also be concerned with the extent to which each nation was constrained in its efforts toward expansion, and thus how likely it was to perceive its demands as generally satisfied or unsatisfied.

The drawing up of capsule national profiles seems important for three reasons. First, they should enable us to assess national capabilities and demands, domestic pressures, and the directions in which each nation was pressing its interests and influence. Second, they may suggest the conditions that gave rise to competitions and conflicts that led to WWI. (If national attributes are as important in explaining the behavior of great powers as we have postulated, then analysis of these attributes is basic to further, more complex, investigation.) Third, they should illustrate the dynamic nature of the international system. Nations do not stand still in terms of population, technology, access to resources, or military capabilities—even though a given country may keep the same name, government, and legal status.[4]

After the Conference of Berlin in 1884 all the major powers of Europe pursued policies of expansion.[5] There were many critics of this tendency, including William Gladstone in England,[6] but for the most part expansion "in all its modes seemed not only natural and necessary, but inevitable; it was pre-ordained and irreproachably right. It was the spontaneous expression of an inherently dynamic society."[7]

In Chapter 1 we suggested that the tendency toward lateral pressure and the expansion of a nation's interests can be accounted for by many different public and private motivations. Moreover, lateral pressure can be manifested in several ways. And different countries can move toward the same outcome—the outbreak of war in 1914, for example— by different "paths", i.e., by different sequences of events. In view of these considerations, debate over the "true motives" of expansionism or "the real cause" of war may not be particularly enlightening. The problem should be to understand the multifaceted dynamics of lateral pressure, international competition, and international conflict. Once this has been done, it remains to devise ways for determining which of the elements in a particular equation of expansion are most influential in a given situation at a specific time. Debate over residual influences can then proceed within established boundaries of reference.

---

[3]This perspective provides a basis for the major propositions in the introduction. See Appendix A for the sources of the data presented in this chapter and for an indication of measurement error or bias.

[4]Taylor, 1954, p. xxiii.

[5]Robinson and Gallagher, 1961, p. 3.

[6]For examples of Gladstone's criticism, see Parliamentary Debates, Third Series, May 7, 1877, 234:414-415, 437-438.

[7]Robinson and Gallagher, 1961, p. 3.

In any case, expansionist activities are most likely to be associated with relatively high-capability countries, and to be closely linked with growth in population and advances in technology. Also, growth tends to be associated with intense competition among countries for resources and markets, military power, political influence, and prestige. Thus, attention to the levels and rates of advance of these variables is crucial in an analysis of expansion.

Population

During the years between 1870 and 1914, the average population of Russia (91.9 million) was nearly equivalent to that of the next *two* most populous powers. Germany had an average of 52 million for this period, in comparison with an average of 43 million for Austria-Hungary, 39 million for Britain, 38 million for France, and 31 million for Italy. All were growing, as can be seen in Figure 2-1, but there were notable variations in rates. Of the major powers during 1870–1914, Russia displayed a fairly high annual rate of population growth (1.6 percent), followed by Germany (1.15), Britain (.89), Austria-Hungary (.80), Italy (.65), and France (by far the lowest, .10).[8] If population growth were the major (or only) factor contributing to lateral pressure,

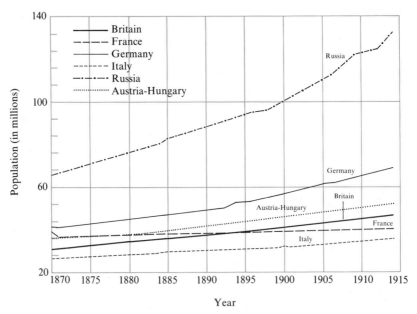

Figure 2-1. Home population, 1870–1914.

---

[8]Growth rates here are the calculated annual percentage increases in the 45-year period, rounded off.

we would expect Russia to have been the most expansionist of the powers.[9] Russian expansion may have been reduced, however, by the vast expanses of nearly empty territory already possessed by the tsarist empire. Filling this expanse would postpone any necessity for overseas territorial expansion. At the same time, if the rate of population growth were the major (or only) factor contributing to lateral pressure, France should have been the least expansionist of the major powers. Since this was not the case, there are, clearly, other important considerations.

If we measure the population *density* of the six nations, we get a somewhat different ranking (see Figure 2-2). As might be expected, the density in Russia was very low, although increasing: 34.5 persons per square mile in 1870, 52.0 in 1900, and 70.6 in 1914. If population density were the primary factor contributing to lateral pressure, we would expect Russia to be among the least expansionist of the major powers. On the basis of *rate of change in density*, however, Russia (1.64 percent) and Germany (1.12) would rank as most likely to expand, followed by Britain (.86), Austria-Hungary (.70), and Italy (.69).

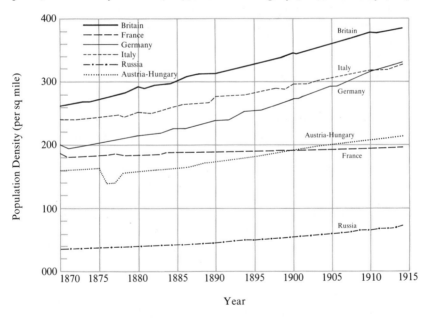

Figure 2-2. Population density, 1870–1914.

[9]Of course, population increases must be related to levels and rates of change of technology, as well as access to resources, if a correct assessment of the relationship between population and lateral pressure is to be made. The relationships modeled in Part III are based on levels rather than rates of change (see Chapter 10 for an explanation). However, some notion of change is incorporated in the analysis by the use of lagged variables and through the use of time-series data.

The rapid increase in density in Germany is noteworthy: by 1900 Germany was the third densest of the powers (269.9 persons per square mile), being surpassed only by England (342.8) and Italy (293.5). By 1914 the German level (324.7) had surpassed that of Italy (321.8) and was approaching that of England (378.7). French population density changed more gradually (from 186.4 in 1870 to 194.6 in 1914), at an average annual rate of .10 percent. If lateral pressure were generated primarily by the rate of increase of population density, we would again expect France to have been the least expansionist of the major powers.

Iron and Steel Production

Population growth is not the only factor in lateral pressure. Both population and technological advancement contribute to increases in demands, which, in combination with national capabilities, contribute to lateral pressure. All of the major powers experienced some advances in technology, as measured by production of iron and steel.

Until 1850 Britain was the only industrial power of any importance. Although industry in France had made some advances of consequence, England was clearly in front.[10] During the later part of the nineteenth century, however, in the course of about thirty years, Germany experienced "what England required over one hundred years to complete—the change from a backward and primarily agrarian nation to a modern and highly efficient industrial and technological state."[11]

In 1870 the British output of iron and steel was almost three times the German output; by 1913, however, the volume of German production had increased by a factor of more than eight. Despite this rapid rate of increase, Britain continued to maintain a somewhat narrow lead over German production until around 1900. After that, Germany overtook Britain in overall production and then continuously increased its lead. In 1913 Germany produced almost 45 million metric tons of iron and steel compared with Britain's 24 million metric tons. Figure 2-3 shows the levels of production of the six nations between 1870 and 1914.

Russian output of iron and steel, although considerably lower than that of Britain or Germany, increased remarkably. Output of steel in 1870 was merely 363 thousand metric tons; by 1914 it was 3.6 million metric tons. These advances are hardly consistent with the image of nineteenth-century Russia as a backward, unproductive country. Al-

---

[10]Taylor, 1954, p. xxx.
[11]Pinson, 1954, p. 219.

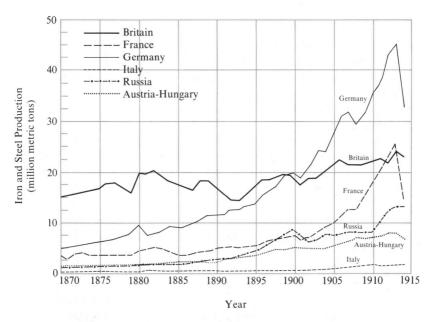

Figure 2-3. Iron-and-steel production, 1870–1914.

though some sectors were underdeveloped, even primitive, Russia's industrialization was well under way.

Despite a comparatively low output of iron and steel, Austria-Hungary almost quadrupled her production between 1880 and 1914, from approximately 1.6 to 6.2 million metric tons. (Output of combustible material, especially coal, increased well over six times, from 6,130 to 40,358 thousand metric tons, between 1870 and 1914.) Nevertheless, compared with the other powers, production levels were quite low.

Between 1870–1914 the average annual output in iron and steel for Britain was 18.6 million metric tons, compared with 16.5 million for Germany, 7.4 million for France, 4.6 for Russia, and 3.6 for Austria-Hungary. Italy produced by far the smallest output, with an average annual volume of only 0.6 million metric tons.

Differences in *rates of increase* in iron and steel production were even more diverse: Germany and Italy, starting from vastly different base levels, increased at mean annual rates of 5.0 and 9.1 percent, respectively, followed by Russia (5.6 percent), Austria-Hungary (3.6), France (4.2), and Britain (1.2). Of course, these rates of growth should be considered with one eye on the levels of production; still, the contrast between virtually stagnant British production and the German boom is apparent.

National Income

Iron and steel production is an incomplete measure of technology, omitting many crucial dimensions generally included in national income. We experimented with both national income and iron and steel production as measures of technology. We consider national income and per capita national income better indicators of the levels and growth of technology.

As can be seen from Figure 2-4, all powers experienced increases in national income during this period. Although German national income was initially somewhat higher than that of England, Britain's income rose steeply, surpassing Germany by 1878 and retaining the lead until 1906. Starting from a much lower base in 1870, French national income in the early 1880s about equaled that of Germany. But this momentum was soon lost and France finally fell sharply behind even Russia. Italian national income lagged behind that of France. The national income for France, although high compared with the income of many countries, tended to remain considerably lower than that of Britain or Germany. None of the six European powers experienced unconstrained growth. To one degree or another, all suffered declines at some point—although Britain's growth was perhaps the steadiest.[12]

In average annual *rates of increase* of national income, France ranked first (3.04 percent), followed by Italy (2.84), Germany (2.49), Britain (2.42), and Russia (2.32). It should not be inferred from these figures that France and Italy were "doing better" than Germany and Britain—absolute levels must also be examined. But by combining these data with population growth rates we can acquire a greater perspective on rising demands.

Figure 2-5 shows the growth of per capita national income for the great powers (except Austria-Hungary). In average annual *rates of increase* Britain maintained a slight but secure lead (1.53 percent) over Germany (1.34). The highest growth rate is that of France, 2.95 percent, compared with 2.17 percent for Italy and 0.73 for Russia. In *levels* of per capita national income, Britain was first (169.2 1906 US

---

[12]National income (in million US dollars, standardized to 1906).

	1870	1890	1900	1914
Britain	3,413	6,730	8,170	9,068
Germany	3,631	5,034	7,011	10,020
France	1,742	4,344	5,109	6,135
Austria	*No series (see Appendix A)*			
Italy	1,167	2,020	2,331	3,642
Russia	3,435	4,446	6,570	6,147

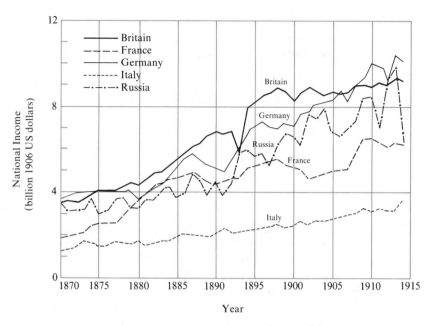

Figure 2-4. National income, 1870–1914.

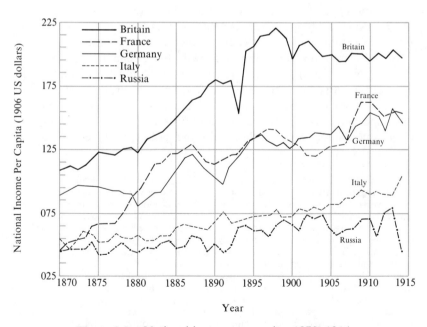

Figure 2-5. National income per capita, 1870–1914.

dollars per capita), followed by Germany (116.9), France (114.4), Italy (68.7), and Russia (55.9).

In the long run, Britain and Germany showed similarly high rates of growth and levels of national income. However, the national incomes of France and Italy increased at higher rates than those of Germany and Britain, even though levels were lower than those of the latter two. Britain greatly surpassed the other five nations in the level of per capita national income. However, the rate of growth of per capita income in the French and Italian economies was more impressive than that of the other great powers.

Trade

You will recall that in Chapter 1 we stated that demands generated by population growth and technological advances are met through development of national capabilities. This can be done by increasing domestic resources (agricultural yields, mineral deposits, water power), acquiring new territories, or developing trade.[13]

In average annual values of exports between 1870–1914 (standardized to 1906 US dollars) the powers ranked as follows: Britain (1.57 billion), Germany (1.02), France (.74), Russia (.38), Austria-Hungary (.34), and Italy (.24). The ranking is different with respect to average annual increases: Italy, with the lowest base, ranked first with a mean annual increase of 3.44 percent, followed by Germany (3.31), Russia (2.87), Austria-Hungary (2.62), Britain (2.18), and France (1.88). Figures for total trade (Figure 2-6) show a similar ranking.

In 1879, in order to encourage growth in German agriculture (for a growing population) and shelter new German industries from foreign competition, Bismarck turned from free trade to protectionism. "For a time German agriculture did relatively well, and German industry developed steadily."[14] During the late 1880s and early 1890s, however, it became increasingly evident that the policy designed to further

---

[13]The model developed in this study used imports plus exports as an indicator of trade without regard to either direction (imports vs exports) or the nature of trade (raw materials versus finished goods). The choice of this indicator was preliminary. In future studies we shall use trade quite differently, separating imports and exports and trying to distinguish between trade patterns that are likely to bring countries together and those that may contribute to conflict. Trade may serve to meet a considerable part of a country's demands and thus reduce lateral pressure. But trade—the "reaching out" for resources and markets—can itself be viewed as a manifestation of lateral pressure. In rewriting the equations for future analysis, we shall try to incorporate more satisfactorily *both* of these functions. This adjustment should add important dimensions to the analysis. It should be possible, for example, to specify the related attributes of a country engaged in unequal or exploitative trade, i.e., the creation of economic dependency, and to see how such economic exploitation may relate to other aspects of a country's behavior.

[14]Nichols, 1958, p. 137.

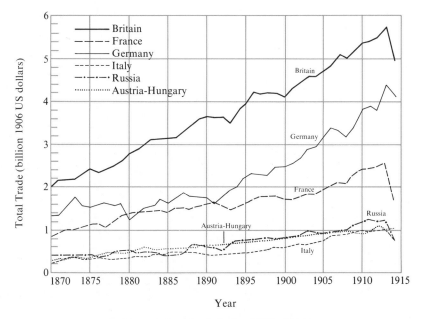

Figure 2-6. Total trade, 1870–1914.

German economic growth in fact tended to hamper it; Germany thus began to acquire a colonial empire, partly in order to ensure foreign markets.

Merchant Marine

In merchant-marine tonnage and number of commercial ships, Britain by far surpassed both France and Germany, the next two ranking powers. (It should be noted that the number of ships is an unreliable comparison, since the minimum tonnage required for a craft to be counted differed among the nations in our study.) In merchant-marine tonnage, Germany surpassed France in the early 1870s and retained a substantial lead throughout the entire period (1870–1914). Germany showed a substantial rate of annual increase of 2.28 percent; in comparison, Britain's rate of increase was 1.92 percent. These rates exceeded those of Austria-Hungary (1.43 percent), France (1.43), and Italy (.59), but fell short of the spectacular growth of the Russian fleet (3.32 percent). Nevertheless, Britain maintained the highest level of tonnage, as illustrated in Figure 2-7.

Colonial Expansion

In this study we have relied on colonial expansion as an indicator of lateral pressure. In fact, however, colonial expansion measures only

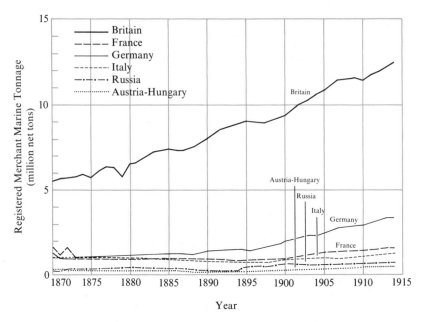

Figure 2-7. Registered merchant marine tonnage, 1870–1914.

one type of lateral pressure, and as an indicator it leaves much to be desired. Nevertheless, the expansion of most major powers during the nineteenth and early twentieth centuries was characteristically colonial, and hence total colonial area should serve as a decent indicator of expansion in our study.[15]

Italy had the highest mean annual *growth rate* in square miles of colonial territory (10.5 percent), followed by France (7.69), Germany (3.8), Britain (.74), and Russia (.23).[16] Austro-Hungarian territorial expansion was limited to the acquisition of Bosnia-Herzegovina, so that a rate of territorial expansion for the Austrian empire would be meaningless. Figure 2-8 shows the growth of colonial territory (measured in total area) for the six great powers.

Britain, which in many ways played the role of the dominant power, manifested the greatest expansion, as indicated by the total area of her colonial possessions, the number of violent conflicts overseas, and the

---

[15]It was exceedingly difficult to obtain consistent estimates of colonial population for the period 1870–1914. Severe inconsistencies across sources and within individual sources, coupled with the difficulties of estimating natural-birth rates, made the development of a consistent series increasingly complex. We therefore preferred to use total colonial area. (The involvement of the European powers in colonial wars also might have served as a rough indicator of expansion during this period. See Appendix A for additional comments on the measure of expansion in our study.)

[16]For Britain, France, and Russia the calculations are based on the whole period, 1870–1914. For Germany, Italy, and Austria-Hungary the calculations are based on a period beginning with the date of initial acquisitions to 1914.

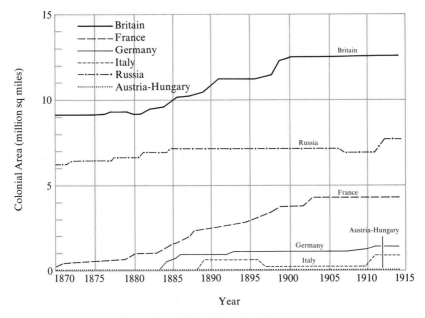

Figure 2-8. Colonial area, 1870–1914.

level of technological advancement (measured by national income, per capita national income, and iron and steel production). Britain more than doubled her merchant-marine tonnage between 1870 and 1914. Similar strides were made in exports. Through a large and growing empire and flourishing trade, Britain (directly or indirectly) controlled a large part of the globe.

Germany, which increasingly played the role of Britain's major rival, had a faster growing home population than Britain and a rapidly advancing technology. Between 1870 and 1914, Germany's commercial activities increased very rapidly; her total trade (imports plus exports) increased from 1.311 to 4,147 million dollars (standardized to 1906 US dollars). Certainly, this demonstrates that there were important outlets for German lateral pressure. Nevertheless, national leaders at the time were particularly sensitive to national differences in colonial area, irrespective of whether existing territory and trade were sufficient to meet economic demands. Although Germany enjoyed great economic success in the mid-nineteenth century, she may have considered herself at a disadvantage in comparing herself with the empires of other nations. Her success as a colonial power was minor in the long run—as late as 1914 the German empire was only about one-tenth the size of the British.

In 1884–1885 Germany acquired her first colonies, Togoland and the Cameroons. Acquisitions increased considerably in the next few years, encompassing territories in Africa, the Southwest Pacific,

China, and other parts of Asia. By 1914 the German empire extended to over 1,207,000 square miles, a little less than six times the size of Germany's territory in Europe, but still only a small fraction of Britain's colonial area. German colonial expansion was closely related to domestic growth; correlations between home population and colonial empire and between national income and colonial empire were at or above .85.

France had a relatively stable home population, a constant home territory (aside from the loss of Alsace-Lorraine), and comparatively high levels of technological advancement. At the same time, France's colonial expansion was spectacular. Although the size of the French empire never came close to that of the British, the rate of her territorial acquisition was very much greater. This advance is especially significant in light of a relatively stable home population. In 1870 France controlled approximately 217,100 square miles outside Europe; by 1885 the total had risen to 1,547,500. In 1900 the French empire extended over parts of Asia, Africa, America, and Oceania, totaling approximately 3,735,700 square miles, and by 1914 the Empire was well over twenty times its size in 1870. Much of this expansion was accompanied by violence. After 1882 France was engaged almost constantly in some overseas war. Of the 45 years between 1870 and 1914, only nine were relatively tranquil.[17]

Russia's population was the largest in Europe, with by far the highest rate of increase. Russian industrial production also increased considerably. Although Russia did expand in territory, expansion was largely within its borders (which, however, were not yet those of the USSR). When WWI broke out, Russia still had vast, contiguous territory into which her people might move. Like the United States in the nineteenth century, Russia was able to extend its control over wide expanses of contiguous territory, and in doing so collide only peripherally with the interests of other great powers. Nevertheless, Russian interests did on occasion collide with those of Britain and other powers. In line with a clearly imperialistic policy, Russia expanded from approximately 502,300 square miles in 1870 to 1,500,000 in 1914.[18] This territory was in addition to European Russia, which included Finland and Poland.[19]

---

[17]This estimate is based both on Richardson's data (*Statistics of Deadly Quarrels*, 1960) and on sources noted in Appendix A.

[18]This territory included Central Asia, Caucasia, Bessarabia, Manchuria, Sakhalin, Kurile, and Persia.

[19]Russian continental expansion presents special problems in distinguishing between "home" and "colonial" territory. According to some statistical sources, all territory other than "European" Russia is considered "colonial." In other references, only territories with legally distinct status (e.g., Finland and the Asian protectorates of Khiva and Bkhara) are considered "colonial." Any division into "European" and "Asian" Russia is thus purely arbitrary. For our study, we have considered all Russian territory other than "European" Russia to be colonial. See Appendix A for additional comments.

In 1914 Russia's Asian population acquired through territorial expansion amounted to approximately 32,504,410. The population density in the acquired territories was much lower than in the European portions of the Empire.

The population of Austria-Hungary was growing at a rate similar to that of Britain (and surpassed only by Russia and Germany), but its territory was fairly constant. Its level of technology (measured by the production of iron and steel) was, next to Italy's, the lowest of the powers; its rate of increase in technology was by far the lowest. Although the increases in population and the relatively small advance in technology generated increases in demand, compared with Germany, France, or Britain, Austrian technology was not sufficiently developed to support the economic and military capabilities needed for successful expansion. Moreover, the empire suffered a shortage of open-sea ports, and the merchant marine was for a long time almost negligible. Throughout the period 1870–1914, imports were consistently higher than exports. Flanked by a powerful and expansionist Germany on the north and a generally weak, overcrowded, and frustrated Italy on the southwest, Austria-Hungary, seeking to capitalize on declining Turkish power, found herself continually threatening the interests and ambitions of Russia.

Territorial expansion by Austria-Hungary was generally not feasible, although the Empire did improve its territorial position by taking over Bosnia and Herzegovina. Efforts toward expansion were limited to the Balkans. Some neighboring areas in the Balkans were densely populated, and ethnic divisions presented further obstacles to penetration. Austro-Hungarian efforts at increasing political power and influence were generally unsuccessful, leaving the empire's leadership frustrated and dissatisfied. Austria-Hungary had limited access to the sea (and limited maritime capabilities) and Serbia lay directly across a main avenue of the empire's expansion into the Balkans. Thus contained, the extension of the Austro-Hungarian empire was largely confined to Bosnia and Herzegovina. On the whole, the possibility of alleviating demands through territorial expansion was seriously constrained.

As will become evident in Part II, the course of events involving the European powers during the decade prior to WWI cannot be discussed without considering Serbia. Although Serbia is not considered a great power for the purpose of our study (data on Serbia for the period 1870–1914 would have been inadequate, in any case) it will help to understand Serbia's role in the drift toward war by touching upon a few of the country's major attributes. The Treaty of Bucharest, signed July 25, 1913, allocated to Serbia a total area of 33,891 square miles, well over twice her size in 1870 when the country was granted independence by Turkey. This increase in Serbia's territory further constrained territorial expansion by Austria-Hungary. There was also growth in Serbia's population, which increased almost one and one-half times between 1870 and 1895 (when the official census reported 2,312,484 people) and almost another one and one-half times by 1914.[20] These increases in territory and population encouraged Serbian aspirations for a Greater Serbia. Although the data are too limited for systematic analysis, we can infer increasing Serbian demands from the facts of rising population and territorial increases.

Although Italy's population was comparatively of moderate size, the growth rate was considerably higher than that of France and not too much lower than that of Britain or Austria-Hungary. Since home area was constant, population density rates rose; Italian home territory was relatively unproductive, and resources were scarce.[21] The level of technology was low but rising—slowly at first, but by the turn of the century at much higher rates. The volume of production, however, remained quite low. Because of a rising population, constant area, and limited resources, Italy's technological advances made a colonial program seem increasingly desirable. Pressures generated by rising demands initially found an outlet in territorial expansion around 1890. The first Italian acquisitions of any appreciable size preceded by a few years the remarkable increase in technology and productivity around the turn of the century.

Of the six nations in our study, the most rapidly growing in the period 1870–1914 were those whose expansionist activities had been lowest at the beginning of the period. Because two nations may achieve equivalent gains in production over different periods, the Italian and German performances are not entirely comparable to the British, French, or Russian.

The size of the British empire far exceeded that of the French, but the rate of French territorial growth—which started from a much lower base—surpassed that of Britain. Britain and France were clearly the most expansionist of the powers (if measured only by territorial gains) and thus the most likely to be reasonably satisfied with the status quo—which presented them with opportunities for continuing acquisitions.[22] Russia's rapid expansion eastward, in combination with considerable

---

[20]The *Statesman's Yearbook* of 1916 reports an estimated population of 4,547,992 for that year, a figure that most likely reflects a lag of at least two or three years between the time the estimate was made and the date it was reported. Additions in territory obviously account for considerable population growth. In the absence of adequate data on technology, production, commerce and so on, it is difficult to assess the full significance of Serbia's population increases and territorial expansion.

[21]Since much Italian land was either not arable or of low yield, it could not itself provide an adequate base for a growing population. Italy lost 3,000 square miles on the northern border between 1870 and 1890, stabilizing at approximately 110 thousand square miles.

[22]Louis, 1967, pp. 10–11.

advances in technology and production, suggests that it, too, might have been relatively satisfied—until countered and blocked by Japanese expansion.[23] Although Germany and Italy did expand their colonial territory, the possibilities open to them fell considerably short of the advantages enjoyed by Britain, France, and, to some extent, Russia. Austro-Hungarian expansion was of course limited to the acquisition of Bosnia and Herzegovina.

Colliding National Interests

As suggested in the previous chapter, lateral pressure, whatever its manifestation (exploration, commerce, investment, conquest), tends to establish extraterritorial national interests that a country then feels ought to be defended. In attempting to protect their interests in lower-capability regions, major powers are likely to find themselves involved in armed conflict with local rulers or groups rebelling against foreign intrusion. For the period 1870–1914, great-power involvement in colonial wars would be a further measure of expansion.

A generation ago Lewis Fry Richardson collected data on "deadly quarrels" in all parts of the world from 1820 to 1914. Included in the data are statistics on casualties inflicted in each war.[24] Richardson's data can be used to measure the extent and intensity of British, French, German, Austro-Hungarian, Russian, and Italian violence in gaining influence or control over lower-capability societies. On the basis of Richardson's data, the greatest violence was exercised by Britain and France—the behavior of Germany, Italy, Russia, and Austria-Hungary was scarcely comparable.

According to Richardson's calculations, during 1870–1914 there were only three years when Britain was not engaged in at least one war over the acquisition or maintenance of territory.[25] Africa was a major battleground for Britain, with wars against Egyptians, Sudanese, Zulus, and Boers (resulting in tens of thousands of casualties) and wars against Ashanti, Kaffirs, Basutos, Arabs, and others (resulting in somewhat lower casualty levels).[26] Britain was also deeply involved militarily in Afghanistan (adjacent to Russia), along the northwestern frontier of India, in Tibet, and Burma. British interests in Thailand, Malaysia, China, and elsewhere were advanced and defended at lower levels of violence.[27]

---

[23]See Wolfers, pp. 141–142, for a discussion of "satisfied" and "dissatisfied" powers. Davies (1962) suggests that "satisfaction" is transitory.

[24]Richardson, 1960b, pp. 52–69.

[25]*Ibid.*

[26]*Ibid.*

[27]Our estimates are based in part on Richardson's calculations of "deadly quarrels," and in part on the chronology issued annually by the *Statesman's Yearbook* and the sources listed in Appendix A.

France was similarly involved in extensive violent conflict with colonial populations. The most violent manifestations of French expansion prior to WWI were in Africa and Indochina. There were armed conflicts with Algerians, Tunisians, and Moroccans in North Africa, and with Tuaregs, Senegalese, Nigerians, and Dahomeyans further south. The fighting in Indochina was principally against Tonkinese. Most hostilities involved casualties in the hundreds; only the wars with the Tonkinese and engagements against the Novas of Madagascar resulted in somewhat higher casualties.

In the pursuit of colonies Germany involved herself in fewer wars than either Britain or France. There were substantial levels of casualties in only two conflicts, one establishing authority over the Hottentots, the other subduing the Wangoni. There were smaller wars against the Waheme. In only four of the 45 years under study was Germany actively engaged in substantial armed conflict with colonial populations.

Russia was actively engaged in hostilities of significant magnitude during only eight years in the period 1870–1914.[28] Even the Afghan War produced comparatively few casualties. Generally, Russian expansionism proceeded at *comparatively* low levels of violence. In this and other respects, Russian expansion in the nineteenth century was comparable to the expansion of the United States westward to the Pacific. When Russia pressed her influence into the Balkans, she collided with Turkish interests and increasingly with those of Austria-Hungary. Russia collided with Britain at the Dardanelles, in Persia, Afghanistan, Tibet, and China, and with Japan in Korea. The Russo-Turkish War, the Sieges of Geok-Tepe, and the Russo-Japanese War were hostilities of considerable magnitude.

Although Italian expansion was accompanied by violence, the total area in question was relatively small—approximately 886,800 square miles in 1914—and casualties were relatively low. The two most serious armed conflicts were both in Africa—Ethiopia, in the east, and Libya, in the north. In the course of these territorial acquisitions Italy's interests collided with those of other powers, especially those of France and Britain. By the mid-1900s the interests of Italy overlapped most critically with those of others in North Africa, giving rise to a series of acute crises there.

Major international crises of this period—the Fashoda Incident, the Moroccan Crises, and the Bosnian Crisis of 1908–1909—may be viewed as tests of changing national capabilities and relationships among the great powers. It should be kept in mind, however, that throughout the period 1870–1914 relations among the powers were in

---

[28]The estimates for Russia are derived from the Richardson data, historical accounts listed in Appendix A, the *Statesman's Yearbook* (volumes for 1870 to 1920), and Langer, 1962.

large part relatively cordial. Major crises unfolded within the context of a universal political ethos; diplomacy among the powers was effective enough to contain, if not to resove, conflicts without recourse to war. In this respect at least, historians are correct in pointing out that the nineteenth century was relatively tranquil. The international crises of the late nineteenth and early twentieth centuries, which did not involve direct armed conflict between the major powers, might be considered as tests of strength, intended to "verify" changes in relative power. In this sense, WWI was a final test of shifts in power among the great powers, a test to "resolve disagreements as to whether such shifts had indeed occurred" and determine "whether the political adjustments pressed for" were "really warranted."[29]

In this chapter we have presented summary profiles of the six major powers included in our study. The more prominent attributes, such as population, technology, merchant marine, military budgets, colonial territory, and the like, tend to be highly correlated and difficult to untangle in the search for the causes of international violence. For this reason we shall examine the *links* among domestic growth, expansion, and interaction among major powers. In this connection it should be noted that no one attribute explains great-power behavior — none correlates highly with our measure for violence-behavior. It would be incorrect, therefore, to assert that population growth or technological advancement or military expenditures or colonial expansion, taken singly, explains violence-behavior in any satisfactory way. Our problem is to see what combinations of these attributes will provide clues to violence among great powers.

These interactive relationships will be examined first in Part II by reviewing the international political history of the period 1870–1914. In Part III these same relationships are then investigated quantitatively. In the next chapter we shall consider some of the ways in which growth and expansion affected great-power relations during the Bismarckian era, when European colonialism was becoming increasingly competitive.

---

[29]Kuznets, 1966, p. 345.

Part II

3 European Politics and Overseas Expansion

In this chapter and the rest of Part II we will trace the changing relationships between the major European powers in 1870–1914. In doing so, we will show the extent to which historians have already pointed out links between national growth, expansion, and international violence. We shall see how increasing demands within each country contributed to territorial expansion; conflicts of expanding national interests; competition for resources, markets, arms superiority and strategic advantage; alterations in the alliance system; and the creation in general of conditions conducive to war.

During the first three-quarters of the nineteenth century, Britain—because of her strength at sea, her industrial capabilities, and the fact that she had relatively little foreign rivalry to contend with—greatly extended her imperial domain, enjoying an effortless supremacy in the world outside Europe.[1] As a great sea power with possessions on five continents, Britain found herself (if only through the pursuit of her normal affairs of commerce, administration, and diplomacy) more and more in friction with other powers, thus inviting alliances against her.[2]

In their book *Africa and the Victorians*, Ronald Robinson and John Gallagher describe British expansionism in Africa.[3] They offer several explanations, implying that all were pertinent, and without attempting to relate them systematically or rank them in terms of importance. (1) Britain claimed colonies and protectorates in tropical

---

[1]Robinson and Gallagher, 1961, p. 471; see also Landes, 1969, pp. 238–239.
[2]Langer, 1951, pp. 67–96.
[3]In line with the Treaty of Berlin (1878), but against "all precept and prejudice against the experience and trends of previous expansion," the British occupied Egypt (1882) and staked out a huge tropical empire on the African continent. What was more (to the bewilderment of some), "they were ready by the end of the century to fight major wars for Sudanese deserts and South African *Kopjes*" (Robinson and Gallagher, 1961, p. 17).

Africa "not because they were needed as colonial estates," but for strategic reasons—although in the long run "they had to be developed as colonial estates to pay the costs of their administration."[4] (2) British leaders were determined to deny possession of African territories to rival powers—a policy that sometimes generated even further territorial expansion.[5] (3) The purposes of the close official circle making African policy were often visionary, and their actions were usually inspired by notions of the world situation and calculations of its dangers which were peculiar to the official mind.[6] (4) The new African empire was an "offshoot of the total processes of British expansionism throughout the world and throughout the century."[7] (5) British penetration of tropical Africa was an involuntary response to developments arising from the decline of Turkish authority from the Dardanelles to the Nile.[8] (6) Gladstone and Granville "drifted into the Niger like a couple of imperial Micawbers looking for something to turn up." (7) Britain advanced into the Niger as a consequence of minor trade rivalries in West Africa and major changes in the European configuration of power provoked mainly by British blunders in Egypt.[9] (8) "The Liberals claimed the Lower Niger merely to prevent an existing field of British trade from disappearing behind French tariff walls. . . ,"[10] (9) ". . . The majority of the Cabinet . . . was not prepared to let . . . Bismarck beat them out of doors again in Africa." (10) Salisbury and Chamberlain were prisoners of their own conception of what conditions were like in South Africa.[11] Furthermore, Britain was frequently confronted with *faits accomplis* from her colonial administrators, who were inclined to annex whatever was available "if only to keep out newcomers."

In due course, many Englishmen, including Gladstone, opposed further expansion of the British empire, but others considered it a necessity. "We could not produce in foodstuffs enough to sustain the

---

[4]*Ibid.*, p. 409.

[5]*Ibid.*, p. 284. Increasingly, during the 1880s, Egypt became the pivot of Britain's Mediterranean strategy. "A foreign power astride the Upper Nile would be in a position either to levy blackmail or to lever [the British] out of Egypt." On behalf of British interests in India, Lord Granville asserted, "I regard it as of very serious importance that no foreign power should oust us from [Egypt]" (quoted p. 190). Gladstone to Lord Granville, 28 December 1884: "I agree with you that there is something absurd in the scramble for colonies, and I am as little disposed to join in it as you can be; but there is a difference between wanting new acquisitions and keeping what we have; both Natal and the Cape Colony would be endangered . . . if any foreign power chose to claim possession of the coast lying between the two . . . . I want to secure the coastline all round South Africa from the mouth of the Orange River on the west. . . ." (quoted p. 208).

[6]*Ibid.*, p. 466.

[7]*Ibid.*, p. 471.

[8]*Ibid.*, p. 466.

[9]*Ibid.*, pp. 179–180.

[10]*Ibid.*, p. 180.

[11]*Ibid.*, p. 427.

population that lives in this island," Lord Salisbury asserted in 1892, "and it is only by the great industries that exist here and which find markets in foreign countries that we are able to maintain the vast population by which this island is inhabited. . . ."[12] Lord Rosebery expressed concern over the loss of Britain's earlier "monopoly of colonies,"[13] and Chamberlain thought that half the British population would starve if the empire were reduced to the dimensions of the United Kingdom "by a stroke of a pen."[14]

Britain's overall trade was the highest among the powers, and it continued to grow throughout most of the period under study. After a decline in the early 1870s, Britain's net capital exports began to rise around 1877 and continued to increase through the middle 1880s. The German trend at this time was somewhat downward.[15]

There was a high correlation between British trade and colonial expansion. The feeling was strong in England, as among other colonial powers, that control of sea routes and colonial territory was an important safeguard for a country's survival. As industrialism developed on the Continent, Britain's economic supremacy became more and more threatened. Moreover, during the 1870s the countries of continental Europe tended to swing from free trade to protectionism, and Britain found continental markets closing against her. At about the same time, some of the new industrialized countries began to feel the pressures of overproduction and to demand new markets for their surplus goods.[16]

Conceivably, Britain, as the preeminent imperial power, felt relatively satisfied with the status quo and thus highly sensitive to French, German, or other challenges to British colonial supremacy. At the same time, domestic growth in Britain (as well as in rival nations) may have exacerbated the competition. For however fast England was losing her long-time advantage on many dimensions, she was still growing on most — in population, in technology, and in her commercial, financial, and naval capabilities. Colonial expansion, whether or not it proved profitable overall for the economy, offered a variety of profitable challenges for adventurers, traders,[17] professional soldiers, investors, bureaucrats, and others.

If Britain's success in building an empire stimulated other powers to emulate and even surpass her, this was part of the price Britain paid for greatness. For a while she coped with rival nation challenges by

---

[12]Langer, 1951, p. 79.
[13]*Ibid.*, p. 77.
[14]Chamberlain, 1897, p. 202.
[15]Bloomfield, 1968, pp. 7–13.
[16]Langer, 1962, p. 284.
[17]Cecil Rhodes, for example, was a major beneficiary of exploitation in southern Africa.

shrewd diplomacy and skillful manipulation of the balance of power; but after 1885 British leaders became increasingly sensitive to new pressures. Britain found herself increasingly at odds not only with France (which had ambitions in Africa and Madagascar) and Russia (which was pressing its own interests into central Asia), but also with Germany. The possibility of these countries collaborating against Britain was a nagging anxiety.[18]

A major objective of British leaders was to maintain and defend the Empire's lines of communication with the Indian subcontinent, which was of great strategic as well as political and economic value.[19] The Indian empire provided Britain with "a uniquely self-financing army, which allowed Victorian governments to exert power in the Far and Near East without always having to foot the whole bill." Another major objective was to develop positions of strength against Russia "as she sprawled out westwards and eastwards from the Asiatic heartland."[20]

Russian expansionist inclinations increasingly found expression and justification in Pan-Slavism.[21] The Pan-Slavic movement had emerged from the original notion that all Slavs of Eastern Europe constituted one great cultural family. Pan-Slavic sentiments were eventually incorporated into tsarist Russia's foreign policy; they were thus perceived by Austrian leaders as a threat to their own empire. It seemed highly likely to German and British leaders that the historic Russian drive to control Constantinople and other parts of the declining Ottoman empire would conflict with Austrian and German aspirations in the same area and also threaten the British "life line" to India.

The Russian policy was that Constantinople, strategically located on the Bosphorus Strait leading to the Black Sea, should in no instance fall under the control of another power. Regarding the Black Sea as her own *mare clausum*, Russia had come to view the closure of the Dardanelles in 1841 to all but Turkish warships as important to her own national security. Since the closure was regarded as essential to Russia's defense, the tsarist government wanted no alteration in subsequent treaties that preserved this state of affairs.[22] On the other hand, Russian leaders felt deeply humiliated by treaty clauses that excluded their own warships from passing through the Bosphorus Strait; the exclusion was considered inconsistent with Russia's status as a great power.[23]

---

[18]Langer, 1962, p. 297.
[19]Robinson and Gallagher, 1961, p. 13.
[20]*Ibid.*
[21]Medlicott, 1963, pp. 4–6.
[22]Price, 1956, pp. 9–16, 18–19.
[23]Fay, 1966, p. 362.

Between 1870 and 1890 German Chancellor Bismarck dominated European politics much as the Austrian statesman Metternich had done during the first half of the century. His policies contributed in important ways to the relative tranquility that prevailed in Europe during those two eventful decades. In general, his purpose was to achieve a system of military alliances assuring maintenance of the status quo after the Franco-Prussian War and to prevent the formation of any coalition that might threaten his country. His initial aim was to isolate France, which desperately wanted to regain Alsace and Lorraine, but increasingly he developed what amounted to a unipolar concert of Europe. The German defeat of France had been the result of spectacular advances in German technology, production, and other capabilities. Although these advances continued between 1870 and 1890, accumulation of German power was also based on shrewd negotiations and the manipulation of alliances.

To protect Germany's vulnerable eastern frontier and to further isolate France, Bismarck in 1872–1873 organized the League of Three Emperors, which amounted to a Holy Alliance against revolution in all its forms. Nothing about specific political problems was said in any of the agreements; critical questions of the Ottoman empire and the Balkans were not touched on. Within a few years the arrangement proved unable to withstand the strain of new conflicts in the Balkans, although Bismarck "evidently considered it better than nothing."[24]

The decline of the Turkish empire disturbed the whole balance of power in Europe, Until 1829 the Turks had maintained control of the entire Balkan peninsula. At the conclusion of the first Russo-Turkish War (1829) the Ottoman empire was forced to recognize the independence of Greece, grant autonomy to Serbia, and transfer Wallachia and Moldavia to Russian protection. For the Ottoman and Austrian empires this was like prying the lid from Pandora's box. Thereafter, the continuing decline of Turkey, the pressure of Russia in the Balkans, the Russo-Turkish War of 1877–1878, and the continuing upsurge of nationalism among subject nationalities in the Balkan regions further destabilized the balance of power. Of particular importance, with respect to events leading to WWI, was the Serbian achievement of independence through the Treaty of Berlin.[25]

Austrian leaders had been watching the disintegration of the Ottoman empire in the Balkans with covetous eyes, but their aspirations were in conflict with those of Russia, which had long-standing aspirations of her own in the region.[26] In many respects Austria-Hungary was "scarcely more than a huge, economically under-developed

---

[24]Langer, 1962, p. 25.
[25]Medlicott, 1963, pp. 10–11.
[26]Medlicott, 1956, pp. 253–265.

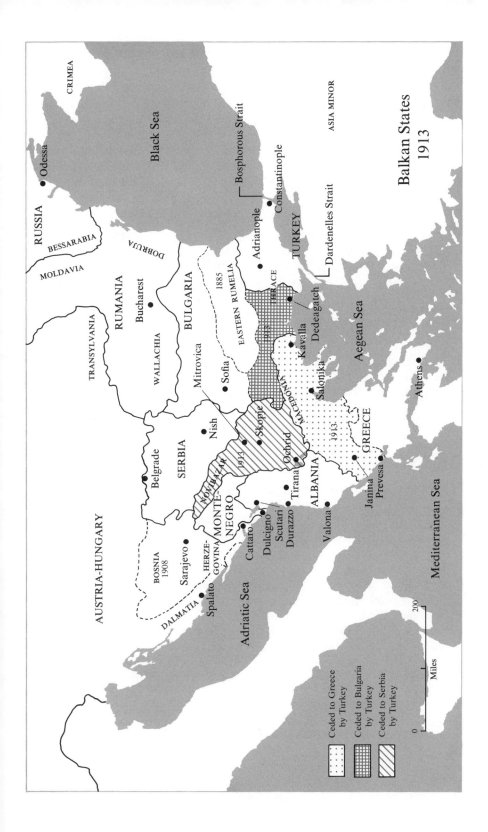

Balkan States
1913

RUSSIA

CRIMEA

Black Sea

Odessa

BESSARABIA

MOLDAVIA

DOBRUJA

RUMANIA

Bucharest

WALLACHIA

TRANSYLVANIA

BULGARIA

1885

EASTERN RUMELIA

Sofia

Mitrovica

Nish

SERBIA

Belgrade

1913

NOVI-BAZAR

MONTE-
NEGRO

Skopie

Ochrid

MACEDONIA

THRACE

Adrianople

Bosphorous Strait

Constantinople

TURKEY

Dardenelles Strait

ASIA MINOR

Dedeagatch

Kavalla

Salonika

1913

Aegean Sea

Athens

GREECE

Janina

Prevesa

ALBANIA

Tirana

Valona

Durazzo

Scutari

Dulcigno

Cattaro

HERZE-
GOVINA

Sarajevo

BOSNIA
1908

Spalato

DALMATIA

Adriatic Sea

AUSTRIA-HUNGARY

Mediterranean Sea

Ceded to Greece
by Turkey

Ceded to Bulgaria
by Turkey

Ceded to Serbia
by Turkey

0   200

Miles

area."[27] The empire was among the most populous of Europe, yet its industrial resources were comparatively meagre and its standard of living was low. But in particular fields, the industrial capabilities of the empire were "substantial and technically up-to-date," and Austrian and Hungarian industry served a sizeable market.[28] Austrian population, industrial production, and trade were growing, but the empire was not able to expand territorially as were the other powers; acquisitions were limited to Bosnia and Herzegovina.

With the decline of Turkish power, Russia found herself competing with Austria for trade in Rumania, Bulgaria, Greece, and Serbia. From the Austrian viewpoint it was vital that these Balkan kingdoms should not become dominated exclusively by Russia, and Russian encroachments were observed in Vienna with apprehension.[29] After the Crimean War against Turkey, Russia felt increasingly checked by England and France and by the hostile attitude of Austria.[30]

The Turkish decline created new opportunities for the other great powers. During the Russo-Turkish War of 1877–1878 Bismarck, in an effort to prevent any union between France and Russia, encouraged the tsar to push his conquests around the Black Sea, at the same time encouraging Austria to acquire a Balkan empire.[31] Through the military convention of January 15, 1877, and a subsequent political agreement, Austria had pledged neutrality in the event of a Russo-Turkish war.[32] In exchange for this concession and Russian annexation of Bessarabia, Austria-Hungary would be allowed to annex Bosnia-Herzegovina except for the Turkish *sanjak* (district) of Novibazar, between Serbia and Montenegro. When Russia, confident of Austrian neutrality, declared war and defeated Turkey (1877–1878), matters turned out differently; the Russians imposed on the Turks a treaty that served strictly Russian interests.

The most important provision of the Treaty of San Stefano between Russia and Turkey (March 3, 1878) was the proposed creation of a large autonomous Bulgaria, stretching from the Danube to the Aegean Sea and from Albania to the Black Sea. This Greater Bulgaria, which was to include most of Macedonia and Thrace (thereby splitting European Turkey into two parts), was to be occupied by Russia, according to the treaty, for two years.[33] Montenegro and Serbia would receive their independence and territorial increases. Rumania, despite

---

[27]Marz, 1953, p. 124.

[28]*Ibid.*, pp. 125–126. "The output of pig iron per high furnace, for instance, was before the war twice as great in Austria as in Great Britain, and the cotton mills were . . . equipped to a much greater extent with modern ring frames than in the British mills."

[29]Langer, 1962, p. 98.

[30]Medlicott, 1956, pp. 72–73.

[31]Langer, 1962, p. 77.

[32]Medlicott, 1963, p. 2.

[33]Fieldhouse, 1966, p. 183; Bridge, 1972, p. 86.

the fact that she had assisted Russia during the war, was to cede Bessarabia to Russia in return for independence and the Dobruja region. In addition to Bessarabia, Russia was to receive territory in the Caucasus, strategic land in northern Armenia (commanding the descent to Mesopotamia), and part of a caravan route into the heart of Persia.[34] Contrary to Russia's pledge to Austria, Bosnia and Herzegovina were to be semi-autonomous.

If carried out, these arrangements "portended the annihilation of Austro-Hungary's prestige and influence on the Balkan peninsula."[35] However, the Dual Monarchy was not willing to absolve Russia from her promise to turn over Bosnia and Herzegovina, and both the Austrian and British governments were fearful of a huge Russian-controlled Bulgaria stretching to the Aegean.[36] The tsarist government soon discovered that the Treaty of San Stefano had been too bold a challenge to those powers that had been predisposed to support Turkey.[37] The virtual destruction of Ottoman sovereignty in Europe assured resistance from Britain and Austria, who feared that Russian interests would move deeper into the Balkans.[38]

Britain immediately protested the treaty, and Austria also expressed indignation. Through a secret treaty between Britain and Russia, the latter renounced the caravan route from the Black Sea toward Persia. The boundaries of the proposed Greater Bulgaria were redrawn to allow for three states: Bulgaria, Eastern Rumelia and Macedonia. Bosnia and Herzegovina were awarded to Austria-Hungary as protectorates. By a secret treaty between Britain and Turkey, however, Britain was to receive Cyprus in return for a pledge to defend Asia Minor against further advances by Russia.[39]

Within the course of a month (June 13–July 13, 1878), representatives of the powers at the Congress of Berlin were able to achieve a complete "paper settlement" of the Balkan and Near Eastern questions—an outcome so speedy as to suggest that the solutions were neither as original nor as final as the more optimistic of its authors supposed, although the settlement lasted for the next twenty-two years. However, over the next thirty years or so, the nationalistic ambitions of Serbia, Bulgaria, Rumania, and Greece increasingly "brought them into constant conflict with Turkey, Austria-Hungary or one another."[40] The Austrians viewed these nationalistic tendencies—especially in Serbia—with considerable apprehension.

[34]Sontag, 1933, pp. 15–16.
[35]Bridge, 1972, p. 86.
[36]Langer, 1962, pp. 142–143.
[37]Taylor, 1954, pp. 216–217.
[38]Medlicott, 1963, p. 12.
[39]Austro-Hungarian Monarchy, 1878, p. 157.
[40]Fay, 1966, pp. 353–354.

The Treaty of Berlin provided Austria with an opportunity for exercising a preponderant influence in the Balkan states. Russia found herself badly outmaneuvered, and Russian capital soon went to more profitable investments in Asia. The later attempt in Bulgaria to compel acceptance of Russian loans only caused suspicion and undermined Russian influence there. Austria, on the other hand, as the beneficiary of unequal trade arrangements with Bulgaria, could easily command that country's markets; in other Balkan states without Russian-controlled governments, Austria's position was even stronger.[41]

Britain agreed to accept French occupation of Tunis, and Bismarck suggested that Britain herself should acquire Egypt. The German Chancellor's support of French acquisition of Tunis angered Italy, which went away empty-handed (although it was later offered Tripoli).

These conflicts of territorial interest caused increasing friction among the powers. Good relations with Russia had been a basic aspect of Prussian foreign policy since the time of Frederick the Great. By the summer of 1879, however, Bismarck had become unsure of Russia and was persuaded that Austro-German unity provided a strong guarantee for the peace of Europe. From the Chancellor's viewpoint, if Austria were seriously defeated or deprived of her position as a great power, Germany risked being caught between Russia on the one side and a revanchist France on the other. On October 7, 1879, the Austrian and German empires concluded a Treaty of Alliance pledging the two powers to mutual support if either were attacked by Russia. If one were attacked by another power, however, the other was obliged only to observe benevolent neutrality — unless the attacker was supported by Russia.[42] Austria reserved the right to annex the provinces of Bosnia and Herzegovina at whatever moment she should deem opportune. Other articles dealt with Bulgaria, Eastern Rumelia, and the *sanjak* of Novibazar.[43]

Despite unanimity over the terms of the Dual Alliance, Germany and Austria construed its ultimate purpose differently. Bismarck soon came to believe that a conflict with Russia was not as probable as he had thought. Austria stood for a strong anti-Russian policy, and hoped to enlist British support in forcing the tsarist government to observe the Treaty of Berlin.[44] Until the collapse of the Hapsburg and Hohenzollern empires in 1918, however, the Austro-German Alliance of 1879 served as "the very mainspring of Bismarckian and Wilhelminian policy."[45]

Two years later, on June 18, 1881, Austria-Hungary, Germany, and Russia established the Three Emperors' Alliance, based on the Three

---

[41]Bridge, 1972, p. 108.
[42]*Ibid.*, p. 106. For the text of the treaty see *ibid*, pp. 396–398.
[43]*Ibid.*, pp. 399–402.
[44]Langer, 1962, p. 450.
[45]*Ibid.*, p. 196.

Emperors' League of 1873. In case one of the three powers should find itself at war with a fourth power, the other two were to maintain benevolent neutrality and seek to localize the conflict. Russia, in agreement with Germany, declared her firm resolution to respect Austrian interests arising from the Treaty of Berlin. The three powers recognized the principle of the closing of the Bosphorus Strait and the Dardanelles.

On the basis of the Austro-German Alliance and the Three Emperors' Alliance. Bismarck proceeded to develop a systematic web of diplomatic arrangements that involved all the major powers (with the exception of France) and many secondary powers.[46]

Further efforts were made to bring some order to relations between the Balkan countries and Austria and other great powers. In 1881 Serbia and Austria agreed not to tolerate intrigues against one another on their respective territories.[47] The Austrian empire stood ready to countenance Serbian expansion southwards with the provision that the *sanjak* of Novibazar should not be penetrated. Serbia, in return, placed her foreign policy under Austrian control, remaining a virtual puppet until 1903. A five-year secret alliance between Rumania and Austria provided reciprocal support in case of outside attack. Italy joined the treaty five years later, and thereafter the treaty was periodically renewed.[48]

With the temporary solution of Balkan problems, Germany began to shift her attention to Africa and the Pacific. Until about 1883, Bismarck's overriding purpose seems to have been to establish the hegemony of Germany on the European continent, and at first he opposed the idea of an overseas empire.[49] In 1884 he withdrew his opposition to the acquisition of colonies and established German protectorates in Africa and the South Seas[50]—in spite of considerable opposition from Great Britain.[51] Indeed, supported by a surge of public opinion, Bismarck assumed a leading role in the tide of German colonialism that characterized the years 1883 to 1885.[52]

This basic alteration in Bismarckian policy has been explained in different ways—as a way of increasing German power, as a tradeoff for the support of German industrialists on other issues, and as a response to the Great Depression of 1873–1896.[53] The idea that Bismarck's colonial policy was an outgrowth of the Great Depression has much

---

[46]Healy and Stein, 1971.

[47]Langer, 1962, pp. 326–327.

[48]Petrie, 1949, p. 35; cf. Martens, 1920, p. 21.

[49]Aydelotte, 1937, p. 21.

[50]Territories acquired by Germany during the 1880s included Togoland, Cameroon, Southwest Africa, East Africa, German New Guinea, the Bismarck Archipelago, and the Solomon Islands.

[51]Brandenburg, 1927, p. 98.

[52]Langer, 1962, p. 287.

[53]See Brandenburg, 1927, pp. 18–19; Taylor, 1954, p. 295; Turner, 1967; and Townsend, 1921, p. 106.

appeal; overproduction and a fall in domestic prices make better sense than more esoteric explanations of Bismarck's colonial program. Nevertheless, more fundamental explanations for German expansion seem to lie beneath the ebbs and flows of the domestic economy.

According to William Langer, if we accept the doctrines of expansion and imperialism as they were put forward at that time, it cannot be denied that "Germany's needs were greatest."[54] Unless she were willing to continue "exporting" population to the United States and elsewhere, Germany needed new area for her growing population. Also, she "needed markets for her growing industrial output, and she needed sources for raw materials."[55]

Germany was growing rapidly on a number of critical dimensions, and demands for raw materials and markets were rising. In 1871 the new German empire, despite its spectacular defeat of France and other successes, was still largely an agrarian society, "only slightly less rural in character, a trifle more industrialized, than the Prussia of 1816."[56] Then, over the next thirty years "all the forces stimulating industrial growth made their combined force felt."[57] This transformation from an agrarian state to the most advanced industrial economy in Europe — "one of the wonders of economic history"[58] — created new demands.

German economic growth depended more and more on the importation of enormous quantities of raw materials, foodstuffs, and luxuries, paid for through the exportation of manufactured goods. For this and related reasons, important sectors of German industry were becoming restive under Bismarck's policy of trade protectionism; there was a strong consensus for expansion into foreign markets. As German industry and overseas commerce grew, the attention of the government was increasingly directed overseas. German traders and merchants appeared along African coasts, in the Pacific, and elsewhere. At the same time, large numbers of missionaries who went out to serve among colonial "heathens" often combined "trading activities with their spiritual duties and established important economic interests in remote parts of the world."[59] The feeling grew that such private interests ought to be supported and defended.

Hans Delbruck and other nineteenth-century apologists for German colonialism "were impressed by the *national prestige* (not the eco-

---

[54]Langer, 1962, p. 289.

[55]*Ibid*. See also Landes, 1969, p. 240.

[56]*Cambridge Modern History*, 1962, XI:58.

[57]*Ibid*.

[58]*Ibid*.

[59]Langer, 1962, pp. 287–288. By the 1880s some fifteen German firms had established sixty trading stations on the west coast of Africa, and there were hundreds of German religious missions. The German firm of Goddefroy established a virtual monopoly in Samoan trade, and German interests were deeply involved in the Fiji Islands. These extensions of German interests abroad "necessarily involved new claims on the imperial government." Soon German traders and missionaries were "clamouring for protection and agitating for annexation of this or that territory by the home government."

nomic advantages) achieved by England as a result of her empire. 'What was and is valid for England is also valid for us.'"[60] In view of the constantly diminishing area of unclaimed colonial territory, the desire for colonies was almost certain to collide with the same desire by other powers.

As Germany's overseas holdings increased, she became involved in colonial disputes with Britain, which had already acquired the largest part of the colonial pie. Bismarck believed that the English, holding tenaciously to what they had and expanding further, were unwilling to allow the Germans a fair chance in the colonial field. For Bismarck a central question was whether Britain, in return for greater German support for her policies, would be willing to allow Germany to expand her holdings.

Imperialist policies attracted active support from various sectors of German society. In January, 1884, the *Kolonialzeitung* was founded, and it soon began disseminating colonial propaganda and providing a central organization for previously scattered efforts at colonial expansion. Within a year the organization had acquired more than 10,000 members. Bismarck notified the powers that German imperial protection had been extended over settlements on the northern coasts of New Britain Archipelago and that plans were being made to expand German interests from this nucleus.[61] As Bismarck tended more and more to consider England Germany's principal commercial rival, he tried to isolate her in the struggle for overseas trade and colonial power.

An Anglo-German dispute arose in 1883 when German subjects established themselves at Angra Pequeña in southwest Africa. When Bismarck first inquired of the British whether they claimed authority in the area, the reply was evasive. Later, after the German flag had been raised, Britain asserted that she considered any claim to sovereignty over areas between Portuguese territory in the north and the territory of Cape Colony in the south as an infringement of her rights. Britain eventually recognized Germany's claim, but Anglo-German frictions in the area continued for several decades.[62]

During most of the 1870s British overseas interests collided more often with French than with German interests. France, like Britain and Germany, had undergone rapid technological and economic growth, and French overseas activities, interests, and colonial holdings expanded at a comparable rate.

---

[60]Langer, 1962, p. 289–293; see also Landes, 1969, pp. 240–242.

[61]Aydelotte, 1937, pp. 18, 23–24. Bismarck received news December 23, 1884, that the German flag had been raised over parts of New Britain, New Ireland, and New Guinea. The announcement came during a parliamentary deadlock over Bismarck's colonial policy and added further strength to German imperialist impulses. Soon a series of treaties of "protection" and friendship were concluded with back-country chiefs in Africa and elsewhere. Colonies, Bismarck said, would mean the winning of new markets for German industry, the expansion of trade, and a new field for German activity, civilization, and capital.

[62]Langer, 1962, pp. 292–300.

At the time of the Franco-Prussian War (1870–71) France and Germany were largely equal in both population and income. During the following thirty years, however, Germany's birth rate became the highest in Europe, France's the lowest, and the German economy expanded at almost twice the rate of the French.[63] We may ask, then, given these conditions, whether the spectacular expansion of French overseas interests before WWI can be accounted for in terms of the propositions outlined in Chapter 1. The question cannot be answered as yet—indeed, it will persistently arise throughout the whole book. Nevertheless, the French economy did continue to grow throughout the 1870–1914 period, so that it may be possible to account for French colonial expansion by French technological and economic growth.

The tendency in recent years, outside the Marxist-Leninist tradition, has been to treat economic explanations of history with caution and even skepticism. Two leading scholars, Christopher Andrew and Henry Brunswhig, present considerable economic evidence for French colonial expansion, only to discount it or explain it away. This may be the result of the failure to take into account the indirect ways in which French expansionist interests, both in and out of government, were able to override the economic arguments against expansion. That is, even if French colonial policies were not profitable to the nation *as a whole*, economic interests may still account for these policies. In accounting for colonial expansion, therefore, one must take into consideration *private benefits* (to entrepreneurs, investors, bureaucrats, and military officers) as well as social costs (e.g., taxes).

Brunschwig, for example, in his book *French Colonialism, 1871–1914*, seems to recognize the importance of economic considerations even while minimizing that importance. The notion that colonialism was profitable was, he says, "nothing more than a myth." But the myth was believed "by those moved by nationalist emotions and also by those opponents of the policy who condemned the capitalists for the profits they were making out of colonial expansion."[64] Clearly, Brunschwig confuses private and public profit. It would seem that an economic influence is no less economic because it benefits only certain interests rather than the national interest as a whole.

Similarly, Andrew and Brunschwig do not accept economic explanations for the colonial policies of Théophile Delcassé, undersecretary of state for colonies in 1893, minister of colonies from 1894 until mid-1895, and appointed foreign minister just before the Fashoda Incident (1898). Andrew quotes Delcassé to the effect that Europe at the time was "stifling" within her boundaries, with production everywhere outstripping the European demand for manufactured products.

---

[63]Andrew, 1968, p. 16.
[64]Brunschwig, 1964, pp. 182–183.

All Europe was therefore "driven by necessity to seek new markets far away," and "what more secure markets" could a nation possess than "countries placed under its influence"?[65] Yet, according to Andrew, Delcassé's own passionate support for French expansion had "far less to do with economic necessity than with national prestige."[66] But national prestige—like national security—tends to be closely connected with economic considerations, especially for countries "stifling" within their boundaries and "driven by a necessity" for secure markets. Why so many analysts are reluctant to accept economic variables, even while recognizing their existence, is difficult to understand.

French colonial expansion led to competition and conflicts of interests with other powers—with Italy, England, and, especially after the turn of the century, with Germany. Although he was not in any sense "the passionate anti-German portrayed by some historians," Delcassé viewed Germany with suspicion and looked forward to the eventual return of Alsace-Lorraine to France.[67] Yet at all points of the globe that most occupied Delcassé's official attention—Siam, the Nile, the Mediterranean, and West Africa—it was Britain, not Germany, that he saw as France's main competitor.[68] For this reason, Bismarck hoped to improve relations with France and persuade the French to pursue a common policy against Britain, rendering England "helpless when opposed by a united continent."[69]

When English statesmen stood up to Bismarck, they were all but challenging him to establish a coalition against Britain.[70] The chancellor asserted that he did not seek war with Britain, but wanted her to understand that if the navies of other nations were to unite, they would counterbalance her on the ocean and compel her to reconsider the interests of others. Although Germany lacked the maritime capabilities, Bismarck contemplated an "equilibrium of the seas" directed against England.[71]

One of Britain's major disabilities was Egypt, where a whole range of financial irregularities had created something approaching an international scandal. Under an 1880 international arrangement for solving Egyptian monetary problems, the powers could cause Britain considerable embarrassment by raising questions about her involvement in

---

[65]Andrew, 1968, p. 26.
[66]*Ibid.*, p. 27.
[67]*Ibid.*, p. 16.
[68]*Ibid.*, pp. 12, 48.
[69]Langer, 1962, p. 297.
[70]*Ibid.*, pp. 301–302.
[71]"For a young people," asserted Prince Albert of Prussia, "there is no prosperity without expansion, no expansion without an overseas policy, and no overseas policy without a navy." (Quoted in Townsend, 1930, p. 57.) Without a strong navy, Germany's threats against Britain lacked credibility (Robinson and Gallagher, 1961, p. 207).

Egypt's financial status.[72] Under these circumstances, Bismarck took advantage of an overlap of German and French interests. French willingness to collaborate with Germany against Britain probably emerged less from any serious expectation of annexing Egypt than from the hope of seeing it detached from British control, thus enhancing French security in the Mediterranean.[73]

From the time of Napoleon's expedition in 1798 until de Lessep's construction of the modern Suez Canal (1869), France had been the dominant European influence in Egypt. England acquired a direct stake in the region in 1875 when the government purchased 40 percent of Suez Canal shares.[74] During the next year, France and England established "dual control" over Egypt's unstable finances, and there followed a period of Anglo-French cooperation.[75] Faced in 1882 with a threat of a nationalist rebellion, France and England agreed on joint military intervention. When parliamentary opposition forced France to withdraw at the last moment, Britain alone intervened and established a "temporary" occupation that lasted for seventy years.[76] During the 1890s Germany and especially France were disturbed by Britain's use of Egypt as a base for military expeditions into the Sudan to the south.

For Germany and France, the Egyptian question was useful in forcing Britain to modify her opposition to the colonial aspirations of other powers, thus allowing the Germans and French to press their claims more vigorously in Africa and elsewhere.[77] France emerged as a threat to British predominance in the Mediterranean and, as a consequence, it became increasingly important to Englishmen to hold onto Egypt.[78]

Had these maneuvers actually resulted in a naval combination against Britain, the Franco-German collaboration could have presented a serious threat to Britain. It is doubtful, however, that Bismarck intended to achieve so close an alliance with France or to risk permanent estrangement with England.[79] Moreover, French leaders were wary of Bismarck's long-term proposals, being content to accept German support for France in Egyptian affairs.[80]

While seeking a limited entente with France, Bismarck worked at completing his grand diplomatic scheme by inducing Britain to play a more positive role in meeting a perceived Russian threat. He argued

---

[72]Langer, 1962, p. 298.
[73]Robinson and Gallagher, 1961, p. 271.
[74]Andrew, 1968, p. 21.
[75]*Ibid.*
[76]*Ibid.*, pp. 21–22.
[77]Langer, 1962, p. 299.
[78]Robinson and Gallagher, 1961, pp. 268, 271.
[79]Langer, 1962, p. 303.
[80]*Ibid.*, p. 304.

that if Russia increased sufficiently her influence in Turkey, British ships would soon find it impossible to pass through the Bosphorus Strait. The chancellor had three immediate goals: British support of Austria, reestablishment of British influence in Turkey, and Italian support in the Mediterranean.[81]

Bismarck's negotiations with Italy are evidence of how closely the activities of the major powers in North Africa and the Near East were tied to their relations on the European continent. Situated as she was, and with a rapidly growing population and some technological growth (especially in the north), Italy tended to extend her interests in two directions, eastward along the Adriatic coast, and across the Mediterranean into North Africa. Italy's disappointment over her failure to acquire Tunis has already been noted. It has been said that her quest for alliances was really a quest for recognition as an equal, a recognition rarely accorded.[82] Italy's desire to expand into the near-Balkan area and in various parts of Africa was not supported by sufficient capabilities, and thus she was not in a favorable position to successfully maintain an imperialistic policy. Despite having come away from the Congress of Berlin empty-handed, Italian leaders continued to seek predominance in Tunis, but succeeded only in provoking intense French competition.

When Tunis became a French protectorate in 1881, the Italians felt compelled to seek new international support. In October of that year King Humbert paid a visit to Vienna. Austria was not hospitable to his proposal for a mutual guarantee, but Bismarck, who was afraid that Russia might not remain loyal to the League of the Three Emperors, picked up the negotiations as a diplomatic precaution. On May 20, 1882, an embittered Italy joined Germany and Austria to form the Triple Alliance. The Alliance pledged to guarantee the general peace, fortify the monarchical principle, and maintain existing social and political orders in the three participating states.[83]

The crucial clause for the Alliance for Germany was an Italian promise to remain neutral in a war between Austria and Russia. Bismarck considered that Italian neutrality would save the Germans four army divisions in the event of such a war, since Germany was pledged to preserve the territorial integrity of the Austrian empire and it was felt that Italy would exploit an Austro-Russian war to advance her own ambitions in the Balkans. Through the Alliance Germany hoped to inhibit France from a revanchist war and Austria sought security against an attack by Russia. Italy looked for enhanced prestige, protection against any attempt by France to restore the temporal power

---

[81]Langer, 1931, p. 435.
[82]*Cambridge Modern History*, XII:553.
[83]Langer, 1962, pp. 244–247; for the text of the treaty see de Martens, X:17–20.

of the pope, and above all, the support of the other two powers in her ambition to establish an Italian colonial empire in northern Africa and the Adriatic.

Toward the end of 1886 Bismarck was faced with the impending expiration of the Triple Alliance. According to one calculation in Berlin, Germany, Austria, and Italy as a bloc "probably weighed as much as Russia and France together."[84] But Italy's price for renewal of the Triple Alliance included German support for Italian opposition to French expansion in North Africa and a share in Balkan and Turkish shores whenever these regions should be partitioned by the major powers. Bismarck was prepared to negotiate, but the Austrians objected, proposing that Italy join the other two powers in guaranteeing the status quo in the Balkans. Bismarck objected to this arrangement and the Austrians refused to accede to Italian demands; negotiations reached an impasse.[85] In the end, Bismarck presented an acceptable formula involving two agreements distinct from the Triple Alliance agreement: one between Austria and Italy, the other between Germany and Italy.

In the Austro-Italian agreement Italy achieved the right to be consulted on any partition of the Balkans or the Ottoman empire; in return, she pledged to oppose any territorial modification in these regions that might be injurious to either nation. The Italo-German treaty also contained a provision for maintaining the status quo in the Balkan region, excluding Bulgaria. Germany agreed to support Italy in the event that France tried to extend her sovereignty in North Africa.[86]

Bismarck felt that it was vital to secure British support for Austrian interests in the Balkans. This was achieved early when Italy and Britain concluded the First Mediterranean Agreement (February 12, 1887) preserving the existing order in the Mediterranean area. In case of encroachment by an outside power, Britain bound herself to support Italy in Cyrenaica, Tripolitania and elsewhere on the North African coast, and the British position in Egypt was recognized in return.[87]

Eight days after the conclusion of the First Mediterranean Agreement, Germany, Austria, and Italy renewed the Triple Alliance for five more years. The new arrangement specified Austrian recognition of Italian interests in the Balkans and an Italian claim to compensation in the event of a partition of the Ottoman empire. Also, Austria pledged to achieve an understanding with Italy and offer compensation before occupying any Balkan territory—a clause calculated by Bismarck to inhibit Austrian expansion to the southeast. Germany, however, refused to assist Italy's expansionist ambitions in North Africa.[88]

---

[84]Rich, 1965, I:193.
[85]*Ibid.*, I:195.
[86]*Ibid.*, I:196.
[87]*Ibid.*, I:21.
[88]See de Martens, 1920, X:30–34.

Italy was committed to support England in Egypt, while Britain agreed to support Italy against the encroachments of any third power in North Africa. The two countries also adhered to maintenance of the status quo in the Mediterranean, Adriatic, Aegean, and Black Seas. Germany thus secured the aid of Britain in supporting Italy against France in North Africa, and Austria was assured of both Italian and English support in keeping Russia out of Bulgaria.[89] A month later Austria acceded to the First Mediterranean Agreement. All three powers asserted that it was in their mutual interest to preserve the status quo in the Mediterranean and Near East and to prevent the aggrandizement of any one power at the expense of the others.

Despite these various arrangements, Bismarck remained dissatisfied, particularly with respect to German relations with Russia. Therefore, during 1887 he negotiated a secret Treaty of Reinsurance with the tsar's government. The treaty stipulated that if either signatory should find itself at war with a third great power, the other would preserve benevolent neutrality and try to localize the conflict. This provision was not to apply, however, in the event of an offensive war against France or Austria by either party. Germany recognized historic Russian rights in the Balkans and the legitimacy of Russian influence in Eastern Rumelia and Bulgaria. Germany and Russia also agreed that during hostilities the Dardanelles whould be closed to warships of all nations.[90]

Because of his support for Russian interests in the Balkans, Bismarck was accused by Austrian leaders of disloyalty toward Austria. However, Bismarck had frequently made clear in Vienna that Germany would not support Austrian interests in the Balkans. It is probably more accurate to say that Austrian leaders had been mistaken in their understanding of German intentions. On the other hand, the British government seemed pleased with Bismarck's assurance that German troops were committed for defense against France; they would have been less than pleased if they had known that Bismarck also had assured Russia of diplomatic support. The Russians would have been equally unsettled, however, if they had been aware that— almost on the eve of the Reinsurance Treaty in 1887—Bismarck had maneuvered the Mediterranean coalition against them and that Field Marshal Moltke was busily advising the Austrians (not without encouragement from Bismarck) on how they might increase their military power in Galicia. The Reinsurance Treaty was thus "a fraud on the Russians . . . ."[91] Along with other alliance arrangements in Bismarck's diplomatic web, it served the purpose of securing Germany against both France and Russia and inhibiting a bipolarization of European power.

---

[89]Rich, 1965, I:202.
[90]Martens, 1920, X:37–41; Langer, 1962, pp. 416–425.
[91]Taylor, 1954, pp. 318–319.

With the signing of the Reinsurance Treaty, Bismarck's alliance system had reached completion and, on paper at least, German security had been provided for. By this time, moreover, the European powers were "so enmeshed in an elaborate scheme of insurance treaties, reinsurance treaties, agreements, and understandings that it was almost impossible for any one of them to act without bringing all the others upon the scene." Under the circumstances there was, as Bismarck himself said, "a premium upon the maintenance of peace."[92]

However, Bismarck's alliance system could not itself maintain the balance of power for long. Among the great powers, population growth and technological and economic development were contributing to changes in the international configuration of power. Nevertheless, during his chancellorship Bismarck was able to achieve a considerable balance of power in Europe. At the same time, there was a fundamental contradiction between Bismarck's policies of economic protectionism and the imperial expansion of German, British, French, Russian, and Austrian interests.[93] In the next chapter we will consider how Bismarck's Concert was transformed into the *Weltpolitik* that increased the probability of war among the great powers.

---

[92]Langer, 1962, p. 459.
[93]Rosenberg, 1943, p. 72.

Competition, Crisis, and the Search for Stability

4

This chapter is concerned with the ways in which the competitive expansion of the major powers contributed to the breakdown of the complicated alliance network Bismarck had labored to build. We shall focus on the accelerated extension of European activities and interests throughout the world, the disruption of the Bismarckian concert, the Franco-Russian alignment, the beginnings of *Weltpolitik*, the Anglo-Japanese alliance, and the failure of the great European states to achieve a stable configuration of power. We shall consider some of the ways in which a nineteenth-century alliance system generally associated with peace in Europe gave way to bipolar conflict and the conditions for the outbreak of world war in 1914.[1]

The power available to a country is the result of a complex combination of human and material resources, and its exercise may involve political, economic, military, or psychological considerations, or a combination of all four. In Chapter 1 we indicated that a country may increase its power relative to other countries by concluding alliances or by denying a rival the possibility of favorable alignments. The formation of alliances is a diplomatic rather than military undertaking and is normally thought of as a peaceful activity. On the other hand, an alliance for military purposes, while presumably drawing the signatory parties closer together, implies the existence of a rival or enemy country or bloc and therefore conflict. Although alliances are considered advantageous in the struggle for position in the hierarchy of power, a country may find itself burdened with responsibilities and drawn into conflicts that it might otherwise have avoided.

---

[1]Our discussion is based largely on Singer and Small, 1970.

The question is frequently raised whether or not within an international system there is an optimal number of countries and/or alliances as well as perhaps an optimal distribution of capabilities for the maintenance of stability. Is there some balance-of-power formula that will greatly diminish the probabilities of war? Several different views have been put forward.[2] "Historically speaking," according to one of these, "the balance of power scheme appears to have been of most use when applied to a situation in which there were three main elements, France and Austria, for example, with England as the balance."[3] Others have held that five is the optimal number, and so forth.

In an effort to examine this problem quantitatively J. David Singer and Melvin Small raised the following question:"Do alliance aggregations in general, or bipolarity tendencies in particular, correlate in any meaningful way with the onset of international war in the nineteenth and twentieth centuries?"[4] This question suggested two specific hypotheses: (1) "The greater the number of alliance commitments in the system, the more war the system will experience;" and (2) "the closer to pure bipolarity the system is, the more war it will experience."[5] In testing these hypotheses, Singer and Small divided the span between 1815 and 1945 into two 65-year periods. This analysis left the two hypotheses essentially unresolved. During the second period the international system seemed to operate as predicted, whereas between 1815 and 1900 it did not. So we are still left with uncertainties about the effects of bipolarity and increasing numbers of alliances and whether they aggravate or ameliorate the probability of war.

Changes in population, technology, access to resources, or military capabilities increase or decrease the relative power of a major country, altering the prevailing configuration of international power. Alteration of this sort takes place continuously. As increments of change add up in one or several countries, those countries that feel themselves weakening in relative power will cast about for some means of catching up. Alliances (or the denial of alliance possibilities to rivals) constitute a way whereby a country may increase its capabilities quickly and at relatively little cost. Such commitments are normally concluded to serve the national interests of the contracting parties (these interests being self-defined); the overall effect on the configuration of international power may not be considered, or, if considered,

---

[2]For representative views, see Burns, 1961, p. 356; Kaplan, 1970, p. 8; and Kaplan, 1957, p. 130; Deutsch and Singer, 1964, p. 386; and Groennings et al., 1970, especially the contribution of Dina Zinnes, "Coalition Theories and the Balance of Power."
[3]Scott, 1961, p. 375.
[4]Singer and Small, 1970, p. 61.
[5]*Ibid.*, p. 66

may not be accurately assessed. Thus, what appears to be in the common interest of two countries not only may be contrary to the interests of other countries but may, in the long run, threaten the welfare of the signatories themselves by creating a greater risk of conflict and violence.

During the late nineteenth and early twentieth centuries many factors influenced events both in Europe and in overseas arenas—old rivalries, struggles for status, the pursuit of strategic advantage, and so forth—but the rise of a strong and vigorous Germany was a powerful factor both in altering the configuration of power in Europe and in intensifying the struggle for colonies.

After 1890 the Bismarckian Concert gave way to a new set of conditions, resulting from the interaction of three centers of power: the Triple Alliance (Austria, Germany, Italy), the Dual Alliance (Russia, France), and the British empire. This arrangement became increasingly unstable, and as a consequence, the powers sought a new and more viable alliance system. The concert that Bismarck had achieved through personal diplomacy was disrupted and replaced by two alliance blocs. This new arrangement did not emerge directly. Between 1890 and 1900 Anglo-French conflicts were more intense than Anglo-German conflicts. It was not clear until after the turn of the century what role Britain was to play in the trend toward bipolarization of the great powers. A strong factor in deciding the outcome was the rapid pace of German industrial and commercial growth.[6]

Germany soon broke loose from the system of alliances Bismarck had forged. In fact, the system had already become a source of tension in relations among the great powers. The initial cracks appeared with the conclusion of the Franco-Russian alliance and Bismarck's own fall from office. Actually, however, the intricate system of alliances was inadequate for maintaining stability not only in Europe, but also across the vast colonial territories of Asia, Africa, and the Pacific.[7] With the erosion of the Bismarck Concert, Germany sought agreements country by country—now with Britain, now with Russia, now with France—but without an intricate web like that established by Bismarck.

With these changes, European leaders were not at all certain who to consider as friends or enemies. The historical rivalries between Britain and France and between Britain and Russia continued, while Germany continued to feel threatened by her central location between France and Russia. An Anglo-German alliance might establish and maintain a stable balance, but this was impossible because of German growth and expansion, which meant further conflicts of German and British interests and eventually an Anglo-German naval race.

---

[6]Rosecrance, 1963, p. 161.
[7]Taylor, 1954, p. xxxii.

In 1890 the new Kaiser, Wilhelm II, forced Bismarck to resign as chancellor. Energetic, flamboyant and dedicated to religion, the army, and the theory of the divine right of kings, the new Kaiser resented Bismarck's prestige and dominance in German affairs. At the time of Wilhelm's accession, the recently initiated German colonial policy had grown "within modest limits, but in a manner that determined subsequent developments."[8] With Bismarck's retirement, German policies became less cautious and more conspicuously ambitious and aggressive.[9]

To succeed Bismarck as chancellor, Wilhelm II appointed a Prussian general, Georg von Caprivi, who served until 1894, when he was followed by Chlodwig Hohenlohe-Schillingsfürst. Caprivi's priorities in foreign policy were the Triple Alliance and a strong German army.[10] In 1890 Wilhelm, at the advice of his ministers, refused to renew the Reinsurance Treaty with Russia, "an agreement which was, in every sense of the term, the cornerstone of the Bismarckian alliance system."[11] During the last decade of his regime, Bismarck had succeeded in building up the Triple Alliance and in maintaining viable relations with St. Petersburg. At the same time, through the Mediterranean Agreements of 1887, he had established a link with Britain by way of Vienna and Rome. The lapse of the Reinsurance Treaty disrupted the balance of this arrangement.

With the expiration of the Reinsurance Treaty in 1890, Germany and Britain concluded an arrangement whereby Germany made extensive concessions in East Africa in return for Helgoland, a small island in the North Sea, considered of great value for the defense of the German coast. This agreement caused some consternation in Russia, since the Anglo-German treaty was signed almost at the same time as the Reinsurance Treaty was allowed to lapse.[12] Indeed, the Anglo-German agreement was "so favorable to Britain that it was generally interpreted as a sign of Germany's desire to purchase British friendship. . . ."[13]

Germany's failure to renew the Reinsurance Treaty was partly the outcome of personal conflicts within the government, but also the result of a reassessment of German interests in relation to the other European powers.[14] In place of Bismarck's elaborate system of diplomatic checks and balances, the Caprivi administration proposed to build an alliance of states with interests similar to those of Germany — one in which Britain would take the place of Russia.[15] In Southeastern

---

[8]Helfferich, 1914, pp. 81–82.
[9]Schmitt, 1918, p. 137; see also Röhl, 1967, pp. 276–277.
[10]Nichols, 1958, pp. 40, 375.
[11]Langer, 1951, p. 3.
[12]Langer, 1951, p. 6.
[13]Rich, 1965, 1:327.
[14]Langer, 1962, pp. 480–502.
[15]Rich, 1965, 1:323.

Europe the Germans shifted their policy from support of Russia without injuring Austria to support of Austria without injuring Russia. From the viewpoint of Austria, Germany's support seemed to provide more freedom of action in Balkan and Near Eastern affairs and encouraged Austria to engage in further flirtations with Russia, in order to procure still more German support in the east.[16] Thus, by severing their previous arrangement with Russia, the Germans decreased their bargaining power with Austria and Italy and "lost perhaps their most effective lever for prying the British out of their isolationism."[17] Moreover, Germany was obligated to support Italy as well as Austria. If she failed to do so, the Triple Alliance might be in jeopardy.[18] This meant that Germany had increased her vulnerability, since a French attack on Italy would bring Germany into the conflict.[19] If Russia, in turn, were to achieve an alliance with France, Germany would be threatened from her eastern as well as her western flanks. Because of their pivotal position in the alliance, Austria and Italy could demand more of Germany in return for their friendship.[20] But the disposition of Britain was even more critical. Britain could align herself with Germany and the Triple Alliance, or she had the possibility of bringing her naval power in support of France and Russia and of blocking off the Mediterranean from effective use by the Triple Alliance.

Changes in German foreign affairs were the result also of German trade protectionism, a slump in 1890 that deepened the following year into a severe depression, and a famine in Russia that led to a ban on the export of Russian grain. The predominantly pro-agrarian orientation of Bismarck's protectionist policy may have contributed to the 1893 Russo-German "tariff war" and the growing alienation between Germany and Russia.[21] In any case, the German tariff on grain began to be acutely felt in Russia. In response to Russian complaints, Caprivi negotiated trade treaties focusing on the Triple Alliance and based on mutual concessions.[22] The objective was to consolidate central Europe economically in order to create "a trading area for German industrial exports against the brutal tariff barriers of Russia" (and of the United States) and "to defend the Triple Alliance and Italy in particular," against a French economic offensive.[23]

As viewed from Berlin, Italy had always been the weakest element in the Triple Alliance. Italian interests were primarily in the Mediterranean, whereas the area was a secondary concern for Austria and of

---

[16]Nichols, 1958, p. 115.
[17]Rich, 1965, I:323.
[18]*Ibid.*
[19]Nichols, 1958, p. 283.
[20]Rich, 1965, I:323.
[21]Rosenberg, 1943, p. 72.
[22]Nichols, 1958, pp. 141–144.
[23]*Ibid.*, p. 140.

minimal interest for Germany. Nevertheless, Italy's partnership in the Triple Alliance compelled German and Austrian attention to Mediterranean affairs and thus Italy played a "largely decisive role" in the course of European diplomacy.[24]

In 1890 France offered Italy a partition of Tripolitania in return for the abandonment of Italian claims on Tunis. This offer made German leaders uneasy because Turkey might then conclude an alliance with Russia. Yet any German attempt to prevent Italy from joining with France in such a partition might lead to her withdrawal from the Triple Alliance. A middle course might be a promise by Germany, Britain and Austria that no other European power should acquire Tripolitania – a promise that would constitute a lesser evil for Germany and Austria than a flare-up in the Balkans and the loss of Italy. In any case, the French offer was viewed in Berlin as "the beginning of a world crisis," whereby Italy would be "brought into a false position, isolated and finally left at the mercy of Russo-French domination and caprice in the Mediterranean.[25]

Germany urged Britain to recognize this French threat to her position in the Mediterranean and to offer Italy assurance that the status quo would be maintained. Lord Salisbury, secretary of foreign affairs and prime minister, promised Italy support in Tripoli, and the French offer of partition was refused by Rome.[26] The French continued their efforts to detach Italy from the Triple Alliance; their lack of success probably stemmed from Germany's improved relations with Britain. The Italians needed British goodwill because of their vulnerability to naval attack, and British support if they were to advance their colonial ambitions in North Africa.[27]

Meanwhile, Germany's failure to renew the Reinsurance Treaty had increased Russia's freedom of action and thus opened the way for the Franco-Russian Alliance – an arrangement that "radically altered the position of Germany," forced "an entire reconsideration of the policy of Great Britain," "completely upset the European system" as it had been in the time of Bismarck, and contributed to the emergence of two antagonistic great-power blocs.[28]

The 1890 Helgoland Treaty had led to what some Germans felt was a "sacrifice" of colonial claims in the hope of achieving better relations with Britain.[29] Later in the decade, however, "an increasingly colony-minded public opinion," encouraged by the Kaiser and many of his advisers, forced the German government to "consider the acquisition of overseas territory for its own sake."[30] After 1894 the Pan-

---

[24]Nichols, 1958, p. 115.
[25]Ibid., p. 116.
[26]Ibid.
[27]Rich, 1965, I:335.
[28]Langer, 1951, p. 4.
[29]Ibid., p. 416.
[30]Rich, 1965, I:367.

German League promoted the idea that all Teutonic peoples of Central Europe ought to be incorporated into one German nation. Some especially enthusiastic leaders of the new *Weltpolitik* envisaged the extension of German boundaries to encompass the Netherlands, Denmark, Luxemburg, Switzerland, Austria, and Poland as far east as Warsaw. There were also dreams of reaching deep into the Balkans, and thus building outward into a huge colonial empire with possessions in Africa, Asia, and Oceania.[31]

The unprecedented expansion of German foreign trade in turn provided new impetus for even greater industrial development.[32] Imperialist expansion became increasingly important to many segments of the German population and played a greater part in the foreign policies of the empire itself. The most eminent German economists regarded the question of expansion as "nothing less than a question of life and death."[33] The best way to guarantee access to raw materials and markets, many Germans felt, was to control the necessary sea routes and also the territories where natural resources were found. The government found itself increasingly called upon to protect German commerce and colonial interests.

Beginning about 1896, a new prosperity followed the Great Depression, and the decade, overall, was characterized in Germany by a further surge of industrialization accompanied by a relative decline of the agricultural sector.[34]

During the early 1890s Caprivi's foreign policy had come under severe attack as being designed only to maintain the position of Germany on the continent while ignoring the requirements of German growth and denying her possibilities of becoming a great world power. Such a limited program led quite logically to strengthening the German army while neglecting the navy, and to seeking good relations with England as a defense against the continental threat of Russia. Germany now had to choose between the safer course of maintaining herself as a continental power and the admittedly riskier policy of *Weltpolitik*, which meant vigorous competition with Britain and other powers.[35] Many Germans felt that what the country desperately needed was a powerful navy. Admiral Georg von Müller asserted that central Europe was getting too small and that the free expansion of people

[31]Albertini, 1952, I:95. Many of these visions were without serious basis or support, but the idea of a powerful German imperium became a very real projection. "The German Empire has become a world empire," Wilhelm II declared on January 18, 1896, the twenty-fifth anniversary of the Empire's founding. "Everywhere at the most distant points in the globe dwell thousands of our fellow countrymen. German merchandise, German science, German energy sail the oceans. The value of our trade amounts to thousands of millions. It is your duty to aid me in creating firm links between this greater Germany and our fatherland."

[32]Nichols, 1958, p. 150.
[33]Langer, 1951, p. 416.
[34]Ritter, 1965, p. 115.
[35]Röhl, 1967, p. 162.

living there was being constrained by the distribution of power in the "inhabitable" areas of the world, and particularly by Britain's world domination.[36] Müller saw the possibility of war with the objective of breaking this domination, although he expressed preference for an Anglo-German alliance — an alignment of two Germanic empires against the Slavic and Romance peoples, whereby the former might coexist peaceably and use their combined political power to further the predomination of the Germanic race.[37]

The Kaiser also was a strong advocate of a powerful German navy. It had been folly, he declared, to initiate a colonial policy without a war fleet. German trade was "waging a life and death struggle" with English trade, but "the great merchant navy" that sailed all the seas under the German flag was "quite helpless before the 130 British cruisers," to which the Germans could "proudly oppose" only four.[38] Yet the Kaiser was confident that Germany could hold her own on the seas.[39]

Despite the extension of German interests into Africa, the Near East, the Pacific, and elsewhere, the great rival powers in the world appeared to be France and Britain. After the Berlin Conference on Africa (1884–85), France had extended her interests and power from Senegal and Guinea deep into the Western Sudan, and by the late 1880s was confronting (from the English viewpoint, "enveloping") the British settlements of Gambia and Sierra Leone.[40] During the 1890s the French pushed their interests further into the heart of the African continent. In due course Delcassé embarked on a vigorous colonial policy in Morocco. Taking advantage of the proximity of Algeria and continued unrest in Morocco, he set out to enhance French influence in the Moorish kingdom and complete France's empire in North Africa.[41]

The potential for Anglo-French conflict existed in Egypt and the headwaters of the Nile, and in Southeast Asia. In 1893 an Anglo-French crisis developed in Siam, where the British hoped to preserve a buffer state between English Burma and French Indochina. In seeking to extend their Indochinese possessions at the expense of Siam, the French clashed with Siamese troops at the border and then sent two gunboats to bring pressure to bear on Bangkok. A French ultimatum to Britain demanding withdrawal brought steadily worsening Anglo-French relations to a critical point.[42]

Meanwhile, Franco-Russian negotiations progressed, and in January, 1894, the two countries formally accepted a secret military

---

[36]*Ibid.*

[37]*Ibid.*, p. 163.

[38]Kaiser Wilhelm to von Hohenlohe, 25 October 1896, in Dugdale, II:471.

[39]It has been asserted that winning support for the monarchy was a major ulterior purpose behind this drive for a larger navy (Röhl, 1967, p. 254).

[40]Robinson and Gallagher, 1961, p. 379.

[41]Williamson, 1969, p. 6.

[42]Rich, 1965, I:350.

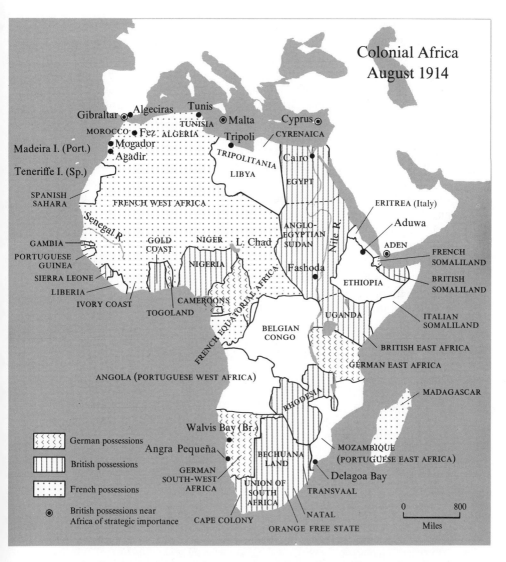

Colonial Africa
August 1914

German possessions

British possessions

French possessions

British possessions near
Africa of strategic importance

convention that bound each to come to the aid of the other in case of attack by Germany, or by Austria or Italy supported by Germany. The convention also provided that in case of mobilization by Germany, Austria, or Italy, both France and Russia should immediately mobilize and move their forces as close to their frontiers as feasible. This Dual Alliance between France and Russia became the foundation for later alliances, leading to the 1904 Entente Cordiale between Britain and France.[43] Although the original focus of the Dual Alliance was on European relationships, the signatories became fearful of Germany's

---

[43]For texts of various documents leading into the Entente Cordiale, see Gooch and Temperly, II:285–407.

growing power and influence overseas — France being concerned with the threat of a new rival in the Mediterranean and Russia with growing German interests and influence in Turkey.[44]

In 1896 the Triple Alliance was again renewed. Early in that year Austria followed up earlier attempts to reactivate the Near Eastern agreements of 1887 with Britain and Italy; however, even with German support the negotiations were unsuccessful. Both Italy and Austria held Germany responsible for the failure. In an attempt to bolster the Triple Alliance after the Italian defeat in Ethiopia at the Battle of Aduwa, Wilhelm II approached England with the suggestion that she should either join the Alliance or at least come to the aid of Italy. This overture was not received well in London, but instead provoked an angry outburst in the English press.[45]

In South Africa, where Germany and Britain were acutely competitive, trouble was continually breaking out between England and the quasi-independent Boer states.[46] In late December, 1895 the Jameson raid, an unauthorized attempt to support insurgent British nationals in Transvaal, presented Germany with a possibility of challenging British expansion into the Boer republics and establishing German protection over Transvaal.[47] It also provided an issue that could be used to justify large increases in naval appropriations from the Reichstag.[48] With the failure of the raid, Wilhelm dispatched a telegram congratulating Transvaal President Krüger for having succeeded in restoring peace and preserving independence without having to appeal to "friendly powers" for aid.[49] It has been said that this telegram "probably did more to influence British and German public opinion against each other than any other single act before 1914."[50] The British resent-

---

[44]Andrew, 1968, pp. 134 and 285; see also Nichols, 1958, p. 234.

[45]Rich, 1965, II:474.

[46]Röhl, 1967, p. 165.

[47]Langer, 1951, p. 224. Conflict in South Africa stemmed not only from the expansion of European interests there, but also from the fundamental antagonism between the British and Dutch in the region, a conflict between local republican sentiment and British imperialists, and the discovery of the Witwatersrand gold fields (*Ibid*, p. 213). The Kaiser, watching these developments, had encouraged Transvaal President Krüger to count on German support.

[47]Langer, 1951, p. 224.

[48]Rich, 1965, II:469.

[49]Langer, 1951, p. 240; Dugdale, 1929, II:387–409 ("The Krüger Telegram and Its Consequences, January–March, 1896"). For British responses, see *Parliamentary Debates*, 1896, 36:282–331, 362–406.

[50]Rich, 1965, II:469. The German intent had been to prevent a linking of Transvaal, Rhodesia, and the Cape Colony, to make clear to Britain that Germany would not allow extension of the British empire without some advantage to herself, and to suggest that it would be within English interests to improve relations with the Triple Alliance (see Brandenburg, 1927, pp. 88–89). In reality, there was nothing Germany could do to help the Boers, and dispatch of the telegram was an ill-advised act. To many Germans, however, it seemed a "glorious, dramatic demonstration that Germany had become a power of the first rank" (Taylor, 1954, p. 366).

ment over the telegram merely reinforced the feeling of many Germans that they had to strengthen their economic and military position.[51]

During June, 1898, the German government drew up a list of colonial territories that might be considered payment for a benevolent attitude toward Britain if the latter insisted on further colonial expansion. Relations between Britain and the Boer Transvaal Republic worsened; if the British were to obtain control of strategic Delagoa Bay on the coast of Portuguese Mozambique, the Boers would no longer enjoy unfettered access to goods from abroad.[52] Thus, British control of the bay might mean control of the Transvaal Republic.[53]

To prevent this, the Germans succeeded on August 30, 1898 in negotiating a treaty with Britain that arranged for loans to Portugal; the Portuguese colonies were to serve as security and the treaty provided for a division of the colonies should Portugal default the loan. In an accompanying secret convention, Britain and Germany agreed to oppose the intervention of any third power in Portuguese Mozambique, Timor, or Angola.[54] The pattern of European alliances was again becoming complex.

For Germany, the value of the Anglo-German treaty over Portuguese colonies was soon nullified, however. Britain concluded a secret treaty with Portugal, promising to protect all Portuguese conquests and colonies in return for a Portuguese guarantee not to allow the passage of war materials to South African forces in the event of war between Britain and the Boers—which finally erupted in October, 1899.[55] "The Germans had thus been thoroughly cheated, or, from another point of view, thoroughly outwitted."[56]

If Anglo-German relations improved somewhat during the summer and autumn of 1898, those between Britain and France were subjected to considerable stress. Indeed, from Paris it often appeared that whichever way French leaders faced, they confronted some clash between the interests of their country and those of Britain.

In the Mediterranean the situation was especially complex as long as Britain was uncertain whether her best interests lay in some arrangement with the Triple Alliance, on the one hand, or with France or Russia, on the other. Britain dared not risk an abdication of power in this region to either France or Russia as long as she had no alliance arrangements with either country. Such a loss of power would force Italy to seek some agreement with France in the Mediterranean, and thus weaken Italy's commitment to the Triple Alliance. Britain feared

---

[51]Tirpitz, 1919, I:65.
[52]Langer, 1951, p. 216.
[53]Rich, 1965, II:586.
[54]*Ibid.*, p. 588.
[55]*Ibid.*, p. 589.
[56]*Ibid.*, p. 600.

that to the extent that Italy's part in the Triple Alliance was weakened, Austria would be left "to face alone the intermittent pressures of Russia in the Balkans and at the [Dardanelles]."[57]

Lacking official understandings either with Germany and the Triple Alliance or with France and Russia, Britain saw no alternative in strengthening her interests in the Mediterranean and North Africa but to act as the "balancing power." Any French expansion in these regions was certain to be interpreted as a challenge to Britain. Although most of the desirable coast lands of Africa had already been claimed by England, France had successfully established herself in Algeria and Tunis (to the consternation also of many Italians), at the mouth of the Senegal River, along the Ivory Coast, and north of the Congo. From these bases the French pushed inland, making treaties with local chiefs, claiming the headwaters of important rivers, and cutting off the coastal colonies of other nations from communications with the hinterland.[58] The imperial vision which came more and more to dominate Delcassé's foreign policy was of a "Greater France built around the shores of the Mediterranean, with an African hinterland stretching toward the Congo."[59]

For years the French government had tried to effect British evacuation from Egypt.[60] As French activists in Central Africa expanded eastward, British leaders became more and more apprehensive.[61] Once in possession of the Nile Basin, France not only could control Egypt's water supply by damming headwater lakes, but also connive with Italian and Russian interests in Ethiopia and perhaps obtain an outlet to the Red Sea, where she already held a footing.[62]

Toward the end of 1893, as British and French rivalries became critically intense in Nigeria, Britain and Germany concluded a treaty delimiting the western frontier of Cameroon and permitting German territory to extend northward as far as Lake Chad. This arrangement would have allowed Germany to expand eastward, blocking French advancement toward the Nile but without threatening British interests. France, alarmed by such implications, some months later concluded an agreement with Germany stipulating further delimitations of the eastern frontier, so that French expansion became feasible not only northward into the Chad region, but also eastward toward the Nile.[63]

---

[57]Nichols, 1958, p. 284. In fact, this weakening of the Triple Alliance took place in 1900 and 1902 with secret agreements between France and Italy. Italy's alliance with Germany and Austria had come about largely because of Italian-French conflicts in the Mediterranean.
[58]Sontag, 1933, pp. 63–64.
[59]Andrew, 1968, p. 87.
[60]Langer, 1951, p. 538.
[61]Andrew, 1968, p. 44.
[62]Langer, 1951, pp. 129–130.
[63]Ibid., p. 131; see also Andrew, 1968, pp. 41 and 547.

In July, 1898, after an epic journey from the Congo to the Nile, a French expedition reached Fashoda in the Sudan.[64] There it found itself confronted by an Anglo-Egyptian force under Lord Kitchener, which had undertaken to reconquer the Sudan region. French leaders asserted that they had no desire to thwart British policy in the Nile Valley, but badly needed a commercial outlet for Central Africa.[65] The British maintained, on the other hand, that French forces had no right to be in Fashoda.[66] Briefly, there was talk of war. For six weeks the issue remained in doubt; British diplomatic pressure, backed by naval power, eventually forced France to renounce her attempt at controlling the headwaters of the Nile.[67]

An important outcome of the Fashoda Incident was French determination to strengthen the Franco-Russian alliance in order to gain more positive support against Britain.[68] After Fashoda, Delcassé saw reinforcement of the alliance as a safeguard against German acquisition of Hapsburg holdings along the Adriatic.[69] In view of the Emperor Franz Joseph's advanced age and the absence of a direct heir to the throne, the French foreign minister was afraid that Germany might undertake annexation that would result in a vast German state in the center of Europe. The acquisition of Trieste would be enough to turn Germany into a Mediterranean power.

In Berlin the Fashoda Incident left Kaiser Wilhelm and his advisers with the impression that there was no chance of real agreement between Paris and London and that Germany was in a very strong position with respect to Britain. The view in Berlin was that "the history of the eighteenth century would be repeated in that differences which separated London and Paris overseas would prevent them from coming together in Europe."[70] Undoubtedly, this and other assumptions by the Germans adversely affected Anglo-German negotiations around the turn of the century.

Britain's relations with the Boers were now approaching a crisis, the Russians were exerting pressures in the Near and Far East, and France and Britain had not yet recovered from Fashoda—Anglo-French relations reached a low point. The possibility existed that

[64]Langer, 1951, pp. 266, 268, 538–539; Andrew, 1968, p. 44.

[65]Monson to the Marquess of Salisbury, Paris, 9 October 1898, in Gooch and Temperley, I:176–177.

[66]Monson to the Marquess of Salisbury, Paris, 18 September 1898, in Gooch and Temperley, I:165–166.

[67]Williamson, 1969, p. 2.

[68]Andrew, 1968, p. 124. Delcassé persuaded the Russians to undertake, with a large loan, the construction of a railway between Orenburg and Tashkent (see the map, p. 78), which was completed in 1904. The strategic implications of this line—conceived as a threat to India—"dominated the military thinking of the British Raj during the early years of the twentieth century."

[69]Williamson, 1968, p. 5.

[70]Petrie, 1949, p. 246.

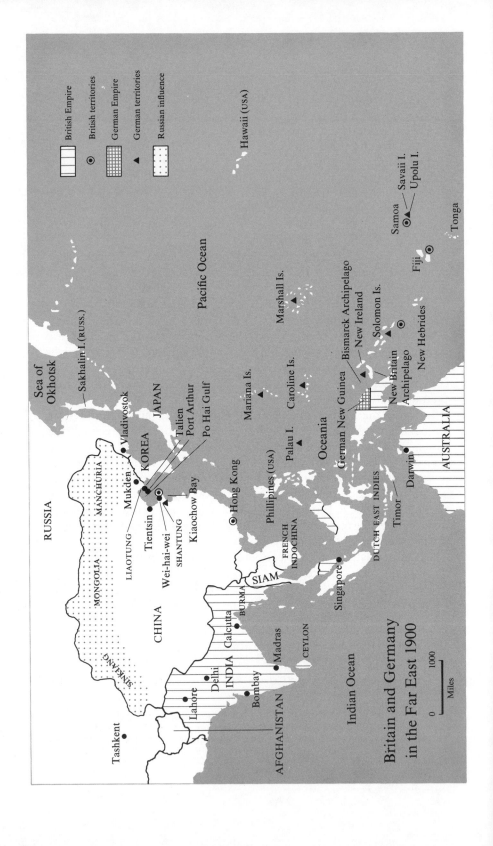

Britain and Germany
in the Far East 1900

France or Russia might take advantage of England at a vulnerable juncture in the Boer conflict, and that Germany might even collaborate with France "to limit the insatiable appetite" of Britain.[71] At this time Delcassé was concerned primarily with the questions of Egypt and Morocco, and he wanted German support in each. Also, although hoping to detach Italy from the Triple Alliance, he considered it important to deflect Italy from cooperation with Britain in the Mediterranean.[72]

Britain's position in the world configuration of power depended largely on her relations with Germany, since France and Russia were not likely to involve themselves in a conflict if Germany were on the English side. Under these circumstances, Lord Salisbury decided to forestall an anti-British coalition by making concessions to Germany in Samoa. Through a treaty of November 14, 1899 Germany acquired the islands of Upolu and Savaii, the Tonga and Savage Islands, some small islands in the Solomons, and the British received a disputed part of Togoland in Africa.[73] Nevertheless, Germany, which by now had learned of British duplicity in the Anglo-German loan to Portugal (and moreover exaggerated the importance to British policy-makers of German support), was still quite prepared to exploit British difficulties throughout the world, including the Transvaal Republic, provided the gains were adequate and the risks acceptable.[74]

Early in 1900 Delcassé asked the Russians to make inquiries in Berlin about Germany's attitude toward the Boer War; he also made some unofficial overtures of his own.[75] He hoped for direct intervention by the three powers in South Africa, but German responses to this proposal were for the most part equivocal. At one point the Kaiser suggested that as a preliminary condition for any further negotiation there be a guarantee of the status quo of the existing territory of the European powers.[76] This proposed condition alerted France to the German attitude toward Alsace-Lorraine and thus had a profound effect on subsequent French relations with Germany.

The failure of the plan for three-power intervention in the Boer War marked a turning point in French relations with both Britain and Germany. Delcassé concluded that further French expansion near the headwaters of the Nile had no chance of success without German support—which France had no reason to expect.[77]

Great-power expansion continued through the turn of the century, as did the search for a new alliance system. With the defeat of China

---

[71]Andrew, 1968, p. 158.
[72]*Ibid.*, p. 140.
[73]Rich, 1965, II:600.
[74]Langer, 1951, pp. 618–619.
[75]Rich, 1965, II:617.
[76]Andrew, 1968, p. 172.
[77]*Ibid.*, p. 179.

by Japan in 1895, the European powers became alarmed at the extent of Japanese successes. Britain and Russia, feeling particularly threatened, entered into discussions about the future of Korea and China, and were soon joined in these discussions by Russia's ally, France. Thereafter, as international competition extended into China and adjacent areas of the Far East, the tendency of the great powers was to acquire leaseholds, concessions, and other special privileges rather than colonial territories. Thus, while the powers competed in Africa for the few remaining unappropriated lands of the continent, competition in China was over railway concessions and definitions of spheres of influence.

Wilhelm suspected Britain of intending to seize Shanghai, concluding that such an eventuality would encourage similar seizures by France and Russia. Should this come about, the Kaiser proposed that Germany, too, should expand her interests in China, where German trade was already substantial.[78] Wilhelm hoped to acquire at least a naval base as a center for expanded German operations in the Far East.[79] On November 19, 1897 German troops were landed in Kiaochow Bay, which lay in the Russian sphere of influence.[80] Germany sounded out British attitudes toward the landing. Perhaps believing that the Germans in Kiaochow would counterbalance the Russians further north, the British raised no objections and thus strengthened the German government in its dealings with Russia over the presence of German troops.

During the spring of 1898 European leaders were watching events in China, which appeared to be on the verge of partition, with utmost care. When news reached London of a Russian determination to take Port Arthur and Talienwan on the Liaotung Peninsula, several members of the British cabinet began looking with new interest on a possible arrangement with Germany. The British colonial secretary, Joseph Chamberlain, sounded out the Germans on the possibility of an alliance; but this overture was discouraged not only in Berlin but also by the prime minister, Lord Salisbury.[81] At the same time Britain moved her Far Eastern Fleet into the Gulf of Pechili in order to occupy the port of Wei-hai-wai on the northern coast of the Shantung Peninsula—a response to Russian advances and an important step in the ensuing dismemberment of China. Britain later admitted that she had

---

[78]Rich, 1965, II:435–436.

[79]Ibid., p. 555.

[80]Ibid., p. 556. The murder of two German Catholic missionaries in Shantung Peninsula, where Kiaochow lay, provided the opportunity. Russia asserted that she would do everything possible to induce the Chinese to give satisfaction for the murders, but at the same time set out to reassert her own claim to Kiaochow. See Langer, 1951, pp. 452–453.

[81]Williamson, 1969, p. 2.

desired a treaty with Germany primarily in hope of halting Russian domination of China.

Germany, on the other hand, saw Russian expansion in the Far East as perhaps relieving Russian pressure on German and Austrian interests in Europe. German leaders also doubted that an Anglo-German alliance would be accepted by the British parliament. If the anti-Russian implications of such an arrangement were perceived, and if parliament rejected the treaty, then Germany would be left to confront the resentments that were certain to be felt by the Russians and their French allies.[82]

With the autumn and winter months of 1900–1901, European statesmen focused more and more attention on the activities of Russia, especially those in the Far East. There were 50,000 Russian troops in Manchuria, the strategic rail line from Peking to Tientsin and north was in Russian hands, and in early November the announcement was made that the Chinese government had conceded land to the Russians at Tientsin. This news led to an immediate scramble for similar concessions by the Germans, French, Austrians, Belgians, and Japanese.[83]

During the Boxer Rebellion in 1900 all the European powers and the United States sent troops to China, thus enhancing the probability of territorial partition. To German leaders it was evident that any parceling out of so large an area might lead to a major shift in international alignments. Britain might make extensive concessions to Russia elsewhere in the Far East as well as in the Near East in exchange for Russian recognition of British rights in the Yangtze Valley.[84] On the other hand, German leaders thought that if the British were reassured about German expansion in the Yangtze, Britain might be persuaded to take a firm stand against Russian expansion into Manchuria. In the end, an Anglo-German treaty on China was signed on October 16, 1900.[85]

Meanwhile, German leaders were becoming increasingly concerned about their country's relations with Japan. In view of the widely recognized Japanese policy of aggrandizement, a direct alliance between Germany and Japan would arouse suspicions and further aggravate relations with Russia.[86] If Britain were to join the Triple Alliance and

---

[82]Rich, 1965, II:568–571.

[83]Langer, 1951, p. 711.

[84]Rich, 1965, II:620.

[85]*Ibid.*, pp. 623–624. According to this agreement, the open-door principle was to be applied to the Chinese littoral and river ports for as far as the British and German governments could exercise their control. This last stipulation was meant to disallow any implication that Russia was to be allowed a free hand in Manchuria, but the wording was so vague that the German and British governments were not able to agree on where the open-door zones ended and where the Russian sphere began. These ambiguities led to misunderstanding between the German and British governments and to uncertainties in their dealings with Russia.

[86]Langer, 1951, p. 721.

Japan were included as an ally of Britain, the implications of such an indirect alliance with Japan would be entirely different. Britain might then operate as a control on Japan; but even if she did not, this expansion of the Triple Alliance would be so powerful that for Berlin, at least, the attitudes of other powers toward Germany would be of far less significance.[87] The likelihood of an Anglo-German accommodation in the Far East was dampened on March 15, 1901 when Bülow declared in a Reichstag speech that the Anglo-German Yangtze Agreement did not provide for any united opposition to Russian expansion in Manchuria.

For the most part, the British foreign office failed to understand what Germany desired from an Anglo-German alliance. For Germany, an Anglo-German alliance would be a defensive arrangement that would apply to the *British Empire as a whole* and also to the *Triple Alliance as a whole*, with its terms becoming operative in the event that any one of the contracting powers were attacked by two or more great powers.[88] Lord Salisbury objected to an agreement with the whole Triple Alliance. He claimed that in the event that Italy or Austria came under attack and Germany rendered assistance under provisions of the Triple Alliance, Britain, under a defensive alliance with Germany alone, would not be obligated to join the conflict. Germany could not possibly agree to an arrangement that left England so uncommitted while requiring German aid to Britain should any part of the latter's far-flung empire come under attack.

Partly as an outcome of Anglo-German competitions, partly as the consequence of the Franco-Russian alignment, the European balance of power reached such a delicate, volatile state that moves by any one of the major powers sent disturbing reverberations throughout the whole system. The one central and relatively stable relationship was that between France and Russia. Having failed to achieve an arrangement with Germany, British leaders tried to negotiate with Russia. When these attempts collapsed, they turned first to Japan and then to France in order to end the "disquieting isolation" that would have characterized her position in the event of a conflict with Russia or France.[89]

After March, 1901 many English leaders thought that Germany had raised "the mirage of an Anglo-German alliance" only as a means of distracting them from the real aims of German policy.[90] Britain's hostility toward Germany was undoubtedly based on "far more than naval or imperial rivalry." From the viewpoint of English leaders,

---

[87]Rich, 1965, II:641.
[88]*Ibid.*, p. 652.
[89]Albertini, 1952, I:145.
[90]Andrew, 1968, p. 204.

"German statesmen often seemed to believe that Germany could find security only in a world in which the other powers were prevented by their mutual hostility from combining against her."[91] As viewed from London, German leaders had a vested interest in exploiting conflicts among the other powers.

From Germany's standpoint, however, her position on the Continent had not essentially changed. In 1901, as in 1887, Germany could not afford to alienate Russia without being certain of British support in the event of a two-front war—Germany was regarded as a threat by both countries. Because of her technological advancement, industrial production, merchant marine tonnage, imports, and, increasingly, her naval budget, Germany was surpassing France, thus becoming Britain's principal rival. At the same time, she could not settle her differences with Russia, since one condition for a Russo-German alliance was a guarantee of existing German boundaries. This guarantee would mean preserving the status quo in Alsace-Lorraine, which Russia could not condone because of her relations with France.

Britain, on the other hand, was wary of any arrangement between herself and the whole Triple Alliance.[92] The British also had reservations about any relations with either Austria or Italy.[93] Command of the English Channel was a crucial consideration; "the liability of having to defend the German and Austrian frontiers against Russia" were heavier than that of "having to defend the British Isles against France."[94] The British fear of Russia—"a fear caused principally by India's apparent vulnerability to overland attack"—was a major element in the growing disposition in London toward an accord with Russia's ally, France.[95]

British interests continued to collide with those of Russia and France throughout the world. Russian activities and interests were steadily expanding in Persia and elsewhere in the Middle East, and British representatives in the area "felt quite helpless and useless" in the face of these advances.[96] Yet in Britain the idea was growing that opposition to Russia in the Persian Gulf and elsewhere was increasingly "out of date," since Germany appeared more and more to be England's foremost rival.[97]

British attitudes toward Russia and France were increasingly influenced by Japan, whose own position was strongly affected by her relations with European powers. For Japan the critical questions were

[91]*Ibid.*
[92]Rich, 1965, II:680.
[93]Langer, 1951, p. 732.
[94]*Ibid.*, p. 734.
[95]Andrew, 1968, p. 125.
[96]Langer, 1951, pp. 752–753.
[97]*Ibid.*, p. 734.

whether France would support Russia in a Far Eastern war and whether Britain, in turn, would use her fleet to support Japan. In Tokyo the assumption was that France would not dare enter such a conflict if Britain supported Japan. In due course, negotiations between London and Tokyo led to the Anglo-Japanese Alliance of 1902 whereby the two countries promised to maintain the integrity and status quo of Korea and China.[98] If, in the pursuit of these ends, either ally became involved in a defensive war with a single power, the other ally would remain neutral and try to limit the conflict. But if more than one power fought either signatory, the other was obligated to give assistance. And in a secret note, each country agreed "in so far as possible" to maintain a naval force superior to that of any third country in the area.[99]

The conclusion of the Anglo-Japanese Alliance marked a new departure in British diplomacy — a break with the tradition of "splendid isolation" in which Britain had tried to maintain sufficient independence to shift her influence and support as circumstances dictated. The Anglo-Japanese treaty became an important factor in shaping subsequent alliance arrangements. It committed Britain to official discouragement of further Russian expansion in Manchuria — with the obligation of taking action if Russia did not desist. Although it simplified British problems in Asia, however, it had the effect of complicating relations in Europe. For by "eventually facilitating" a Japanese victory over Russia, the alliance "enhanced France's need for British support."[100] Indeed, the signing of the Anglo-Japanese Alliance was perceived in Paris as a serious threat to French foreign policy. "To protect the Dual Alliance, to avoid trouble with Britain, and to gain a 'free hand' in Morocco: these considerations [from a French viewpoint] dictated the improvement of Anglo-French relations . . . ."[101] At the same time, English leaders were growing increasingly anxious over the possibility of a Russo-Japanese war and the danger of its escalating into hostilities between the Anglo-Japanese and Franco-Russian alliances.[102] This concern contributed directly to the Anglo-French Accords of 1904, which are discussed in the next chapter.

Whatever tradeoffs Britain and France might achieve would be viewed unfavorably by Germany if they succeeded in bringing Britain and France closer together. For Germany, fearing a two-front war, could not afford to alienate France without some certainty of British support; the very real possibility now emerged of alienating both. German leaders thus had some foundation for the feeling that they

---

[98]*Ibid.*, p. 720.
[99]Williamson, 1969, p. 4.
[100]*Ibid.*
[101]*Ibid.*, p. 7.
[102]Andrew, 1968, p. 211.

were being "encircled" — although Russia was to be seriously weakened by her defeat at the hands of the Japanese in 1905. By working toward a clear demarcation of their overseas activities and interests, France and Britain together divided the great powers essentially into two blocs, and thus greatly enhanced the probability that a clash between any of the powers would involve all the powers.

5 Collisions of National Interests

Germany's central geographical position, with France on one flank and Russia on the other, greatly enhanced the risk for Germany of a two-front war. Under these circumstances some type of treaty arrangement with Russia was highly desirable; lacking such a safeguard, German security required an understanding with Britain. Yet Germany allowed her Reinsurance Treaty with Russia to lapse in 1890. Then, after more than a decade of intermittent and deeply ambivalent discussions between Britain and Germany, an Anglo-French accord was signed, leaving Germany strategically vulnerable in both the west and the east. Moreover, an accelerating naval competition was beginning to exacerbate already strained relations between London and Berlin.[1]

The persistence of this unfavorable situation can be explained in part by poor diplomacy. But the explanation seems to lie by and large with rapid German industrial and commercial growth and with extensive German expansionism, beginning in the early 1870s with the annexation of Alsace-Lorraine and continuing in West, Central, and South Africa, in the Pacific Islands, the Far East, Turkey, and Arabia. As a consequence of this growth, German interests increasingly collided with those of France, Russia, and Britain. Germany's growing military, naval, and commercial capabilities tended more and more to threaten, and to be threatened by, the capabilities of the same three powers.

After the turn of the century Germany made further attempts at improving her relations with Russia; by then, however, the configuration of European power had been changed too greatly to make this

---

[1]Williamson, 1969, p. 28.

feasible. The realities of the emerging power structure increasingly forced Germany to look to Austria as her major ally.

In 1905 one more attempt was made to bring about a Russo-German understanding. On July 24 the Kaiser and the tsar signed the Treaty of Björkö (never officially concluded), whereby Germany and Russia pledged themselves to mutual defense in Europe against an attack by any European power. They also agreed not to conclude a unilateral peace in the event that they became allies in a defensive war. The proposed arrangement made little sense at a time when Russia and France were already aligned and the foundations of a Triple Entente with Britain were beginning to take shape. Under the circumstances, any military cooperation between Germany and Russia in a war against Britain would have to take place in *Asia* rather than Europe. And, of course, the Russian government insisted that the treaty would not apply in the event of war between Germany and France. This was to be Germany's final attempt to compensate for its failure to renew the Reinsurance Treaty.[2] Meanwhile, German diplomatic prospects had worsened even further with the historic agreement in 1904 between Britain and France.

French and British interests had frequently collided in many parts of the world, especially in Egypt, Newfoundland, Siam, Nigeria, and Morocco.[3] Three conflicts were especially difficult to resolve: Egypt, fishing rights off the shores of Newfoundland, and Morocco.[4] These questions were settled in the Anglo-French Accords of April 8, 1904.

The Accords amounted to a "diplomatic revolution of the first magnitude."[5] They brought to a close one of the oldest national rivalries in Europe, and meant that France, whose animosities had fluctuated between Britain and Germany, would now be able to focus on her problems with the latter.[6] In the Accords France recognized British occupation of Egypt but was given guarantees with respect to the Egyptian debt. Britain agreed to make effective the Treaty of 1888, providing for free navigation of the Suez Canal. France relinquished long-standing rights in Newfoundland but retained fishing rights there; in return, she was given territory near French Gambia and east of the Niger. French and British spheres of influence were delimited on the frontiers of Siam, and disputes with respect to the New Hebrides and Madagascar were adjusted.[7]

But the most important agreement, from the viewpoint of both countries, concerned Morocco. The agreement over Morocco emerged

---

[2]Albertini, 1952, I:159–161.
[3]Williamson, 1969, p. 10.
[4]*Ibid.*
[5]Andrew, 1968, p. 211.
[6]Rich, 1965, II:681.
[7]Langer, 1952, p. 752.

in large part from the requirements of British global strategy. French penetration of Morocco, establishing a strong naval power across the Strait of Gibraltar, presented a potential threat to the movement of British ships into and out of the Mediterranean. By bringing Britain and France into agreement, the Accords secured British access to the North African coastline.[8]

France had hoped to acquire in Morocco a "privileged situation" that might compensate for the loss of her former position in Egypt.[9] French proponents of colonialism saw Morocco as the last chance to "extend the space" occupied by Frenchmen on the earth — an important future part of a "greater France" built around the Mediterranean.[10] In 1900 France and Italy had negotiated a secret North African Accord that recognized French rights in Morocco and Italian rights in Tripolitania.[11] In secret articles to the Anglo-French Accords Britain recognized French interests in Morocco and promised diplomatic support of French efforts to realize them. The two powers agreed to eventual termination of the independence of Morocco and partitioning of the country between France and Spain. In October, 1904 Spain agreed in general terms to the provisions of the Accords concerning Morocco, and in a secret agreement with France signed the same day settled on the respective zones of influence in Morocco if the authority of the sultan could no longer be maintained.

Delcassé's sense of urgency over an agreement with Britain on Morocco resulted from a fear of German rivalry there.[12] With the globe almost wholly parceled out among the powers, Morocco was seen as "the last imperial chance" remaining for the French.[13] In view of the tendency of the "German race" to "expand and overrun," Delcassé concluded that France urgently required a comprehensive settlement with Britain on the Egyptian and Moroccan questions.[14]

---

[8]Williamson, 1969, p. 15.

[9]Hale, 1931, p. 99.

[10]See Andrew, 1968, p. 105. "It is in Morocco that you will find phosphate deposits and iron ore, wheat fields and olive plants!" the leader of the French *Parti Colonial* told a banquet of the Union Cordiale in 1903. "It is there that you will find markets for the cotton goods of Rouen and the Vosges! Wool to supply our weavers in Roubaix and Tourcoing! Railways to build and harbours to develop!"

[11]Prior to 1904, insofar as relations between France and Britain were uncertain, if not antagonistic, Italy confronted a certain risk in becoming allied too strongly with either country. At the same time, Germany was apprehensive that Italy would use her partnership in the Triple Alliance as a bargaining power with France and Britain in the Mediterranean. Because of Italy's interests in North Africa, as well as territorial disputes with Austria along the Austro-Italian border, Germany believed that an Anglo-French entente would offer a strong attraction to Italy. Thus, by the time of the 1904 Anglo-French Accords the Triple Alliance had been seriously weakened by the Secret Franco-Italian agreement on Morocco in 1900, and later by another secret Franco-Italian agreement in 1902 (even though neither were known to Germany at the time).

[12]Andrew, 1968, p. 204.

[13]Brunschwig, 1966, pp. 118–119.

[14]Andrew, 1968, p. 211.

Germany did in fact have interests in Morocco. As early as August, 1902, the British foreign secretary, Lord Lansdowne, had recognized that Germany might demand participation in any settlement of the Moroccan problem. Yet only a few months later he acceded to Delcassé's insistence that Germany not be allowed to intervene in Morocco. In the 1904 Anglo-French Accords this policy of exclusion was reaffirmed by Lansdowne. This British decision decisively affected Anglo-German relations.[15]

Having gained British, Italian, and Spanish assent to the "peaceful penetration" of Morocco, Delcassé now tried to force the Sultan of Morocco into accepting reforms for the police, the banks, and the army, all to be carried out with French assistance.[16] This French pressure raised deep anxieties in Germany. For a time, Kaiser Wilhelm had hoped that if France became sufficiently entangled in Morocco, she might become less concerned over Alsace-Lorraine and also weaken herself militarily. Chancellor Bülow pursuaded Wilhelm to change his view because of the extent of German political and economic interests in Morocco.[17] As Bülow saw the situation, France was impairing Moroccan independence in defiance of the Madrid Conference of 1880, which had established most-favored nation treatment for Morocco. This consideration gave the Moroccan question international significance.[18] Bülow maintained that it was not only the extent of German economic and political interests in and about Morocco that prompted him to advise the Kaiser to turn against France, but also "the conviction that in the interests of peace we must no longer permit such provocations."[19]

The German intention was to inflict a series of humiliations on France, forcing her to give up her aspirations in Morocco.[20] On the chancellor's advice Wilhelm landed at Tangier from his yacht (March 31, 1905) for a speech to the German colony there.[21] The Germans were encouraged in this undertaking by the fact that Russia, France's only ally, was preoccupied in the Far East (as the Kaiser landed,

---

[15]Williamson, 1969, p. 14.

[16]*Ibid.*, p. 30.

[17]Albertini, 1952, I:153. Early in 1903 a Moroccan Association had been founded in Germany; the new organization demanded that the German government seize a foothold in Morocco (Andrew, 1968, p. 210).

[18]Sontag, 1933, p. 103. The chancellor's aim was to make France answer for her aggressive policies before a conference of the signatory powers. Bülow saw in the Moroccan situation a way to weaken or destroy the Anglo-French entente and break the "iron ring" that the Germans felt Britain was forging around Germany (not only on the Continent but also overseas, with respect to access to raw materials and markets).

[19]Bülow, 1931, II:121.

[20]Albertini, 1952, I:153.

[21]Bülow to Kühlmann (Tangier), Berlin, 3 April 1905, and Bülow to Kaiser Wilhelm II, Berlin, 4 April 1905, in Lepsius *et al.*, XX:295, 301–303; see also Rich, 1965, II:703–704. For French documentation, see *Documents Diplomatiques Francais (1901–1911)*, *2ᵉ Serie*, VIII.

Russia was withdrawing from her defeat by the Japanese at Mukden). Britain, moreover, was engaged in reorganizing her armed forces – and in any case her navy would be useless in a defense of Paris.[22] Thus, Germany could conceivably fight France without risking war on two fronts. Wilhelm promised to do all in his power to safeguard German interests in Morocco. He visited the sultan, treating him as a free and independent sovereign, and discussed with him the security of German interests.[23] For the time being it looked like a victory for the Kaiser's personal diplomacy.

Whether or not German diplomats were bent on forcing the Moroccan crisis to a breaking point is not entirely clear. As pointed out by Norman Rich, a distinction must be drawn "between the possibility of war that lies behind every diplomatic action, and the deliberate use of diplomatic action to provoke a war."[24] In any case, the French cabinet was not willing to risk war, and Delcassé was forced to resign as foreign minister.[25]

Refusing to settle the issue through direct Franco-German negotiations, Germany pressed for an international conference. Wilhelm put forward the demand only four days after the defeat of the Russian fleet at Tsushima. At Algeciras in January, 1906 the powers – including the United States – arranged a compromise that reaffirmed the integrity of Morocco but authorized France and Spain to police the coastal towns.[26] Germany and France later (February 8, 1909) achieved an agreement that recognized France's special interests in Morocco in return for recognition of Germany's economic interests and a promise to associate German nationals in future concessions. Nevertheless, Wilhelm and Bülow had overplayed the German hand during the 1905 crisis. France, through clever diplomacy (and despite the fall from office of Delcassé) had scored a triumph. Germany's attempt to establish a special position in Morocco had failed. Italy, without the knowledge of Germany or Austria and in spite of her partnership in the Triple Alliance, had agreed in 1902 to undertake no aggressive actions against France if the latter should become involved in war. The Anglo-French entente thus emerged stronger than ever.

At the same time, however, the division in Europe was deepened. The British emergence from isolation, which had given rise to the

---

[22] Also, there were serious doubts in Berlin whether England would fight for France at all (Rich, 1965, II:697).

[23] Bülow, 1931, II:125. For an English account of Wilhelm's visit to Tangiers, see White to Marquess of Lansdowne, Tangier, 2 April 1905, in Gooch and Temperley, III:63.

[24] Rich, 1965, II:699.

[25] *Ibid.*, p. 711.

[26] For British documents on the Algeciras Conference see Gooch and Temperley, III:204–349 (for a British summary of events in Morocco during 1906 see Enclosure No. 42, Lowther to Grey, Tangier, 5 January 1907, pp. 346–349); for German documents, see Lepsius *et al.*, XX, Ch. 147; for French documents, see *Documents Diplomatiques Francais (1901–1911), 2e Serie*, IX.

1904 Anglo-French Accords, along with the developing arms race between Germany and Britain, also led to the settlement of Anglo-Russian differences (August 31, 1907) — an eventuality German leaders thought impossible and hence inconceivable. The Anglo-Russian agreement demarcated the interests and spheres of the two powers in Persia, Afghanistan, and Tibet, and created the Triple Entente (Britain, France, and Russia).[27] The process that Germany called "encirclement," but which the British referred to as "insurance," now began in earnest. The first test of the new Triple Entente was the Bosnian Crisis of 1908–1909.

The course of Austro-Hungarian development at this time offers evidence that a country can continue to grow on important dimensions and at the same time suffer serious domestic malaise and disability. Much of the Austrian difficulty stemmed from the fact that, on the whole, Austro-German sectors of the population enjoyed comparatively greater wealth, income, and influence than Slavic and other minorities.[28] The Dual Monarchy was frequently referred to as the "sick man of Europe," or as a broken pot held together with wire. Yet Austrian industry served a sizeable European market, and the empire had sufficient capabilities to extend its interests and activities into the Balkan region. This expansion, by conflicting with the interests and activities of other powers, threatened peace in Europe and much of the world on a number of occasions.

Because of Austria's relative weakness among the great powers, particularly in merchant marine and naval capabilities, overseas expansion of the empire proved unrealistic. The Balkans, on the other hand, offered a ready market for Austrian industry, and Austria-Hungary had generally higher capabilities than the smaller Balkan states. Historically, the Dual Monarchy had been constrained there by Turkish sovereignty and Russian influence and interests. However, Ottoman power was steadily declining, and the defeat of Russia by Japan in 1905 effectively precluded the possibility of Russian aid to Serbia and other countries in the region. The Balkan Peninsula thus became vulnerable to Austro-Hungarian exploitation.[29] At the same time, however, other countries were making ever greater inroads into Balkan trade.[30] During 1908 and 1909, conflict between the interests of Austria-Hungary and those of Russia and other powers in the Balkan region gave rise to an acute international crisis.

In Chapter 3 we learned how revolts in the two most northwesterly provinces of the Ottoman empire, Bosnia and Herzegovina, gave rise to the Russo-Turkish War of 1877–1878, the Treaty of San Stefano,

---

[27]Albertini, 1952, II:188–189; Petrie, 1949, p. 297.
[28]Marz, 1953, p. 135.
[29]Helmreich, 1938, p. 4.
[30]Among these were Britain and, ironically, Austria's ally Germany. (Bridge, 1972, p. 269).

and the Congress of Berlin. During the Russo-Turkish War Russia conceded the two provinces to Austria, but later (through the Treaty of San Stefano) the tsarist government reversed itself on this issue. For a time (until 1908), Austria achieved occupation of, but not sovereignty over, Bosnia and Herzegovina.

More and more, Austria-Hungary saw its ambitions blocked by Serbia, whose population was increasing and whose territory had expanded moderately but persistently. Generating some amount of lateral pressure of its own, a growing Serbia under Russian protection could seriously inhibit the expansion and protection of Austro-Hungarian interests in the Balkans. Every Serbian gain was perceived in Vienna as a loss to Austria-Hungary. Germany, informed of the Austrian feeling, proclaimed noninvolvement (declaring at the same time an unshakable loyalty to the Dual Monarchy). Meanwhile, the continuing decline of Turkish power raised the question of which country might fill the vacuum should Turkey withdraw from Macedonia. The Austrian foreign minister, Alois von Aehrenthal, saw in the new Russian foreign minister, Alexander Izvolsky, an ardent champion of Russia's mission in the Near East.[31] Through some quid pro quo with Russia, Aehrenthal hoped to inaugurate an expansionist policy that would reinvigorate Austria's economy and at the same time greatly strengthen its position among the great powers.[32]

For the immediate future Aehrenthal proposed to reduce the influence of Serbia in the Balkans by annexing Bosnia and Herzegovina, which Serbia had long hoped to make part of a large Serb state. His long-range objective was "the economic and eventually the political, subjugation of Serbia to the Empire."[33] Magyar leaders were generally opposed to the transformation of Austria-Hungary from a Dual to a Triple Monarchy. Nevertheless, Aehrenthal sought a bargain with Izvolsky. Aehrenthal was willing to negotiate the question of egress through the Dardanelles, an issue of fundamental interest to St. Petersburg, if Izvolsky would not oppose the annexation of Bosnia and Herzegovina.

While negotiating the Anglo-Russian Convention of 1907, Izvolsky had received assurances that Britain would be willing to negotiate the question of the Dardanelles. By opening the Dardanelles, Izvolsky also hoped to increase Russian influence in the Mediterranean. Now, with improved relations between the two countries, he hoped for an Anglo-Russian military move against Turkey. Possibilities for action were limited, however, in that Russia's defeat by Japan in 1905 had weakened the Russian military and strained the empire's finances. Any adventurous and aggressive undertaking might precipitate

---

[31]Schmitt, 1937, pp. 4–5.
[32]*Ibid.*, p. 4.
[33]Bridge, 1972, p. 317.

revolution and jeopardize the tsarist dynasty. Whatever Izvolsky hoped to gain would have to be acquired by diplomacy, not by armed force. Meanwhile, without previous consultation with Izvolsky, Aehrenthal announced in January, 1908 a program for constructing a railway from the Bosnian frontier across the *sanjak* of Novibazar to Mitrovica in Old Serbia (see the map, p. 51). Possession of the *sanjak* was important to Austria as a means of making certain that Serbia and Montenegro remained isolated from one another. The plan for the railway aroused indignation in St. Petersburg, where it was interpreted as marking the end of the Austro-Russian accord that had been achieved in 1897.[34]

Deprived of the possibility of using armed force because of Russian weakness, Izvolsky addressed an *aide memoir* to Aehrenthal, promising to abstain from obstruction of the Austro-Hungarian railway project and requesting Aehrenthal to support in Constantinople a Russian application for authorization of preliminary studies for a Danube-Adriatic railway line.[35] Since Aehrenthal seemed to have no objection, Izvolsky decided to go further.[36] On July 2 he raised the possibility that Russia might consent to the annexation of Bosnia and Herzegovina in return for Austrian support for the opening of the Dardanelles to Russian warships.[37] He also proposed discussions of Near Eastern affairs, which took place when he and Aehrenthal met September 15 and 16 at Buchlau, a private estate in Moravia. The details of the agreement reached by Aehrenthal and Izvolsky at Buchlau were not recorded (nor have they been fully established since). Within a few weeks "each statesman was calling the other a liar."[38]

On October 5, with the encouragement of Austria, Bulgaria declared her independence from Turkey, a move welcomed by Aehrenthal in the hope that the Bulgarians might throw in their lot with Austria-Hungary. The following day the Emperor Francis Joseph proclaimed the annexation of Bosnia-Herzegovina. To compensate for the annexation, Austria-Hungary declared her intention of withdrawing altogether from the *sanjak* of Novibazar, thus abolishing the dual Turko-Austrian administration that had governed the province since the Treaty of Berlin and removing the barrier that had separated Montenegro from Serbia.[39]

---

[34]*Ibid.*, pp. 7–8.

[35]*Aide memoire* of the Russian foreign office, 27 April 1908, in Bittner and Uebersberger, I: 3–4.

[36]Schmitt, 1937, p. 8.

[37]*Aide memoire* to the Russian government, 7 May 1908, in Bittner and Uebersberger, I: 5–6.

[38]Sontag, 1933, p. 118.

[39]Memorandum, London, October 3, 1908, in Gooch and Temperley, III:377–378.

These events did not result in any major political or territorial alterations in the Balkans. Austria-Hungary had occupied and administered Bosnia and Herzegovina for thirty years, and Turkey had never exercised any control whatsoever over Bulgaria, an autonomous principality since 1878. Nevertheless, the "deal" between Aehrenthal and Izvolsky was a violation of the Treaty of Berlin and was widely resented among the other signatories of the treaty because they had not been consulted. Moreover, Bulgaria's formal assertion of independence could be viewed as altering the balance of power among the Balkan states, and in the long run disturbing the larger European balance.

The response to the Austro-Hungarian annexation of Bosnia-Herzegovina (and to the Izvolsky-Aehrenthal agreement, as rumors began to spread) differed from capital to capital, but was generally negative. Suggestions were put forward for an international conference, but none of the powers was prepared to take action in this direction. Turkey protested both the annexation and the Bulgarian declaration of independence, and Serbia, certain that Austria would attack as soon as possible, ordered mobilization.[40]

In London Sir Edward Grey, the foreign secretary, described the annexation and the Bulgarian declaration of independence as a great shock and a damaging public insult to Turkey.[41] With regard to Izvolsky's bid for the opening of the Dardanelles to Russian warships, he conceded that the international denial to Russia of all egress was "a thing which could not be maintained forever."[42] But Sir Edward was resolutely opposed to Izvolsky's plan for opening the Dardanelles only to Russian warships while leaving them closed to the warships of other great powers. Such a one-sided modification would in time of war give Russia the advantage of using the whole Black Sea as a *mare nostrum* from which her cruisers and destroyers "could issue, and retire at will from pursuit by a belligerent."[43]

Aehrenthal of course hoped to head off any great-power debate of the annexation. He confided to the German ambassador in Vienna that "it would be best to speak as little as possible" about a conference so that "neither this power nor that would hit upon the idea to make a proposal relative to this."[44] Izvolsky, faced with his own government's stern disapproval of his prior consent to the annexation, was forced to demand that the annexation issue be submitted to a great-power conference. Aehrenthal informed Izvolsky that Austria would agree to

---

[40]Pallavicini to the foreign office, Istanbul, October 6, 1908, in Bittner and Uebersberger, I:138–139.

[41]Grey to Goschen, London, October 9, 1908, in Gooch and Temperley, V:420–421.

[42]Grey to Lowther, London, October 9, 1908, *ibid.*, pp. 418–419.

[43]Grey's memorandum, London, October 14, 1908, *ibid.*, p. 441.

[44]Tschirschky to the foreign office, Vienna, October 7, 1908, in Lepsius *et al.*, XXVI: 133.

a conference only on the condition that Turkey first recognize the annexation of Bosnia-Herzegovina and that the conference take account of such recognition without debate.[45]

Sir Edward found it difficult to see how so many questions raised by "the illegal actions" of Austria and Bulgaria "could well be solved in a peaceful manner" except by a conference along the lines suggested by Izvolsky. He emphasized, on the other hand, that before going into such a conference it would be necessary to achieve preliminary agreement "as to what subjects should be discussed, how they should be dealt with, and in what form." Turkey should receive some advantage "to compensate her for advantages gained by other powers at her expense."[46]

Italy's position seemed confused. In a meeting prior to the proclamation of annexation Aehrenthal assured the Italian foreign secretary, Tittoni, that Russia considered the annexation a matter between Austria and Turkey. Tittoni agreed to support the annexation in return for Austrian demilitarization of Novibazar. A few days before the proclamation, Izvolsky visited Tittoni seeking his support for opening the Dardanelles to Russian warships; Tittoni agreed in return for Izvolsky's pledge of support for Italian expansion in North Africa. Thus, when the idea of a great-power conference was first publicly proposed, Tittoni opposed it. However, once the details of the Tittoni-Aehrenthal agreement became known, the Italian parliament protested loudly and Tittoni was forced to change his mind.

In France Premier Clemenceau thought that Turkey would not actively oppose the annexation of Bosnia and Herzegovina, since "she had ceased weeping over the loss of those Provinces [*elle en a fait son deuil*], but that with regard to a declaration of independence by Bulgaria it did not seem at all probable that the Porte [Ottoman government] would accept it without opposition." He supported the idea of a conference of the treaty powers on the subject and hoped that Russia, France, and England might propose such a conference together—with the possibility that Italy might "be brought to act with the three proposing powers."[47]

Although Bülow insisted that Germany was not responsible for Austria's policies in Bosnia, the German response was solidly behind Austria.[48] Germany wanted good relations with Turkey, but not at the expense of her alliance with Austria;[49] she must make certain to

---

[45]Aehrenthal to Mensdorff, Vienna, October 11, 1908, in Bittner and Uebersberger, I (No. 242): 192.

[46]Grey, in a Minute written upon communication from the ambassador to St. Petersburg, London, October 5, 1908, in Gooch and Temperley, V:390–391.

[47]Bertie to Grey, Paris, October 6, 1908, in Gooch and Temperley, V:395.

[48]Bülow to the foreign office, Norderney, October 7, 1908, in Lepsius *et al.*, XXVI: 137.

[49]Bülow to the Kaiser, Norderney, October 5, 1908, *ibid.*, p. 51.

retain Austria as a true alliance partner.[50] As Bülow perceived the situation, Russia hoped to drive a wedge between Germany and Austria by using the annexation issue to "shake the trust that unites us." Germany must not risk the loss of Austria-Hungary, with her fifty million inhabitants and "her strong and efficient army." Still less, however, could Germany allow herself to be dragged by Austria into the midst of an armed conflict that, the chancellor was convinced, "would be very difficult to localize and might lead to a general war," one in which Germany had "certainly nothing to gain."[51] The alliance would be shaken if Germany did not back Austria in her effort to expand in the Balkans,[52] and Germany's position would be "a serious one if Austria should lose her faith and lean away from Germany."[53] Although there were risks for Germany in this policy, they were unavoidable.[54] Thus, Bülow reiterated that Germany could not afford to equivocate with respect to Austria-Hungary.

Turkey was opposed to discussing the question of the Dardanelles,[55] and Britain felt that she could not participate in a conference contributing "to the further dismemberment of Turkey, or [allow] for the overthrow of the liberal administration recently established" there.[56] Wilhelm emphasized that the Germans would refuse to participate in a conference unless the annexation of Bosnia and Herzegovina were excluded from discussion.[57] From the German point of view there were indeed advantages to be gained from a discreet handling of the controversy. But Austria's activities made discretion difficult. By mid-November 1908, preparations were underway in Austria for mobilization, and in Serbia there were powerful pressures for countermeasures. Austrian military activities began to cause alarm among European leaders.[58]

Early in 1909 Austro-German relations were strengthened by a series of written exchanges between German Field Marshal Moltke and Austrian Field Marshal Conrad.[59] According to Moltke, in the event of Russian mobilization in response to an Austrian invasion of

---

[50]Bülow to the foreign office, Norderney, October 5, 1908, *ibid.*, pp. 102–104.

[51]Bülow, 1931, II:380.

[52]Bülow to the foreign office, Norderney, October 5, 1908, in Lepsius *et al.*, XXVI: 102–104.

[53]Bülow to Kaiser Wilhelm, Norderney, October 5, 1908, *ibid.*, pp. 50–54.

[54]Bülow, 1931, II:366.

[55]Grey to Lowther, London, October 12, 1908, in Gooch and Temperley, V:425.

[56]Grey to Bertie, London, October 6, 1908, *ibid.*, pp. 399–400.

[57]Szögyény to the foreign office, Berlin, October 8, 1908, in Bittner and Uebersberger, I:156–157.

[58]Grey to Carnegie, London, November 16, 1908, in Gooch and Temperley, V:499; see also Berchtold to Aehrenthal, St. Petersburg, November 18, 1908, in Bittner and Uebersberger, I:470–471.

[59]Conrad to Moltke, January 1, 1909, in Conrad, I:379–394.

Serbia, Germany would mobilize her entire army. In the case of a major war, moreover, German forces would launch their principal attack against France.[60]

The Austrian intent, meanwhile, was to get the Serbs to agree to annexation — by threat if possible, otherwise by armed force. The annexation issue had to be settled quickly, since the prolonged military preparations were seriously damaging the economic life of the empire.[61] In January the Dual Monarchy came to an agreement with Turkey with respect to the annexation. Austria renounced all rights to the *sanjak* of Novibazar, assured complete religious freedom and equality for Muslims in Bosnia and Herzegovina, and declared a readiness to negotiate concerning the protectorate in Albania.[62] Turkey signed a separate agreement with Bulgaria.[63]

On February 19 Sir Edward proposed that the great powers meet to discuss averting any Austrian action against Serbia. France, Russia, and Italy supported the proposal, but Germany took exception on the grounds that Serbia, not Austria, was causing the difficulties. Aehrenthal offered assurances to Britain that Austria would "make use of no sudden or violent action against Serbia" and that she had no "wish to humiliate Serbia." He demanded, however, that the Serbian government publicly demonstrate a willingness for peaceful relations with the Dual Monarchy.[64]

Meanwhile, Russian leaders still faced the grim reality that their country was not in a position to go to war. Military authorities considered it would take three to five years to prepare the army, which was itself opposed to involvement in a war at this time. Russian leaders thus faced a choice between abandoning Serbia or embarking on war under notably unfavorable circumstances.[65] Izvolsky's advice to the Serbian government was to draw up a short circular asserting friendliness toward Austria, to drop all territorial and political claims, and to leave its case in the hands of the great powers.[66]

On March 14 the Austrian government decided that if no satisfactory response arrived from the Serbian capital by the next morning, the transportation of additional troops to the southeastern part of Austria would begin on March 16.[67] Aehrenthal, with support from

[60]Moltke to Conrad, January 21, 1909, *ibid.*, pp. 379–394.
[61]Bridge, 1972, p. 316.
[62]Schmitt, 1937, pp. 118–119.
[63]*Ibid.*, pp. 123–143.
[64]Cartwright to Grey, Vienna, March 4, 1909, in Gooch and Temperley, V:654–655.
[65]Berchtold to Aehrenthal, St. Petersburg, February 24, 1909, in Bittner and Uebersberger, I:827–828, 877–878.
[66]Grey to Nicolson, London, March 9, 1909, in Gooch and Temperley, V:665–666.
[67]Tschirschky to the foreign office, Vienna, March 14, 1909, in Lepsius *et al.*, XXVI: 659.

Bülow, informed Izvolsky that the details of the Buchlau discussions (between Aehrenthal and Izvolsky) would be published forthwith unless Serbia agreed to an early settlement.[68] This amounted to political blackmail. Bülow was even more explicit in his instructions to the German ambassador in St. Petersburg, Pourtàles. "Tell Izvolsky in a definite way that we expect a precise answer—yes or no: any evasive, conditional or unclear answer would be regarded as a refusal. We would then withdraw and let events take their course."[69] Izvolsky replied that his government was willing to join with the other powers in securing an early settlement. He still hoped that if the powers could be induced to hold a conference, some concessions could be obtained from Austria. Aehrenthal was of the opinion, however, that the moment for rapprochement among the three imperial powers (Germany, Austria, and Russia) had "not come by a long shot." He therefore thought that it would be useful "to lay—cautiously and without showing any haste—the groundwork for rapprochement" when the opportunity presented itself.[70]

The deadlock was broken "by the diplomatic collapse of Russia." As an invasion of Serbia became more and more imminent, Izvolsky "lost his nerve and appealed desperately to Berlin . . ."[71] Germany replied with a request that Russia recognize the Austrian annexation of Bosnia and Herzegovina forthwith or Germany would not restrain Austria from an attack on Serbia. Izvolsky complied, playing in Paris and London "the role of victim of a German 'ultimatum'."[72] Yielding to Russian pressure, Serbia proclaimed that her rights had "not been infringed upon by the *fait accompli* in Bosnia and Herzegovina" and that it would consequently conform to a decision of the powers with respect to the annexation. From that moment on, Serbia would "abandon the attitude of protest and opposition" to the annexation and "undertake to change its present policy towards Austria-Hungary in order to live henceforth in friendship with this power."[73] Major war was thus averted, essentially because Russia was not prepared to fight and Austria sought satisfaction by threat, bluff, and diplomatic blackmail instead of by armed force.

What was the outcome of the Bosnian crisis of 1908 and early 1909? Most notably, the Triple Alliance had held firm. Britain, until now the most important element in the balance of power, had chosen sides;

---

[68]Szögyény to Aehrenthal, Berlin, March 14, 1909, in Bittner and Uebersberger, II: 101; Aehrenthal to Szögyény and Berchtold, Vienna, March 24, 1909, *ibid.*, pp. 174–175.
[69]Bülow to Pourtales, Berlin, March 21, 1909, in Lepsius *et al.*, XXVI:693–695.
[70]Tschirschky to foreign office, March 30, 1909, *ibid.*, pp. 726–727.
[71]Bridge, 1972, p. 318.
[72]*Ibid.*, p. 419.
[73]Serbia, official note, March 31, 1909, in Bittner and Uebersberger, II:225.

thus, the solution of the annexation issue also strengthened the Entente. As a result, the two blocs became "so evenly balanced that it became extremely important on which side the small powers would align themselves, especially if there was the possibility of uniting them."[74] The combined strength of the small powers might be decisive in any test of strength.

Russia suffered severe diplomatic losses. Having failed to secure an opening of the Dardanelles, Izvolsky was then forced to abandon Serbia and submit to humiliation at the hands of Austria and Germany.[75] Against the background of defeat in 1905 at the hands of the Japanese, this may well have aggravated in St. Petersburg a desperate feeling of "falling behind." By winning general recognition of the annexation without recourse to an international conference, Germany and Austria had "carried off a great diplomatic victory," whereas Russia and Italy had "bowed to their will" in a way that was especially humiliating to St. Petersburg.[76] Yet the Bosnian crisis further strengthened the Anglo-Russian alliance. When the Russian submission to Germany first became known in St. Petersburg, there was "a storm of indignation" that Britain and France had let Russia down. In time, however, this ill feeling was directed against Germany, where in turn the tendency was to hold Izvolsky responsible.[77] Under these circumstances Russia naturally drew closer to England. Moreover, the Bosnian crisis contributed to the reorganization and strengthening of the Russian army and, in some measure at least, to an acceleration of the British naval program.

The Serbs came out of the crisis with a new viewpoint, convinced that the Austrian attack had only been postponed; consequently, they took up an anti-Austrian policy in earnest. The crisis also had a unifying effect on Serbs in and out of Serbia and on Balkan Slavs in general. Hitherto, Serbs in Serbia had seldom troubled themselves about Serbs in Austria-Hungary, nor for that matter about Serbs in Bosnia and Herzegovina. In a sense, Aehrenthal had taught the Serbs to be "Yugoslavs." Many Serbs became more determined than ever to wrest the Slavic provinces from the Austrian Empire.[78] Izvolsky also had lent a hand, of course, by encouraging Serbian nationalism.

In many respects, the Austrian position in Europe, already ambiguous and difficult, was further weakened. Bulgaria, which Aehrenthal had hoped "to harness . . . to the chariot of Austrian policy," passed

---

[74]Helmreich, 1938, p. 12.
[75]Schmitt, 1937, p. 244.
[76]Albertini, 1952, I:293.
[77]Schmitt, 1937, pp. 245–246.
[78]Bridge, 1972, p. 321.

over to the Russian camp.[79] In trade with the Balkan countries and Turkey, Austria found herself losing out more and more to competition from Germany.[80] And the deterioration of Austria's relations with Britain, Russia, and Italy made her all the more dependent upon Berlin—"at least if she ever wished to embark on a policy of action."

The crisis had even more far-reaching consequences. By binding herself to Austria in what amounted to an offensive alliance (largely through the efforts of Fieldmarshals Conrad and Moltke), Germany critically altered the configuration of power in Europe and assumed a degree of responsibility for the rigid, unrealistic, and compulsive ambitions of the Dual Monarchy that proved fatal in 1914.

Meanwhile, relations between France and Germany over Morocco were still under negotiation. In mid-January, 1909 news of the impending conclusion of a Franco-German agreement on Morocco caused surprise and apprehension in London. British fears were dispelled only as it became evident that British economic interests were not in jeopardy. Franco-German relations over Morocco, having been smoothed out in 1909, were severely aggravated later by the Agadir Incident, which developed after insurgent tribes threatened Fez during March, 1911. The sultan had appealed to Paris for help in defense of the city and the French had complied.[81] This unilateral action alarmed Spain, which (with German encouragement) concluded that France was undertaking the partition of Morocco specified in the 1904 Anglo-French Accords. Resolving to secure her own share of the spoils, Spain landed troops on the Moroccan coast, and the partition began.[82] The penetration of Morocco by French troops and the occupation of Fez were regarded in Germany as a violation of the Algeciras Act, reopening the whole Moroccan question.[83]

The 1909 Franco-German agreement on Morocco had allowed Germans equal standing with Frenchmen in commercial and financial affairs; in return, Germany recognized the special political position of France. Although the exploitation of mineral resources, development of public works, and building of railways promised possibilities for economic cooperation, from the German viewpoint the actual outcome was far from satisfactory.[84] France had been steadily extending her "political grip on Morocco" and probably intended to convert it eventually into a French protectorate.

Germany felt she had the right to peacefully station ships in Mogador and Agadir in order to protect Germans—just as France protected her

---

[79]*Ibid.*, p. 322.
[80]*Ibid.*, p. 323.
[81]Albertini, 1952, I:327
[82]Williamson, 1969, p. 142.
[83]Albertini, 1952, I:327.
[84]*Ibid.*

citizens in Fez.[85] The German gunboat *Panther* and, later, a cruiser were sent to Agadir "to protect German interests." In fact, however, no German interests of importance had been established anywhere near Agadir—although there was considerable sentiment in Germany favoring the annexation of some part of the Atlantic seaboard of Morocco. It was also common knowledge that German syndicates were seeking coaling stations in Teneriffe or Madeira.[86] It seems reasonable to assume that German leaders expected the threat of the presence of a German gunboat to increase with the growing strength and prestige of the German navy. The German deployment of the *Panther* was an unmistakable attempt to practice coercive diplomacy. On July 15 the German foreign secretary, Alfred von Kiderlen-Wachter, suggested to the French ambassador that Germany ought to have the whole of the French Congo. Astonished, the ambassador replied that no French government could give up a whole colony, but suggested that some of it might be surrendered in return for Togo and some of the Cameroons.[87]

British officials were in disagreement over whether to support France in its drive for Morocco.[88] According to Sir Edward Grey, France had two alternatives: to adhere to the Act of Algeciras or to render Germany adequate compensation—inside or outside of Morocco—although Sir Edward thought that the partition of Morocco might encourage Germany to demand concessions elsewhere.[89] As far as Britain was concerned, the whole complexion of the Moroccan question was transformed once the issue of naval bases arose—even if over an insignificant African port.[90] The arrival of the *Panther* seemed to confirm Sir Edward's fears about German intentions.[91] On July 20 the British ambassador in Paris presented the French foreign minister with a note announcing Britain's intention, in the event of a deadlock, of calling an international conference. The British government, he said, would not treat the admission of Germany to Morocco as an unconditional *casus belli*. Nevertheless, Britain would not deal with such admission except in concert with France and in terms that France found satisfactory, although Britain expected to be consulted about any step involving serious consequences for herself, including, presumably, any partition of Morocco.[92] In an address at Mansion House in London, Lloyd George, long-known as a radical and pacifist, warned that Britain's national honor was at stake. The security of

[85]Fay, 1947, p. 280.
[86]Woodward, 1935, p. 311.
[87]Fay, 1947, p. 285.
[88]Williamson, 1969, p. 148.
[89]*Ibid.*, pp. 142–149.
[90]Chamberlin, 1939, p. 43.
[91]Fay, 1947, pp. 286–287.
[92]Williamson, 1969, p. 151.

Britain's international trade was no partisan question. It was, Lloyd George declared, "in the highest interests, not merely of this country, but of the world, that Britain should at all hazards maintain her place and her prestige amongst the Great Powers of the world (cheers)."[93]

This assertion of British interest in Morocco was both a public pledge of British support of France and a restatement of Britain's strong policy toward Germany.[94] For Britain to stay out of the negotiations, Germany would have to renounce any territorial ambitions she might have in Morocco.[95] As German leaders saw it, Lloyd George had not only rejected satisfactory compensations for Germany in Morocco, but in Central Africa as well.[96] In Germany and Britain there were rumors of sinister fleet movements — and in Germany talk of war.[97] The British fleet prepared for action. Morocco, which at one point had been the site of potential reconciliation between France and Germany, became more and more the focus of Anglo-German conflict.

Toward the middle of August, 1911 Churchill went to the country for a few days. "I could not think of anything else but the peril of war," he recalled in subsequent years.[98] But Germany decided to back away — she and France reached a settlement. Part of the French Congo was added to the German Cameroons, and France was allowed to do as she pleased in Morocco. The *Panther* was withdrawn from Agadir in late November.[99]

The Agadir Incident was an historic turning point. Not only did it consolidate the Entente Cordiale, it also provoked both Britain and Germany to make preparations for a sudden outbreak of war.[100] It also had the effect of sharpening German feelings of insecurity. In the next chapter we shall see how this sense of insecurity contributed to the Anglo-German naval race — and how, in turn, that race contributed to further feelings of insecurity in both Germany and Britain.

---

[93]Lloyd George, speech at the Mansion House, 21 July 1911, in Gooch and Temperley, VII:391–392; for the full text, see *The Times of London*, July 22, 1911. To some extent Lloyd George's assertions may be dismissed as rhetoric, but, as we have noted, leaders of great powers (especially of the strongest power) often seem to assume that what is good for their country is good for all.

[94]Williamson, 1969, p. 153.

[95]*Ibid.*, p. 154.

[96]Hale, 1940, p. 395.

[97]Woodward, 1935, p. 313.

[98]Churchill, 1924, p. 63.

[99]Brandenburg, 1927, pp. 382–383.

[100]Churchill, 1924, p. 65.

The Anglo-German Naval Race

6

Europe in the last quarter of the nineteenth century and the first quarter of the twentieth witnessed a spiraling competition among the powers that was manifested in diplomacy, commerce, colonization, and, especially after 1900, naval and arms races. Along with other authorities, Hans Morgenthau considers the European arms race before 1914 a classic example of the dynamics of competition.[1] The propositions in Chapter 1 may have suggested, misleadingly, that lateral pressure gives rise to conflicts of interest that in turn contribute to competition, crises, and war. In fact, however, as our presentation of history so far has shown, two processes occur simultaneously — expansion of national interests and competition.

In this chapter we shall be concerned with some of the events contributing to the Anglo-German arms race prior to WWI.[2] We do not discount altogether the effect of the personal predisposition and idiosyncrasies of individual leaders — no doubt Kaiser Wilhelm's ambitions, obsessions and feelings of inadequacy contributed to the Anglo-German arms race. Nevertheless, larger, deeper, more pervasive factors were at work, and it seems quite possible, even probable, that these factors would have created an Anglo-German conflict even if the character of the Kaiser had been quite different.[3]

An arms race is "an immense social, political, legal and economic process."[4] It is also a technological process. In his study of the

---

[1]Morgenthau, 1967, p. 170; see also Huntington, 1971, p. 501: "Arms races are an integral part of the international balance of power. From the viewpoint of the participants, an arms race is an effort to achieve a favorable international distribution of power."

[2]For some of the background of Germany's entry into the arms race, see Ritter, 1965, p. 137.

[3]See Steinberg, 1965, pp. 23, 28.

[4]*Ibid.*

German navy and its contribution to the Anglo-German naval race, Jonathan Steinberg asserts that "technology has no life of its own." He believes, therefore, that the causes of the Anglo-German race must be looked for elsewhere. The conclusion that the Anglo-German race was caused not by technology but by the politics of the participants may be correct in a narrow sense. However, national policies are significantly shaped by relative differences in technology (as well as differences in other capabilities). Indeed, Steinberg himself grants that national differences in technology tended to "shift the lines of force and the relative positions of the great powers and thus to change the framework of diplomacy."[5]

By the late nineteenth century, the countries that enjoyed political, economic, and military power, as well as diplomatic prestige, were for the most part those countries with relatively advanced technologies. Differing rates of economic and industrial growth and inequalities of political and military power contributed to "a greater political disequilibrium on a wider scale than men had perhaps ever to contend with."[6] Tirpitz shared the view with other German leaders that the major source of Anglo-German antagonism was Britain's jealousy of Germany's increasing industrial experience—even though Britain continued to maintain a comfortable lead in industrial production.[7]

The early phases of the German naval program caused little anxiety in Britain.[8] More direct manifestations of German economic growth were unsettling. As early as 1885 Germany's "upward climb in industry and commerce" had become a prominent topic of public discussion in Britain, both in parliament and in leading articles of the press.[9] The emergence of Germany as a serious commercial rival of Britain was relatively sudden, and the German industrial advance was "almost sensationally rapid."[10] (German export trade came close to matching the British around 1897, and again in 1904.) To some political and economic leaders in Britain, the outlook for British commerce was dark.[11]

German leaders felt that a powerful battle fleet would be an important adjunct to German commerce and foreign policy. According to a memorandum issued in June, 1894 by the German Executive Command (written chiefly by Tirpitz), a nation with world interests "must be able to uphold them and make its power felt beyond its own territorial waters." Therein lay "by far the most important purpose of the German fleet."[12] Until just before the turn of the century there had

---

[5]*Ibid.*, p. 24.
[6]Hinsley, 1963, p. 218.
[7]Tirpitz, 1924, I:254–258; Hale, 1940, p. 238.
[8]Woodward, 1935, p. 2.
[9]Hoffman, 1933, p. 74.
[10]*Ibid.*, p. 77.
[11]*Ibid.*, pp. 93–94.
[12]Woodward, 1935, p. 17.

not been much expectation in Germany of rising above the level of a second-rate naval power. Thereafter, however, the Germans continually compared their navy with that of Britain.[13]

In Britain, concern for the navy stemmed in large part from the fact that Britain was an island.[14] To most Englishmen the defeat of the British navy meant the threat of starvation.[15] Britain therefore required "absolute naval superiority," and "an uncommitted posture which allowed her to keep the great Continental powers 'in balance' and thus to protect herself."[16] One factor in the Moroccan crisis of 1905 was British apprehension that German coaling stations on the Atlantic coast of Morocco would increase the danger in time of war to British commerce routed via the Cape. Any expansion of German naval forces was certain to generate apprehension in Britain.[17]

Yet the growth of Germany's naval power did not keep pace with her growth in other areas.[18] Indeed, around the turn of the century the German fleet "bore no reasonable relation to Germany's growing trade and overseas interests.[19] After his appointment to the admiralty, Tirpitz pressed even further than the Kaiser himself the methods by which it was hoped to convert German public opinion to support for a powerful navy. Within less than a year he had persuaded the Reichstag to accept the Navy Bill of 1898. In 1900 Britain possessed 47 battleships, Germany only 14. By the beginning of 1908, however, the totals were 53 and 24, respectively — Britain having increased her naval power by 13 percent, Germany by 71 percent.[20]

It was not long before the German program created new concern in England. The 1900 law proposed a German fleet that, if combined with that of some other nation, might be *superior* to that of Britain.[21] If the proposed fleet were achieved, the two-power standard that constituted the foundation of British control of the sea would be in serious danger — unless England chose to undertake a naval program of such magnitude as possibly to strain the patience of the British taxpayer. "The determination of the greatest military power on the continent to become at the same time the second naval power," wrote Winston Churchill after the war, "was an event of the first magnitude in world affairs. It would, if carried into full effect, undoubtedly reproduce those situations which at previous levels in history had proved of such awful significance to the Islanders of Britain."[22]

---

[13]Hislam, 1908, p. 19; see also Schoen, 1922.
[14]*Parliamentary Debates*, 1896, XXXVII:1523; cf. Ritter, 1965, p. 136.
[15]Woodward, 1935, p. 13.
[16]Ritter, 1965, p. 136.
[17]Marder, 1961, p. 115; and Ritter, 1965, p. 136.
[18]Steinberg, 1965, p. 158.
[19]Hurd and Castle, 1913, p. 118.
[20]Hislam, 1908, p. 28.
[21]*Ibid.*, p. 21.
[22]Churchill, 1924, I:12–14.

From the Germans' point of view, there was nothing unreasonable about German needs and ambitions.[23] Germany wanted a navy "not merely for the protection of her coasts and her commerce, but for the 'general purposes of her greatness'."[24] Without a strong fleet, Germany might find herself at the mercy of Britain, a "grasping and unscrupulous nation which, in the course of history, had taken opportunity after opportunity to destroy the trade of its commercial rivals."[25] The German fleet would therefore have to have the capability of inflicting serious damage on the British fleet.[26]

German and British naval objectives increasingly clashed. Britain was determined to maintain her supremacy at sea at any cost, and she accomplished this by watching the naval programs of other powers and shaping her own plans accordingly.[27] After the turn of the century, the German naval program increasingly "determined the programmes of Great Britain."[28]

The Boer War had marked something of a turning point in Anglo-German relations. The position of the German government in this conflict was legally correct, but Germany's persistence in taking advantage of Britain's preoccupation with pressing her claims in South Africa and elsewhere was deeply resented in England. The German press and many public figures condemned Britain's "buccaneering adventure in South Africa, criticized the British Army as a pack of mercenaries, and slandered Queen Victoria in gross caricatures."[29] At one point in this conflict British vessels seized two German mail steamers bound for South Africa. Many Germans suffered profound feelings of humiliation, feeling that their country was being "kicked around" again.[30]

The close connections between increases in industry, shipping, trade, colonial enterprise, and naval strength, on the one hand, and feelings of anxiety, suspicion, fear and sometimes even panic, on the other, have been described by the German diplomat Baron Schoen.[31] German demands for raw materials and markets contributed to the extension of German interests in many parts of the world. To some extent this expansion and the overall growth of German trade were perceived as a challenge by British commercial interests. This contributed to Anglo-German competition but not, generally, to serious feelings of hostility in Britain. Nevertheless, many Germans felt that German economic growth was blocked by unrestrained expansion of British interests.

---

[23]Tirpitz, 1924, I:10.
[24]Woodward, 1935, p. 10.
[25]*Ibid.*, p. 11.
[26]*Ibid.*, p. 24.
[27]*Ibid.*, p. 31.
[28]*Ibid.*, p. 12.
[29]Marder, 1961, pp. 105, 122.
[30]Cf. Wilhelm II, 1922, p. 233.
[31]Schoen, 1922, p. 224.

The rapid growth of German trade and the far-flung extension of German interests first encouraged in Germany a demand for a larger merchant marine, and then for a larger and more effective navy. Eventually, the systematic development of German naval power had the effect of exacerbating British anxieties and thus contributing to the strengthening of the British fleet. Thereafter, each increment in the development of one navy stimulated comparable development in the other.[32]

The Anglo-German naval race was not the only arms competition in the years prior to WWI; the military and naval budgets of all major European powers increased (see Figures 7-1, 7-2, and 7-3, as well as Table 7-1, in the next chapter). The Anglo-German naval race commands particular attention, however, because of its influence in setting the stage for WWI. The German naval program, beginning with the Navy Law of 1898, was conceived as a direct challenge to British diplomatic and military hegemony. The immediate purpose was to give Germany an instrument for influencing and even coercing Britain.[33] Since Germany had allowed her alliance with Russia to lapse in 1890, "she had no other reliable diplomatic means of exerting pressure on England, as Bismarck had been able to do."[34]

The Kaiser thought that if war with Britain could be avoided until the critical phase of the German naval program was completed — around 1904 according to Tirpitz's calculations — the navy would be strong enough to cause anxiety in Britain. The danger of a British attack would then diminish as English leaders perceived that war with Germany would incur great risk to their country.[35]

In 1904, however, Britain settled her differences with France. This improvement of Anglo-French relations was in considerable part attributable to growing German military and naval power, even though the immediate reasons were Anglo-French conflicts in Asia. The Anglo-French accord made sense for Britain as a form of reinsurance, but it also had the effect of isolating Germany.[36] Because Germany was particularly sensitive to being "flanked" by France and Russia, any change in relations involving France or Russia, to say nothing of Britain, was bound to have repercussions in Berlin. Lacking a reinsurance arrangement with Russia, and with Russia and France drawing closer together, German leaders looked to Britain for detente. Yet Germany did not want an Anglo-German arrangement that did not also encompass the Triple Alliance. Britain, however, was intensely wary of committing herself to Italy and Austria as a condition for alliance with Germany.[37] Both nations were suspicious. German leaders feared that

[32]See Tirpitz, 1924, I:61–105.
[33]Steinberg, 1965, p. 18.
[34]*Ibid.*, p. 18.
[35]Albertini, 1952, I:151.
[36]*Ibid.*, p. 3.
[37]Albertini, 1952, I:149.

Britain might draw Germany into a war with Russia; Britain feared that Germany might bring her into a war with France.[38]

Tirpitz thought that a strong German fleet would attract either Britain or the Franco-Russian alliance in her direction, and thus significantly limit the risk of a sudden attack by Britain.[39] In effect, however, the Anglo-French Accords made both possibilities extremely unlikely. For the Accords relieved Britain of the need to reckon with the French navy, thus robbing Tirpitz's "risk theory" of part of its threat.[40]

In fact, Britain's newly achieved accord with France tended to irritate Anglo-German relations. Although English leaders viewed the Anglo-French and Anglo-Russian ententes as defensive measures, the Germans believed that the new alignment of the powers was directed specifically against their country. From the German viewpoint, unless the alliances were dissolved, any arms limitation would be folly.[41] German leaders therefore hoped to detach Britain from her moral if not her written commitments to Russia and France. Indeed, the Moroccan crisis represented an early German attempt at testing and, if possible, breaking the Anglo-French Accords.

Tirpitz and the Kaiser expected the strength of the German fleet to influence British policies:[42] In fact, however, a naval threat was "the least likely way to force an alliance on the English."[43] What Tirpitz and other German leaders did not foresee was that every increase in the German navy increased the risk of war not only for Britain, but for Germany as well.[44] Since all the major powers were rapidly building ships, "British naval supremacy was threatened every time a keel was laid by any one of them." Thus, instead of drawing Britain or the Franco-Russian alliance toward Germany, German naval expansion pressed the three powers into closer association.[45]

Most British observers had regarded the expansion of the German fleet in its early stages "not as a threat in itself but as a new factor in what the First Lord called 'the balance of power in the navies of Europe.' . . . Germany had to keep up with the latest naval developments if she were to remain a great power."[46] British leaders became less tolerant, however, as German naval growth began to threaten the two-power standard.[47] The two-power standard dated back as far as 1770. It had been reinstituted after the Crimean War and

---

[38]Woodward, 1935, p. 3; Brandenburg, 1927, p. 13; Woodward, 1935, p. 3; and Albertini, 1952, I:324.

[39]Steinberg, 1965, p. 21; Marder, 1961, pp. 171–172.

[40]Woodward, 1935, p. 69; see also Huntington, 1971, p. 526.

[41]Ibid., p. 256.

[42]Albertini, 1952, I:151; Huntington, 1971, p. 526.

[43]Ritter, 1965, p. 137.

[44]Steinberg, 1965, p. 21.

[45]Ibid., pp. 18, 21.

[46]Ibid., p. 196. The first lord of the admiralty quoted is George Goschen (1895–99).

[47]Ibid., p. 27.

officially accepted by Britain's first lord of the admiralty in 1889, when it was stated that the British naval establishment should "at least be equal to the naval strength of any two other countries," with a margin of 10 percent for "eventualities." Over the next 15 years or so this standard was confirmed again and again by both Liberal and Conservative spokesmen.[48] As a consequence of the Anglo-French Entente, the ineffective showing of the Russian fleet in the war with Japan, and the development of the German fleet to the degree that it posed a greater threat than the French or Russian navies, a revision of the standard was made in 1904. Thereafter, the two-power standard was based on comparisons with Germany and France rather than Russia and France.[49]

Between 1900 and 1905 Anglo-German relations deteriorated steadily. In July, 1904 the German ambassador in London reported to Berlin that most English newspapers viewed the growth of the German fleet "as a menace to England."[50] In many respects, German views of Britain's "threatening activities" were a mirror image of English perceptions of Germany's hostile attitude. For the sake of her empire, Britain felt that she had to be more considerate of France (as a major colonial power) and Russia (as a major Asiatic power) than she was of Germany. Those two countries had "more to offer her, and also constituted a greater potential threat, than landlocked Germany."[51]

Many Englishmen considered the navy their best if not an indispensable security. At the same time, a strong German fleet was increasingly perceived by Germans "as a means of getting colonies and for coping with England."[52] Germany felt compelled to build a more powerful navy whenever Britain began strengthening hers, and vice versa. Spiraling arms contributed to spiraling anxieties and hostilities.[53] Instead of a sense of security, there emerged a sense of suspicion, apprehension, and fear.

Not long after the turn of the century, Britain decided to build a more powerful and expensive ship, the Dreadnought. This ship had been designed to "outrange in the heaviest armament, and to outpace in speed and maneuver, any other type of battleship."[54] The development of the Dreadnought was immediately perceived by German leaders as a serious threat. British leaders, too, were concerned that construction of the new ship would imply a new threat to other powers. At a public meeting in Albert Hall, Prime Minister Campbell-Bannerman warned against an arms race as "a great danger to the

---

[48]Marder, 1961, p. 123.

[49]*Ibid.*, pp. 107, 123–124.

[50]*Ibid.*, p. 109.

[51]Ritter, 1965, p. 134.

[52]Langer, 1951, p. 246.

[53]Grey, 1925, II:271; Brandenburg, 1927, p. 272; and Lt. General Moltke, chief of the central staff, to Bülow, 23 February 1906, in Dugdale, 1931, III:239–240.

[54]Woodward, 1935, p. 106.

peace of the world." It was, he said, the outcome of policies that stimulated the belief that force is the best if not the only solution to international differences.[55] These were brave and hopeful words, but in themselves they could not alter the fact that different nations had different rates of growth, nor could they deter the expansion and conflict of national interests.

In May, 1906 the Reichstag passed a supplementary naval law, introduced by Tirpitz, which increased the size and armaments of all the new classes of battleships. From the German viewpoint it "would have been foolish to incur a vast expenditure on ships not of the very best technique." In other words, Germany felt that she too must build Dreadnoughts.[56]

In an effort to slow down the naval rivalry, Britain announced reductions in her shipbuilding program and promised further cuts in the event of a general agreement at the Second Hague Conference, which opened June 17, 1907. At the First Hague Conference in 1899 the major powers had been anxious to avoid any move toward limiting defense capabilities or any proposals for disarmament. The Second Hague Conference provided Britain with an opportunity for proposing a general reduction in armies and navies. To the Germans a British proposal on this issue looked like a scheme for preventing Germany from enhancing its sea power at a time when England still enjoyed a considerable superiority.[57] Tirpitz charged that the colossus England, "already more than four times as strong as Germany, in alliance with Japan, and probably so with France," was asking "little" Germany to disarm.[58] With Austria weakened by internal disorders and Italy behaving like a dubious ally, the German government could scarcely afford to accept limitations on its army. Although France and Russia shared this reluctance to a considerable degree, the delegates of these two countries allowed the Germans to take the lead in blocking British (and American) proposals. As a consequence of these reservations and apprehensions, the question of reducing expenditures on armaments was not discussed at the conference.[59]

This failure to check naval competition had disastrous consequences; the outcome was a sense of diminished security. This was reflected in the exacerbated Anglo-German rivalry, which henceforth became "the dominant factor in the European situation."[60] After the Second Hague Conference all hope of a reduction of European armaments vanished.[61] In Britain it appeared that the navy would have to

[55]*Parliamentary Debates*, 1906, CLII:1335.
[56]Brandenburg, 1927, p. 273.
[57]Fay, 1947, p. 234.
[58]Marder, 1961, p. 131.
[59]*Ibid.*, p. 133.
[60]*Ibid.*, p. 134.
[61]Woodward, 1935, p. 5.

prepare for an Anglo-German naval conflict that "more and more Englishmen came to regard as inevitable."[62] These developments nurtured the well-developed trend toward a division of Europe into rival camps. In July, 1907 the Triple Alliance was renewed, followed the next month by the signing of the Anglo-Russian agreement over Persia, Afghanistan, and Tibet. This latter arrangement had the effect of reconciling conflicts of British and Russian overseas interests much as the 1904 Accords had done for Britain and France.

During the spring of 1908 *The Times* of London obtained and published a letter from the Kaiser to the British first lord of the admiralty, Lord Tweedmouth, which discussed British and German naval policies. In it Wilhelm chided the British for their apprehension over Germany's naval policy. It was "absolutely nonsensical and untrue" that the purpose of the German Navy Bill was to provide a navy as a "challenge to British naval supremacy." The German fleet was being built "against nobody at all"; it was being built solely for "Germany's needs in relation with that country's rapidly growing trade."[63] Moreover, the Kaiser asserted, the extraordinary rapidity with which improvements were being introduced in various types of battleships, armaments, and armor made the commissioned German fleet obsolete even before the building program had been half finished.[64]

The Kaiser's letter seemed to be a clear attempt to influence the British minister responsible for naval estimates. Englishmen were shocked when the document appeared in print, and King Edward was astonished that his nephew sovereign would write directly to a British public servant.[65] Fantasies of German espionage and invasion, "questions and answers in parliament, and continuous agitation of the fleet question in the press produced an atmosphere charged with tension and alarm."[66]

Plagued by ill health, Campbell-Bannerman resigned as prime minister on April 1, 1908, and was succeeded by Herbert Henry Asquith. Reginald McKenna followed Lord Tweedmouth as first lord of the admiralty; David Lloyd George moved from the board of trade to the exchequer; and Winston Churchill entered the cabinet as president of the board of trade. For the next three years Lloyd George and Churchill led the wing of the cabinet that favored social reform and arms reduction.[67] Later, however, as first lord of the admiralty, Churchill would demand and receive the largest naval budgets in English history.

---

[62]Marder, 1961, p. 122. In general, we would expect that the greater the perceived threat from a rival country, the more likely will be the tendency of a people to see the alternatives narrowing and to reconcile themselves to the "inevitability" of a violent conflict.

[63]Wilhelm II to Lord Tweedmouth, Berlin, 16 February 1908, in Tirpitz, 1924, I:58.

[64]*Ibid.*, pp. 58–59.

[65]King Edward VII to Kaiser Wilhelm II, Buckingham Palace, 22 February 1908, in Lepsius *et al.*, XXIV:36.

[66]Hale, 1940, p. 312.

[67]Marder, 1961, p. 142.

In August, Lloyd George and Sir Charles Hardinge accompanied King Edward on a visit to Germany. The objective of Lloyd George's visit was believed to be an attempt to lay foundations for an under-standing about reduction of naval armaments.[68] Edward met the Kaiser privately on August 11. He reported to Sir Charles that he had touched on the question of naval expenditures, and had mentioned to Wilhelm that Sir Edward Grey had provided him with a paper on the views of the British government. Wilhelm, however, asked neither to see the paper nor to know its contents, and the king concluded that it would be tactless to force a discussion his nephew seemed anxious to avoid. "There are no frictions between us," Edward declared, "there exists only rivalry."[69] Nevertheless, Wilhelm asserted that Germany intended to fulfill her naval plans—not for aggressive purposes, but in order to defend her interests if that became necessary.[70] The Kaiser added—unwisely it would seem—that "he considered it doubtful if England could permanently keep up the two-power standard.[71]

The Germans perceived an ambivalent British attitude that they felt should not be overlooked. On the one hand, the British proclaimed their willingness to be reasonable, but on the other, as Lloyd George had assured Commons, the British naval position was one of "unassail-able supremacy, and such it must remain."[72] Supremacy was the corner-stone of British policy, and both Conservative and Liberal statesmen were inflexible on this point. Thus, every official British proposal for a limitation of the German fleet was regarded in Berlin as a hostile proposal.

Lloyd George and Sir Charles returned to England with the convic-tion that no agreement could be reached. The government thus saw no other alternative than to apply to Parliament in the spring for large credits for the navy. This action would at the same time demolish the policy of retrenchment advocated by the Liberals and strengthen the conviction of Conservatives that Britain's defenses had been sorely neglected.[73]

In 1908, at a time when tensions were already high in Europe be-cause of the annexation of Bosnia and Herzegovina by Austria, the Kaiser again proclaimed Germany's need for a strong navy in sensa-tional terms. In an interview published October 27 in the London *Daily Telegraph,* Wilhelm referred to Germany as a young and growing empire with a rapidly expanding worldwide commerce to which "the legitimate ambition of patriotic Germans" refused to assign any

---

[68]Bülow to the German foreign office, Norderney, 22 August 1908, in Dugdale, III:297.

[69]Lepsius *et al.,* XXI:456.

[70]Brandenburg, 1927, p. 275.

[71]*Ibid.*

[72]Metternich to Bülow, London, 1 August 1908, in Lepsius *et al.,* XXIV:113.

[73]Brandenburg, 1927, p. 289.

bounds.[74] In a sense, Wilhelm was demanding only a larger share of what Britain and France already had — access to resources and markets and the armed force required to protect trade routes. But the dynamics of domestic growth, foreign trade, colonial expansion, and naval competition were such that any major effort to "catch up" had the effect of challenging rivals to even greater efforts and thus intensifying the struggle for power, status, and strategic advantage.

---

[74]Quoted in Hale, 1940, p. 314.

7 Arms Competition and the Failure of Negotiations

As a country grows in population, technology, industrial production, territory, and the like, military expenditures are likely to increase more or less commensurately. A nation's extension of its interest beyond its home territory may also stimulate increases in army and/or naval expenditures. There is a further possibility that organizational and bureaucratic elements within a country may push the development of armaments for purposes of their own, which may be remote from the actual requirements of defense and quite independent of what a rival power may be doing. To isolate the contribution of great-power rivalry and competition from other possible causes of armament growth is an extremely difficult undertaking. These problems are compounded by the complexities of alliances. For example, the decisions of Austria and Italy to build Dreadnoughts added to British apprehensions over Germany and influenced the decision of the admiralty to build the four additional ships authorized by parliament.[1]

Combined army and naval expenditures as a percentage of the total national budget over the period 1870-1914 ranged from a high of 89.9 percent for Austria-Hungary[2] to only 19.8 percent for Italy (see Table 7-1). The highest rates of change, on the other hand, were by France and Italy. As constituent states of Germany were absorbed by the national government, the ratio of military expenditures to the total German budget actually decreased, despite a consistent rise in level.

A related measure of military expenditures is the ratio of (army and navy) expenditures to total national income. The quotient yields a

---

[1]*Parliamentary Debates,* 1910, XV:86.

[2]The Austrian Imperial government was responsible for defense and foreign affairs; domestic responsibilities remained with the separate administrations of Austria and Hungary.

rough approximation of a nation's allocations to military needs proportionate to overall productive output. In these terms, France was first, followed by Russia, Italy, Britain and Germany.[3] By far the highest rate of increase in military expenditures relative to national income was by France, followed by Russia, Britain, Italy, and Germany. Army expenditures alone also showed considerable variation among the powers, although the general upward swing did not assume as great a momentum as that of navy budgets. In terms of *absolute levels*, the largest army expenditures were incurred by Russia, followed by France, Germany, Britain, Austria and Italy. In terms of absolute levels of naval expenditures, the powers ranked as follows: Britain, France, Russia, Germany, Italy and Austria. Britain increased at the most rapid rate. Specific data, other indices of military expenditures, and rates of change are presented in Table 7-1, and Figures 7-1, 7-2, and 7-3.

In the preceding chapter we saw how German naval increases raised British apprehensions and led, in spite of continuing British negotiations with Germany, to major increases in British naval expenditures. Over many of the same years, however, the British army was also undergoing reorganization and development.

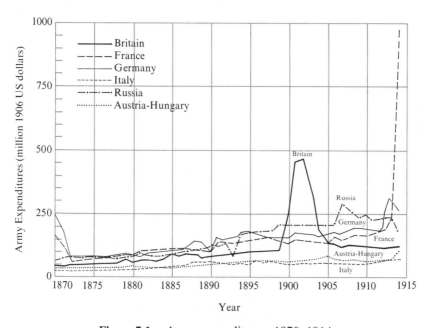

Figure 7-1. Army expenditures, 1870–1914.

---

[3]As noted before, longitudinal data for Austro-Hungarian national income is not available, although estimates for specific years have been computed.

Table 7-1. Mean levels and mean annual rates of change of military expenditures, 1870–1914.

	Britain	Germany	France	Russia	Italy	Austria-Hungary
Expenditures[a] (in thousands)						
Army	$114,004	$145,699	$146,473	$146,842	$49,571	$55,658
Navy	95,405	33,709	51,562	34,500	19,154	7,101
Total	209,409	179,408	198,035	181,343	68,725	62,759
Annual Change						
Army	*4.7%*	*1.8%*	*9.7%*	*3.8%*	*3.1%*	*2.7%*
Navy	*4.5*	*4.6*	*3.7*	*6.0*	*7.2*	*26.9*
Total	*4.4*	*1.8*	*7.6*	*3.9*	*3.8*	*3.3*
Percentage of National Budget	37.6%	60.6%	27.7%	27.8%	19.8%	89.9%
Annual Change	*.82*	*−2.78*	*1.95*	*1.08*	*1.35*	*.10*
Percentage of National Income	2.95	2.86	4.52	3.32	3.15	—
Annual Change	*2.1*	*−.6*	*4.8*	*3.3*	*1.3*	—
Per Capita Expenditures[a]						
Army	$2.85	$2.75	$3.78	$1.53	$1.59	$1.28
Navy	2.35	.59	1.33	.34	.60	.16
Total	5.20	3.34	5.11	1.88	2.19	1.44
Annual Change						
Army	*3.8%*	*.6%*	*9.6%*	*2.2%*	*2.4%*	*1.9%*
Navy	*3.6*	*3.4*	*3.6*	*4.4*	*6.5*	*26.0*
Total	*3.5*	*.6*	*7.5*	*2.3*	*3.2*	*2.4*

[a]US dollars standardized to constant 1906 prices. Native currencies were first deflated by each nation's wholesale price index, then converted to equivalent US dollars by individual conversion rates (see Appendix A). The rate of change is the mean of the series: change in expenditures divided by previous expenditures.

During the years 1906-1910 the war office and the admiralty reformed and perfected the organization, weaponry, and war plans of the British army and navy.[4] Much of the impetus for developments in the army was the Anglo-French Accords of 1904 and the new relations between the two countries that began to develop. Responsibility for a large part of this military reform and development was assigned to Richard Burdon Haldane, who served on the committee of imperial defense from 1906 to 1914 and was minister of war for more than six of these eight years.

Along with the attempts at armament reduction noted in Chapter 6, Anglo-French military and naval discussions began in December, 1905, as the Liberal government of Campbell-Bannerman came into office. In a speech some weeks earlier, Sir Edward Grey had defined the future foreign policy of the Liberals as maintenance of the Entente

---

[4]Williamson, 1969, p. 89.

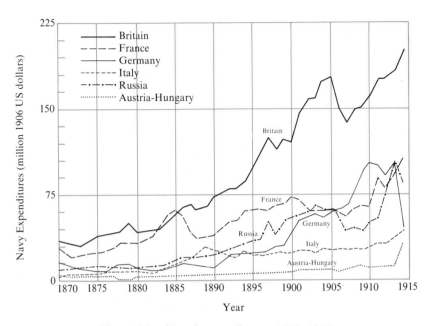

Figure 7-2. Naval expenditures, 1870–1914.

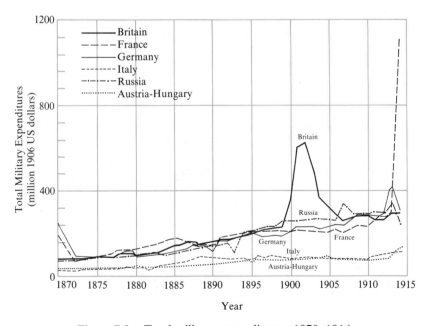

Figure 7-3. Total military expenditures, 1870–1914.

Cordiale, coupled with hopes for more satisfactory relations with Russia and Germany. But better relations with Berlin, he cautioned, could not be pursued at the expense of British relations with France.[5]

France feared a German attack through Belgium, and hoped that British forces would be available to strengthen the Belgians in such an eventuality.[6] In the event of a continental war, a British expeditionary force might be required to make up for the inadequacy of French forces for defending "the entire French frontier from Dunkirk down to Belfort, or even farther south, if Italy should join the Triple Alliance in an attack."[7]

There were three major uses to which British forces might be put: defense of the home islands, defense of the colonies, and intervention to influence the outcome of a war on the Continent. By late 1905 it had become evident that Britain was not prepared for the third eventuality. Under conditions as they then existed, she could not put more than about 80,000 men in Europe, and more than two months would be required to deploy even that limited number.[8] Britain had excellent troops in India and elsewhere, highly trained for their specialized tasks, but required for defense of the empire and not "organized in the great self-contained divisions" that would be required for fighting against armies prepared for rapid warfare on the Continent.[9] For home defense Britain depended primarily upon the Royal Navy to defend the islands from attack. British forces were not sufficient to provide whatever home defense might be necessary and at the same time provide France with anything like adequate support. Nonetheless, it was felt that a highly trained, efficient British expeditionary force of 120,000 troops "might just have the effect of preventing any important German successes on the Franco-German frontier."[10] Whether the force that in fact emerged would be adequate in the event of the country's involvement in a full-scale war was a different matter. Depending on how its role was perceived, some critics attacked the expeditionary force for being too small, others for being too large.[11]

French authorities were "attentive observers of every stage of Haldane's army reforms."[12] Anglo-French staff talks were pursued from time to time throughout all the years of army reform and the debate on strategy in Britain.[13] In view of the Franco-Russian alliance, not only

---

[5]*Ibid.*, p. 60; Wainstein, 1971, pp. 153–155.

[6]Fay, 1947, p. 206.

[7]Lord Haldane, 1920, p. 30.

[8]*Ibid.*, p. 32.

[9]*Ibid.*, p. 31.

[10]Memorandum to Col. Charles Caldwell, October 3, 1905, quoted in Williamson, 1969, p. 50. See also Fay, 1947, p. 211; Haldane, 1920, pp. 33, 166.

[11]Williamson, 1969, p. 99; Haldane, 1920, pp. 171–176.

[12]Williamson, 1969, p. 101.

[13]*Ibid.*, p. 112.

France but also Russia stood to benefit from an improved British army and from British seapower and the British expeditionary force.[14]

From 1905 on, Izvolsky and other Russian leaders saw two main threats to their country's security—renewed hostilities with Japan and confrontation with British interests in the Near and Middle East.[15] Hostilities with Britain would push Russia into the arms of Germany and thus threaten the Franco-Russian Alliance, which was viewed, in spite of its inadequacies, as the foundation of Russian policy. If Russia could improve her relations with Britain, she could pursue an active Balkan policy—while pursuing the expansion of her interests in the Far East—and preserve and even improve her ties with France.[16] The Anglo-Russian Treaty of 1907 not only reduced tensions along the northwest frontier of India and arranged a potential division of spoils between the two countries in Persia, it also paved the way for a coordinated Anglo-Russian strategy in Europe.[17]

Both Russia and Britain feared the possibility of clashes in the Near and Middle East, especially in Persia. Moreover, British leaders understood that it was no longer possible to be a friend of France and an enemy of Russia.[18] Under terms of the 1907 Treaty, Russia and Britain recognized the territorial integrity of Tibet under the suzerainty of China and agreed to refrain from interference in that country's domestic affairs and from securing special concessions there. An agreement was also reached over Afghanistan. With respect to Persia, the accord differentiated a Russian sphere in the rich and populous north and a British sphere in the barren south, which encompassed land routes of strategic importance to English-dominated India.[19] Between these two spheres lay a neutral zone, including the upper reaches of the Persian Gulf, in which neither country was to seek concessions except in agreement with the other.[20] In view of these provisions of the 1907 Treaty, Britian and Russia greatly reduced the possibility of clashes over spheres of interest.

In August, 1911 the French offered assurances to Russia that in the event of war with Germany, the French army would be ready to take the offensive, with support from the British army on its left wing, along the Belgian frontier.[21] Such an understanding would strengthen the positions of Britain, France, and Russia, but any British naval agreement with Germany would tend to threaten the alignment.

---

[14]Fay, 1947, p. 215.
[15]Albertini, 1952, p. 188.
[16]Fay, 1947, p. 216.
[17]Williamson, 1969, p. 95.
[18]Albertini, 1952, I:188–189.
[19]Fay, 1947, pp. 219–220.
[20]Albertini, 1952, I:189.
[21]Fay, 1947, p. 213.

During the autumn and winter of 1908-1909 there was growing anxiety in Britain over continuing rumors of acceleration in the German shipbuilding program.[22] This consideration added to the discontent of those Englishmen who thought that their government was neglecting the navy in the face of a growing foreign threat.

German leaders, meanwhile, were reassessing the British "threat." In a secret communication to Tirpitz, the chancellor urged consideration of enlarged coastal defenses as an alternative to the naval race, and a concomitant slowing down of the shipbuilding program. On the other hand, the introduction of the Dreadnought by Britain made it increasingly feasible for Germany, through qualitative changes in her own program, to consider aiming for parity. On January 27, 1909 the chancellor informed Tirpitz that the English would certainly follow the two-power standard and warned that if further exasperated by Germany's determination to go on with her program, Britain might actually make a preemptive attack on Germany before the latter was ready to fight her at sea. England was opposing Germany all over the world, and the growing anti-German feeling in England was considered a danger for Germany.[23]

In London the possibility that Britain "might have fewer Dreadnoughts than Germany in the spring of 1912" led to greater panic during March, 1909.[24] This consideration suggests one subtle way in which an arms race (or other conflict) can be generated and exacerbated by anticipation of something that *may* happen in the future.[25] Clearly, if two sides respond to such perceptions, the "future" becomes self-fulfilling.

The view of the British government was presented by the first lord of the admiralty, Reginald McKenna, and by Prime Minister Asquith during parliamentary debates on the naval estimates in March, 1909. In order to secure passage of the bill, McKenna exaggerated the rate at which German warships were being turned out.[26] He described in general terms the state of British naval construction during the preceding year, and added, "the difficulty in which the Government finds itself placed at this moment is that we do not know, as we thought we did, the rate at which German construction is taking place."[27] British construction, he warned, ran the risk of being keyed less to the actual rate of German construction than to the Admiralty's underestimate of that construction.[28]

---

[22]Marder, 1961, p. 151.

[23]Tirpitz to Bülow, 4 February 1909, ibid., pp. 341–342; see Huntington, 1971, p. 56.

[24]Woodward, 1935, p. 13; Wainstein, 1971, pp. 155–157.

[25]Cf. Hale, 1940, p. 342.

[26]Fay, 1947, p. 297; Moll, 1971.

[27]*Ibid.*, pp. 933–934; Woodward, 1935, p. 223.

[28]*Parliamentary Debates*, 1909, II:939; Moll, 1971, pp. 435–437.

The vital connection between Britain's colonial interests, sea routes, and naval bases, on the one hand, and the home islands and their defense, on the other, tended to impel the British government toward a policy of naval strength. Because of Britain's dependence on imports, British security and British overseas commerce were considered inseparable. Even if Britain were to retain full command of the sea at home, any interference with her overseas foreign trade would be greatly disruptive.

Prime Minister Asquith tried to assess for parliament the implications of the Anglo-German competition. "Diplomatic intercourse between us is now open and friendly," he conceded, "and we see no reason why it should not continue to be so." That being the case, why should there exist what appeared to be an increasing competition between the two countries in naval expenditures? Why was no mutual arrangement possible? Asquith thought that the answer was clear-cut: ". . . we, whose whole national defense and security depend upon our supremacy at sea, cannot afford to go behind, to slacken our efforts, or to put ourselves in such a position that any contingency that might occur could possibly menace that independence and supremacy."[29]

Some days later, on March 29, a vote of censure on the government's shipbuilding program was moved in the Commons. During the debate that ensued, Sir Edward Grey made explicit reference to the way in which Britain was "locked into" the escalation process. The great countries of Europe were raising enormous revenues for naval and military preparations, Sir Edward said. This might be called national insurance, but it amounted to a satire and a reflection on civilization, which, if the trend continued, would surely be submerged sooner or later. Yet Sir Edward himself saw no possible escape from the competition in armaments. If Britain alone among the powers were to undertake a unilateral reduction, she would sink into a position of inferiority and "cease to count for anything amongst the nations of Europe."[30] It is perhaps even clearer in retrospect than it was to Sir Edward that although withdrawal from the race appeared tantamount to a national disaster in both London and Berlin, continued competition made armed conflict increasingly likely.

Britain had not only Germany to worry about. The Austrian program had already given the Italians "an attack of nerves," with the result that Italy also developed a Dreadnought plan. Together, the Austrian and Italian programs now had a decisive effect on British naval policy.[31]

Three issues were becoming more and more prominent in Anglo-German negotiations: a mutually satisfactory Anglo-German naval

---

[29]*Ibid.*, pp. 956–957; Huntington, 1971, pp. 508–510.
[30]Woodward, 1935, pp. 230–233; Wainstein, 1971, pp. 162–164.
[31]Marder, 1961, pp. 170–171.

arrangement, a workable program for exchanges of information, and some kind of political understanding, which German leaders considered essential if relations between their country and Britain were to be improved. All of these issues were complicated by increasing tensions and mutual fears.

In July, 1909 Bülow retired as chancellor, to be followed by Theodor von Bethmann-Hollweg, who was prepared to negotiate the arms issue on condition that Britain promise "at the very outset" that her policy would be "peaceful and friendly" toward Germany and that she guarantee that British alliances were not directed against Germany.[32] What many German leaders had difficulty understanding was that Britain, as a power that continued to reap advantages from the status quo, had little or no reason for aggressing against Germany—unless Germany herself threatened that status quo. In a sense, then, the harder German leaders pressed for their own country's advantage and security, the more they aroused hostilities in Britain.

Bethmann-Hollweg's proposal had two parts: first, the possibility of a British guarantee of neutrality in the event that France and Russia, singly or together, attacked Germany, or if Germany went to the help of Austria; second, a reduction of three ships in the German program before 1914 and a ratio of 4:3 in new British and German ship construction. This proposal favored Germany in that her program for 1909-1910 would remain unaltered, whereas Britain would lose the four "contingent" ships that parliament had cleared the way for.[33] As might have been expected, the German package deal was coolly received in Britain.[34] As viewed in London, such a general political understanding would have to be negotiated between the two great power blocs and not between Germany and Britain alone. "I want a good understanding with Germany," Sir Edward declared, "but it must be one which will not imperil those we have with France and Russia."[35]

Tirpitz's initial naval plan provided for a ratio of 4:3 in capital ships—32 British to 24 German ships either completed or under construction by 1914. Later he suggested 28 British to 21 German ships by 1913. Subsequent German proposals required British recognition of German sovereignty over Alsace-Lorraine—an arrangement that might destroy the British entente with France.[36] The British foreign office was not enthusiastic over either the political or the naval proposals.[37] Nevertheless, Germany demanded that a political agreement accompany any naval agreement. The British response was that England did

---

[32]Woodward, 1935, p. 268.
[33]*Ibid.*, p. 269.
[34]Marder, 1961, p. 174.
[35]Woodward, 1935, pp. 269–272.
[36]Marder, 1961, p. 174.
[37]*Ibid.*

not have formal understandings with Russia and France and could hardly go further in the matter with Germany than with them.[38]

The negotiations were thus at an impasse and the escalation continued. In November, 1909 it was decided in Britain that four capital ships would be sufficient for the following year, but that six would be needed in 1911–1912. Around December 1, the program was increased to six after it was learned that Austria had laid two Dreadnoughts, meaning that Britain would have to send more Dreadnoughts into the Mediterranean (thus reducing her advantage against Germany in that type of ship). A cabinet crisis ensued, but it was quickly smoothed over when the admiralty proposed a 5:5 program for the two years: one battle cruiser and four Dreadnoughts each year.[39]

The Anglo-German competition arose not from a German demand for parity with Britain, but from a German desire for a fleet sufficiently strong to "deter" Britain by making extremely expensive any attack on Germany by the Royal Navy. Germany acknowledged British supremacy at sea, Admiral Müller told British Ambassador Goschen, but could not accept a supremacy so overwhelming that Britain could attack at any time without real risk. "We want a navy strong enough," he declared, "to knock about the British navy sufficiently in case of an attack so that other nations do not have to fear it any more."[40]

In August, 1910 the British government made explicit two ways of arresting the naval race, both dependent on a change in German policy: an alteration in the German Navy Law, which German leaders had made perfectly clear they were unwilling to undertake, or a "reduction of the tempo" in German shipbuilding without any alteration in the navy law. Thereafter, a year and a half of "intermittent, fruitless negotiations" took place.[41]

On a more general level, the same three issues continued to disturb Anglo-German relations: the naval race, an arrangement for exchanging information, and a German desire for a "political understanding." Among German leaders themselves there were some differences over the first issue. Bethmann-Hollweg seemed inclined to propose a stabilization of the naval competition through a building tempo of 2:3 per year for the next six years, but Tirpitz demurred. Much of the German fleet consisted of ships and armament that were out of date, if not obsolete. Moreover, the navy law after 1917 "would be endangered" if Germany tied herself down as the chancellor proposed.[42]

---

[38]Woodward, 1935, p. 273.
[39]Marder, 1961, p. 214.
[40]*Ibid.*, p. 223.
[41]*Ibid.*, pp. 222–223.
[42]*Ibid.*, p. 223.

The British admiralty's position on the issue of exchange of information was generally acceptable to the Germans, but with three important stipulations: information should be exchanged simultaneously, at a particular date each year, and the exchanged information should include a binding agreement on the number of ships to be laid down by the two governments each year.[43] As for a German proposal that neither power should use the information exchanged for the purpose of amending its building program, this was viewed by the British admiralty as "manifestly absurd."[44]

Bethmann-Hollweg asserted that Germany was prepared to agree with any practical plan for exchanging information, but maintained that the condition of peace was strength — the weak would always be prey to the strong. Any nation that did not continue to spend enough on armaments to make their way in the world would fall into the second rank, whereupon there would always be another, stronger power ready to move into the place they had vacated.[45]

From the German viewpoint a political agreement of some kind was still "an indispensable preliminary condition for any naval agreement." Thus, with respect to any reduction of tempo, German leaders wanted to know what "equivalent" would be offered in return for a pledge not to increase the building program in the Navy Law.[46] Essentially, the obstacles to a naval limitation agreement were the same as they had been in 1909. Germany insisted on British neutrality as a condition for concessions in the German building program, whereas the British refused to extend a guarantee that would have destroyed their alignments with Russia and France.[47]

The British ambassador in Berlin reported on February 3, 1911 that a substantial increase in the German navy was expected in the very near future. He also expressed his belief that Britain's future expenditures could regulate German allocations — that Germany could be deterred from further increases. The British government believed it could best convince Germany of the futility of trying to compete in naval construction by increasing English naval estimates for the coming year.[48] Overlooked was the strong probability that increased British expenditures, perceived in Berlin as a strengthening of British advantage, would merely stimulate Germany to redouble her own efforts.

During debates on the British naval estimates in March, Sir Edward himself warned Commons of the growing burden of naval and military armaments. Specifically, he referred to the paradox that European

[43]Marder, 1961, p. 225.
[44]*Ibid.*, p. 227.
[45]Woodward, 1935, pp. 304–305.
[46]Marder, 1961, p. 223.
[47]*Ibid.*, p. 232.
[48]Goschen to Grey, February 3, 1911, in Gooch and Temperley, VI:581–583.

armaments were increasing rapidly at a time when great-power relations seemed to be improving otherwise. But there was also a "much
greater paradox," namely, that the "growing and enormous burden"
of naval and military expenditures was coincident "not merely with
friendly relations between the powers, but with the growth of civilization as a whole." Indeed, it was the "most civilized nations" who
were spending the largest amounts, and their armaments were not for
protecting themselves against the less civilized, but were constructed
"in rivalry with each other."[49] Sir Edward supported the idea, under
discussion for so long, of systematic exchanges of information between Britain and Germany. In the long run, he said, the remedy for
arms competitions lay in negotiation and limitations agreements rather
than appeals to force.[50]

Paradoxically, Sir Edward's speech was widely interpreted in
Germany as a sign that Britain was "at the end of her financial resources."[51] This reaction demonstrates another pernicious characteristic of the escalation process: with intensified competition
between two countries interacting in such a spiral, not only is an increase in the advantage of one party likely to be viewed as a threat to
the other, but also any tendency on the part of one country to compromise, reduce its effort, back away, or withdraw is likely to be interpreted by the other country as either a sign of weakness or a trick.

While the first lord of the admiralty was invoking the "German
menace" in order to ensure a strengthening of the Royal Navy,
Tirpitz was having difficulties of his own in organizing sufficient support for an accelerated German naval program. In the Reichstag the
Socialists — a considerable bloc — stood bluntly opposed to the German
armaments program. Other deputies were uncertain.

Although the Anglo-French entente remained secure, French leaders became apprehensive whenever Anglo-German naval talks were
underway.[52] French diplomats and military men were well aware
that Anglo-German antagonisms made France a more valuable ally
to England. French leaders were also aware that the continuing naval
competition drained funds from the German army budget. They seemed
less concerned that the naval race also deprived the British army
of money.

The proposals of late 1910 and early 1911 for Anglo-German exchanges of information were disturbing to France; ". . . for the first
time some type of Anglo-German agreement appeared likely."[53]
Rumors of an impending accord between Germany and Russia on the
Near East also made French leaders apprehensive, despite assurances

---

[49]Woodward, 1935, p. 299.
[50]*Ibid.*, pp. 301–302.
[51]*Ibid.*, p. 303.
[52]Williamson, 1969, p. 135.
[53]*Ibid.*

from Russia that the Triple Entente would not be in jeopardy. French policy-makers came under increasing domestic attack for not maintaining closer communication with Britain.

At a meeting of the German Conservative party in Breslau, one speaker proclaimed that German prestige had reached a low point when a pacifist British Liberal minister could "shake his fist" in Germany's face and declare that Britain alone "had to give orders to the world."[54]

In Hamburg on August 27 the Kaiser referred to the German navy as a defense for German commerce and expressed the wish that it should be strengthened in the future, "to ensure that nobody should dispute with Germany her place in the sun."[55] The launching of each new German warship meant that Germany's adversaries would be that much less-inclined to pick a quarrel, he asserted, and thus was one more guarantee of peace. Not only that, he said, but each ship rendered Germany more valuable as an ally.[56]

During an audience with the Kaiser on September 26, Tirpitz explained his ideas about the naval law that he had begun designing. Specifically, he proposed offering England a political agreement, for which the Kaiser had frequently expressed a hope, in return for a guarantee that Germany would not attack England. The British government, he hoped, would accept a 3:2 fleet ratio in place of the old two-power standard.[57] The argument put forward by Tirpitz was a familiar one: since Germany was behind in naval strength, it was vital to make up for lost time.[58] Without sea power to protect her industry, Germany felt she would soon cease to be a great European power.[59]

Prime Minister Asquith declared that Britain did not want "to stand in the way of any power" wishing to find a place in the sun. "We have no sort of quarrel with any of the great powers in the world. The first of all British interests remains, as it has always been, the peace of the world, and to the attainment of that great object diplomacy and our policy will still with single-mindedness be directed."[60] In fact, however, the overriding British policy was not the preservation of world peace, but the safeguarding of her own security and overseas interests. Viewed from the German standpoint, preservation of "the peace of the world" amounted to an inequitable status quo, a permanent British strategic advantage, the preservation of a lion's share of limited resources and markets, and Britain's continued world dominance.

In October, 1911 an alteration was made in the British cabinet: Winston Churchill replaced Reginald McKenna at the admiralty.

---

[54]Bethmann-Hollweg, 1920, p. 37.
[55]*The Times*, London, August 28, 1911, p. 6.
[56]Schmitt, 1918, p. 198.
[57]Jenisch to Kiderlen, Romintern, September 28, 1911, in Lepsius *et al.*, XXXI:5–6.
[58]Tirpitz, 1924, I:125.
[59]*Ibid.*, p. 111.
[60]*Parliamentary Debates*, 1911, XXXII:110.

"The new first lord of the admiralty was a friend of Germany, but first of all he was champion of absolute naval supremacy for England."[61]

The year 1912 was to be a critical one; Germany's *Dreiertempo* (three large ships per year) would terminate, to be followed by a six-year *Zweiertempo* of two large ships per year.[62] The Supplementary Naval Law of 1912 has been described by Waldo Chamberlin as "the final effort of the German empire to adjust itself to the imperialism of the nineteenth century and its prototype, the British empire."[63] Whether or not this is an accurate assessment, German and British attitudes toward the naval race in general were now interlocked.

British feelings about the naval race with Germany were still mixed in 1912. The government insisted—and a majority in parliament and probably large numbers of private citizens agreed—that Britain must maintain preeminence in naval power at any cost. Of course, the British government hoped to achieve a naval limitation agreement with Germany, insuring British superiority at no added cost.

Among many Germans there was a reciprocal concern for some sort of agreement with Britain. The German foreign office informed London of a willingness to pursue conversations "in a friendly sense." With respect to the 1912 supplementary law, the Germans thought it possible "to meet British wishes" if at the same time Germany were to receive sufficient guarantee that British policy would be friendly.[64]

During February, Churchill and Kaiser Wilhelm presented, within a few days of one another, their views on the arms race. Wilhelm opened the Reichstag on February 7, 1912 with a speech in which he proclaimed his determination "to maintain the solid fabric of the empire and of state order unimpaired, to increase the welfare of all conditions and classes of the people, and to preserve and raise the strength and prestige of the nation."[65]

Speaking in Glasgow, Churchill, who in previous roles had often criticized increases in naval expenditures, sought to justify Britain's expanding program. It was sea power that had made Britain a great power. By contrast, Germany had become a great power, was respected and honored all over the world, before she had a single ship. For Britain a navy was a necessity, whereas from some points of view a navy was something of a "luxury" for Germany. British naval power meant British survival. For Germany, on the other hand, a strong navy meant "expansion."[66] There could be no hesitation, Churchill asserted. The British navy must be preeminent. "As naval competition

[61]Chamberlin, 1939, p. 50.

[62]*Ibid.*, p. 36; Tirpitz, 1924, I:195–196.

[63]*The Annual Register*, 1913, p. 319.

[64]*The Times*, London, February 10, 1912, p. 9. Many Germans were unhappy to find their navy referred to in German translation as a "luxury fleet."

[65]*Ibid.*, p. 10.

[66]*Ibid.*

becomes more acute," Churchill declared, "we shall have, not only to increase the number of ships we build, but the ratio which our naval strength will have to bear to other great naval powers, so that our margin of superiority will become larger, and not smaller, as the strain grows greater. Thus we shall make it clear that other naval powers, instead of overtaking us by additional efforts, will only be more out-distanced in consequence of the measures which we ourselves will take."[67]

On the day of Wilhelm's speech to the Reichstag, Lord Haldane, whose military experience had been confined almost wholly to army affairs, arrived in Berlin on a mission of naval negotiations. He met first with Bethmann-Hollweg on February 8 — at almost the same time that the German Navy League was convening and demanding a large increase in the German navy and continuation of the Dreiertempo.[68] There had been a "drifting away" between Germany and England, Lord Haldane said, and it was important to ask what the cause was.[69] "Germany had built up, and was building up, magnificent armaments, and with the aid of the Triple Alliance she had become the center of a tremendous group. The natural consequence was that other powers had tended to approximate." The problem was not insuperable, however. Two powers might maintain very friendly relations "if there were only an increasing sense of mutual understanding and confidence." The present seemed to be a favorable moment of new departure in a more peaceful direction.

Bethmann-Hollweg suggested that some formula be agreed upon for neutrality between the two nations. Lord Haldane agreed on the principle, but suggested that a range of other topics should be opened up.[70] The British were free-traders. They believed that the more trade Germany developed the more would English trade develop in response. Bethmann-Hollweg agreed. "Yes, we each give each other the open door." Lord Haldane suggested that the two nations could work together in the world a great deal more.

"In Africa, for instance?"

"In Africa particularly."

The two then discussed the possibility of divisions of territory, although Lord Haldane warned that he could not commit his government on the matter.[71] He observed also that "a spreading out of time" of the new German naval program might make a difference. "Perhaps eight or nine years?" Bethmann-Hollweg asked. "Or twelve," Lord Haldane suggested, if not even more.[72]

---

[67]Maurice, 1937, I:294. For German documentation on the Haldane mission and its consequences, see Lepsius et al., XXXI, Ch. 243.

[68]From Haldane's diary, February 10, 1912, in Gooch and Temperley, VI:676.

[69]Ibid., p. 677.

[70]Ibid., p. 679.

[71]From Haldane's Diary, in Gooch and Temperley, VI:600.

[72]Ibid., pp. 680-681.

The discussion closed on a note that was to lead eventually to serious misunderstanding between the two nations.[73] Wilhelm regarded Lord Haldane's suggestion for a political agreement "as a practically official proposal" and hoped that Sir Edward would negotiate on the basis of these suggestions. Unfortunately, Lord Haldane failed to make it clear that no political accord with Germany would be possible unless Germany agreed to drop the Navy Law. In his discussions with the Kaiser, Lord Haldane had asked only for a "spreading of the *tempo*." Although the British considered "slowing down" an insufficient concession, the Germans, interpreting Lord Haldane's position as a moderation of earlier British demands, left the discussion believing that Britain "was willing to enter into a political agreement in return for a slowing down in the rate of construction of large German ships."[74] As a result, in the course of further negotiations, Wilhelm felt that Britain was not living up to her "offer."[75]

The issue of naval competition had other complications beyond Anglo-German relations. The French ambassador in London, Paul Cambon, told Arthur Nicolson in the British foreign office that the Russians were reorganizing their military and changing their mobilization plans and were therefore "in a transition state." In the Russians' view, "they would not be ready for taking a *serious* part in a campaign . . ." until mid-1913. The Germans were aware of this, according to Cambon, and were also fully aware that another six French divisions would bring the two alliances "practically to an equality." The Germans were hastening military increases in order to obtain superiority before France could field the six divisions.[76] The whole European system tended to be delicately sensitive and responsive to whatever direction Anglo-German relations took.[77]

Churchill, after studying a copy of the German Navy Law brought back by Lord Haldane, submitted a report to the cabinet that underscored "the extraordinary increase in the striking force of all [German] ships of all classes."[78] On February 22 Sir Edward asked Lord Haldane to meet with him and German Ambassador Metternich at the foreign secretary's private residence. While reiterating the "genuine desire" of the British government for cordial relations, Sir Edward underscored the difficulty of reaching any agreement that coincided with a substantial increase in the German fleet. Two days later Sir Edward presented Metternich with a memorandum that put forward his government's viewpoint in considerable detail.[79]

---

[73]Chamberlin, 1939, p. 104.
[74]Schmitt, 1918, p. 251, see also Halperin, 1930, p. 190.
[75]Minute by Sir A. Nicolson, London, February 15, 1912, in Gooch and Temperley, VI:693–694.
[76]Chamberlin, 1939, p. 104.
[77]Churchill, 1924, I:104.
[78]Enclosure No. 524, February 24, 1912, in Gooch and Temperley, VI:698–699.
[79]Chamberlin, 1939, p. 121.

As the British cabinet heard Churchill's report on the dangers to England resulting from the German Navy Law, Ambassador Metternich was drafting a message to Bethmann-Hollweg in Berlin emphasizing once more that there could be no Anglo-German agreement of a political nature unless the new Navy Law were abandoned. Bethmann-Hollweg thus opposed the proposed German naval increase on the ground that it would prevent any possible accord with England, but also because the funds were urgently needed for domestic programs.

Although British leaders desired some kind of accord with Germany, they also held a deep and growing distrust of the German political situation. There was considerable anxiety that Admiral Tirpitz might succeed Bethmann-Hollweg as chancellor. British leaders were also concerned about what they perceived as a general lack of continuity in German foreign policy and a division in policy control among the Kaiser, the chancellor, and foreign secretary Kiderlen.[80]

While Wilhelm was still in doubt over the fate of the Navy Law in the Reichstag,[81] he prepared an offer to King George for an offensive and defensive alliance that France might also join.[82] Wilhelm anticipated that refusal of such a proposal might make Britain look responsible and fasten upon her the onus of wrecking negotiations.[83] Before Bethmann-Hollweg could forward the offer to Ambassador Metternich, Kiderlen and Tirpitz intervened. In the end the Kaiser's proposal was not presented.

Churchill also had a plan for peaceful settlement of the naval question. He suggested to Commons that both nations might "take a holiday" for a year. "Supposing we both introduced a blank page in the book of misunderstanding; supposing that Germany were to build no ships" in any given year. This would provide a single arrangement whereby "without diplomatic negotiation, without any bargaining, without the slightest restriction upon sovereign freedom of either power, this keen and costly naval rivalry" could be abated. The indirect results to the welfare of the entire world would, Churchill thought, be measureless in terms of "hope and brightness." It was evident, however, that Churchill was requiring Germany to take the crucial first step.[84]

Churchill's proposal for a shipbuilding "holiday" and the Kaiser's suggestion that an alliance be drawn up that included France both struck at the root problem. "These two volatile men," according to Waldo Chamberlin, "presented the only ideas that went to the heart of

---

[80]*Ibid.*, p. 115.
[81]The Kaiser's handwritten comment on Metternich's dispatch to the foreign office, 17 March 1912, in Lepsius *et al.*, XXXI:183.
[82]Schmitt, 1918, p. 277.
[83]Chamberlin, 1939, p. 140.
[84]*Parliamentary Debates*, 1912, XXXV:1557.

the troubles in the world of that day. The Kaiser would do away with the 'rival camps' then existing in Europe; Churchill would halt the construction of armaments. Perhaps neither plan was an all-inclusive panacea, but both were steps so far beyond anything else tried or suggested that the world may well regret that neither was attempted."[85] Unfortunately, neither side was prepared to take the first step.[86]

Before he knew whether or not the German Navy Law of that year would pass the Reichstag, Winston Churchill spoke to Commons: "The spectacle which the naval armaments of Christiandom afford at the present time will no doubt excite the curiosity and the wonder of future generations." The most optimistic interpretation that could be placed upon the escalating arms race was that naval and military rivalries were *the modern substitute for what in earlier ages had been actual wars,* he declared. Just as credit transactions had in the present day so largely superseded cash payments, so the jealousies and disputes of nations might be decided more and more by the mere possession of war power without the necessity for its actual employment. If that were true, the grand folly of the twentieth century might be found to wear a less unamiable aspect. On the other hand, war itself, if ever it came, would not be an illusion—even a single bullet would be found real enough. Consequently, the admiralty must leave to others the task of mending the times, and confine themselves to the more limited and more simple duty of making quite sure that whatever the times might be "our Island and its people" would come safely through them.[87]

Churchill thus found himself in a dilemma familiar to many men of power: a vigorous exercise of that power might propel his own nation and other nations, even mankind, toward the brink of catastrophe; yet not to exercise that power might invite serious disability for one's country, even national disaster.

As first lord of the admiralty, Churchill used the German Naval Laws as one more impelling justification for maintenance of British naval superiority. Indeed, whereas Tirpitz had wanted to alter the balance to 3:2, Churchill was now determined to strengthen Britain beyond the two-power level. "When the next two strongest naval powers were France and Russia," he asserted during the March 1912 debates in the British parliament and before the last German Navy Law had been passed, "and when those two powers were also what one might call the most probable adverse diplomatic combination, the two-power standard was a convenient rule, based upon reality, for us to follow as a guide." The passage of time and the rise of the German navy had changed this. Now Britain faced "a very powerful homogeneous navy, manned and trained by the greatest organizing people of

[85]Chamberlin, 1939, p. 148.
[86]*Ibid.,* p. 91; see also *Annual Register,* 1912, p. 323.
[87]*Parliamentary Debates,* 1912, XXXV:1573–1574.

the world, obeying a single government and concentrated within easy distance of our shores." As a consequence, the two-power standard, if applied to Europe alone, would be wholly inadequate and inapplicable.[88]

A further reason Britain should have an ample margin, Churchill said, was that the consequences for Britain of a naval defeat were so much greater than they would be for Germany or France. "We are fed from the sea; we are an unarmed people; we possess a very small army; we are the only power in Europe which does not possess a large army. We cannot menace the independence or the vital interest of any great continental State; we cannot invade any continental State. We do not wish to do so, but even if we had the wish we have not got the power."

Germany saw the problem quite differently, of course. Despite her rapid growth, Germany saw herself "encircled" by Britain, France, and Russia, "deprived" with respect to colonial holdings, and blocked in her efforts to achieve a navy more nearly equal to that of Britain.

The Anglo-German naval race did not cause the outbreak of war in 1914, but the competition—in addition to the uncertainties and frictions it generated—kept the major powers in a state of imbalance so that any seeming advantage gained by either bloc tended to stimulate efforts by the other bloc to make good the difference. In the next chapter we shall see how the major powers collaborated during the Balkan wars of 1912–1913 in order to keep the European peace. But the arms race persisted in the meantime, and when the Balkan wars were over, the imbalance among the powers seemed even greater than previously.

---

[88]*Ibid.*, col. 1555.

The Tripolitanian and Balkan Wars

8

In preceding chapters we dealt with the expansion of European interests into Africa and other far-flung regions of the world and some of the ways in which the conflict of national interests in these places contributed to commercial and naval competitions and other conflicts among the major powers. In Chapter 4 we discussed the extension of national interests (especially those of Russia and Austria) into the Balkans and considered how conflicts of interests there gave rise to the Bosnian Crisis of 1908–1909. We can see some parallel characteristics in the Balkans and the overseas colonial regions in that both were relatively low-capability areas that higher-capability countries found attractive for commercial, political, and strategic reasons.

In this chapter we shall be concerned with two major conflicts: the Tripolitanian War of 1911 and the Balkan Wars of 1912–1913, both involving conflicts of interest among the powers. The first of these is of interest both because the Italian victory contributed to the further weakening of Turkey and because the Italian strategy had implications for the balance of naval power in the Mediterranean. The Balkan Wars are of concern to us here because they disturbed the European configuration of power and because the great powers were unable to settle their differences over the Balkans even though they managed to restrain themselves from direct involvement in the Balkan Wars.

A major aspect of Bismarck's strategy at the Congress of Berlin had been support of Britain's aspirations in Egypt and Russia's aspirations in Bulgaria as a means of holding a balance between Russia and France and preventing the establishment of a Franco-Russian combination directed against Germany.[1] The Congress had sanctioned French

---

[1] Langer, 1962, p. 429.

occupation of Tunis and British domination of Egypt. Italy, on the other hand, which had aspired to possession of Tunis, had gone away empty-handed—although as far as Germany was concerned Italy could take Tripoli at any time.[2]

When the Triple Alliance was renewed in 1887, Germany pledged that it would recognize war between Italy and France over the North African territories of Tripoli or Morocco as a *casus foederis*. That same year Britain promised (in return for Italian support of Britain in Egypt) to support Italian action anywhere along the North African coasts, particularly in Cyrenaica and Tripolitania. With the renewal of the Triple Alliance in 1891, Germany agreed to support any Italian action in the event that maintenance of the status quo in Tripolitania, Cyrenaica, or Tunisia became impossible.[3] In December 1900 Italy arranged with France to reserve the right to develop her interests in Cyrenaica and Tripolitania in the event of a modification of the political or territorial status of Morocco.

When the Triple Alliance was again renewed in 1902, Austria pledged not to interfere with any Italian action in the area if there were a change in the status quo there. The Italians were also able to secure Russian recognition of their rights in Cyrenaica and Tripolitania in return for Italian support of Russia on the question of the Dardanelles.[4] Germany, while ostensibly supporting Italy's ambitions, hoped at the same time to restrain any Italian action in North Africa that might further antagonize Britain, France, or Turkey.[5]

The Tripolitanian War was in large measure the outcome of Italy's determination to take advantage of her agreements with France and to counter-balance French gains in Morocco. Although Italy was a lesser member of the great-power system, she was growing in population and industry.[6] Many Italians, feeling that other powers, especially France, had gained at Italy's expense, aspired to economic, political, and strategic expansion in North Africa and along the Adriatic.

When Italy launched her attack against Turkish forces in Tripoli on September 28, 1911, the other powers were considerably displeased, but all were bound in one way or another not to oppose the undertaking.[7] Russia was probably the least opposed, having pledged herself to recognize Italian aspirations in Tripoli in exchange for Italy's support of the opening of the Dardanelles. Whatever aspirations one or another of the powers may have cherished in the past for the exploitation of Turkish holdings in Europe, each now had reasons of its

---

[2]Fay, 1947, p. 81.
[3]*Ibid.*, p. 143.
[4]Albertini, 1952, 0:340–341.
[5]Fay, 1947, p. 144.
[6]See *ibid.*, Ch. 3.
[7]Helmreich, 1938, p. 33.

own for safeguarding Turkey against sudden and total collapse. Russia, which had not yet recovered from her defeat of 1905, was scarcely ready to assume the risks that were almost certain to accrue if Turkish power in Europe disintegrated altogether. Britain and Germany were competing for Turkish friendship. France was apprehensive of any situation that pitted Russia against any member of the Triple Alliance. From the outset, however, Austria was especially unhappy with the Italian attack since it would disturb the status quo in the Balkans and thus threaten the Dual Monarchy at a time when it was not adequately prepared.[8]

British commercial interests in the Near East were already well entrenched when, in 1909, British capitalists had begun to take an interest in Mesopotamian oil fields.[9] French financial interests were also firmly established in the eastern Mediterranean and other regions of the Near East. Germany's activities and interests in Turkey and adjoining areas dated largely from the late nineteenth century. During 1890 a German company had undertaken plans to build a Berlin-to-Bagdad railway.[10] Since rail connections already existed between Berlin and Constantinople, the task was to construct an extension from the Bosporus to Bagdad. There were even hopes of laying track all the way to the Persian Gulf and thus having a shorter route from western and central Europe to India. At one point German financiers invited French and British bankers to participate, but cooperation among the three powers was not easily achieved.

In Britain there was some fear that a Berlin-to-Bagdad railway might damage English interests in Mesopotamia and Persia; French officials were sensitive to Russian anxieties that the railroad might infuse the "sick man of the East" with new vigor and thus delay division of the Ottoman empire. Nevertheless, the Germans, French, and British did begin negotiations for cooperative construction of Turkish railways and for the division of the empire into spheres of interest. By this time, however, Germany had completed nearly four hundred miles of the line, and the damage to the Germans in international goodwill had been done.[11]

Meanwhile, despite some setbacks, Italian forces made rapid progress against the Turks, and by November 1911 Tripoli and Cyrenaica had been annexed. The war demonstrated the importance of sea power, since Italy was able to control the eastern Mediterranean and prevent the Turks from moving reinforcements to their African possessions.[12] These naval operations and Italy's closing of the Dardanelles during

---

[8]Albertini, 1952, I:350–351.
[9]Fisher, 1967, p. 70.
[10]For British views of the railway, see Gooch and Temperley, VI:227–282, 327.
[11]Fay, 1947, I:503.
[12]Woodward, 1935, p. 316.

hostilities increased Russian sensitivity to the issue of opening Dardanelles to Russian warships.[13]

Italy's occupation of Tripoli and seizure of islands in the Aegean Sea were viewed by some Englishmen as having threatened their country's naval position. There was the further apprehension, shared by many Frenchmen, that the Italians might provide their German allies with naval facilities in Tripoli or the Dodecanese. These anxieties in Russia, Britain, and France strengthened Italy's ties with the Triple Alliance.[14] This, along with the deployment of a German squadron in the Mediterranean, made it "more important than ever for England to retain the friendship of Turkey and keep her out of the Triple Alliance."[15] Anxiety over the Italian victory also led to closer Anglo-French naval relations.[16]

Understandably, the Balkan countries perceived the Italo-Turkish War as a favorable opportunity for fulfilling their own aspirations. Of particular interest was Turkish Macedonia, of which all the Balkan states claimed large areas on the basis of ethnic ties.[17]

The propositions presented in Chapter 1 referred almost entirely to major powers. However, we would expect lesser powers to follow the same principles of competition among themselves and to expand their interests into regions with lower capabilities than their own. A major difference between relations among great powers and relations among lesser powers is the very significant restraint imposed on the latter by the superior capabilities of the great powers.

Although there is not sufficient data for analysis, we do know that the Balkan states grew considerably in population and on other dimensions and that there was a tendency toward the expansion of territory and interests.[18] Not only did the activities and interests of the great powers collide with each other in the Balkans, but the expansion of the Balkan countries themselves produced conflict in that region — with each other and with the major powers, especially Austria. In addition to economic expansion, Serbia, Bulgaria, Greece, and Rumania all had nationalistic aspirations for territories beyond their borders.

---

[13]Fay, 1947, p. 325.

[14]Marder, 1961, pp. 299–300.

[15]Ibid., p. 301.

[16]Ibid., pp. 303–304.

[17]Albertini, 1952, I:364; and Helmreich, 1938, p. 33.

[18]In 1878 the population of Serbia is believed to have been about 1,670,000; by 1912 it had reached the neighborhood of 2,912,000. Density increased from approximately 878 persons per square mile to 1,337. The population of Bulgaria in 1878 was probably about 1,859,000; by 1912 it was in the neighborhood of 4,544,000. Population density had more than doubled over that period of time from around 502 persons per square mile to about 1,228; Bulgaria gained slightly in territory in 1913 and density decreased somewhat (ca. 1,161 persons per square mile). The population of Greece increased between 1870 and 1912 from about 1,458,000 to 2,733,000 (with a small increase in territory in 1881). Since Greek home territory more than doubled during the same period of time, density increased from about 729 to 1,093 per square mile.

The Balkan ferment, as well as Austrian and Russian connections with it, dates back long before WWI.[19] Inside the Austro-Hungarian empire subject peoples had been stirring expectantly for years. In the Austro-Serbian Treaty of 1881 Serbia had consented to Austrian control of her foreign policy.[20] Until 1903 she remained virtually an Austrian puppet. In 1904, as a safeguard of national security, the Kingdom of Serbia and the Principality of Bulgaria concluded a treaty of alliance.[21] In effect, Bulgaria pledged herself to oppose Austrian annexation of the *sanjak* of Novibazar, which at the time was occupied by Austria. Relations between Bulgaria and Serbia could never be truly cordial, however. According to the British minister in Belgrade at the time, the two countries would not have friendly relations "until the competition between the two nationalities for an eventual acquisition of the Slav countries under Turkish rule" was ended.[22]

Austria took advantage of the unrest and uncertainties of Balkan affairs to strengthen and expand her own interests. In Chapter four we saw how Austrian policies contributed to the Bosnian Crisis of 1908–1909. Thereafter, Aehrenthal pursued a policy of diplomatic (and to some extent military) bluff. Taking into account antagonisms between Serbia and Bulgaria, Aehrenthal had thought in 1908 that if Austria were to further the creation of a Greater Bulgaria at the expense of Serbia, it might become possible to gain control of Serbia during some future crisis. In due course Austria might secure an independent alliance, under Austrian leadership, with a friendly Montenegro and a Greater Bulgaria obligated to the Austrian Monarchy. The annexation of Novibazar would bring Austria "no real advantage," and might involve more risk than it was worth. From the Austrian viewpoint, therefore, the empire had more to gain by controlling Serbia than by possessing Novibazar.[23]

As had been evident during the Bosnian Crisis of 1908–1909, any considerable attempt by Austria to safeguard or extend her interests in the Balkans was certain to involve Russia — and thus, sooner or later, the other major powers. Russia used her influence in the Balkans as a diplomatic lever in her attempt to open the Dardanelles to her warships. Yet as early as 1897 Russia had begun to shift her attention more and more toward Persia and China, and after the turn of the century her Far East concerns absorbed much of the attention of the foreign ministry. For a decade, then, Russia's demand for the opening of the Dardanelles was not vigorously pressed.

---

[19]Gooch and Temperley, IX:xiii.
[20]Martens, X:45–49.
[21]Helmreich, 1938, pp. 5–6.
[22]*Ibid.*, p. 11.
[23]*Ibid.*, pp. 172, 176.

Izvolsky had made two abortive attempts to open the Dardanelles to Russian warships, once during negotiations for the Anglo-Russian Convention of 1907, and again during the 1908 Buchlau discussions with Aehrenthal. Both had failed because of British opposition and the lack of French support.[24] Despite the Franco-Russian military agreement on mutual defense in Europe, Russia and France were unable to come to terms on the question of the Dardanelles.[25] In the autumn of 1911, with the strengthening of Anglo-French ties (after the Agadir Incident) and Germany's abandonment of all claims in Morocco, Izvolsky thought the situation was more favorable for pressing the opening of the straits.[26] At the same time, Russia became actively involved in a secret alliance of the Balkan states — an alliance that was a major contributor to the first Balkan War.

During the early part of the war between Turkey and Italy over Tripolitania, Russian diplomats tried to exploit Turkey's difficulties in the Balkans by encouraging a Balkan League.[27] At first, Russia's efforts to realize such an alliance failed, largely because of the mutual jealousy and suspicion separating Serbia and Bulgaria. Ever since the abortive Treaty of 1904, Serbia had been seeking an alliance with Bulgaria in order to strengthen her position in opposing Austria.[28] In Serbia there was growing apprehension that when Francis Ferdinand came to the Austrian throne, he might seek to transform the Dual Monarchy into a tri-partite empire encompassing additional Slavic regions. Serbia might then be too weak to avoid being absorbed into the empire.[29] Aehrenthal was convinced that a Balkan League was no more than a utopian dream, since he felt Serbia and Bulgaria would never succeed in reconciling their conflicting claims to Macedonia.[30]

With the news of Italy's declaration of war on Turkey in September, 1911, the proposal for a Balkan League was reinvigorated with Russian encouragement. On February 29, 1912, Bulgaria and Serbia signed a treaty guaranteeing each other's territory and independence; each agreed to support the other in the event that any of the great powers should try to acquire by force, however temporarily, any Balkan territory.

---

[24]See Gooch and Temperley, IX:xiii.

[25]Essentially, the difficulty was a confusion between strategic and colonial issues, From the French point of view, France's expansion in North Africa was strategic as well as colonial, as strategic to her as the Dardanelles were to Russia. In order for France to support Russia on the opening of the Dardanelles, therefore, Russia would have to support French interests in North Africa. From the Russian point of view, however, France's stake in North Africa was entirely colonial. This impasse illustrates the reluctance of the major powers prior to WWI to commit themselves to the risk of full national support for one another's colonial enterprises.

[26]*Ibid.*, p. 413.

[27]Fay, 1947, p. 427; Helmreich, 1938, p. 25.

[28]Helmreich, 1938, p. 57.

[29]Albertini, 1952, I:371; see also O'Beirne to Grey, October 20, 1910, in Gooch and Temperley, IX:224–225.

[30]Helmreich, 1938, p. 27.

The Serbo-Bulgarian Treaty was directed against Austria as well as Turkey. Specifically, Serbia was protected against any Austrian attempts to seize parts of Macedonia or Albania that Serbia coveted or attempts to reoccupy Novibazar. In effect, the arrangement was designed to establish Russian hegemony in the Balkans by drawing the small Slavic states directly into the Russian orbit. This meant that in the eventuality of a general war, these states would be drawn to the side of the Triple Entente.[31] Because of this, the treaty was not entirely acceptable to Bulgaria, which was not well-disposed toward Serbian acquisition of Bosnia and Herzegovina or other Austrian territory. Bulgarian interests lay in the direction of Macedonia, Thrace, and even Constantinople. The Bulgarian disposition, therefore, was to direct the new alliance against Turkey rather than Austria.[32]

On May 16, 1912 the Serbo-Bulgarian Treaty was followed by a Graeco-Bulgarian Treaty (which carried no provision for the sharing of Turkish territory but was of a purely defensive character).[33] During the early autumn of 1912 Serbia and Montenegro also concluded a treaty of alliance, similar to the Serbian-Bulgarian treaty and directed also against both Turkey and Austria.[34]

The Balkan bloc was then complete. Formal alliances provided ties between Serbia and Bulgaria, Bulgaria and Greece, and Serbia and Montenegro, and there was an oral agreement, tantamount to an alliance, between Bulgaria and Montenegro. Greece was allied with Bulgaria, but probably had only oral agreements with Serbia and Montenegro.[35]

The conclusion of these alliances had great significance for Europe as a whole, in that they signified a "decided swing in the balance of power to the Entente."[36] Yet despite the advantage that the Entente seemed to have gained and despite Austrian apprehensions over Serbian expansion and Austria's desire to further its interests in the Balkans, the Austrian predisposition was for nonintervention and the avoidance of risky ventures. Indeed, the major powers in general shared a strong desire to avoid in the Balkans any kind of undertaking that might exacerbate the competitions and conflicts that already existed among themselves on other issues.

---

[31]Helmreich, 1938, p. 56.

[32]Fay, 1947, pp. 403–431. A secret annex of the treaty provided that if disorders broke out in Turkey and the status quo in the Balkans was threatened, Bulgaria and Serbia would discuss plans for joint military action. Provided Russia did not object to their plan of action, the two countries would then undertake military operations as agreed. If a dispute were to arise between them, it was to be referred to the tsar for arbitration, and his decision would be binding. A division of spoils in Macedonia was set forth in detail. See Helmreich, 1938, pp. 48–49, 55–56.

[33]Albertini, 1952, I:365.

[34]Helmreich, 1938, pp. 88–89.

[35]*Ibid.*

[36]*Ibid.*, p. 89; see also Nekludov, 1920, p. 45. Nekludov, the Russian minister in Sofia, "personally did not dread an Austrian *military* invasion," but expected "penetration by intrigue, economic stratagems and other means. . . ."

Unlike their counterparts in other capitals, Russian officials knew that the Balkan League had been formed with the aim of destroying European Turkey.[37] Russia's major concern in the Balkans was to make certain that no other great power achieved domination there, an eventuality that Russian policy-makers believed would threaten the very existence of Russia as an independent state. Thus, ". . . fear of being strangled at the Straits was the dominant motive of Russian policy."[38] From a Russian viewpoint, the union of Serbia and Bulgaria contained one dangerous element: "the temptation to use it for offensive purposes."[39] The Serbo-Bulgarian Treaty had provided Russia with a veto right, but even the tsar himself lacked confidence in it.[40]

Under the Franco-Russian Treaty of 1891 the two governments were to consult "on all questions of a nature to affect the general peace." In the event that peace was endangered, and especially if one of the parties were threatened with aggression, the two governments were to consult on measures to be taken if war broke out. The Franco-Russian military agreement of 1892 explicitly declared that the two countries had no aim other than mutual defense in the event of war provoked by any member of the Triple Alliance.[41] Presumably, the arrangement relieved France of the obligation to support Russia in the event that the latter were attacked by Germany in response to Russian aggression against Austria. Similarly, Russia had indicated her unwillingness during the Agadir Incident to go to war in defense of French interests in Morocco.[42]

Only gradually did the Austrians learn about the Serbo-Bulgarian treaty. Being unaware of the secret annex, Berchtold and others in Vienna were inclined to view it as a purely defensive instrument and a means for maintenance of the Balkan status quo. German knowledge of the arrangement was similarly limited, with the consequence that Kiderlen saw it as a means of "keeping the Balkans in hand" and of preventing "their independent action."[43] However, German leaders were apprehensive over the ever-present danger of being drawn too far into the confused Balkan situation because of Germany's alliance with Austria. Bethmann-Hollweg was responsive, therefore, when in early August the Russian government, beginning to fear open war in the Balkans, informed Berlin of its determination to prevent war by curbing the actions of the Balkan League.[44] As disturbances mounted during the summer of 1912, and as the Balkan states prepared for

---

[37]Mutius (Constantinople) to the German foreign office, 19 July 1912, Lepsius, 1922, IV:109.

[38]Taylor, 1954, pp. 283–284.

[39]Helmreich, 1938, p. 33.

[40]Albertini, 1952, I:370–372.

[41]*Ibid.*, pp. 368–369.

[42]*Ibid.*, p. 569; and Fay, 1947, pp. 326, 370, 407, 343.

[43]Helmreich, 1938, pp. 63–64.

[44]Bethmann-Hollweg to the German foreign office, 7 August 1912, in Dugdale, IV:110.

war, Austria, Russia, and France took various diplomatic steps in an effort to localize and pacify the enlarging conflict through united action.[45]

Sensitive to the close interdependence of critical issues in the Near East, Poincaré in late August provided his minister of war, Alexander Millerand, with a series of questions on the probable Austrian reaction toward an insurrection in Montenegro or Albania, toward an Italian naval action in the Dardanelles, and toward a conflict between the Balkan states and Turkey. The French chief of staff replied that Austrian intervention in a Macedonian or Albanian insurrection would trigger a war under conditions favorable to the Entente. A break between Austria and Italy would probably occur, forcing Austria to detach half her forces from her eastern front, a circumstance that would be advantageous to either Russian or French operations, depending upon whether Germany stayed clear or seized the opportunity to attack France. Given such an outcome, the Triple Entente might win a victory enabling the map of Europe to be redrawn.[46]

Encouraged by this assessment, Poincaré told Izvolsky that, according to the information available to him, if Serbia were to enter the war Austria would attack Belgrade. Russia might then be forced to intervene against Austria. In such an event, France would provide only diplomatic support—unless Germany gave military support to Austria against Russia.[47] Foreign Minister Sazonov replied to the effect that Russia could not justify support of any French military action provoked by colonial questions—unless France's vital interests in Europe were endangered.[48]

German leaders became increasingly concerned over how Austria would respond to events in the Balkans. Bethmann-Hollweg and Kiderlen agreed that according to their treaties and arrangements, Germany was not bound to support Austria "in her schemes in the East, let alone adventures; and all the less" since Austria had not promised Germany unconditional support against France. Hence, Germany must always reserve her attitude toward Austrian action "in questions of the East and the Balkans as each case arises." Germany would not become the satellite of Austria in the Near East."[49]

In early September, 1912 Bethmann-Hollweg met Count Berchtold at Berchtold's country estate at Buchlau. Apprehensive that Berchtold might involve Germany in an unwanted Balkan conflict, Bethmann-Hollweg tried to make clear to the Austrian foreign minister that Germany's "former passive attitude toward Austrian intentions

---

[45]Helmreich, 1938, p. 116.
[46]*Ibid.*, p. 373.
[47]*Ibid.*
[48]Fay, 1947, pp. 336–338; see also Albertini, 1952, I:374.
[49]Kiderlen to Bethmann-Hollweg, 2 September 1912, in Dugdale, IV:112–113.

against Serbia must not be taken as a matter of course."[50] In his negotiations, however, the chancellor "did not get much satisfaction out of Count Berchtold." From Berlin, Kiderlen urged that the Austrian government keep Germany informed of its intentions in advance and not, as had so often happened, face her with a "fait accompli."[51]

Toward the end of September the Balkan states followed the example already set by Montenegro and mobilized.[52] At the suggestion of Poincaré, now the French premier, Austria and Russia were instructed, as representatives of the great powers, to dissuade the Balkan states from armed conflict and to warn them that territorial changes would be a threat to European peace and stability and could not be tolerated. But Balkan leaders, having heard such warnings before, counted upon disunity and conflict of interest among the powers.[53] On October 8, as the instructions were presented, Montenegro—joined immediately by Bulgaria, Greece and Serbia—declared war on Turkey.[54]

The rapid and overwhelming successes of the Balkan forces took Europe by surprise.[55] European leaders lived in fear from the start that the theater of hostilities might be extended.[56] Pressures from major European powers kept hostilities localized, but the interests of the powers themselves conflicted, and the possibility of escalation was acute—partly because of treaty ties that tended to draw Russia, Austria, and their respective allies into the conflict, and partly because the major powers were becoming increasingly ambitious, competitive, and suspicious of each other. Under these circumstances, France, Germany, Russia, and Britain supported the status quo primarily as a means of keeping Austria from advancing.[57]

The assumption in Austria and elsewhere was that Russia had been responsible for the outbreak. "The Montenegrin army was officered by a Russian mission, and it did not seem possible that the Russian general in command could be completely guiltless." Moreover, if Sazonov himself was guiltless, the Russian minister in Belgrade "certainly was not, nor were the Russian nationalists, military chiefs, and grand dukes, who were longing for war in the Balkans."[58]

In Russian official circles it was widely assumed that by now a general war was inevitable, and yet the leadership was confronted by a serious dilemma.[59] If Russia did not intervene, Austria could be ex-

---

[50]*Ibid.*, p. 112.
[51]*Ibid.*
[52]Albertini, 1952, I:376; also, Helmreich, 1938, p. 130.
[53]Woodward, 1935, p. 395
[54]Sontag, 1933, p. 176.
[55]Helmreich, 1938, p. 196.
[56]Woodward, 1935, p. 396.
[57]Helmreich, 1938, p. 131.
[58]Albertini, 1952, I:377.
[59]Buchanan to Grey, St. Petersburg, October 22, 1912, in Gooch and Temperley, IX: Part II, p. 43.

pected to win against Serbia. On the other hand, there was deep apprehension lest Russia become involved in a major war at a time when she
was not prepared.[60] In the end, the more aggressive leaders were held
in check by Sazonov and others.

The consensus of European powers was that Austria not only would
veto the entry of any of the belligerents into the territory of Novibazar,
but would herself intervene, probably sending troops to block the penetration of Novibazar.[61] Rumors of an occupation spread.[62] In 1909
Austria and Italy had agreed that if Austria were obliged by the course
of events to undertake occupation of Novibazar, this could take place
only after a preliminary accord had been reached with Italy, based on
compensation.[63]

Austria had to choose between nonintervention, which meant no
further territorial expansion (her policy since at least 1908) and re-
occupation of Novibazar and expansion to Salonika. There were dispositions in both directions. The Balkans provided a convenient,
indeed the only readily available, sphere for the extension and development of Austrian interests.[64] Some Austrians, notably Count Conrad,
believed that the empire's survival depended upon vigorous efforts in
this direction. It was widely assumed that Austria would seize the
opportunity to assert herself. Austria not only had ambitions for expansion, it was also in a peculiarly vulnerable position because of the large
numbers of Slavs (as well as other minorities) within the empire who
might make common cause with a Russian-supported Balkan or Pan-
Slavic movement. On the other hand, there were serious risks in such
a policy, as Berchtold well knew, and at this juncture, he thought, the
military capabilities of the Dual Monarchy were not sufficient to justify
taking them. The hope was that by joining with the powers in a cooperative effort, hostilities could be contained, Russian ambitions held in
check, and the possibilities held open for Austrian exploitation in
more favorable circumstances sometime in the future. There was
never therefore any intention in the Austrian foreign office of pursuing an active policy. On the contrary, any undertaking that might
involve the empire in a war would be avoided.[65]

As the Balkan War proceeded, British leaders, especially Sir Edward
Grey, began to play an increasingly important role in continental
affairs. England had a vital stake in stability and the status quo. Sir
Edward's goal was to localize the conflict by keeping Austria and
Russia in touch.[66] In this he was supported by the French, who wanted

---

[60]Helmreich, 1938, p. 153.
[61]Albertini, 1952, I:386.
[62]Helmreich, 1938, p. 177.
[63]Albertini, 1952, I:389.
[64]Helmreich, 1938, p. 162.
[65]*Ibid.*, pp. 185, 189; and Woodward, 1935, pp. 400–401.
[66]Gooch and Temperley, IX:xiii.

Entente solidarity, "success of the Balkan states for the sake of Russia and the Entente," and avoidance of a European war.[67] And German leaders, aware of Sir Edward's intentions, expressed a willingness to cooperate with Britain in order to avert war[68] — although there was some apprehension in Berlin that official British policy might not be entirely congruent with Sir Edward's personal dispositions.[69] The Kaiser thought that the great powers should "form a ring around the scene of battle, where the conflict must remain and run its course."[70]

The war covered three main theaters: along the Turko-Bulgarian frontier in Thrace, on the Graeco-Turkish frontier, and in Macedonia. During the autumn Turkish troops suffered a series of defeats at the hands of the allied Balkan forces. In early November Russia issued a warning to Bulgaria against the occupation of Constantinople, vowing that they would resist with their fleet. Within a week Serbian forces reached the Adriatic after overrunning northern Albania. Turkey suffered defeats on all fronts, but except for the fortresses of Adrianople, Janina, and Scutari, the territories that the Balkan states had hoped to acquire were not in their possession.[71]

Two issues now became critical, not only to the Balkan conflict but to Russo-Austrian relations as well: the appearance of Serbian forces on the Adriatic and the status of Albania. To the Austrians, a Serbian port on the Adriatic would mean in effect a Russian port, something Austria would not countenance.[72] Such Serbian expansion would jeopardize the Albanian state that Austria (and Italy) wanted established.[73]

Britain and Germany, concerned with a larger European war, tried to minimize the issue. Britain did not think a Serbian port was worth a European war.[74] And the Kaiser observed that Serbia merely wanted to get to the sea "as her neighbors and, in fact, all inland nations do." Wilhelm saw "absolutely no risk for Austria's existence or even prestige in a Serbian port in the Adriatic Sea" and thought it "objectionable" to oppose Serbia's wishes.[75] Wilhelm was not disposed to "march against Paris and Moscow for the sake of Albania and Durazzo."[76]

---

[67]Helmreich, 1938, p. 149.

[68]Kühlmann to Bethman-Hollweg, 15 October 1912, in Dugdale, IV:115.

[69]Kiderlen to Kuhlman, 20 October 1912, *ibid.*, p. 118.

[70]Quoted in Helmreich, 1938, p. 184.

[71]*Ibid.*, p. 202.

[72]*Ibid.*, p. 210.

[73]*Ibid.*, p. 209; and Grey, 1925, p. 255.

[74]Helmreich, 1938, p. 220.

[75]Kaiser to Kiderlen, 7 November 1912, in Dugdale, 1931, IV:120–121.

[76]Buchanan to Grey, St. Petersburg, October 16, 1912, in Gooch and Temperley, IX:26. See *The Times*, London, November 11, 1912, pp. 9–10. On November 9 Prime Minister Aquith reported, in a speech at the Guildhall in London, that the great powers were working together on the Balkan question in a "remarkable" manner — although the general European opinion was unanimous that the Balkan victors were not to be robbed of the fruits that had cost them so dearly.

At the time of the Balkan mobilizations Russia had undertaken a trial mobilization that, according to St. Petersburg, had been planned for some time and had no connection whatever with the Balkan crisis. Both the Austrian and German foreign offices accepted these explanations at the time and raised no serious objections. Austrian authorities, however, grew increasingly suspicious that there was in fact a direct connection between Balkan events and the "trial" mobilization. In fact, the mobilization activated certain standing instructions in Austria that were to take effect in case of war.[77]

The Emperor Francis Josef agreed on October 4, 1912 to "preparations for increase in strength of troops. . . ." Later that month, 7,000 reserve troops were dispatched to Bosnia, and arrangements were made for further military measures. On November 19 a decision was made to strengthen Austrian forces in Galicia. "We shall see how Russia reacts to our border measures," the Austrian war minister declared. "If she accepts them quietly, then we shall have a free hand against Serbia."[78] The empire needed about 50 years to bring its Slavs into order, he continued, and this could be realized only if Slavic expectations of Russian support were definitely put aside.

Anxieties were further intensified in European capitals when Count Conrad, who had been forced to resign as chief of staff in November, 1911 because of Aehrenthal's opposition to his proposed attack on Italy, was recalled to his post.[79] Since Conrad was known as a determined enemy of Serbia, war seemed imminent.[80] Sazonov informed British Ambassador Buchanan that if Austrian mobilization continued, the Russian government would be forced to take "counter measures."[81]

Inevitably, the position of Russia in the crisis was worrisome to France. It was no longer simply the Franco-Russian alliance that was at stake, observed Paul Cambon, the French ambassador in London — the supreme interests of France were in jeopardy. "Germanism was aiming at the Mediterranean; the road to it must be barred at all costs."[82]

The Turks, meanwhile, had opened direct negotiations for an armistice, which took effect December 8, although Greece refused to recognize the armistice because Turkey would not cede the fortress of Janina. The focus of attention shifted quickly from the Balkans to

---

[77]Helmreich, 1938, p. 160. Russia did not desire war, according to Helmreich, but may have undertaken the trial mobilization, in part at least, as a way of indicating that she "meant to have her way in coming events and would not suffer a humiliation such as that of 1908–09."

[78]*Ibid.*, p. 138.

[79]Albertini, 1952, I:433.

[80]Cartwright to Grey, November 26, 1912, in Gooch and Temperley, IX:205; and see Conrad, in Albertini, 1952, I:434.

[81]Buchanan to Grey, December 22, 1912, in Gooch and Temperley, IX:311–312.

[82]Albertini, 1952, I:415.

London, as Britain began to play an increasingly active role in the negotiations. Sir Edward Grey, in order to avoid catastrophe, pressed successfully for a conference of powers.

The conference convened in London on December 17, 1912 and continued to meet, as circumstances required, until August, 1913.[83] Concurrently, an ambassadorial conference was held to discuss the boundaries and status of Albania, the disposition of the Aegean Islands, and related issues.

By this time, however, the military measures initiated by Austria in late November and early December were taking effect. In Bosnia and Herzegovina Austrian troops achieved a war footing, and garrisons elsewhere were strengthened. Altogether, Austria had called about 224,000 men (Russia estimated the number to be 300,000). The Russian army had been increased by about 350,000 reservists, of whom around 150,000 were deployed near Austrian frontiers. Without a special edict from the tsar, these troops would have to be dismissed on January 1. But unless Austria reduced her forces, Russia was not prepared to allow these reservists to demobilize.

Russia insisted on mutual disarmament as a precondition for negotiations, whereas the Dual Monarchy refused to reduce its forces until the Serbian army withdrew from Albania and a satisfactory frontier for Albania had been assured.[84] Moreover, the plan for a Serbian port on the Adriatic and a strip of territory, even if both were neutralized, was unacceptable to Austria.[85]

The Austrian refusal to allow access to the sea frustrated and enraged Serbian leaders and made them even more defiant. Serbia agreed to withdraw from the Adriatic, but the issue of frontiers for an independent Albania presented further threatening problems: the situation would become "very serious" if Albanian frontiers were pushed far east or north to include villages with a majority of Serb-speaking population.[86] Conversely, Austria, pressed for an autonomous Albania "large enough to stand by itself" with a seaboard touching Greece on the south and Montenegro to the north and following ethnographical lines inland.[87] Both Austria and Italy favored establishment of an Albanian state, but for different reasons. The two allies were also rivals, and they shared a hope that the creation of Albania would serve to exclude Serbia from the Adriatic, which both wanted to dominate. Each was suspicious of the other, however, and each had sought secret support from Russia to exclude the interests of the other from Albanian territory.

---

[83]*Ibid.*, pp. 255–256.

[84]Helmreich, 1938, p. 259; Schmitt, 1918, p. 361; and Bax-Ironside to Grey, Sofia, January 6, 1913, in Gooch and Temperley, IX:360; Bridge, 1972, p. 350.

[85]Schoen to the German foreign office, 24 November 1912, in Dugdale, IV:123.

[86]Paget to Grey, December 21, 1912, in Gooch and Temperley, IX:310.

[87]Cartwright to Gery, December 21, 1912, *ibid.*, p. 309.

By January 1913 the Serbs were insisting on retention of Debra and Jakova, which they had occupied; the Montenegrins were determined to possess Scutari, which they had under siege; and the Austrians, having given up Prizend and Ipek, were unwilling to make further concessions.[88] Feeling that she had been denied the fruits of her military successes, including an outlet to the Adriatic, Serbia now wanted a revision of the Serbo-Bulgarian Treaty to give her a part of Macedonia.[89] In order to save Scutari for Albania, Berchtold made wide concessions in favor of Serbia and Montenegro on the northeastern frontier of Albania, "giving up not only all the areas which he had originally listed as possible bargaining counters, but the important market towns of Dibra and Djakova, which were notoriously Albanian in character."[90] But Montenegro refused to accept the decision on Scutari.

After two months of negotiations, a coup d'etat in Constantinople brought the armistice to an end, and on February 3, 1913 hostilities were resumed. Again, the powers were confronted with the problem of keeping the conflict localized. France and Britain feared a Russian demonstration of force on the Armenian border. Italy was apprehensive lest Russia might raise the question of the Dardanelles again. Germany would not stand aside if Turkish territories in Asia were endangered. Russia warned that she would intervene if, as seemed possible, Rumanian troops were to exploit the situation by crossing the Bulgarian border.[91]

By the latter part of April hostilities against Turkey, except for the Montenegrin siege of Scutari, had come to an end. Despite protests from the powers, Montenegrin forces on April 24 took Scutari, which had been assigned to Albania and which, from an Austrian viewpoint, was vital to Albania's existence.[92] Turkish forces withdrew to Tirana. The powers now faced the problem of how to pry the Montenegrins out of Scutari.[93]

Austria immediately informed the powers that if they failed to fulfill their responsibility in the matter, she would act alone — possibly landing troop detachments or bombarding coastal cities.[94] She also demanded special satisfaction and an apology from Montenegro for incidents that had occurred in connection with the Scutari hostilities.[95]

Berchtold was inclined to think that Russia would not go to war. But he hesitated to expose Austria to the risk of armed conflict with Russia without the support of Italy, with whom Austria had special

---

[88]Albertini, 1952, I:435.
[89]Fay, 1947, p. 443.
[90]Bridge, 1972, pp. 350-351.
[91]Helmreich, 1938, pp. 277-278; see also Gooch and Temperley, IX:xiv, 608.
[92]Albertini, 1952, I:435.
[93]Helmreich, 1938, p. 314.
[94]*Ibid.*, pp. 315-318; and Albertini, 1952, I:443.
[95]Helmreich, 1938, p. 318.

agreements on Albania. Without an understanding, unilateral Austrian action in the area might bring on a war with Italy as well as Russia. The Italians were unsettled and equivocal: there was discussion of a possibility of Italy acting in southern Albania if Austria were to proceed against the Montenegrins at Scutari.[96]

The Austrian assessment of Russia's position was essentially correct. Sazonov thought that, as an outcome of the capture of Scutari, Montenegro was entitled to territorial as well as financial compensations. At the same time, the Russians were "most anxious to avoid being dragged into a war." Russia was "not afraid of Austria," but she also recognized that Germany had to be reckoned with. In case of hostilities, France would support Russia, but "it was not known what England would do," and she alone had the capability for striking Germany a mortal blow."[97]

At an ambassadorial conference on April 28, 1913 Austria declared that unless the powers undertook concrete measures to bring Montenegro to terms, she would definitely act alone. The Triple Alliance urged a landing of troops under international sponsorship, but the Entente considered such action premature. Austrian patience had come to an end. Although Berchtold himself opposed the idea, a meeting of the council of joint ministers in Austria approved the dispatch to Montenegro of a 12-hour ultimatum.[98]

Austria began calling up reserves; forces in Bosnia, Herzegovina, and Dalmatia were put on a war footing despite Russia's warning that she would not tolerate an attack on Serbia.[99] By May 3 mobilization was in full swing, "even if it was not so labeled."[100] On May 3 Berchtold dispatched a "warning telegram" rather than an ultimatum to the Montenegrin government. This offered Montenegro the possibility of avoiding hostilities with Austria if she acted immediately. On the following day the Montenegrins "marched out of Scutari, tension relaxed, Austria-Hungary's latest military measures were countermanded, and Conrad lamented that yet another opportunity for war had been lost."[101] The crisis came to an end, and on May 14 an international naval landing force occupied the city.[102] The crisis over Scutari had demonstrated once more that although Austria preferred to avoid military action, she was at least prepared to use the threat of force to protect an interest that was considered vital.

The first Balkan war ended on May 30 with the Treaty of London, whereby Turkey ceded all territory west of a line between Midia and Enos and renounced all claim to Crete.[103] The status of Albania and

---

[96]Albertini, 1952, I:447–448.

[97]Helmreich, 1938, p. 319.

[98]Ibid., p. 318; Albertini, 1952, I:448.

[99]Bridge, 1972, p. 352.

[100]Helmreich, 1938, p. 322.

[101]Bridge, 1972, p. 352.

[102]Albertini, 1952, I:448; and Helmreich, 1938, p. 325.

[103]Grey to Lowther, April 23, 1913, in Gooch and Temperley, IX:709–710.

the Aegean Islands was left to the decision of the powers. In general, the settlement was accepted by the Balkan allies with great reluctance.[104]

Serbia, long dissatisfied with the constraints of the Serbo-Bulgarian Treaty, joined with Greece, Turkey, Rumania, and Montenegro against Bulgaria in the second Balkan war of June and July, 1913 — a case of the victors quarreling over the spoils. Again, the Austrian position was a difficult one. Berchtold hoped to curb Serbia and lessen the attraction of that country to Slavic peoples within the empire, preferably without intervention.[105] In case of a Bulgarian defeat, Austria could not countenance an "excessive strengthening of Serbia."[106] She had also more or less promised to support Rumania with the hope of drawing that country away from Russia, the assumption being that Vienna could expect support from Italy. It soon became evident, however, that Italy had no intention of being drawn into the conflict, and Austria realized that she might be left to fight alone.[107] Once Rumania had entered the war, moreover, Austria could not attack Serbia without opposing her own ally.[108] On July 10 Rumanian forces began invading Bulgaria, which then wired the Russian government for help; Turkey took advantage of the situation by reconquering Adrianople. Fearing that Russia might attack Turkey, Austria reserved to herself the right to intervene to protect Bulgaria from being overthrown by the Turks.[109]

A dispute then arose among the powers with respect to what territory should be allotted to Greece. The consequent division was a peculiar one: France and Germany supported Greek claims, whereas Russia and Austria favored Bulgaria. Sir Edward was prepared to agree with whatever was finally settled.[110]

The brief but bloody struggle, in which Bulgaria was forced to succumb "to a crowd of enemies," was ended with the Treaty of Bucharest on August 10, 1913. At the same moment the Conference of London adjourned for the summer holidays; its meetings were never resumed.[111] As Sir Edward later recalled, "There was no formal finish; . . . . We had not settled anything . . . but we had served a useful purpose. . . . We had been a means of keeping all the six powers in direct and friendly touch. The mere fact that we were in existence, and that we should have to be broken up before peace was broken, was in itself an appreciable barrier against war."[112] Nevertheless, war was

---

[104]Woodward, 1935, p. 395; Grey to Bax-Ironside, May 21, 1913, in Gooch and Temperley, IX:807; Elliot to Grey, May 23, 1913, *ibid.*, p. 809; Bax-Ironside to Grey, May 31, 1913, *ibid.*, p. 827.

[105]Helmreich, 1938, pp. 377–378; Fay, 1947, p. 443.

[106]Albertini, 1952, I:455.

[107]Dugdale, 1931, IV:183.

[108]Helmreich, 1938, p. 379.

[109]Jagow to Tschirschky, 25 July 1913, in Dugdale, IV:185–186.

[110]Lichnowsky to the German foreign office, 22 July 1913, *ibid.*, p. 185.

[111]Gooch and Temperley, IX:xv.

[112]Grey, 1925, p. 263.

avoided primarily because neither Russia nor Austria was disposed
then, as they were less than a year later, to make a decisive move.
Thus, Sazonov sought to avoid escalation of the Balkan Wars and persuaded Serbia to drop demands that Austria would not have granted
without war.[113] In the first Balkan War Austria "never had any intention or desire to profit by the occasion to attack Serbia." So, too, in
the second Balkan War, "the failure of Berchtold's purpose of preventing the rise of a Greater Serbia out of the utter defeat of Bulgaria
was due, not to the veto of Germany and Italy, but to the fact that
the Austrian ministry never had any intention of carrying out his purpose by resorting, if need be, to force . . ."[114] According to Berchtold,
although his "heart" was disposed toward reliance on force at this time,
his "head" was not, since he "felt no confidence that authoritative
quarters would stand firm.[115]

The immediate effect of the Treaty of Bucharest was a worsening
rather than strengthening of Austro-German relations.[116] Through
December, 1912 Germany and Austria had been in basic agreement
over Balkan policy, but by August, 1913, this harmony had given way
to discord.[117] Although Germany's sympathies for Turkey, as well as
for Rumania, might be tolerated in Vienna, there were complications.
Fearing any outcome that might enhance Serbia's territory or national
capabilities, Austria had come to hope that Bulgaria would acquire the
greater share of Turkish territory. A "large and saturated Bulgaria"
would arouse Serbian antagonisms and thus dispose Bulgaria to help
the Dual Monarchy to keep Serbia in check.[118] Moreover, "there was
not one point where the interests of Bulgaria and the Dual Monarchy
collided."[119]

Increasingly, Germany encouraged Austria to seek an agreement
with Serbia rather than with Bulgaria. Indeed, the Kaiser thought
that a combination of Serbia, Rumania, and Greece under Austrian
leadership would be "the most natural and best" because Turkey
would prefer to join such a union rather than an alliance with Bulgaria.
But Austria would have nothing to do with a Serbian-Rumanian-
Greek combination.[120] Berlin and Vienna thus found themselves pursuing contradictory policies in their efforts to preserve the status quo
for Austria.

From the Austrian viewpoint, Bulgaria's defeat not only further
upset the balance of power, but had the additional effect of encour-

---

[113]Albertini, 1952, I:486.
[114]*Ibid.*, 467.
[115]*Ibid.*, 471.
[116]Helmreich, 1936, p. 143.
[117]Fay, 1947, p. 496; and see Helmreich, 1936, p. 141.
[118]Helmreich, 1938, p. 370.
[119]Helmreich, 1936, p. 134.
[120]*Ibid.*

aging the aspirations of Serbia (as well as those of Rumania). Minorities within the empire itself, especially in Bosnia and Herzegovina, grew more and more restive.[121]

Conrad, who thought that time was running out for the Dual Monarchy, "had wanted war for years past." Asked whether the Austrian army was capable of meeting an enemy, Conrad responded on April 24, 1913: "Now, yes. Whether this will be so in a few years, I am doubtful."[122] The general predisposition among German, Austrian, and Russian leaders, on the other hand, was to defer a large-scale war by every means possible until some further time when, each hoped, the position of his own country would be significantly improved. At meetings of the Austrian ministerial council on October 3 and 13 the choice was between accommodating further Serbian expansion or presenting Serbia with an ultimatum requiring the evacuation of Serbian troops from Albania.[123] The conclusion was that "very energetic measures would be required to get Serbia to evacuate."[124] Some hoped that diplomatic action would be sufficient; others, especially Conrad, thought that military action constituted the only realistic alternative. Berchtold wavered.[125] Conrad was delighted that in this instance so many other Austrian leaders inclined toward his recommendations.[126]

Differences in German and Austrian interests had been reflected for some time by inconsistencies in German policies with respect to the Serbian question.[127] Germany had urged the Dual Monarchy to make friends with Serbia, but at various times she also promised support in the event that Austria felt obliged to take military measures against Serbia.[128] Now, as a new crisis unfolded, Germany provided Austria with assurances, and the Kaiser himself conceded to Conrad that ". . . in the end situations arise in which a great power can no longer stand aside; it must grasp the sword."[129] But what the Germans really had in mind, according to Fischer, was to apply an additional deterrent — to put off Russian intervention "by stressing the German-Austrian alliance."[130]

The German foreign office advised its chargé in Belgrade to support Austrian demands, and measures were undertaken to secure similar action by Britain and France.[131] In an effort to prevent a full-scale

---

[121]Fay, 1947, pp. 462–464; according to Helmreich, "the Austrian foreign office certainly desired peace in this region," but not at any cost.
[122]Woodward, 1935, pp. 400–401.
[123]Fay, 1947, p. 467; also Helmreich, 1938, p. 423.
[124]Helmreich, 1938, p. 423.
[125]Fay, 1947, p. 469.
[126]Helmreich, 1938, pp. 423–424.
[127]Fay, 1947, p. 472.
[128]Helmreich, 1936, p. 141.
[129]Conrad, 1922, III:470.
[130]Fischer, 1967, p. 43.
[131]Helmreich, 1938, p. 424.

European war from breaking out at that moment, Arthur Zimmerman, German undersecretary of state for foreign affairs, dispatched telegrams to Vienna, London and Belgrade to the effect that Germany was taking "a firm attitude" and publicly announced that a viable Albania was of vital interest to Germany's ally, Austria.[132]

Austria rejected as inadequate an assurance by Serbia on October 15 that an order to halt further advances had already been issued. Reinforced by Germany's promise of support, Berchtold during the night of October 17–18 dispatched an ultimatum demanding a complete evacuation of Albanian territory by Serbian troops in eight days.[133] This was followed on October 30 by an Austro-Italian note to Greece demanding the evacuation of southern Albania by December 31. Against the background of recent Austrian vacillations, Berchtold's "unexpected exhibition of decisive energy took all Europe aback with surprise." There could be no doubt but that "Austrian diplomats meant business this time"; the Serbian government decided forthwith to meet Austria's demands and Austria achieved "an easy diplomatic victory."[134] In St. Petersburg Sazonov complained of Berchtold's "policy of surprises" and *fait accomplis* that her allies were unable to prevent.[135]

No doubt these events "help to explain Austria's course of action, under much greater provocation, in July, 1914."[136] The fundamental problem faced by the Dual Monarchy—a growing and expansionist Serbia—was persistent: between Austria and "the present Serbian state" stood the "great South Slav problem" which then and in the future would increasingly demand "a final solution" around the idea of a Great Serbia. Such a solution would undoubtedly involve armed force that would "either leave few traces of the present Serbian state" or would "rock Austria-Hungary to its very foundations."[137] The delays and ineffectiveness of the conference of powers "in protecting Albanian interests, when defied by the Montenegrins at Scutari and the Serbians at Dibra, explain to some extent why Austria was absolutely unwilling, after the murder of Archduke Franz Ferdinand at Sarajevo some eight months later, to submit her . . . complaint against Serbia to another conference of powers." Only when Austria had acted quickly and energetically on her own account, by sending a peremptory ultimatum, had Serbia "heeded her demands immediately." Russia, moreover, had not interfered, and the foreign office in Vienna had "accomplished its immediate purpose."[138]

German leaders had offered assurances to Vienna that in the efforts to achieve a viable Albania they stood "firmly behind Austria." Yet

[132]Fischer, 1967, p. 43.
[133]Fay, 1947, p. 473; Helmreich, 1938, p. 425; and Fischer, 1967, p. 43.
[134]Helmreich, 1938, p. 427.
[135]Fay, 1947, p. 473.
[136]*Ibid.*, p. 474.
[137]Helmreich, 1936, p. 144.
[138]Fay, 1947, I:474–475.

German leaders remained uneasy and indecisive on the whole issue. Those who saw a struggle approaching would see clearly that "the concentration of all forces [and] the utilization of all possibilities" were called for.[139] Thus, from the viewpoint of Berlin, only an aggressive move by Russia would fully justify full-scale German military action in a European war. With this in mind, it becomes easier to understand why in July, 1914 German leaders were so deeply concerned over developments in St. Petersburg and so predisposed to counter any Russian mobilization with aggressive actions of their own.

There were, however, two more elements in the equation of conflict: France, ally of Russia, and, even more critically, Britain, whose powerful navy remained a crucial factor in the world balance of power. Germany could afford to engage Russia, and, by invoking the Schlieffen Plan, even a Russia supported by France. But a general war remained a high risk unless British neutrality could be counted on.

Helmreich, Fay, and others, have noted how the procedure followed in October, 1913 was later duplicated in July, 1914: the warning to Serbia, the general promise of support from Germany, the independent presentation of the ultimatum, and the subsequent notification of ally and rival. To the major powers in 1913 the desired end of Austria's action, Serbia's compliance with an international decision, seemed "manifestly so correct that the danger of a general war was slight."[140] In fact, armed conflict among the great powers was averted. What then distinguished the crisis of October, 1913 (and others in 1908-1909, 1912, and early 1913) from that of July, 1914, which produced a major war?

The conclusion was widespread in European capitals that the actions of the powers in the Balkan Wars had further upset the precarious balance of power among them. Germany's attempts to acquire a "continuous colonial empire in central Africa" had persuaded her leaders that this could not be accomplished "without a fundamental regrouping of the contractual and sentimental relations between France, Britain, and Russia."[141] Indeed, viewed from Berlin, the grouping of the powers since the turn of the century increasingly limited the possibilities for Germany's development in a number of directions. The Germans believed that events in the Balkans during 1912 and 1913 had the effect of further tipping the balance of power in favor of the Entente. During the months immediately following the crisis of October, 1913, Germany and Austria unsuccessfully tried through diplomatic means to "reestablish an equilibrium" more favorable to themselves.[142] In July, 1914, therefore, the prevailing opinion among the great powers

---

[139]Quoted by Fischer, 1967, p. 33.
[140]Helmreich, 1938, p. 426.
[141]Fischer, 1967, p. 38.
[142]Helmreich, 1938, p. 59.

was that they lacked the diplomatic flexibility to localize the crisis in the Balkans.

In addition to the Austro-Serbian conflict and the disagreement over Albanian territory, a significant change had come about with respect to Rumania. Through a secret treaty in 1883, Rumania joined the Triple Alliance; the treaty was renewed at various intervals, the last time being February, 1913.[143] At first there had been no question about Rumania's loyalty to the treaty, but by early 1914 the situation had changed considerably. A major factor in moving Rumania away from the Triple Alliance and closer to the Entente had been the "astonishing victories over Turkey in the first weeks of the [first Balkan] war," whereby Bulgaria, Serbia, and Greece had "occupied wide stretches of territory, which vastly extended their frontiers and greatly increased their prestige, power and population." Having maintained a "dignified neutrality" in the first war, Rumania had gained no new territories, while "her rivals were growing strong."[144] Subsequently, Rumania joined Serbia and Greece against Bulgaria in the second Balkan War, acquiring a considerable amount of Bulgarian territory as a result. Austria now found herself threatened not only by Serbian nationalism but also by Rumanian nationalist sentiments for the incorporation of Rumanian portions of Transylvania. Although the Russian government itself ruled over Rumanian populations in Bessarabia, Russia seized upon this opportunity to increase her influence over Rumania.

Seeking to recover from the painful circumstances the Balkan Wars had created, Turkey had been casting about for ways of westernizing and modernizing her administration and renewing her military capabilities.[145] Even while the Balkan Wars were still in progress, secret negotiations were carried on between Germany and Turkey over a special military mission for the training of Turkish troops.[146] Toward the end of 1913 it was learned in St. Petersburg that General Liman von Sanders, together with 42 other German officers, had been given a five-year commission to train the Turkish army, control Turkish military training establishments, serve in the Turkish war council, supervise the promotion of higher Turkish officers, exercise the disciplinary powers of a commanding general, and actually command the Turkish First Army Corps in Constantinople.[147]

From the Russian perspective, a German general was not only virtually in command of Constantinople, but of the Dardanelles as well. It seemed to level a mortal blow at Russia's position in the Black Sea and her aspirations for control of the strait. In the end, Liman was removed from command of Constantinople without serious loss of prestige to either Germany or Turkey, but not until after the major

---

[143]Hale, 1940, p. 436.
[144]Fay, 1947, I:476.
[145]Albertini, 1952, I:541.
[146]*Ibid.*, p. 507.
[147]Albertini, 1952, I:541.

capitals of Europe had all become involved to one degree or another. Conrad thought it highly probable that Russia would seize this opportunity to strike, and, to Conrad, this was not undesirable. Austria's position was not improving, and the sooner Russia struck, the better would be the advantage to the Central Powers.[148]

German leaders hoped to exploit the crisis to "make capital" out of "Anglo-Russian tensions and thus detach France and Russia." In the end, however, Britain "made common cause with France and Russia against Germany," which was thus forced to retreat. Encircled, so it seemed, by the Entente, Germany "saw her isolation becoming more and more total." From this point forward, "the more Germany's enterprises ran aground and the more her cards got over-trumped in the international imperialist game between the powers, the louder grew the cry that she should break out from the threatened encirclement before it was complete. . . ."[149]

In the relatively restricted fields of commerce and finance, "Germany was unmistakably willing to play the junior partner to Britain as a world power. German public opinion, on the other hand, in the knowledge of the nation's power and economic potential, was not prepared to accept such a position: it claimed nothing short of fully independent status, equal to England's, America's, and Russia's." Agreements between Germany and Britain on the Bagdad Railway, Persian Gulf ports, and problems of Mesopotamia reveal the extent to which Germany was trying "to reach an understanding—and ultimately an 'alliance'—with Britain, even at the cost of sacrifice."[150]

Although perhaps a grossly oversimplified metaphor, one can imagine a trip wire or lanyard laid through Vienna, Belgrade, Bucharest, St. Petersburg, Berlin, Rome, Paris, and London—with less "sensitive" extensions into Africa, the Near and Far East. A crisis almost anywhere in the world might trigger hostilities. By far the most sensitive stretch was the Vienna-Belgrade loop passing through the Serb-inhabited regions of the Austrian empire. In this sector any annexation, almost any threatening event, could result in a serious escalation of conflict. Germany hoped (or preferred to believe) that Britain was not "wired in," that if the lanyard were tripped, she would remain neutral. Believing this, German leaders underestimated the risks of any incident or crisis involving the powers.

On several critical occasions during the Balkan Wars, the cooperative efforts of Germany, Britain, and France had been impressive— much to the surprise of European diplomats and statesmen. "The Concert of Europe had at last taken form."[151] In January, 1913 Bethmann-Hollweg told Goschen that Anglo-German cooperation on

---

[148]Conrad, 1922, III:670.
[149]Fischer, 1967, pp. 43, 45–46, 48.
[150]*Ibid.*, p. 41.
[151]Woodward, 1935, p. 398.

the Near Eastern question was "worth more than any naval agreement or political understanding as a starting point for future good relations."[152]

World War I was not mechanistically predetermined or "fatalistically inevitable" as various otherwise impeccably nondeterministic authorities have frequently asserted. Presumably, a firm policy of restraint or other exercise of firm political will in Vienna, Belgrade, St. Petersburg, or Berlin might have prevented the outbreak of war during the summer of 1914 — as firmness had served to constrain the Balkan crises in 1908–1909 and in 1912–1913. By 1914, however, changes in the relative capabilities of the major powers, changes in the configuration of international power, and the resulting intensification of competition had made policies of restraint more difficult.

---

[152]*Ibid.*

Europe on the Eve of World War

9

Scholars have often identified international competition and alterations in the alliance structure as important factors in creating the conditions for war. Less attention has been paid to the underlying processes that contribute to international competition and to major alterations in the configuration of power.

As indicated in Chapter 1, population growth and technological advancement create demands within a society. In order to meet these demands, a society develops appropriate capabilities. Germany in the early 1870s is a prime example of this tendency. During the 1870s and 1880s she developed a wide range of commercial and industrial capabilities in order to meet the demands created by a growing population and advancing technology. These capabilities contributed, in turn, to Germany's emergence as the dominant political and military power on the European continent.

Bismarck made use of this power to create a network of alliances on the European continent. This network served to contain the conflicts that were generated as German demands for resources and markets increased and as her military and political power surpassed that of France and began to challenge that of Britain. With continuing growth in population and technology, however, Germany was forced to reach farther and farther beyond her own territorial limits in order to acquire needed resources and markets. This "reaching out" had three effects. It contributed to further domestic growth (and thus even greater demands for resources); it led to conflicts between expanding German interests and those of other powers; these conflicts of interest in turn contributed to more acute competition among the powers that threatened the Bismarckian alliance system. After 1890, the system began to break into two blocs, the Triple Entente and the Triple Alliance. The blocs emerged from the increasing instability in the configuration of power, but the emergence of the blocs themselves contributed to that instability.

In contrast to Germany's rapid emergence as a dominant power, Britain had been a powerful force in European and world affairs for decades. Britain, relying on her superior technology, economic capabilities, and powerful navy, had dominated the seas and maintained a certain independence in continental affairs, throwing her weight now on one side of the European "balance," now on the other. But although Britain's technology and production continued to advance, Germany began to overtake her; for example, after 1898 Germany rapidly surpassed Britain in iron and steel production. By that time, moreover, British leaders were feeling increasingly threatened by the expansion of the German navy.

Prior to the turn of the century, France had been Britain's major rival, and the rapid expansion of both French and British territories led to collisions between the two powers in Africa, Southeast Asia, and other parts of the world where their spheres of interest intersected. But partly in response to German economic growth, the rapid growth in the German navy, the lapse in the Russo-German Reinsurance Treaty, and the expansion of German influence in Mediterranean colonial affairs, Britain and France drew closer together and finally resolved their major differences through the Accords of 1904.

While the Anglo-German naval race escalated, the German and French land armies competed for military supremacy. The Russian military establishment suffered a severe setback as an outcome of the Russo-Japanese War, and this disability became a critical factor during a series of Balkan crises in 1908–1909 and in 1912–1913.

The colonial powers succeeded in regulating many of their overseas conflicts by concluding local agreements in Africa, Asia, and the Pacific. In Europe, however, as Turkish power receded, the interests of Russia, Austria, Germany, and Italy tended to collide in the Balkans, where a resurgent Serbia was perceived as a threat by Austria. No satisfactory great-power agreement in this region could be reached. Any serious disturbance there was viewed with anxiety by all the powers, including Britain. But when Russia and Austria reached the brink of war in 1908–1909 and 1912–1913, Russia could not afford to commit herself to hostilities, and Austria, although suffering domestic disabilities of her own, was able to gain what she wanted by diplomatic maneuvering and threats.

Austria's population was growing, her economy was expanding, and her unsatisfied demands were increasing. But she was constrained from territorial expansion by limited access to the sea and by her reluctance to become involved in a war with powers that were stronger than herself. Under these circumstances, Austrian leaders tried to exploit any disturbance in the Balkans that might open the way for Austrian advantage.

The demands generated by both the domestic growth of the major powers and the competition between them were reaching a threshold where diplomatic constraints were no longer adequate to ensure stability. Each country felt compelled to enhance its military strength as rapidly as possible and to put its war-making capabilities in order.

During 1912 and 1913, while the major powers were cooperating to keep the Balkan conflicts localized, each was strengthening its armaments against the possibility of a major war. From observations made during the first Balkan War, the German general staff in the autumn of 1912 asked for an increase of 50 percent in Germany's active standing army.[1] Although the number was reduced by the cabinet, the resulting budgetary increase was the largest in German history.[2] As a result, France felt compelled, even while the Reichstag was still in session, to reimpose the three-year term of service, which had been reduced in 1905 to two years.[3] Despite these increases, French military leaders felt that French military strength was less than it should be in view of German increases.[4]

Toward the end of 1913 Russia adopted a military program that would increase the number of reserve formations and strengthen her peacetime army, which had grown considerably over the previous three years.[5] Although inferior in equipment and training, the Russian peacetime army was now twice the size of the German forces – even slightly larger than the combined German and Austrian armies. In March, 1914 Austria passed a law increasing her annual military draft.[6]

The total strength of the British Expeditionary Force was only 120,000 men;[7] but Britain, characteristically, relied on her navy.

Ever since the lapse of the Russo-German Reinsurance Treaty, any serious discussion of the possible outbreak of war had drawn the attention of German military planners to the dangerous implications of a two-front war against Russia on the east and France on the west. The problem was intensified by the Franco-Russian Alliance (1893). Thereafter, timing became a crucial element for Germany in the event of a general war. In 1899 Alfred von Schlieffen, chief of the German general staff, had begun devising a plan for avoiding the heavily fortified Franco-German border by attacking France through Belgium.[8] The object was to crush France quickly before the slow-moving Russians could reach German borders from the east. Despite the bold conception of the plan, there was a certain ambivalence in German military attitudes and planning, a confusion of audacity and caution.

---

[1]Fischer, 1967, p. 35.
[2]*Ibid.*, p. 36.
[3]*Ibid.*
[4]Albertini, 1952, I:551.
[5]Ritter, 1956, pp. 141–178.
[6]Barnett, 1966, p. 38.
[7]Ritter, 1956, pp. 153–157.
[8]Fischer, 1967, p. 37.

Even the basic memorandum of 1905, which presented Schlieffen's "enticing and gigantic vision," contained undertones of "doubt and pessimism." In line with the experience of earlier conquerors, Schlieffen wrote, the Germans would find in attacking France that aggressive war consumed the energy and resources of the invading power while tending to strengthen the defending country. Success therefore depended upon a rapid German advance. If French forces were allowed to retreat beyond a limited distance toward Paris, the situation would "lead to an endless war."[9] "This concentration on the west made Germany's plans entirely dependent on the Austro-Hungarian army, which would have to hold the first Russian thrust until the German army had won its anticipated victory in the west and could turn east."[10] German ambivalence in this matter was aggravated when Moltke became chief of the general staff. Moltke himself, when he was being considered as Schlieffen's successor in 1905, confessed to Bülow that he was "too reflective," "too scrupulous," "too conscientious," and too lacking in "the power of rapid decision" for the post to which he was in due course appointed.[11] In spite of all its "tremendous implications and consequences," the Schlieffen Plan was never—during the nine years after it was drafted (1905)—"the subject of a general conference" by the German government or "the subject of formal approval by the Kaiser, chancellor, and foreign secretary."[12]

A memorandum of December 12, 1912, prepared by Ludendorff and signed by Moltke, declared that Germany was no longer comparable with Russia as a land power or with Britain as a sea power. She would therefore have to employ all the resources at her disposal in order to maintain the relative position she enjoyed before other nations had built their forces to their current level.[13]

Moltke estimated that on mobilization "the enemies of Germany and Austria would have a superiority of 12 army corps."[14] On May 12, 1914 the Austrian field marshal Conrad asked Moltke how long it would be after the outbreak of a two-front war against Russia and France before German armies would be able to support Austria's forces in the east. Moltke hoped to be "finished with France in six weeks after the commencement of operations, or at least to have got so far" that main German forces could then be transferred to the east.[15] Moltke considered that a German settlement with Britain was not likely. In the event of a major war, Britain would join France and Russia. Any further delay in an outbreak of war, Moltke thought, now

---

[9]Ritter, 1956, pp. 153–157.
[10]Fischer, 1967, p. 37.
[11]Barnett, 1966, p. 20.
[12]*Ibid.*
[13]*Ibid.*, p. 37.
[14]*Ibid.*
[15]Conrad, 1922, III:674.

reduced German chances, "for we cannot compete with Russia when it is a question of masses."[16]

In May, 1914 Moltke drafted a message to Bethmann-Hollweg that was to be the basis for a proposal to the Kaiser for strengthening German forces (although the message was never sent). The message claimed that increases in German military capabilities recommended earlier by the General Staff had still not been implemented; as a result, Germany's relations with her potential enemies had taken "a decided turn for the worse."[17] Germany's relations in the Balkans had undergone a complete alteration during the two Balkan wars, and Austria could not be depended upon for effective action in support of Germany. A future war would present a threat to Germany's survival. Therefore, it would be necessary to train every able-bodied man for military duty.[18]

The German ambassador in St. Petersburg reported on June 13 that Russia had been "making exertions for the strengthening of her defensive power" such as had never been made by any other country, and was now expecting France — through introduction of a three-year service system — to also strengthen her army.[19]

According to Sir Edward Grey, in retrospect, the object of the armaments race had been the security of each of the powers, but perversely, "instead of a sense of security there had been produced a sense of fear which was yearly increasing." Sir Edward thought that "exceptional expenditure on armaments, carried to an excessive degree, must lead to catastrophe" and even "sink the ship of European prosperity and civilization."[20] Preparations for war among the major powers "had produced fear," which predisposed the course of events toward "violence and catastrophe."[21] The forces making for these increases and for the feelings of fear and hostility were "really beyond control."[22]

Against such a background of mounting pressures, increasing armaments, and interlocking alliances, an incident wherever vital interests collided (especially in the Balkans) was likely to trigger a major war. Possibilities still remained for the exercise of political will to avoid such an outcome. But in view of the past, it did not seem likely that European leaders would be able to devise any long-term solution.

On June 28 the Archduke Francis Ferdinand was assassinated in Sarajevo. Austro-Hungarian leaders immediately associated the tragic

---

[16]*Ibid.,* p. 597; Fischer, 1967, p. 49.
[17]Germany, Reichsarchiv, 1930, Supplement to Vol. I, No. 65, pp. 192–193.
[18]Kautsky, 1924, pp. 53–54.
[19]Pourtalès to Bethmann-Hollweg, No. 1, St. Petersburg, June 13, 1914, in Kautsky, 1924, p. 53.
[20]Grey, 1925, II:271.
[21]*Ibid.*
[22]Woodward, 1935, p. 426.

event with the Pan-Slavic movement and with Russia. Serbia was perceived as part of a Slavic conspiracy and a direct threat to the empire. This time Austria was determined to punish Serbia "no matter what the cost"—by armed invasion if necessary. Once this determination had been made, events compounded rapidly to the outbreak of World War I.[23]

---

[23]See Ole Holsti, 1971.

Part III

10 Theory and Method of Analysis

In Part III we use statistical analysis as a probe into the processes of expansion, competition, and conflict in order to be able to identify some of the long-range antecedents of war. Our concern is not with specific events, such as the actual outbreak of war, but rather with general trends — the constellation of factors that may alter the range of possible national decisions in critical ways, enhance the predisposition toward conflict and violence, and thus produce conditions conducive to war. We have proceeded from the view that no single factor generates conflict among nations, but that conflict is the result of a complex network of causes.[1] In this chapter we shall describe our approach and touch on its problems.

We have developed and estimated a system of simultaneous equations (Table 10-1) to operationalize the model described in Chapter 1 (Table 1-1). Using the resulting coefficients, we simulated the entire system over time. The simulations (and attendant forecasts) then became the foundation for an experiment in the analysis of policy, which was designed to identify the most likely consequences of alternative policies in similar circumstances. Our approach is based on the assumption that progress in the building and testing of theory lies with the use of several tools and the frequent comparison of findings with "common sense" views of reality. In fact, the very elusiveness of reality provides a powerful argument for using several kinds of analysis. Both the historical approach (which concentrates on unique events) and the social-scientific approach (which concentrates on statistical trends), if used with caution, can complement each other. Unique events, however dramatic, may be only the visible peaks of

---

[1] See Bertalanffy, 1968; Alker, 1969; and Gurr, 1972.

icebergs in currents of change; both the historical and social-scientific approaches may be required for a complete picture.

Implicit in the propositions in Chapter 1 is the idea that significant changes in any fundamental attribute of a major power will affect the behavior of that nation toward other states and thus alter the overall relations among major powers. Any growth (or decline) in population, technology, production, or military capability in one nation will therefore influence international affairs in important ways. We would expect this condition to hold true *without regard to the values, motivations, or goals giving rise to change.* Also implicit in our propositions is the idea that differences in the levels (or rates of change) of critical attributes — or differences in access to basic resources — give rise to competition for survival, influence, status, prestige, security, and so forth.

The complexity of the international system gives rise to the problem of how one is to decide what factors are relevant. If almost anything might have some bearing on the matter at hand, what criteria exist for excluding some factors and examining others? Will not the selection of variables, measures, and method of analysis, or the inclusion of certain data at the expense of other, bias the outcome? The answer is clearly yes. However, all explanations are to some extent partial; the object must be to attain parsimony without oversimplification. Theory, hypotheses, experimentation, and knowledge of history can all be used to provide guidelines for deciding which factors ought to be included and which excluded. Nevertheless, all guidelines are subject to continual scrutiny and modification, and therefore, conclusions themselves are inevitably conditional.

In order to make any progress, there is a fundamental need for investigations that can be replicated. The requirement of replication imposes certain requirements on theory, data, and methods. At a minimum, the theory must be reducible to a manageable number of defensible propositions, and relations must be *operationally* defined so that they can be tested and, whenever possible, falsified. There are comparable requirements for data. "If we cannot combine and aggregate, with due attention to the matter of relevant differences, we cannot make empirical generalizations; and in the absence of such generalizations, we may generate a great deal of speculation, but blessed little theory."[2] The methodology must not only be capable of ordering and managing the data in ways that will test the theory, it must also perform these functions according to procedures that are so defined and standardized that any number of investigators can apply them. Given the current state of systematic inquiry in the social sciences, the importance of precise formulation cannot be over-

---

[2]Singer, 1969a, p. 77. See also C. A. McClelland, 1955, 1960, and 1961.

emphasized. It is as important for the study of international relations as any other study of human behavior. There is almost always more than one theoretical explanation for a situation, and choices between explanations require more empirical evidence than yet exists.

We have tried to account for the interaction of nations in terms of the levels (and rates of change) of certain national attributes (population, technology, military budgets, and so forth). We are not concerned here with the role of political elites or their decisions in international relations. Rather, we employ statistical methods to examine trends in historical processes, at the same time recognizing that each datum may be viewed as the trace of a human decision.

The operationalization of conceptual variables, particularly the selection of appropriate measures, was a difficult problem for us. In Chapter 1 (Table 1-1) we presented what we believe are the connections between our theoretical concepts and the operational variables we have chosen to represent these concepts. At best, the variables and measures are approximations. It would be an error of great magnitude to assume that each variable's measure is an accurate representation of the social process being considered. We have chosen, for example, to represent expansion in the nineteenth and early twentieth centuries by one of its principal modes: *colonial* expansion, measured by total colonial territory. Although this measure provides only a first-order approximation of expansion, we believe it is a better approximation than others—at least for the historical period in our present study.

Similar difficulties were encountered in selecting an operational variable for technology. No one has yet devised a satisfactory measure of human knowledge and skills. Initially, we used iron-and-steel production, but this choice proved difficult to justify theoretically, and it yielded uneven results.[3] We then substituted national income, which was somewhat easier to justify, particularly since economists and others have often observed that technology correlates highly with economic output. Nations with comparatively high levels of national income (gross national product) do tend to have comparatively high levels of technology. Nonetheless, a considerable discrepancy may exist between the concept 'technology' and our measure; moreover, another measure might have altered our findings somewhat. Similarly, the use of a multiplicative term, population times national income, to represent the interactive effect of a growing population and an advancing technology may also be less than ideal, although as an approximation of the effect the measure appears to be adequate. The same reservations apply to all other variables in our equations. Overall,

---

[3]Iron-and-steel production was retained as a measure of technology for Austria-Hungary, for which no longitudinal series for national income was available (see Appendix A).

the type of analysis reported in this book would be somewhat improved if more precise measures could be devised, particularly for state and empire "behavior." An enormous amount of work needs to be done on the definition and testing of measures.[4]

In this connection, the question of data is also important. Obviously, metric or "hard" data are preferable to metricized or "soft" data. Metric data are naturally measurable phenomena, such as population, men under arms, national income, and military expenditures. Although the sources for such data may be inconsistent or otherwise in error, the units are readily definable — one man, one dollar — and amenable to aggregation. Most of the measures used in this study are metric, but we have not avoided the use of metricized data. In general, metricizing involves systematically assigning numerical values to essentially subjective concepts. In our study "intensity-of-intersections" and "violence-behavior" are metricized variables.[5]

In our ongoing investigations we are trying to identify in a systematic way the long-range factors that account for international violence. In the particular study reported here we have sought to analyze historical trends that set the stage for the outbreak of war in 1914. We believe the most important of these were national expansion, conflicts of national interests resulting from expansion (expressed as "intersections"), military expenditures (and arms competition), alliances, and violence-behavior of nations. Each of these factors is a *dependent variable* in an equation; together they provide a system of simultaneous equations, which is our operational model for exploring the dynamics of international violence. Figure 10-1 illustrates the relationship of the variables in the system. Those variables in boxes are the dependent variables and are *endogenous* to the system; those with no box around them are *exogenous*. An arrow away from a variable (whether boxed or unboxed) indicates that the variable is an *inde-*

---

[4]For example, expansion might also be measured by overseas troops or military bases, foreign trade, foreign investments, and so forth. Violence-behavior could be measured by casualties inflicted and/or suffered, although this would ignore the potential for violence in a country's "normal" activities — casualties might serve as a useful measure for violence in times of war but generally not during peacetime. Similar comments would pertain to the other measures.

[5]A major difficulty in the social sciences is framing useful hypotheses that do not rely entirely on metricized data for testing. Psychological and psycho-political theories involving such concepts as fear, frustration, and hostility are particularly dependent on artificially constructed data, i.e., numerical values that have been assigned to phenomena through some controlled method of (essentially subjective) scaling. In some of the social sciences the tendency is so strong toward building and testing theory in terms requiring soft data that possibilities for using relatively "hard" data (such as population, GNP, budgets and expenditures, flows and distributions of resources) are minimized or even overlooked. This tendency often gives rise to "units" that cannot be measured (or at least widely agreed on), and therefore theories that cannot be tested universally.

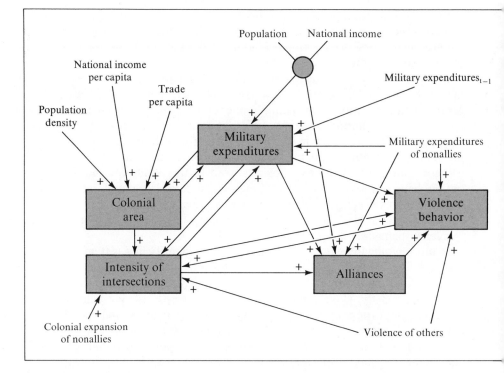

Figure 10-1. Dynamics of international violence: the model. See Table 1-1 for an explanation of the conceptual model.

pendent variable in an equation estimating the dependent (endogenous) variable at the head of the arrow.[6]

Table 10-1 gives the equations that operationalize the system in Figure 10-1. By specifying a system of *simultaneous equations* we are able to take into account the dynamic nature of the real world with its interdependent and reciprocal processes — the dependent variable of one equation can be treated as an independent variable in other equations. The equations were derived from extensive experimentation with data on Britain for the period 1870–1914. Thus, the application of the

---

[6]Each of the five endogenous variables is considered a dependent variable in only one equation — the equation in which it appears on the left side of the equal sign — but may be used as an independent variable in other equations in the system. Variables that are endogenous to the system (model) are to be "explained" by the model. (In this book the five endogenous variables are also termed "jointly dependent" variables.) The exogenous variables help explain the endogenous variables but are not themselves to be explained by the model. They are therefore "exterior" to the system of exogenous variables and are *always* independent.

Table 10-1. System of simultaneous equations used to represent the dynamics of international violence (italic indicates variables endogenous to the system).

---

colonial area $= \alpha_1 + \beta_1$ (population density) $+ \beta_2$ (national income per capita) $+ \beta_3$ (trade per capita) $+ \beta_4$ (*military expenditures*) $+ \mu_1$.

intensity-of-intersections $= \alpha_2 + \beta_5$ (*colonial area*) $+ \beta_6$ (*military expenditures*) $+ \beta_7$ (colonial-area-of-nonallies) $+ \beta_8$ (*violence-behavior*) $+ \beta_9$ (violence-of-others) $+ \mu_2$.

military expenditures $= \alpha_3 + \beta_{10}$ (*military expenditures$_{t-1}$*) $+ \beta_{11}$ (military-expenditures-of-nonallies) $+ \beta_{12}$ (*intensity-of-intersections*) $+ \beta_{13}$ (*colonial area*) $+ \beta_{14}$ (population-times-national-income) $+ \mu_3$.

alliances $= \alpha_4 + \beta_{15}$ (*military expenditures*) $+ \beta_{16}$ (*intensity-of-intersections*) $+ \beta_{17}$ (military-expenditures-of-nonallies) $+ \beta_{18}$ (population-times-national-income) $+ \mu_4$.

violence-behavior $= \alpha_5 + \beta_{19}$ (*intensity-of-intersections*) $+ \beta_{20}$ (*military expenditures*) $+ \beta_{21}$ (military-expenditures-of-nonallies) $+ \beta_{22}$ (*alliances*) $+ \beta_{23}$ (violence-of-others) $+ \mu_5$.

colonial area = in thousand square miles
population = home population, in thousands
population density = home population divided by home area (in thousand square miles)
national income = in thousand US dollars standardized to 1901–1910 = 100
trade = imports plus exports, in thousand US dollars standardized to 1901–1910 = 100
military expenditures = army plus navy allocations, in thousand US dollars standardized to 1901–1910 = 100
nonallies = dummy variable representing dyadic relationship: 1 if two states are not formally allied, 0 if they are
alliances = number of formal alliances
violence-behavior = metricized variable (from 1 to 30) representing the highest intensity of violence of the behavior of the *actor state toward all other states*
violence-of-others = metricized variable (from 1 to 30) representing the highest intensity of violence of the behavior *of all other states toward the actor state*
intensity-of-intersections = metricized variable (from 1 to 30) representing the highest intensity of violence in *specifically colonial conflicts between the actor state and other major powers*
population-times-national-income = multiplicative variable representing the interactive effect of home population and national income
$\alpha_1 \ldots \alpha_5 =$ constant (or intercept) term
$\mu_1 \ldots \mu_5 =$ error (or disturbance) term

Instrument list: iron and steel production, pig iron production, government expenditures, merchant marine tonnage, military expenditures of nonallies, colonial area of nonallies, population density, population times national income, national income per capita, trade per capita, intensity-of-intersections$_{t-1}$, violence behavior$_{t-1}$, violence of others, alliances$_{t-1}$, wheat production, coal production.

---

equations to the other five nations in our study can be considered as independent tests of the model.

Our findings from each equation (applied to the six nations in turn) will be discussed separately in the following chapters. This separate discussion of the variables is for purposes of presentation only. *Each of the five equations discussed separately in the following chapters should be understood to be embedded in a system of equations.*

With simultaneous equations, simple regression analysis in the form of single-equation estimation (ordinary least-squares) is not appropriate. We have employed a combination of generalized least squares and two-stage least squares (described in Appendix B). All statistical results reported in this book, including the regression coefficient estimates, are derived by this combined procedure. All regression methods test the extent to which the dependent variable can be explained by the independent variables in an equation. In our equation specifying the determinants of military expenditures, for example, we postulate that the allocations of one nation are determined in part by the allocations of nonallies, by the intensity of intersections of national interests, by previous military expenditures, and by the combined effects of population and technology. In other words, the dependent variable is a function of these independent variables—together with the constant term and the error or disturbance term (see Table 10-1).

The constant term, α, represents the intercept of the regression function. The constant, like all coefficients in these equations, is an unknown parameter, the value of which is estimated from empirical data. This term can be interpreted substantively as the value of the dependent variable when the values of all independent variables are zero. In many cases the constant may be interpreted as the inertia of the dependent variable, set during the period *before* the initial point of our analysis.

The disturbance term, μ, represents the errors encountered in analysis. There are three major sources of error: (a) misspecification of the functional and structural nature of the equation; (b) systematic measurement error in the data, and (c) random factors or chance.[7] For purposes of estimation it is desirable to minimize the error term. Appendix B indicates the ways in which we have detected significant

---

[7]However, error may also come from data *sources*. Even the standard sources of demographic, production, budgetary, and other data are often inconsistent, and errors and inconsistencies within single sources are not uncommon. The base and criteria for the definition, selection, and compilation of data in one source often change from year to year, sometimes without explanation or even indication. For example, a source may list the area and population of northern Algeria in some editions as components of data on France and in other editions as "colonial" data. Similarly, military reserves and militia may for a number of years be included in the category "men under arms," then suddenly be dropped or shifted to a separate category. We have made adjustments wherever possible to achieve consistency. Thoughtless transcription of data without such care can lead to serious problems.

error and the steps taken to correct for serial correlation in the disturbances.

Statistical analysis of the sort undertaken here is appropriate only for the investigation of relationships of aggregate data. Our data are recorded at annual intervals, so that the methods of analysis used here do not capture day-to-day or other short-range change. Statistical investigations, *insofar as they deal with time-series or longitudinal analysis*, are suitable for the analysis of trends, regularities, and patterns, but not for discrete events.

Regression analysis rests largely on the notions of explained and unexplained variance. The first refers to the extent to which estimated values for the dependent variable — calculated by summing the products of each independent variable and its associated estimated coefficient — coincide with historical data. The second notion refers to the residual, i.e., that portion of the variance in the dependent variable unaccounted for by the independent variables. The higher the amount of variance in the dependent variable accounted for by the independent variables, the greater our confidence in the equation is likely to be — providing, of course, that the coefficients are sharply delineated and are not attributed soley to chance or random factors.[8]

Our investigation has proceeded from these central notions: transformation of the system, phase shifts, and breakpoints. Transformation of the system refers to changes in the *dominant types of relationships* in the system at any point in time — for example, a transformation in the dominant mode of system behavior from expansion to military competition and arms races. Such a transition would mean important changes in the dynamics and type of conflict characteristic of the system. It would not mean that the dynamics of expansion had ceased, but rather that the behavior of the system would now be better-explained by factors other than expansion. The notion of phase shifts is another way of conceptualizing such changes.

Breakpoints are discrete points at which transformations can be identified. They may be viewed in either of two ways: as changes in trend-lines due to nonlinear relationships, or, more commonly, as evidence of change in the system. Such breaks represent changes in the relationships among the variables, which can be either the result of unique events or the cumulative effect of minor changes. In either case, when the change is marked enough, it is referred to as "statistically significant," that is, the magnitude of the coefficients preceding the break may be expected to differ from either those following the break or those of the entire set of observations. We use the Chow test

---

[8]In statistical terms, the regression algorithms involve minimizing the sum of the squared residuals around the regression line. This is the conventional least-square algorithm we have employed, with appropriate modification, as the basis for our statistical analysis (see Appendix B).

to determine the statistical significance of the difference between any two sets of coefficient estimates, and hence the extent to which a transformation of the system (whether hypothesized on theoretical or historical grounds) is statistically significant.[9] In some cases our expectations have been verified; in others they have not. The Chow test is therefore a useful device for guarding against erroneous inferences. Changes in the nature of the coefficients of the nonlinearities involved in time-series data are rarely intuitively obvious. The determination of breakpoints is not predicted entirely from an examination of the data; it depends even more strongly on theoretical specifications of changes in the dynamics of the system.

The issue of time is extremely important in longitudinal analysis. In many instances we are not sure of the time lag—the length of time between a change in a given independent variable (or set of independent variables) and its effect that registers as a change in the dependent variable. This problem is illustrated by our formulation of the dynamics of military expenditures, where we hypothesize that the level of military expenditures during one year is an important determinant of the next year's expenditures. We are not certain that one year is an accurate representation of lag in this case, nor are we entirely certain that a lag exists at all. Whatever lag we do propose is hypothetical, and its validity can only be determined through systematic analysis of the quantitative data.

We have not specified any other lags in our equations (see Table 10-1 and Figure 10-1). This is not because we believe that lags do not operate in the real world—almost certainly they do. The difficulties are: (1) the postulated lag might be inconsistent with the yearly measurement grid, in which case action and reaction, although separate in time, would be measured simultaneously; (2) errors accumulated as a result of erroneous specification of lag structure are likely to be considerable. It seemed unnecessary to introduce such problems into our initial analysis, except in the case of military expenditures, where incrementalist theories of budgetary processes explicitly postulate a one-year lag.

Another important consideration in longitudinal analysis is the question of interdependence among discrete observations. The existence of interdependence violates a critical assumption underlying causal modeling and regression analysis, namely, that successive observations

---

[9]When breakpoints essentially amount to nonlinearities, these can theoretically be captured by nonlinear functions. In practice, however, the exact nature of the nonlinearities is difficult to determine. Breakpoints may also occur at different places in the individual equations of a simultaneous system. In our model—except in the case of the alliance equation, where a breakpoint was predicted in 1896 for historical reasons—the same theoretical breakpoint was tested for *all* equations for each country. In this way, certain of the statistical artifacts associated with a purely data-generated criterion were avoided.

are not dependent on one another. When this assumption is violated, another source of error is added—further necessitating correction of the estimates obtained. This issue is one further element in the problem of measurement error discussed earlier (and more extensively in Appendix B).

In the introduction we argued that levels *and* rates of change in national attributes may be of central importance to setting the level of international violence. In an earlier stage of our analysis we focused exclusively on rate of change for all the variables; however, our estimated coefficients tended to wash out, yielding few statistically significant coefficients. Subsequently, we found that more robust (and statistically significant) estimates of the endogenous variables could be obtained by using only levels. *The results of this analysis, using levels only, are presented here.* For the most part, the estimated coefficients are sharply delineated, and we were able to discriminate with great confidence between those factors that met our expectations of significance and those that did not. This state of affairs is not in itself sufficient to validate (or even adequately test) our hypotheses; however, it does indicate that rates of change are not the most effective way of accounting for the processes we are seeking to understand. (Nonetheless, the rate of change of a particular variable may well be explained by the *level* of another.)

The specific relationships that concern us can be expressed in the form of equations that are expected to fit empirical data. The statistical measures employed to determine the extent to which an equation "fits" historical data include: (a) R^2, the amount of variance in the dependent variable accounted for by the independent variables;[10] (b) the magnitude of both the unstandardized and standardized ("beta," or path)

---

[10]Variance, or the square of the standard deviation, is defined as the average of the squared deviations from the "predicted" value. In its simplest form, it can be written

$$S^2 = \sum_{i=1}^{N} \frac{(Y_i - \overline{Y})^2}{N}.$$

In regression analysis (as in analysis of variance), total variance is divided into two portions: explained variance and unexplained variance. If Y_i = the dependent variable, $\overline{Y}$ = the value of Y that would be predicted given no other information (that is, its mean), and Y_{ip} = the value of Y_i that would be predicted knowing the value of the independent variables (that is, the value on the least-squares regression line), it can be demonstrated that

$$\sum_{i=1}^{N} (Y_i - \overline{Y})^2 = \sum_{i=1}^{N} (Y_i - Y_{ip})^2 + \sum_{i=1}^{N} (Y_{ip} - \overline{Y})^2$$

which, dividing by N, is equivalent to: total variance equals unexplained variance plus explained variance. One principal aim of regression analysis is to reduce the unexplained variance. R^2 is in effect a measure of how successful one has been—it is the ratio of the explained variance to the total variance. See Blalock, 1960, especially pp. 295–299, for further detail.

coefficients; (c) the significance of the individual coefficients, as indicated by the t statistic;[11] and (d) the statistical significance of the equation as a whole, as indicated by the F ratio for the regression. Other important statistics include the partial-correlation coefficient (summarizing the correlation between any one independent variable and the dependent variable, while controlling for other independent variables in the equation); the Durbin-Watson statistic, d, which provides some indication of the degree of first-order serial correlation (ρ) in the error or disturbance term (the estimate of ρ can be obtained by computing $1 - \frac{1}{2}d$; and the Chow test, yielding an appropriate F ratio, which compares two sets of regression coefficients for two time periods.[12] The presentation of data is often a matter of taste and preference. Our objective is to provide the "quantitatively inclined" reader with as much of the relevant statistics as is required for a sophisticated understanding of our procedures. In consideration of other readers, however, much of this evidence is included in footnotes and tables.

One may object that statistical methods are not much more than sleight-of-hand techniques by which data are made to fit curves that may mislead as effectively as they may catch the untutored eye. It is well-known that statistics can tell spectacular and often dangerous lies. The purpose here is not merely to "fit curves," however, but to test our propositions against quantitative data as well as history itself. The fit is never perfect, of course, and a major purpose of any statistical analysis is to identify discrepancies between theoretical expectations and empirical findings.

In the course of these investigations we encountered two important questions and, as a result, a difficulty in methodology. Could we deter-

---

[11]Our usage of the t statistic to derive a significance level does not strictly conform to the usage of significance tests, since we do not have a random sample from which we wish to generalize to a population. The test is appropriate, however, as a general decision rule for accepting and rejecting hypotheses, in the sense that similar decisions would be likely to hold in another body of data. We are grateful to Douglas A. Hibbs for clarifying this point.

[12]These statistics are discussed in some detail in Appendix B. Briefly, the values of the coefficients yield a predictive equation (or transformation) that maps the values of the independent variables into one (predicted) value for the dependent variable. The beta coefficients standardize this value to improve comparability across equations, showing how many *standard deviations* of change in the dependent variable can be expected as a result of one standard deviation of change in a particular independent variable (holding all other independent variables constant). Thus, by definition, the beta coefficient of a constant will always be 0, although its actual size (and significance) may be considerable. The tables in Chapters 11–15 report the R^2, F ratio, and corrected d statistics (in additon to the nature of the correction employed) for each equation, along with the coefficient estimate, beta coefficient, t statistic (with significance level), and partial-correlation coefficient for each independent variable *significant at or above the .05 level* (in some cases we also report the .10 level results). In addition, the Chow test result (along with significance level) is reported for most subperiods, noting whether coefficients for a subperiod differ significantly from those of the full period (1871–1914). Significance levels are denoted here by p (for example, $p = .01$ means that the statistic in question is statistically significant at or above the .01 level).

mine which country was most strongly affecting another over a particular period of time? If this were determined, how successfully could we ascertain the level or extent of the effect? These problems emerged because, with 45 time-points in the data, the statistical analysis suffered more constraints with each increase in the number of independent variables, breakpoints, and phase shifts.[13] Thus, if we wished to identify which nation was directly affecting which, we would have had to enter into each equation the growth, expansion, or competitive activity of all powers as explanatory variables for the behavior of each other power—a procedure we initially followed with "long-form" equations. However, this meant an awkward increase in the number of independent variables required to explain the variance in each dependent variable, which greatly reduced the possibility of obtaining valid coefficients. Despite frequent convergence between this earlier output and theoretical expectations, the results were statistically so weak that they will not be reported here.[14] We then developed "short-form" equations in which one independent variable combined data from all those nations with which the nation under analysis was *not* allied (by use of the dummy variable "nonallies," see Table 10-1). Parenthetically, the coefficient estimates for the other independent variables did not differ markedly between short and long forms of the equations, although significance levels dropped with the reduction in degrees of freedom.

The same model has been tested on each of the six great powers in our study. Undoubtedly, it would have been possible to account for considerably more of the variance by devising distinct models for each country. Our purpose, however, is to see how well *one* general model can account for the behavior of all six nations.[15] Few of the findings presented here will be as simple as the propositions in the introduction may have led the reader to expect. This only reconfirms the fact that reality is more complex than theory—empirical findings are more differentiated and particularized than even operational formulations. In addition, we are profoundly aware that we do not have a complete theory. Our purpose in Part III is to test some *specific links*, and thereby probe the underlying structure of the model (Fig. 10–1).

We have tested for the statistical significance of each of the five equations in our model as well as each variable in each equation. The strength of postulated links among the variables in the model is thus

---

[13]Although our *data* are for the 45-year period 1870–1914, the existence of a lagged variable in the equation for military expenditures necessitated estimation of all equations for the 44-year period 1871–1914.

[14]This weakness resulted from both the loss of degrees of freedom and the multi-colinearity induced by the known tendency of some data (such as military expenditures) to increase with time.

[15]We experimented with several models in the early phases of our work; the present model stems from that experimentation. See Choucri and North, 1969.

examined empirically. Often a high R^2 is generated by only a few statistically significant variables; in such a case our inferences tend to rest more on the statistical significance of a few variables than on that of the equation as a whole.

The more general a theory—as ours clearly is—the more difficult it is to verify empirically, and the less parsimonious is the effort. We are caught in the classic triangle of problems: verification, parsimony, and empirical fit. A theory as general as ours cannot be tested adequately in a single study. In our work presented in this book we have tested some specific aspects of the propositions in Chapter 1. Our findings are reported in the next seven chapters.

Expansion: Colonial Area

11

In the introduction lateral pressure was regarded as the outcome of the interaction of a society's demands and capabilities. Although it can take different forms, this phenomenon is essentially the extension of a nation's activities outside territorial boundaries. During the period 1870–1914 the dominant mode of such extension among the European great powers was colonial acquisitions, which we have measured by the *colonial area* governed or controlled by each nation (disregarding "spheres of influence.")[1] Our initial expectation was that lateral pressure would be explained in large part by a power's population growth and advances in technology, both of which contribute to demands for resources that must be satisfied in some fashion. But the military establishment might also be expected to play an important role, both through its demands for resources and because conquest, colonial administration, the policing of native peoples, and the protection of sea lanes provide admiralties and ministries of war with careers, measures of success, and *raisons d'etre*.

Although we have included foreign trade, itself an important manifestation of lateral pressure, as an independent variable contributing to colonial expansion, it presents a number of particularly perplexing problems in conceptualization and analysis, and thus remains subject to future refinement or reconsideration. For example, it might be preferable to distinguish between import activities, as a mode of lateral pressure concerned with the acquisition of resources, and export activities, as involving the search for markets (although, of course, the two are closely linked.) This study does not focus on the dynamics of

---

[1]Colonial area includes all territories controlled by a nation *beyond its boundaries*. Stated in these terms, Russia presented some difficulties, since it expanded largely by enlarging its national boundaries over contiguous territory (see Appendix A). In this study we have not included other manifestations of expansion, such as investments, extraterritorial privilege, and the like.

trade; therefore, such conceptual refinements were postponed for future analysis.

The colonial-area equation, which emerged after considerable experimentation, should be considered as still partial in its formulation. Initially, we experimented with alternative functional forms. When a satisfactory equation was obtained, we then examined the residuals, introduced breakpoints, reestimated the coefficients, and determined the extent to which these shifts in dynamics were statistically significant. In that connection, the residuals—the difference between historical (actual) and estimated (predicted) values of the dependent variable—contained important information pertaining to shifts in dynamics.

Two basic questions must still be raised: to what extent does this particular formulation as a whole fit empirical data for each of the six powers (to what extent does it approximate reality), and to what extent are the individual terms (that is, the postulated relationships) statistically significant? In addition, important methodological problems must be dealt with, such as the high correlations among the explanatory variables, and also among the disturbance (error) terms. These issues are addressed in Chapter 10 and Appendix B.

Our postulated dynamics of late nineteenth and early twentieth-century national expansion are depicted on the next page. Omitted from the diagram are two factors: the intercept or constant, and the error term. As indicated in Chapter 10, the constant refers to how we would expect the dependent variable (colonial area) to be accounted for *if all the other explanatory variables were zero*. Generally, we would expect the constant term to be greater in the *latter* part of the period under study, i.e., once colonial expansion had been established. In the case of Britain and other powers whose expansion began well before 1870, we would expect the constant to be large and statistically significant throughout the entire period.

The second element omitted from the diagram is the error term (the implications of which were noted in Chapter 10). It is critical to obtain error terms that are as small as possible, either by reanalyzing the data so as to obtain a more correct equation, or by employing statistical methods for purging the analysis of the distorting effects of such errors.

The reader is reminded of these considerations because they bear directly on the results presented from here on, and because both the constant and error terms contain information that is of great importance for interpreting results in Part III.[2]

In the period 1870–1914 all the major powers were increasing the level of their demands and improving their capabilities, but from dif-

---

[2]For the sake of parsimony, actual values of coefficient estimates, beta coefficients, t statistics (with significance level), and partial correlations have been reported in Table 11-1 only for all statistically significant coefficients, along with R^2, F ratio, Durbin-Watson statistics, and results of the Chow test for the equation as a whole. The same format is followed in subsequent tables reporting the results of equations.

Hypothesized Dynamics of Expansion

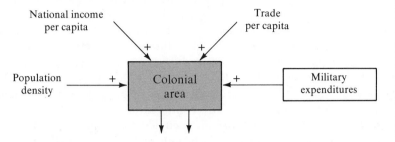

This is represented by the following equation:

$$\text{colonial area} = \alpha_1 + \beta_1 \text{ (home population density)} +$$
$$\beta_2 \text{ (national income per capita)} +$$
$$\beta_3 \text{ (trade per capita)} +$$
$$\beta_4 \text{ (military expenditures)} + \mu_1.$$

The two arrows *from* the colonial area variable indicate that colonial area is an explanatory (independent) variable in two other equations. Throughout our analysis expansion (colonial area) is represented by its logarithmic transformation. This form is more consistent with the dynamics postulated in the introduction in that the independent variables amount to a composite exponent of the dependent variable. Thus, the original theoretical equation is in the form: lateral pressure $= e^x$, where x refers to demands and capabilities, the measures of which are population, national income, trade, and military expenditures. (In the case of Austria-Hungary, for which a national-income series is not available, we employ iron-and-steel production as a measure of technology.)

ferent bases and at unequal rates of change. Thus, all were generating some lateral pressure, and most of them tended to manifest this pressure in colonial expansion. The powers that expanded most rapidly were also those that were growing most rapidly in domestic population and/or technology. Two of the powers, Britain and Russia, extended their territorial holdings at a fairly uniform rate over the whole 45-year period; between 1870 and 1884 these were the only two powers expanding substantially in colonial area. France had acquired considerable expanses of territory prior to 1870, but during the first decade and a half following the Franco-Prussian War and the loss of Alsace-Lorraine her holdings remained essentially constant.

In 1870 Britain had already achieved world preeminence in territorial possession, but she was still growing domestically on critical dimensions and successfully expanding her foreign activities, interests, and colonial holdings. At that time the British Empire contained about 9, 107,000 square miles of territory, an expanse roughly comparable to the total area of North America (9,300,000 square miles). By 1914 she had increased her territory to 12,554,000 square miles, almost equal the size of the entire continent of Europe.

Between 1870 and 1884 Britain occupied Egypt and extended her activities and interests into the Fiji Islands and elsewhere in the Pacific, Southeastern New Guinea, Borneo, Malaya, Burma, Afghanistan, Nigeria, the Sudan, the Gold Coast, Gambia, Sierra Leone, Bechuana-land, and East Africa. In 1875 Britain purchased Egypt's shares in the Suez Canal—a move that not only increased her activities and interests in the immediate area, but also enhanced her strategic concern for Gibraltar, the Mediterranean, the Red Sea and Persian Gulf, and, indeed, almost the whole of the Middle East.

How is this unremitting expansion of the British Empire to be explained? For the period 1871–1914, according to our quantitative analysis, only the constant term, population density, and to a lesser degree, military expenditures, were statistically significant, but these accounted for over 99 percent of the variance in colonial area. The importance of population density is readily understandable because of the impact of increased demands, but what is the meaning of the constant term?[3] It may indicate that conditions prior to 1870 were of great importance to subsequent colonial expansion, the process having already been set in motion by that time. Thereafter, expansion itself may have generated further expansion. Yet (insofar as it is correct) this finding draws attention to fundamental aspects of the process of expansion that the analysis has failed to specify: processes generated by policies and activities initiated prior to 1870, certain bureaucratic factors, the tendency of colonial holdings to encourage or facilitate the acquisition of adjoining territory, and so forth.

Although national income per capita is not statistically significant for the entire period, it and the constant account for 96 percent of the variance in colonial area prior to 1890—population density is not significant in this period. In the period after 1890 national income per capita is again no longer statistically significant, but population density

---

[3]Population density and the constant term were by far the most significant, both at the .001 level. In fact, an excellent approximation of British colonial area (in thousand square miles) could be obtained by adding 2.83 times population density to the constant 8.35, as is indicated by the "parameter estimate-unstandardized" column in Table 11-1. The beta coefficient of density is .85, whereas that of military expenditures is .13 ($p = .05$). No other terms are statistically significant.

once more is a strong contributing factor, as are military expenditures and the constant term.[4]

The tendency of national income per capita to drop out may reflect in part the failure of British industry, frequently noted by historians, to keep pace with innovations in Germany and elsewhere. The increased influence of military expenditures coincides with the Anglo-German naval race and suggests a linkage between arms competition and expansion. The importance of population density during the last decade and a half prior to the outbreak of WWI is a reminder that population growth continued to be an important factor in expansionist activities after attention had to a large extent shifted to the arms race. Nonetheless, the enormous importance of the constant suggests that these are largely variants of a process set in motion prior to 1870.

As will become evident further along, British activities and interests during the first decade and a half after 1870 tended to conflict with those of Russia somewhat more than with those of other major powers. By 1914 Russia's "colonial" territory had increased to 7,011,850 square miles. Between 1870 and 1884 she extended her activities and interests in the Balkans, in the region of the Dardanelles, in the Turkish regions of Ardahan, Kars, and Batum, in Bukhara, Khiva, Krasnovodsk, Kokand, and Merv, and in the Pacific island of Sakhalin. Later she extended her activities and interests into Persia and other parts of the Near East, and into Korea, Manchuria, and parts of China.

For the full period the constant term best explains Russian colonial area. As in the case of Britain, this suggests that Russian territorial expansion during the 45 years prior to WWI may have been in considerable part the outcome of processes set in motion prior to 1870. Some of the inertia might be explained by the usefulness of one territorial addition as a justification and staging area for further acquisitions. Territorial expansion may also stimulate additional expansion through the operations of colonial bureaucracies, in the home government as well as in "the field." Once policies are set and expansionist activities undertaken, bureaucrats at several levels of government, as well as those in industry, commerce and the military establishment, are likely to develop a vested interest in further acquisitions; past programs may therefore be retained and expanded.[5] No doubt there are further considerations along this line that would help to account for the power of the constant throughout this analysis. The two other important vari-

---

[4]Because of the overwhelming importance of the constant throughout, the Chow test shows no significant differences between the period 1891–1914 and the full period (1871–1914), while the coefficients for 1871–1890 are different only at the .10 level. Nonetheless, the beta coefficient for national income per capita is 1.17 ($p = .001$) for the period 1871–1890, whereas population density (beta $= .78$, $p = .001$) and military expenditures (beta $= .36$, $p = .005$) are significant from 1891–1914. The constant remains significant above the .001 level for all periods.

[5]Allison, 1969.

ables for the Russian data were population density and national income per capita, which, along with the remaining variables in the equation (military expenditures, trade per capita), account for 99 percent of the variance in Russian expansion for the full and the subperiods.[6]

Beginning in the mid-1880s, France and Germany began to acquire substantial overseas holdings. Of the two, France obtained the larger territory and more rapidly; one would expect France's expanding interests in many parts of the world to have collided increasingly with those of Britain. In 1870 France had overseas territory of about 217,000 square miles. Between 1870 and 1884 she extended her interests in the South Seas, in Cochin China, Annam, Tonkin, Cambodia, Tunis, northwestern Madagascar, and Somaliland. By 1914 her territorial holdings were about 4,348,000 square miles.

For the full period, 97 percent of the variance in French colonial area can be accounted for by the variables in the expansion equation. In contrast to Britain and Russia, the constant is not as strong an element in explaining French expansion for the full period. Of the variables in the equation, population density and national income per capita are the most significant. France does not fit neatly into the profile of a nation expanding because of increased population, since French population growth during the years under investigation was relatively modest. It is rather surprising, therefore, that French colonial area appears attributable more to population density than to trade per capita, or military expenditures. The importance of national income per capita, however, is entirely consistent with our expectation. It might be inferred from this that if the levels and advances of technology are sufficiently great, even relatively small increments in population may contribute significantly to demands and expansion.

For France, an important breakpoint occurred around 1900. Prior to that year the variables of the equation account for 99 percent of the variance in colonial area. For the later decades (1880–1914), the equation as a whole accounts for 98 percent of the variance, but population density and the constant are the only statistically significant elements. The latter suggests that by 1900 there was in France much the same process that characterized British territorial expansion from 1870 on—that is, expansion generated further expansion. The fact

---

[6]For Russia, as for Britain, the constant is extremely significant for the full period and the two subperiods (1871–1890 and 1891–1914), always at the .001 level. Population density is similarly important throughout (for the full period, beta = .70, p = .025; for 1871–1890, beta = 1.20, p = .001; for 1891–1914, beta = .40, p = .01). However, Russia's military expenditures are important only for the period 1871–1890 (beta = −0.36, p = .025), whereas both national income per capita (beta = .17, p = .025) and trade per capita (beta = −0.19, p = .05) exert a minor impact only for the second subperiod. There is no significant difference between the coefficient estimates for the full period and 1871–1890, but the Chow test is significant at the .001 level for differences between the full period and 1891–1914. Thus, there is a relative shift in importance of population density (in favor of increasing weight to the constant) throughout the full period.

that the technology variable (national income per capita) is not significant means that we were not successful in specifying all aspects of the
role of technology in the model for France.

In view of the vast areas into which France extended her interests
after the mid-1880s, we would expect an increasing number of conflicts
between French and British interests. This did indeed take place, but
with certain important qualifications that will be discussed in a subsequent chapter.

In Part II we noted many times Germany's prewar search for new
materials and markets. Germany did not begin acquiring colonies until
the mid-1880s (although she had seized Alsace-Lorraine as national
territory during the Franco-Prussian War). In 1883 Germany obtained
Angra Pequeña, a 10-by-24 square-mile strip in Southwest Africa, and
the following year she obtained protectorates over Southwest Africa,
Togo, and the Cameroons; in 1885 she annexed Northeast New
Guinea and the Bismarck Archipelago. Around the turn of the century she obtained leaseholds in China, purchased the Marianas and
Palau from Spain, extended her interests in the Near East, and expanded her influence in the Cameroons. During 1911 she acquired a
part of French Equatorial Africa. By 1914 German overseas possessions totaled more than 1,207,000 square miles—an area approximately one-half the expanse of Australia, but only one-tenth the size
of Britain's colonial territory.

The most statistically significant variables for Germany for the full
period are population density, the constant term, and national income
per capita. For the period after 1884, when German acquisition of
colonial territory first took place, the equation accounts for 95 percent
of the variance.[7] These findings are in line with observations made by
historians, particularly economic historians, concerning German
demographic, technological, and resource growth. The essential difference between Germany and Britain or France was that much of the
territorial expansion of Germany that might have accompanied domestic growth was externally constrained.

Over the years 1870–1914, Italy underwent considerable growth in
both population and national income per capita. During the same years
she acquired some territory (and sought much much more), but was
not able to hold on to all of it. For the full period, much of the variance
in Italian colonial area is explained by military expenditures. The

---

[7]For the full period, which includes the 14 years prior to the beginning of German
colonial expansion, the equation explains 58 percent of the variance and is significant at
the .001 level. The key variables are again population density (beta = .65 and $p = .001$
for the full period; beta = .85 and $p = .005$ for 1884–1914) and the constant (significant
at .001 level for the full period and the subperiod, although with widely divergent
values). National income per capita is significant only for the full period ($p = .005$).
Despite the similarity between periods in the particular variables that are important, the
great difference between the estimated values gives a Chow test significant at the .001
level.

Table 11-1. Colonial area—results of estimation from a simultaneous equation system.*

Country	Period	R^2	F ratio	Durbin-Watson statistic	Time-dependent correction	Chow test
BRITAIN	1871–1914	.99	10,100 $df = 4,39$ $p = .001$	1.54	AUTO2	
	1871–1890	.96	90.81 $df = 4,15$ $p = .001$	1.81	None	$F_{24,15} = 2.07$ $p = .10$
	1891–1914	.99	7668.55 $df = 4,19$ $p = .001$	1.93	AUTO2	$F_{20,19} = 1.222$ $p = $ n.s.
FRANCE	1871–1914	.97	321.39 $df = 4,39$ $p = .001$	1.36	MAV2	
	1871–1900	.99	599.262 $df = 4,25$ $p = .001$	1.76	MAV2	$F_{14,25} = 2.20$ $p = .05$
	1880–1914	.98	395.41 $df = 4,30$ $p = .001$	1.22	MAV2	$F_{9,30} = 1.95$ $p = .10$
GERMANY	1871–1914	.58	13.47 $df = 4,39$ $p = .001$	1.35	MAV2	
	1884–1914	.95	119.49 $df = 4,26$ $p = .001$	1.96	AUTO2	$F_{12,20} = 847.0$ $p = .001$

amount of variance explained is greatly increased when subperiods are analyzed—although military expenditures remains the only important variable for the period 1889–1914.[8]

In view of the very limited extent of Austrio-Hungarian colonial territory, our equation is not adequate for capturing Austro-Hungarian expansion, which was manifested largely through commercial and

---

[8]Military expenditures has a beta coefficient of .69 ($p = .001$) for the full period. Both subperiods are far more statistically significant: for 1871–1888 (Chow test significant at .025 level) the significant variables are population density (beta = .93, $p = .005$) and the constant ($p = .001$), whereas the period after a significant increase in Italian colonial area, 1889–1914 (different from the full period at .001 level), is again explained primarily by Italian military expenditures (beta = .44, $p = .005$). With such high R^2 and correspondingly low t statistics, the possibility of multicollinearity in the independent variables should not be overlooked.

Variable	Parameter Estimate		Partial correlation	t statistic	Significance level
	Unstandardized	Standardized (beta)			
Density	2.83	.85	.75	7.1	.001
Mil. Expend.	.128[a]	.13	.29	1.89	.05
Constant	8.35	.00	.99	88.7	.001
Nat. Inc. per cap.	2.96	1.17	.79	5.06	.001
Constant	9.09	.00	.99	42.4	.001
Density	1.81	.78	.75	4.9	.001
Mil. Expend.	.147[a]	.36	.56	2.9	.005
Constant	8.76	.00	.99	90.7	.001
Density	88.71	.44	.54	4.0	.001
Nat. Inc. per cap.	9.19	.35	.38	2.6	.01
Constant	−10.56	.00	−.40	−2.8	.005
Density	105.54	.51	.73	5.3	.001
Nat. Inc. per cap.	7.19	.29	.31	1.6	.10
Constant	−13.69	.00	−.62	−4.0	.001
Density	109.98	.61	.56	3.7	.001
Constant	−13.65	.00	−.44	−2.7	.005
Density	84.45	.65	.47	3.4	.001
Nat. Inc. per cap.	127.13	.53	.40	2.7	.005
Constant	−24.90	.00	−.64	−5.3	.001
Density	5.23	.85	.49	2.9	.005
Constant	5.51	.00	.94	14.5	.001

Table continued

quasimilitary activities in the Balkans. Expressed in terms of colonial area, very little Austro-Hungarian expansion took place, and hence there is almost no change in the dependent variable for the period under study.[9] In view of Austria-Hungary's growth in population and na-

---

[9]Between 1878 and 1914 the "colonial territory" of the Dual Monarchy varied slightly between 19,700 and 22,100 square miles. This left little variance for the regression analysis to explain and thus the possibilities for statistical analysis were limited. For the full period 1871–1914 the limited acquisition of territory by the Dual Monarchy was explained largely by population density. However, after 1878 only the constant term appears to be a statistically significant variable, explaining 97 percent of the variance. From Table 11-1 it is clear that other variables (population density, trade per capita, iron-and-steel production per capita, and military expenditures) have a marginal effect on the dependent variable for some periods. Nonetheless, the constant is the overwhelming factor, always significant at the .001 level. Chow tests suggest the presence of a breakpoint after 1878.

Table 11-1. Continued

Country	Period	R^2	F ratio	Durbin-Watson statistic	Time-dependent correction	Chow test
ITALY	1871–1914	.30	4.25 $df = 4,39$ $p = .01$	1.98	AUTO2	
	1871–1888	.88	22.78 $df = 4,13$ $p = .001$	2.15	AUTO2	$F_{26.16} = 2.62$ $p = .025$
	1889–1914	.70	12.25 $df = 4,21$ $p = .001$	1.88	AUTO2	$F_{8.21} = 8.03$ $p = .001$
RUSSIA	1871–1914	.99	61,400 $df = 4,39$ $p = .001$	2.08	AUTO1	
	1871–1890	.99	66,400 $df = 4,15$ $p = .001$	1.98	AUTO2	$F_{24.15} = .75$ $p = $ n.s.
	1891–1914	.99	261,000 $df = 4,19$ $p = .001$	2.18	AUTO2	$F_{20.19} = 6.57$ $p = .001$
AUSTRIA-HUNGARY	1871–1914	.26	3.46 $df = 4,39$ $p = .025$	1.93	AUTO1	
	1878–1914	.97	296.70 $df = 4,32$ $p = .001$	2.01	AUTO1	$F_{7.32} = 7848.$ $p = .001$
	1871–1890	.65	6.82 $df = 4,15$ $p = .005$	2.01	AUTO2	$F_{24.15} = 0.06$ $p = $ n.s.
	1891–1914	.99	503.62 $df = 4,19$ $p = .001$	2.08	AUTO2	$F_{20.19} = 4229.$ $p = .001$

*All statistics refer to the simultaneous-system estimates using both two-stage least squares and, where indicated in the time-dependent correction column, generalized least squares.

[a]Actual value of unstandardized parameter estimate is multiplied by 10^{-6} for scale purposes.

[b]Iron and steel production used instead of national income; see Appendix A.

tional income per capita, however, we may infer that her demands were relatively high, although she lacked sufficient capabilities for successful territorial expansion. It would be understandable therefore

Variable	Parameter Estimate		Partial correlation	*t* statistic	Significance level
	Unstandardized	Standardized (beta)			
Mil. Expend.	87.0[a]	.69	.54	4.05	.001
Density	213.31	.93	.66	3.2	.005
Constant	−52.27	.00	−.71	−3.7	.001
Mil. Expend.	31.1[a]	.44	.51	2.8	.005
Density	2.03	.70	.32	2.1	.025
Constant	15.61	.00	.999	295.12	.001
Density	12.30	1.20	.86	6.39	.001
Mil. Expend.	−.719[a]	−.36	−.50	−2.23	.025
Constant	15.33	.00	.999	311.477	.001
Density	.71	.40	.53	2.76	.01
Nat. Inc. per cap.	.26	.17	.46	2.29	.025
Trade per cap.	−2.35	−.19	−.41	−1.96	.05
Constant	15.72	.00	.9999	993.99	.001
Density	127.49	.88	.49	3.5	.001
Constant	−22.86	.00	−.48	−3.4	.001
Constant	2.87	.00	.74	6.3	.001
Density	151.76	.34	.49	2.19	.025
Trade per cap.	1477.35	.80	.66	3.36	.005
Constant	−39.48	.00	−.68	−3.55	.001
Iron + Steel per cap.[b]	−1.94	−.92	−.42	−2.05	.05
Mil. Expend.	−1.23[a]	−.30	−.34	−1.6	.10
Constant	3.11	.00	.89	8.47	.001

if Austro-Hungarian leaders, and subjects of the Dual Monarchy, experienced dissatisfaction, frustration, and a feeling of being "blocked" from adjoining regions in the Balkans.

In general, the findings of the statistical analyses reported so far are consistent with history (see Part II) and the propositions put forward in Chapter 1. Population density was confirmed as a strong element in explaining expansion. Technology, measured by national income per capita, was also important but not so consistently as our propositions assert. Military capability contributed significantly in some instances, especially for Italy. Trade emerged as a weaker influence than might have been expected from the propositions, which may be due to the conceptual ambiguities concerning the precise role of trade.[10] Clearly, this formulation does not capture all determinants of colonial expansion—as indicated by the importance in the equation of the constant term—particularly for those countries whose expansion began prior to 1870. Because of its statistical significance, the constant term may represent the outcome of an ongoing (domestic?) process not captured by the equation. It would be preferable to be able to model this process itself.

A major problem with this equation may lie in the measure employed to represent expansion. Colonial area, though undoubtedly theoretically sound, might not be the most sensitive index of the real determinants of expansion. Further experimentation with alternative measures would clearly be advisable. In addition, the determinant of the *beginnings* of expansion (i.e., the step function) has not yet been successfully captured—nor in fact is it understood. Modeling unique occurrences presents severe problems for any probabilistic (or stochastic) mechanism. Nonetheless, the importance of population density and the other independent variables supports our belief that much of the process of expansion has been captured by our theory—although in midstream.

---

[10]The impact of trade on colonial expansion is far more complex than represented here. Trade is also a manifestation of lateral pressure (and hence would be expected to grow along with colonial area, showing a positive relationship). But, if successful, it may also serve to reduce the urge toward colonial acquisitions (showing a negative relationship with colonial area). Since both conditions may hold simultaneously, the different effects of trade may be difficult to untangle. Future analyses treating trade somewhat differently may solve some of these problems.

Intensity of Intersections

12

In this chapter we shall look for the variables that help explain the level of violence in those situations in which the interests of any two countries with high capabilities collide specifically over colonial questions or disputed territory (such collisions are called "intersections" here). We are thus concerned with the processes of both competition and expansion. As noted in Part I, competition is the attempt of one country to surpass another on one or several dimensions, such as military capability. In theory, competition and expansion may be quite independent of each other, although considerable interdependency between the two may be expected in many, if not most, conflicts between major powers.

The intersection variable for any given year, for a given country, is the most intense level of violence of the intersections in that year.[1] The dynamics postulated for this process are depicted in the box on page 190. It would have been desirable to specify these relationships more precisely—in particular, to measure the extent to which a particular power was reacting to each of its rivals. Largely for methodological reasons, we were unable to do so.[2] Therefore, the value

---

[1]See Appendix A for an explanation of the scaling procedure used to determine the numerical values assigned to actions.

[2]For the same reasons, we could not use the dyadic violence variables to identify which nation's activities were being reacted to. There are three specific problems in both cases: (a) the introduction of a separate variable for each nation or pair of nations would greatly increase the number of independent variables in each equation, increasing the loss of degrees of freedom and, by extension, decreasing the reliability of the resulting inferences (particularly since the period under study spans only 45 years); (b) high collinearity exists among the military-expenditures variables of the six powers, further aggravating the loss of precision; and (c) for certain pairs of nations there are many years for which intersections were not reported in the historical sources searched. This last problem is less common when intersections are aggregated across all target nations, rather than remaining dyad-specific. See Appendix A for further comments on the indicators and measures employed, as well as Deber, 1974.

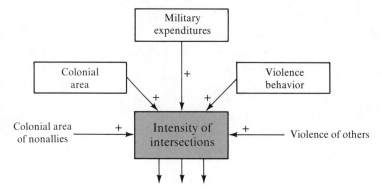

Hypothesized Dynamics of the Intensity of Intersections

This is represented by the following equation:

$$\text{intensity-of-intersections} = \alpha_2 + \beta_5 \text{ (colonial area)} +$$
$$\beta_6 \text{ (military expenditures)} +$$
$$\beta_7 \text{ (colonial-area-of-nonallies)} +$$
$$\beta_8 \text{ (violence-behavior)} +$$
$$\beta_9 \text{ (violence-of-others)} + \mu_2.$$

The three arrows *from* the intersections variable indicate that intensity-of-intersections is an explanatory (independent) variable in three other equations.

for intensity-of-intersections is the highest value of all intersections of one power with *all other powers* in the study. Statistically, we can only draw inferences from the behavior of the aggregate "others."

Nonetheless, the chronology of these intersections can provide insight about specific relationships, and hence allows us to elaborate on the statistical findings. For the years 1870 to 1884, there were many intersections between Britain and Russia, both of whom possessed large and increasing colonial territories (in Chapter 3 we saw that Britain had reasons for being apprehensive of Russia during this period). Thereafter, and roughly until the turn of the century, France replaced Russia as Britain's most frequent challenger. Beginning in the late 1890s or early 1900s, there were an increasing number of intersections between Germany and Britain or France, or between the Austro-German coalition and the emerging Anglo-French-Russian entente. As for Italy, her activities and interests collided first with those of France (until about 1896 or a little after), then with Britain (from after 1900 until the Balkan Wars of 1912–1913) and, increasingly thereafter, with Austria-Hungary. Many of the Anglo-Italian intersections may have resulted from British activities in the Mediterranean and the building of an Italian fleet (allied with the fleets of Austria-Hungary and Germany).

Anglo-Russian relationships reveal many intersections with a particularly high potential for violence. In May, 1877 Britain warned Russia against any attempt to blockade the Suez Canal or to occupy Egypt, and reaffirmed her policy on the Dardanelles. Two months later the British cabinet agreed to go to war if Russia were to occupy Constantinople. During January of the following year the British government sent its fleet to the Dardanelles but recalled it as the situation in the Near East improved somewhat. In March a dispute arose between Britain and Russia over the issues to be discussed at the Congress of Berlin. The British cabinet agreed to call out the reserves and bring troops from India to occupy one or two stations in the eastern Mediterranean.

In order to discourage Russian advances in Asia Minor, Britain in mid-1878 promised to defend Turkey against further attacks on her Asian possessions (for which pledge Britain was given Cyprus, an island of considerable significance for a naval power with growing interests in the Mediterranean). During the autumn of 1878 Russian advances in Central Asia and the determination of Britain to secure its frontier in India led to the Anglo-Afghan War, essentially a client conflict between the two major powers.

Further difficulties arose between Britain and Russia in the early 1880s. Russia occupied Merv (now Mary, Turkmeniya S.S.R.) in 1884 and reached territory ruled by the Emir of Afghanistan. At this point Russia and Britain were brought to the verge of a direct confrontation and war. To prepare the way for a possible attack on Vladivostok, Britain occupied Port Hamilton in nearby Korea. A year later an attack by Russia on Afghan forces led to another severe Anglo-Russian crisis. A projected British counterattack on Russian forces in Central Asia was cancelled when Russia reduced her pressure in Afghanistan.

There were numerous intersections of British and Russian interests just prior to and immediately after the turn of the century. In 1898 a conflict arose over a loan required by China; further intersections resulted from penetration by the two countries into Chinese territory. In 1903 Britain and Russia were involved in a series of disagreements over the partition of Persia. In 1904 naval units of the two countries confronted each other in the Dogger Bank Incident.

The Russo-Japanese War of 1904–1905 greatly reduced the Russian threat to British interests. During the war Russia was too deeply involved to risk serious confrontation with Britain; after the war, the tsarist government was restrained by a depleted treasury, a demoralized military, and recurring domestic political crises. Understandably, therefore, 1905 marked the beginning of Anglo-Russian discussions leading to entente.

British intersections with other major powers tended to be more violent during the earlier part of the period under study and lower after the turn of the century. Only 36 percent of the variance in the intensity of Britain's intersections for the full period can be explained; the significant variables are violence-of-others, colonial-area-of-nonallies, Britain's colonial area, and the constant term. However, for the period 1871–1890, 90 percent of the variance can be explained by the variables in the equation, and for the period 1891–1914, 43 percent. Violence-of-others is an important determinant throughout.[3]

The intensity of Russian intersections for the full period is also explained primarily by the violence variables—the violence-behavior of Russia and violence-of-others. For the period 1871–1890, on the other hand, 75 percent of the variance can be explained by Russian colonial area and military expenditures and the constant term. Both violence variables are statistically insignificant for this first subperiod. By contrast, in the second subperiod (1891–1914) colonial area, the constant, and the violence variables are statistically significant. Better fits can be obtained for the two subperiods than for the full period.[4]

---

[3]For the full period, violence-of-others (beta = .59) is significant at the .005 level, colonial-area-of-nonallies (beta = .34) is significant at the .025 level, and both British colonial area (beta = .53) and the constant are significant at the .05 level. Britain's military expenditures are positively related to intensity-of-intersections for the first subperiod, but negatively related after 1891. This shift in dynamics cancels out the effect of military expenditures for the full period, leaving them statistically insignificant (see Table 12-1). These findings suggest that the intensity of intersections may be better-explained by postulating two separate processes—the earlier period (1871–1890) being more fully captured by our model than the later. Nonetheless, the key element, violence-of-others, remains similar in its effect for all periods. The coefficient estimates for the full period differ from those for 1871–1890 (Chow test significant at .01 level). Although violence-of-others remains at the .005 level (with a slightly increased magnitude), no other variables except British military expenditures (beta = .60, $p = .01$) are significant. For the second subperiod (1891–1914) the coefficient estimates are neither significantly different from those for the full period nor particularly strong (the entire equation is only significant at the .10 level for this subperiod). Violence-of-others remains strong (beta = .72, $p = .01$). Other statistically significant variables are British military expenditures (beta = −.58, $p = .005$), colonial-area-of-nonallies (beta = .03, $p = .05$) and violence-behavior (beta = −.37, $p = .10$).

[4]Our equation explains only 32 percent of the variance for the full period, but is nonetheless significant at the .01 level. Both Russian violence-behavior and violence-of-others are significant at the .025 level, with beta coefficients of .28 and .21, respectively. Although the Chow test shows no significant differences, there does appear to be some kind of breakpoint around 1890, as also occurred in the case of Britain. For the first subperiod, Russian colonial area (beta = 1.36, $p = .001$), the constant ($p = .001$) and Russian military expenditures (beta = −.71, $p = .01$) account for 75 percent of the variance, and the equation is significant at the .001 level. For the second subperiod, 64 percent of the variance is explained by violence-of-others (beta = .54) and the violence-

Since the intensity of Russia's intersections in the early years of the period is partly accounted for by her colonial area, it is again apparent — especially in view of her vast land frontiers facing on Eastern Europe, the Middle East, Korea, and Sakhalin — that these substantial extensions of her interests were almost certain to lead to collisions with the interests of those other powers who were already there. We emphasize this point, even at the risk of belaboring it, because of the tendency among leaders of great powers to express righteous indignation whenever activities in far-flung parts of the world involve them in collisions with other powers. Seldom are national leaders prepared to admit responsibility for their nation's contributions to conflict.[5]

Britain and France, whose colonial territory and other foreign interests expanded rapidly, found their activities colliding in various parts of the world, but for the most part these intersections were not as intense as those between Britain and Russia. A striking characteristic of the colonial conflicts between Britain and France, even during the early years of the period, was the tendency of the two countries to resolve such conflicts through negotiation and often by treaty. This tendency was probably encouraged by the French defeat in the Franco-Prussian War and the subsequent desire of French leaders to avoid serious conflict with Britain.

As early as 1876 Britain and France established a condominium in Egypt. At the Congress of Berlin, Britain offered France a free hand in Tunis as compensation for British acquisition of Cyprus. In 1882 Britain and France acted jointly against a conspiracy in Egypt, although France subsequently refused to cooperate in the bombardment of Alexandria. The British occupation of Egypt in 1882 created an estrangement with France that lasted until 1904. After an 1885 international conference on Egyptian finances, France was able to impede British policies in Egypt. By 1887 Anglo-French differences over Egypt had become great.

By this time French interests had already penetrated central Africa. Alarmed by the implications of British explorations, France dispatched an expedition in 1880 to conclude treaties with local chiefs, founded

---

behavior of Russia (beta = .57), both of which are significant at the .01 level, and, to a lesser extent, Russian colonial area and the constant term (both significant at the .05 level). These coefficients are different from those of the full period only at the .10 level, whereas for the first subperiod there are no significant differences at all.

[5] It is almost a truism that preparations for violence often lead to violence, but since the coefficient of Russia's own military expenditures for the period 1871–1890 is negative, we may infer that the relationship between military expenditures and intensity-of-intersections is not as simple as we would expect. There are at least two possible interpretations of this negative coefficient. Russia could have turned inward, using her military capability for domestic purposes and avoiding direct external confrontation. Alternatively, her conflict with Japan (which is not reflected in this study, since Japan is not included) might have led to a propensity for cooperation with some European powers.

Brazzaville, and organized a protectorate. Five years later Sir Edward Grey asserted that any French expedition to the Upper Nile would be regarded as an unfriendly act. During the 1890s the expansionist activities of France and Britain led to the Fashoda Incident and collisions in other parts of Africa.

In 1894 a Franco-German agreement on the Cameroons facilitated a French advance through the Sudan to the Nile. British efforts to frustrate the French penetration proved ineffectual. Moreover, as Britain struggled to control the Nile, there developed a tendency for Germany and France to collaborate against England in colonial affairs.

During the 1880s British and French interests also clashed in Burma and, increasingly, in Siam. In 1895 an agreement with France delimited the border between Burma and Cochin China and in 1896 an Anglo-French agreement recognized Siamese independence, thus resolving many of the issues between the two European powers. During this period, Anglo-French conflicts in other parts of the world were similarly contained. These arrangements paved the way for the Accords of 1904 and the military arrangements between the two countries prior to the outbreak of war in 1914.

As measured on the intensity scale, French intersections rose to a medium level of intensity around 1880,[6] dropped off in the early 1880s, rose to a moderately high peak in 1888,[7] and rose to another moderately high peak in 1898.[8] After a drop around 1900, the intensity of French intersections rose with each of the Moroccan crises, but declined just prior to 1914.

For the full period 44 percent of the variance in the intensity of French intersections is accounted for by violence-of-others and colonial-area-of-nonallies. A similar pattern emerges for the early subperiod if a breakpoint is introduced in 1900. But the variance accounted for drops to 30 percent for the second subperiod, 1880–1914, and violence-of-others is the only statistically significant variable. Thus, some important factors are apparently not captured by the equation.[9]

Since Germany began acquiring substantial colonial territory later than France, the probability of conflict and violence between Germany and Britain over colonial interests was, for a time, somewhat lower than that between France and Britain. With the German acquisition

---

[6]Reflecting Franco-Italian tensions over Tunis and the resulting protests from Britain.

[7]Reflecting a crisis in Franco-Italian relations.

[8]Reflecting the Fashoda Incident.

[9]The beta coefficient for violence-of-others is .32 ($p = .001$). Colonial-area-of-nonallies was only marginally significant (beta $= .16$, $p = .10$). No other term was significant. The results of the first subperiod differed from those of the full period only in that French military expenditures were also marginally significant ($p = .10$). Nonetheless, since the coefficients retain the same relative significance, they do not differ markedly from those of the full period. Chow tests comparing the two subperiods with the full period indicate that there are no significant differences between the sets of regression coefficients.

of Angra-Pequeña in 1883, the interests of Germany and Britain began to collide with increasing frequency. Between 1883 and 1885 there were numerous Anglo-German intersections in East Africa, the Cameroons, and elsewhere. In 1884 Bismarck established an under-standing with France (particularly with respect to Egypt) and thus became entangled in Anglo-French antagonisms. As long as Bismarck was in power, intersections between Britain and Germany were relatively friendly, tempered by negotiation and diplomacy. The Anglo-German (Heligoland) Treaty of 1890 helped to contain or reg-ulate conflicts between the two powers.

The German landing at Kiaochow in 1897 and the extension of German activities into the Shantung peninsula led to collisions with other powers—especially Britain and Russia—in that part of the world. Similarly, the granting of the Baghdad Railway concession by Turkey to a German syndicate contributed to Anglo-German and other inter-sections in the Near East. German interference in the Boer War and the stopping by the British of the German ship *Bundesrath* were further examples of the intersections that were taking place.

Around the turn of the century efforts were made by both sides to improve relations, but the multiplicity and variety of collisions, to-gether with the growing arms competition, made any satisfactory ar-rangements difficult to achieve. By the time of the Kaiser's visit to Tangier, the Anglo-French Accords of 1904 had brought Britain and France into closer relations, so that German intersections with one were likely to have a damaging effect on German relations with the other, as for example in the Moroccan Crises.

On the other hand, Germany, Britain, and France collaborated rather well during the Bosnian Crisis of 1908–1909 and during the Balkan Wars. Despite colonial conflicts in various parts of the world, the feeling was widespread in both Germany and Britain during the early months of 1914 that a certain stability in relations had been reached.

The intensity of German intersections dropped to a low level after the close of the Franco-Prussian War, rose to a middle level in the early 1880s,[10] then tapered off until 1900, when a medium level was again reached.[11] Thereafter, it dropped to a low point in 1904, rose to a medium level in 1905,[12] increased in 1906, rose moderately in 1909[13] and then sharply in 1911.[14]

About 40 percent of the variance in the intensity of German inter-sections between 1871 and 1914 can be accounted for, primarily by

---

[10]Reflecting in large part Anglo-German intersections in East Africa and the Cam-eroons.

[11]Reflecting primarily the *Bundesrath* affair.

[12]First Moroccan Crisis.

[13]Casablanca affair.

[14]Second Moroccan Crisis.

Table 12-1. Intensity-of-intersections — results of estimation from a simultaneous equation system.*

Country	Period	R^2	F ratio	Durbin-Watson statistic	Time-dependent correction	Chow test
BRITAIN	1871–1914	.36	4.36 $df = 5,38$ $p = .005$	1.73	None	
	1871–1890	.90	26.42 $df = 5,14$ $p = .001$	2.49	AUTO2	$F_{24.14} = 3.69$ $p = .01$
	1891–1914	.43	2.72 $df = 5,18$ $p = .10$	2.07	AUTO2	$F_{20.18} = 1.27$ $p = $ n.s.
FRANCE	1871–1914	.44	5.94 $df = 5,38$ $p = .001$	1.66	MAV1	
	1871–1900	.91	46.13 $df = 5,24$ $p = .001$	1.90	MAV1	$F_{14.24} = 0.52$ $p = $ n.s.
	1880–1914	.30	2.54 $df = 5,29$ $p = .05$	1.50	MAV1	$F_{9.29} = 0.56$ $p = $ n.s.
GERMANY	1871–1914	.40	4.98 $df = 5,38$ $p = .005$	1.66	MAV1	
	1884–1914	.42	3.57 $df = 5,25$ $p = .025$	1.96	AUTO2	$F_{13.25} = 1.11$ $p = $ n.s.

Germany's own military expenditures.[15] The model thus yields only a partial explanation of the intensity of German intersections. Despite the use of variables referring to foreign factors, the model does not seem to uncover any linkage between the intensity of German intersections and violence-of-others. Although it is possible that German intersections occurred "in a vacuum," it is perhaps more likely that the actual process was more complex than the model allows.

---

[15]The only significant explanatory variable is German military expenditures (beta = .45, $p = .05$). The total equation is significant at the .005 level.

Variable	Parameter Estimate		Partial correlation	*t* statistic	Significance level
	Unstandardized	Standardized (beta)			
Violence of Others	.74	.59	.47	3.2	.005
Colonial Area	34.16	.53	.30	1.94	.05
Col. Area Nonallies	.27	.34	.34	2.3	.025
Constant	−309.45	.00	−.30	−1.93	.05
Violence of Others	.76	.69	.63	3.1	.005
Military Expend.	.00015	.60	.58	2.65	.01
Violence of Others	.85	.72	.52	2.60	.01
Military Expend.	−.000034	−.58	−.59	−3.08	.005
Violence Behavior	−.32	−.37	−.33	−1.49	.10
Col. Area Nonallies	3.84	.03	.39	1.77	.05
Violence of Others	.285	.32	.54	3.99	.001
Col. Area Nonallies	.20	.16	.26	1.63	.10
Military Expend.	.000097	.52	.31	1.6	.10
Col. Area Nonallies	.34	.37	.38	2.0	.025
Violence of Others	.196	.21	.49	2.8	.005
Violence of Others	.27	.29	.43	2.60	.01
Military Expend.	.000041	.45	.29	1.9	.05
Military Expend.	.000042	.47	.34	1.8	.05

Table continued

The same findings result when a breakpoint is introduced in 1884.[16] Thus, our estimator for intensity-of-intersections only partially captures reality. Although the general findings are consistent with the historical record, apparently we have failed to include in the equation some of the more significant determinants of the intensity of German intersections. We expected more of the variance to be accounted for

---

[16]The Chow test for the full period and subperiod yielded an *F* statistic of 1.1, which is not statistically significant. For both periods, only German military expenditures are significant (at the .05 level).

Table 12-1. Continued

Country	Period	R^2	F ratio	Durbin-Watson statistic	Time-dependent correction	Chow test
ITALY	1871–1914	.15	1.38 $df = 5{,}38$ $p = $ n.s.	1.95	AUTO1	
	1871–1888	.98	102.26 $df = 5{,}12$ $p = .001$	1.92	AUTO2	$F_{26.12} = 16.51$ $p = .001$
	1889–1914	.55	4.84 $df = 5{,}20$ $p = .005$	1.32	None	$F_{18.20} = -.144$ $p = $ n.s.
RUSSIA	1871–1914	.32	3.54 $df = 5{,}38$ $p = .01$	1.98	AUTO2	
	1871–1890	.75	8.46 $df = 5{,}14$ $p = .001$	1.58	None	$F_{24.14} = .733$ $p = $ n.s.
	1891–1914	.64	6.42 $df = 5{,}18$ $p = .005$	2.30	None	$F_{20.18} = 2.17$ $p = .10$
AUSTRIA-HUNGARY	1871–1914	.66	15.09 $df = 5{,}38$ $p = .001$	1.49	None	
	1878–1914	.62	9.91 $df = 5{,}31$ $p = .001$	2.02	AUTO2	$F_{7.31} = 2.63$ $p = .05$

*All statistics refer to the simultaneous-system estimates using both two-stage least squares and, where indicated in the time-dependent correction column, generalized least squares.

by variables in the model: Germany's colonial area, colonial-expansion-of-nonallies, military expenditures, violence-behavior, and violence-of-others. Conceivably, variables we omitted, such as trade or military-expenditures-of-nonallies, might have accounted for some of the remaining variance in intensity-of-intersections for Germany, but domestic factors are probably the missing links.[17] Nonetheless, our

[17]For example, national unity may have been an important consideration; foreign affairs may have been employed to deflect attention from domestic problems in order to

Variable	Parameter Estimate		Partial correlation	t statistic	Significance level
	Unstandardized	Standardized (beta)			
No significant coefficients					
Violence of Others	1.31	2.02	.91	7.68	.001
Colonial Area	−1.59	−.82	−.80	−4.56	.001
Military Expend.	−.00013	−.55	−.63	−2.78	.005
Col. Area Nonallies	−.16	−.20	−.51	−2.03	.025
Constant	8.04	.00	.69	3.31	.005
Colonial Area	13.39	.95	.66	3.9	.001
Constant	−36.50	.00	−.38	−1.8	.05
Violence of Others	.21	.21	.34	2.2	.025
Violence Behavior	.23	.28	.31	2.0	.025
Colonial Area	356.23	1.36	.78	4.6	.001
Military Expend.	−.00037	−.71	−.56	−2.5	.01
Constant	−5548.59	.00	−.78	−4.6	.001
Violence of Others	.42	.54	.54	2.7	.01
Violence Behavior	.35	.57	.51	2.5	.01
Colonial Area	243.09	.56	.37	1.7	.05
Constant	−3825.30	.00	−.37	−1.7	.05
Colonial Area	.88	.42	.46	3.15	.005
Violence Behavior	.30	.42	.37	2.4	.01
Violence of Others	.26	.29	.31	2.0	.025
Military Expend.	.0001	.38	.31	1.8	.05
Violence of Others	.27	.38	.44	2.8	.005
Violence Behavior	.18	.31	.38	2.3	.025

intention was not to fit an equation to each nation individually, but to see how much of the variance in the variable could be accounted for by a single model. Our equation is quite successful in demonstrating that the intensity of German intersections is related, within the limits of our model, not to the behavior of other powers but solely to German military expenditures.

stimulate patriotism. Such domestic considerations, however important, are beyond the scope of this volume, but are treated in other volumes—see Ole Holsti, 1971, and Nomikos and North, 1975.

Similarly, our explanation of the intensity of Italian intersections is only moderately successful, particularly for the period after 1888. As our historical review showed, early conflicts between Italy and France arose from French actions in support of the pope and from clashes of interest in North Africa. Although Italy had associated herself with the League of Three Emperors as an assurance against France, in the mid 1870s the Italian government also allowed agitation against Austria, aimed at the acquisition of Trieste and the Trentino.

Italian action is Tunis led to establishment of a French protectorate there. This initiated a long period of Franco-Italian competitions and conflicts and modified the Mediterranean situation to Britain's disadvantage. For example, Italy, isolated after the Tunis affair, joined the Triple Alliance. In 1885 she also sought another path to expansion by occupying Assab and Massawa on the Red Sea. Relations between France and Italy became increasingly strained during the late 1880s and early 1890s.

Throughout the entire period 1870–1914, Italian expansion collided with British interests in the Mediterranean and in northeastern Africa. The violence potential of such intersections was increased when Italy joined the Triple Alliance, "locking in" antagonisms into the alliance system. Anglo-Italian intersections acquired a new potential for violence with the escalation of the Anglo-German naval race and the building of an Italian navy. After the turn of the century, the Italian navy, in combination with the German navy, confronted British and French forces in the Mediterranean.

The intensity of Italian intersections reached high levels between 1888[18] and 1894,[19] and then settled into relatively low levels until the Balkan Wars of 1912–1913. The full period is not explained by the equation. If a breakpoint is introduced in 1889, when Italy acquired her first colonies, 98 percent of the variance in the intensity of Italian intersections between 1871 and 1888 can be accounted for by five variables: the constant term and violence-of-others (both positive), and colonial-area-of-nonallies, Italian military-expenditures and colonial area (all negative). There appears to be a strong and consistent tendency for violence-of-others towards Italy to elicit violent responses.[20]

---

[18]Reflecting the Franco-Italian crisis of February, 1888.

[19]This peak marked the outbreak of the Ethiopian War. Since other European powers were not directly involved, it did not count as an intersection in our analysis, although it did figure in violence-behavior.

[20]The period 1871–1888 is significantly different from the full period at the .001 level. Both violence-of-others (beta = 2.02) and Italian colonial area (beta = −.82) are significant at the .001 level; Italian military expenditures (beta = −.55) and the constant are significant at the .005 level. Colonial-area-of-nonallies (beta = −.20) is significant only at the .025 level. The coefficients for the period 1889–1914 are not significantly different from those for the full period, indicating that the coefficients maintained roughly constant relative positions. Only two variables are significant: Italian colonial area (beta =

Since Austro-Hungarian territorial expansion was limited to Bosnia, Herzegovina, and the *sanjak* of Novibazar, we confront difficulties (similar to those described in Chapter 11) in analyzing Austro-Hungarian conflicts with other powers over colonial issues. In many respects the Congress of Berlin set the stage for Austro-Hungarian intersections with Russia, Italy, and other countries in the Balkan region. Decisions made at this time created numerous conflicts and the potential for others. During the years between 1878 and 1914 few agreements were reached between Austria-Hungary and the other powers that successfully constrained or regulated in a lasting way intersections with Austro-Hungarian interests.

Except for certain crises, conflict between the interests of Austria-Hungary and those of Russia and other powers largely resulted in negotiation behind the closed doors of European conference halls rather than military confrontation. Even the Austro-Hungarian mobilization during the Bosnian Crisis of 1908–1909 lacked the real threat of violence ordinarily associated with such an action. Consequently, our data set on Austro-Hungarian intersections is not subtantial enough to warrant drawing conclusions.

Sixty-six percent of the variance in the intensity of Austro-Hungarian intersections with other powers can be accounted for primarily by the empire's colonial area (which, as we indicated earlier, was highly constrained by the activities of Russia and Germany and the lack of sufficient sea power to compete for overseas territory) and two other variables: violence-behavior and violence-of-others.[21]

Since Austria acquired colonies (as we define them) in 1878, that year was designated as a breakpoint. Both violence-behavior and violence-of-others remain salient after that date, but military expenditures replaces colonial area in explanatory power. The importance of violence-of-others in both periods reveals the extent to which the in-

---

.95, as opposed to its negative sign during the first subperiod, significant at the .001 level) and the constant (with a negative sign, significant at the .05 level only). For the second subperiod we are able to account for 55 percent of the variance in the intensity of Italy's intersections. There thus appears to be a marked difference between the first and second subperiods. In particular, the two most significant variables, colonial area and the constant term, both change signs.

These negative relationships are difficult to explain, particularly the effect of Italy's small colonial area. They may indicate that conflict between Italy and other powers tended to be handled through diplomacy rather than violence. Intersections would then be restricted to those situations in which Italy's policies were ineffectual or her ambitions were otherwise blocked. Note that Italy's ambiguous relation to the Triple Alliance, specifically her relations to Austria-Hungary, and to France and Britain, together with relatively low levels of Italian violence-behavior between 1894 and the Balkan Wars of 1912–1913, present a rather complex picture. Perhaps these changes in alignment account for the total failure of the equation to predict the full period, whereas estimation is far more successful for each subperiod.

[21]Colonial area was the most significant variable for the full period (beta = .42, p = .005), but both violence-behavior (beta = .42, p = .01) and violence-of-others (beta = .29, p = .025) were important.

tensity of the empire's intersections were a result of the conflict behavior of other powers.[22]

In the preceding chapter we saw how population and other variables contribute to the expansion of a country's interests beyond its borders. In this chapter we have seen that expansion (along with other variables) contributes to the intensity of conflict between powers over issues of expansion. Both violence-behavior and violence-of-others frequently contribute to this intensity.

An examination of the intensity of intersections among all the major powers between 1883 and 1895 reveals a considerable number of high-intensity peaks, whereas the peaks between 1896 and 1909 tend to be considerably lower. Thus, there is no evidence of any uniform increase from 1870 to the outbreak of war in 1914. It is conceivable, of course, that a particular conflict, such as the Bosnian Crisis of 1908–1909, might have escalated to a major war, as did the six-week Balkan crisis in 1914. From our evidence, however, it is not possible to infer any clear snow-balling process whereby conflicts of lower intensity necessarily give rise to conflicts of higher intensity. A period of high-intensity conflict can be, and often is, followed by a period of relative tranquility.

A considerable number of factors — territorial expansion, violence-behavior, military expenditures, considerations represented by the constant term, and so forth — can contribute to intensity-of-intersections. An analysis of breakpoints shows marked shifts in the determinants of intensity-of-intersection during the period studied; there appears to have been a change midway through the period. The model captures the determinants quite well for earlier subperiods, but fails to include some factors important in later years.

---

[22]The period after 1878 is different from the full period at the .05 level. Although violence-of-others becomes more important (beta = .38, p = .005) and violence-behavior remains roughly the same (beta = .31, p = .025), colonial area becomes insignificant, replaced instead by military expenditures (beta = .38, p = .05). The equation is significant at the .001 level for both periods.

Military Expenditures

13

Most theories of arms races draw upon Lewis Fry Richardson's mathematical treatment of military competition.[1] Richardson linked the rate of change in the military budget of a nation to the defensiveness, economic constraints, and residual grievances of the nation, as well as to the existing level of expenditures, both of the given nation and of its rival. The focus of his study was the spiraling arms competition that seemed to characterize the last decade or more prior to WWI.[2]

Our model proposes that, between rivals, any increase in the strength and effectiveness in one country along a critical dimension is likely to generate new demands in the other, and create a disposition among its leaders to increase national capabilities, either on the same *or a different* dimension. The possibility that competition may occur on multiple dimensions tends to complicate the classical, Richardson-type model of an arms race, in which each country responds to an increase

---

[1]Richardson represents the arms race by the following equations:

$$dx/dt = ky - ax + g$$
$$dy/dt = lx - by + h,$$

where in the first equation t = time; x = the military expenditures of Country A; y = the military expenditures of Country B, A's rival; k is a positive constant representing A's military coefficient; a is a positive constant representing fatigue, expense and other penalties A associates with maintaining defenses; and g is a constant standing for A's initial grievances. In the second equation t = time; y = the military expenditures of Country B; x = the military expenditures of Country A, B's rival; l is a positive constant representing B's military coefficient; b is a positive constant representing the penalties B associates with maintaining defenses; and h is a constant standing for B's initial grievances (Richardson, 1960a, p. 13). See also Wainsten, 1971; and Moll, 1971.

[2]Richardson also dealt (somewhat less successfully) with the pre-WWII period.

in a rival's budget (or tonnage, or whatever) with an increase in kind. Multivariate terms may thus have to be introduced into any refined model. Whereas the Richardson model focuses on rival military or naval budgets as explanatory terms, we go further by adding expansion, conflicts of interest, and the multiplicative effect of population and national income (this does not rule out the classical model, but presents important additional perspectives). Undoubtedly, a large increase in one country's military expenditures is likely to produce an increase in the military spending of rivals, but domestic factors may be a considerable part of the explanation of growth in military establishments.[3]

There are serious methodological problems associated with our analysis of military expenditures. These problems stem primarily from taking into account bureaucratic effects on military growth, i.e., the influence of the previous year's budget on current appropriations. We are confronted with the *coincidence* of two issues: a lagged endogenous variable (military expenditures at $t - 1$) and serial correlation of the disturbances. The problem is a serious one because the significance of this lagged term tends to be overstated; thus, all coefficient estimates become biased and inconsistent unless appropriate adjustments are made.[4] All results reported here include the necessary adjustments.

The military-expenditures equation (depicted on the next page) includes both domestic and foreign factors that contribute (or tend to contribute) to increases in military expenditures. We must ask the following questions: (a) To what extent does this equation accurately represent the dynamics of military expenditures? (b) What are the relative effects of domestic and foreign influences? (c) What differences do we find among the six nations?

The equation includes the variable military-expenditures-of-nonallies, which takes into account the effects not only of alliances, but also, because the identity of nonallies changes, of *changes* in alliances. By including this variable we have incorporated in the equation the effects of breakpoints.

---

[3]See Gray, 1971, p. 78 ". . . there has been so little systematic study of arms race behavior that we cannot reasonably assume the dominance either of action-reaction or of domestic process explanations . . . . it is almost certain that different factors have been of preeminent importance to each competitor during different phases of the race and that different factors are accorded different weights in each country." For one approach utilizing domestic factors, see Allison and Halperin, 1972, pp. 57–58. A large body of literature exists concerning budgetary processes, most notably Wildavsky, 1964.

[4]Many incrementalist theories may be spurious, insofar as they neglect to purge this source of statistical bias. It is all the more notable, then, that incrementalism appears to hold for many of the countries in our study, even after the lagged term has been appropriately deflated and statistical adjustments made. See Hibbs, 1974, for an exposition of the underlying methodological problems; see also Appendix B for our own extension of these correction techniques.

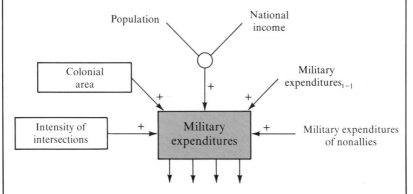

Hypothesized Dynamics of Military Expenditures

This is represented by the following equation:

military
expenditures = $\alpha_3 + \beta_{10}$ (military expenditures$_{t-1}$) +
β_{11} (military-expenditures-of-
nonallies) + β_{12} (intensity-of-
intersections) + β_{13} (colonial area) +
β_{14} (population-times-national-
income) + μ_3.

The four arrows *from* the military-expenditures variable indicate that military-expenditures is an explanatory (independent) variable in four other equations.

Our review of the Anglo-German naval race in Part II described the intricate and subtle way in which domestic growth can combine with commercial and colonial competition to stimulate the building of great fleets. We saw how British and German leaders kept watch over the growth of each other's navies and justified increases of their own on the basis of increases by the other. Because of Italy's partnership in the Triple Alliance, the growth of her navy was also watched with growing concern in London. There was similar competition in the growth of the armies of Germany, France, Russia, Austria-Hungary, and Italy. We do not wish to choose between either international competition or expansion for an explanation of increases in military expenditures. We are concerned rather with how much of the variance in military expenditures can be explained by the variables in our model, and hence in what ways they tend to interact.

The British two-power standard and the German naval program were both keyed to the status of rival forces, yet each was also sensitive to a number of other demands. Because of her insular position, Britain was particularly concerned with the strength of her navy. It was frequently stated in parliament that the nation's naval budget should be compared to the army, not naval, budgets of other powers.[5] Warships were "a matter of life and death" to Britain; they protected her far-flung trade routes and ensured the availability of food supplies.[6] Britain's navy was her sole defense, and her survival depended "on it and on it alone."[7]

In the years just prior to the outbreak of WWI Britain, according to her leaders, stood "as a nation upon the defensive."[8] In the views of King Edward, Winston Churchill, and others, any great increase in the German fleet necessitated a comparable increase in the British navy.[9] German maritime supremacy would be "incompatible with the existence of the British Empire."[10]

In many respects Germany's concerns mirrored those of Britain. A powerful battle fleet was considered a critical adjunct to German foreign policy.[11] One aim was to safeguard food supplies from overseas,[12] but other reasons were offered by German leaders. Security of economic development was a "life question" for Germany.[13] The German Navy had been "the keystone in the mighty system" that had yielded the development of extraordinary wealth and thus was "the basis for the existence of the German people."[14] According to German chancellor Bethmann-Hollweg, a "really great Power with a seaboard *must* have . . . a strong fleet."[15] A strong navy was considered essential for the defense of German colonies, shipping, and overseas commerce in general.[16] Indeed, Germany required "absolute naval superiority" in order to control and protect her far-flung colonial empire.[17]

---

[5]*Parliamentary Debates*, 19 Victoria, 1896, 37:1523.

[6]*Ibid.*, 17 March 1914, 59:1763.

[7]Grey to Rodd, January 13, 1913, as quoted in Marder, 1961, p. 272; see also Chapter 7 here.

[8]*Parliamentary Debates*, Series 5, 20 March 1912, 35:1954.

[9]King Edward VII to Kaiser Wilhelm II, 22 February 1908, in Lepsius *et al.*, 24:36.

[10]Memorandum, in Gooch and Temperley, 3:397–420.

[11]Marder, 1961, p. 121.

[12]Taylor, 1954, pp. 372–373.

[13]"Memorandum of Purpose Appended to the Naval Bill of 1900," Hurd and Castle, 1913, Appendix II, p. 346.

[14]Helfferich, 1914, p. 84–85.

[15]Quoted in Woodward, 1935, p. 373.

[16]Marder, 1961, p. 121.

[17]Ritter, 1965, p. 136.

The dividing line between defensiveness and aggressiveness was sometimes thin, however. According to Tirpitz, a state with oceanic or world interests "must be able to uphold them and make its power felt beyond its own territorial waters."[18] Since her "late entry into the colonial race had left her with what was, in her view, less than her fair share of its prizes," Germany proposed to use her fleet, combined with economic power, as a means of supporting her demand for a revision of the colonial status quo.[19] "National world commerce, world industry, and to an extent fishing on the high seas, world intercourse and colonies" were impossible "without a fleet capable of taking the offensive."[20] The Kaiser himself determined that German power should be used all over the world "to push German commerce, possessions and interests."[21]

The rapid growth of the German navy had sharp repercussions in Britain. After 1905, debates on the issue in parliament were persistent. In 1912, 1913, and 1914 Churchill, as first lord of the admiralty, quoted from provisions of the most recent German Naval Law to justify the maintenance of British naval superiority.[22] The number of vessels Britain felt required to construct each year was thus in part dictated by the German program.

British leaders were as much aware that Germany was responding to British budget increases as German leaders were that Britain was responding to Germany's increases.[23] From a British point of view, a strong German army *and* navy was a lethal combination.[24] For Germany, on the other hand, a growing British navy added to the dread of encirclement, since Germany already felt threatened by the French and Russian armies by her borders. Her uneasiness was further increased by the belief that France might one day try to retake Alsace-Lorraine. Under these circumstances Germany made significant additions to her army in 1905, 1911, and again in 1912.

In 1913 France responded to German increases by reimposing the three-year term of military service, which had been reduced in 1905 to two years. Six months prior to the outbreak of WWI Russia increased the number of her reserve formations, thereby adding a half-million men to a standing army of 1,300,000 (including reserves actually under arms). This was over twice the German army, and stronger by 300,000 men than the combined German and 450,000-man Austro-Hungarian armies. To what extent are these trends in military

---

[18]Quoted in Woodward, 1935, p. 19.
[19]Fischer, 1967, p. 8.
[20]Tirpitz, quoted in Woodward, 1935, p. 18.
[21]Steinberg, 1965, p. 107.
[22]*Parliamentary Debates*, Series 5, 18 March 1912, 35:1555.
[23]*Parliamentary Debates*, Series 5, 20 March 1913, 50:1754.
[24]Woodward, 1935, pp. 375–376.

growth accounted for by domestic growth, and to what extent by the arms-race phenomenon?

Between 1871 and 1914, 74 percent of the variance of British military expenditures can be accounted for by our equation. For the full period, British military expenditures are best-explained by Britain's previous military expenditures and the expenditures of nonallies, although these were not the only significant variables.[25] For the subperiod 1871–1890, the bureaucratic effect (military expenditures$_{t-1}$), intensity-of-intersections, and population-times-national-income are statistically significant. For the second subperiod, only military-expenditures-of-nonallies and military-expenditures$_{t-1}$ are statistically significant. There is some evidence, therefore, of a shift in dynamics — a change from a military capability determined largely by domestic factors to one that was in part a response to the capabilities of other powers.[26] There may also be some evidence, since intensity-of-intersections is replaced by military-expenditures as a significant variable, that colonial concerns may have been overshadowed by conflict in Europe. This, however, is speculative.

In Chapter 6 we saw how the decisions of Austria-Hungary and Italy to build Dreadnoughts added to British apprehensiveness. This raises the questions of whether expansion of the British navy was a reaction to Austria-Hungary and Italy, to Germany, or to the combined capabilities of the Triple Alliance. In some cases an answer might be obtained by disaggregating the data on military expenditures. Here, since there are too few data points in our time series to allow such refinement, such results would be statistically meaningless. Any answer to this question must rely therefore on the historical record, without benefit of multivariate regression analysis.

The model is less successful in accounting for the variance in French military expenditures. Nonetheless, 58 percent of the variance between 1871 and 1914 is accounted for. The most significant variables are France's military-expenditures$_{t-1}$, French colonial area, and the

---

[25]The beta coefficients are: for military-expenditures$_{t-1}$ .46 ($p = .005$), for military-expenditures-of-nonallies .22 ($p = .025$), for population-times-national income .24 ($p = .05$), and for intensity-of-intersections .09 ($p = .10$).

[26]For the period 1871–1890, 99 percent of the variance in British military expenditures is accounted for, primarily by military-expenditures$_{t-1}$ (beta = .43) and population-times-national income (beta = .42), both significant at the .025 level, and by intensity-of-intersections (beta = .21, $p = .01$). These coefficient estimates are significantly different from those for the full period (Chow test is significant at the .001 level.) For the period 1891–1914, on the other hand, the dynamics are not significantly different from those of the full period. Only Britain's military-expenditures$_{t-1}$ (beta = .39) and military-expenditures-of-nonallies (beta = .28) are significant, both at the .05 level. Together they explain 48 percent of the variance. Although a considerable portion of the variance is explained, some factor that has not been captured by our model becomes important in this later period.

constant term.[27] Our analysis suggests that French expenditures were generated less by foreign than by domestic factors.[28] On the other hand, as we have noted in other chapters, French military expenditures themselves contributed to foreign events (particularly to the intensity of French intersections).

Germany is another case of the importance of domestic factors. We can account for 92 percent of the variance in Germany's military expenditures by population-times-national-income, the constant term, and Germany's military-expenditures$_{t-1}$.[29] Again, we find that domestic factors are considerably more important (that is, statistically significant) than foreign factors.

Ninety-four percent of the variance in Russian military expenditures can be accounted for, primarily by Russia's military-expenditures$_{t-1}$, although the effects of population-times-national-income and intensity-of-intersections are also important.[30] The importance of domestic factors is generally consistent with the findings in Chapter 11, in which we reported that Russia's colonial area is accounted for by the constant term and population density.

For Italy, 95 percent of the variance for the full period can be accounted for, almost exclusively by military-expenditures$_{t-1}$, although population-times-national-income is marginally significant. Domestic

---

[27] All three variables are significant at the .001 level.

[28] This is true in general for the full period. For subperiods, however, the statement must be modified. For the period 1871–1900, for example, the key variables are basically domestic: military-expenditures$_{t-1}$ ($p = .001$), French colonial area ($p = .05$), and population-times-national income ($p = .025$), although military-expenditures-of-non-allies are also significant (at the .01 level). The period 1880–1914 also shows some effect from military-expenditures-of-nonallies (beta $= -.19$, $p = .05$) and from French intersections ($p = .05$), but these are overshadowed by the internal effects of population-times-national income and the constant, both significant at the .005 level, and French colonial area and military-expenditures$_{t-1}$, both significant at the .001 level. Foreign factors seem to be statistically significant for this second period, but they remain far less significant than domestic factors.

[29] The most important determinant was German domestic growth — population-times-national income ($p = .001$). Both German-military-expenditures$_{t-1}$ and the constant term are significant at the .05 level. Very similar results are found for the period 1884–1914, except that the constant is no longer significant and population-times-national income exerts a proportionately greater impact; foreign influences are again insignificant in this subperiod.

[30] For the full period, Russia's military-expenditures$_{t-1}$ are significant at the .001 level, population-times-national income at .025, and intensity-of-intersections at .10. The period 1871–1890 is quite different (Chow test significant at .001 level), although military-expenditures$_{t-1}$ remains the most significant variable, and in fact increases in size (remaining at the .001 level). Military-expenditures-of-nonallies is marginally important (beta $= .20$, $p = .025$), but only for this subperiod (it drops out for the period 1891–1914). The second subperiod is virtually identical to the full period, except that intensity-of-intersections is not even marginally significant (the R^2 and t statistics are correspondingly lower).

Table 13-1. Military expenditures — results of estimation from a simultaneous equation system.*

Country	Period	R^2	F ratio	Durbin-Watson statistic	Time-dependent correction	Chow test
BRITAIN	1871–1914	.74	21.52 $df = 5,38$ $p = .001$	2.07	AUTO2	
	1871–1890	.99	196.91 $df = 5,14$ $p = .001$	2.00	AUTO2	$F_{24.14} = 36.37$ $p = .001$
	1891–1914	.48	3.33 $df = 5,18$ $p = .05$	2.13	AUTO2	$F_{20.18} = .125$ $p = $ n.s.
FRANCE	1871–1914	.58	10.38 $df = 5,38$ $p = .001$	1.58	AUTO2	
	1871–1900	.95	82.51 $df = 5,24$ $p = .001$	1.94	None	$F_{14.24} = 303.227$ $p = .001$
	1880–1914	.71	14.20 $df = 5,29$ $p = .001$	1.64	AUTO2	$F_{9.29} = 2.309$ $p = .05$
GERMANY	1871–1914	.92	87.67 $df = 5,38$ $p = .001$	2.26	None	
	1884–1914	.71	12.51 $df = 5,25$ $p = .001$	1.99	AUTO2	$F_{13.25} = 1.58$ $p = $ n.s.

factors are thus the most important; previous allocations tend to shape current allocations independent of foreign or other domestic factors.[31]

These findings are generally consistent with those of Chapter 11, where we reported that, although the variance in Italy's colonial area

---

[31]Military-expenditures$_{t-1}$ contribute most ($p = .005$, beta $= .76$), although population-times-national income is significant at the .10 level. The findings for the period 1889–1914 are very similar to those for the full period (except the coefficients are more statistically significant); only domestic factors, with the exception of military-expen-

Variable	Parameter Estimate		Partial correlation	t statistic	Significance level
	Unstandardized	Standardized (beta)			
Mil. Expend.$_{t-1}$	.46	.46	.45	3.09	.005
Mil. Ex. Nonallies	.18	.22	.36	2.36	.025
Pop. × Nat. Inc.	.000295	.24	.26	1.69	.05
Intersections	1492.72	.09	.26	1.63	.10
Mil. Expend.$_{t-1}$	.45	.43	.53	2.3	.025
Intersections	818.83	.21	.58	2.7	.01
Pop. × Nat. Inc.	.00027	.42	.52	2.3	.025
Mil. Expend.$_{t-1}$	.38	.39	.40	1.8	.05
Mil. Ex. Nonallies	.22	.28	.40	1.9	.05
Mil. Expend.$_{t-1}$	4.28	1.47	.58	4.34	.001
Colonial Area	−122,808.0	−.66	−.56	−4.16	.001
Constant	497,316.0	.00	.51	3.63	.001
Mil. Expend.$_{t-1}$	.58	.58	.80	6.49	.001
Mil. Ex. Nonallies	−.19	−.43	−.47	−2.62	.01
Colonial Area	23813.10	.42	.37	1.93	.05
Pop. × Nat. Inc.	.00036	.40	.44	2.38	.025
Mil. Expend.$_{t-1}$	5.95	1.52	.74	5.94	.001
Mil. Ex. Nonallies	−.19	−.19	−.34	−1.94	.05
Intersections	4220.42	.20	.33	1.88	.05
Colonial Area	−105,558.0	−.33	−.59	−3.92	.001
Pop. × Nat. Inc.	−.004	−.70	−.51	−3.19	.005
Constant	624,608.0	.00	.52	3.28	.005
Pop. × Nat. Inc.	.0003	.72	.67	5.60	.001
Mil. Expend.$_{t-1}$	.30	.29	.29	1.87	.05
Constant	19103.30	.00	.29	1.89	.05
Mil. Expend.$_{t-1}$	−.85	−.85	−.49	−2.78	.005
Pop. × Nat. Inc.	.0078	1.72	.84	7.87	.001

Table continued

until 1888 (the first subperiod) was largely accounted for by population density and the constant term, for the second subperiod and full period it was accounted for by military-expenditures. The intensity of Italian intersections is also explained differently in different time

ditures-of-nonallies (the least significant coefficient, with $p = .025$), are statistically significant. For the period 1871–1888, military-expenditures$_{t-1}$ are significant at .001, population-times-national income at .05, and the foreign factors military-expenditures-of-nonallies at .05 and intensity-of-intersections at .025.

Table 13-1. Continued

Country	Period	R^2	F ratio	Durbin-Watson statistic	Time-dependent correction	Chow test
ITALY	1871–1914	.95	134.65 $df = 5,38$ $p = .001$	1.99	None	
	1871–1888	.99	47.483 $df = 5,12$ $p = .001$	1.90	AUTO2	$F_{26.12} = 7.54$ $p = .001$
	1889–1914	.72	10.23 $df = 5,20$ $p = .001$	2.30	None	$F_{18.20} = 1.55$ $p = $ n.s.
RUSSIA	1871–1914	.94	110.46 $df = 5,38$ $p = .001$	2.26	None	
	1871–1890	.93	36.28 $df = 5,14$ $p = .001$	2.00	None	$F_{24.14} = 26.58$ $p = .001$
	1891–1914	.77	11.79 $df = 5,18$ $p = .001$	2.20	None	$F_{20.18} = 0.19$ $p = $ n.s.
AUSTRIA-HUNGARY	1871–1914	.94	125.54 $df = 5,38$ $p = .001$	2.12	None	
	1878–1914	.87	42.45 $df = 5,31$ $p = .001$	2.06	None	$F_{7.31} = -1.61$ $p = $ n.s.

*All statistics refer to the simultaneous system estimates using both two-stage least squares and, where indicated in the time-dependent correction column, generalized least squares.
[a]Iron and steel production used instead of national income; see Appendix A.

periods: the full-period equation is not statistically significant, yet in the first subperiod the variance is well-accounted for by violence-of-others, colonial-area-of-nonallies, Italy's colonial area and military-

Variable	Parameter Estimate		Partial correlation	t statistic	Significance level
	Unstandardized	Standardized (beta)			
Mil. Expend.$_{t-1}$	.77	.76	.50	3.5	.005
Pop. × Nat. Inc.	.00012	.12	.24	1.5	.10
Mil. Expend.$_{t-1}$	.81	.65	.82	4.93	.001
Mil. Ex. Nonallies	−.02	−.07	−.45	−1.76	.05
Intersections	700.99	.16	.59	2.55	.025
Pop. × Nat. Inc.	.00037	.17	.48	1.88	.05
Mil. Expend.$_{t-1}$	.70	.535	.60	3.36	.005
Mil. Ex. Nonallies	.02	.53	.46	2.33	.025
Colonial Area	9754.54	.69	.63	3.63	.005
Pop. × Nat. Inc.	.0002	.44	.55	2.96	.005
Constant	−61838.80	.00	−.51	−2.66	.01
Mil. Expend.$_{t-1}$	.62	.63	.62	4.8	.001
Pop. × Nat. Inc.	.00009	.30	.35	2.3	.025
Intersections	−1313.03	−.12	−.26	−1.6	.10
Mil. Expend.$_{t-1}$	.98	.89	.81	5.16	.001
Mil. Ex. Nonallies	.04	.20	.52	2.27	.025
Mil. Expend.$_{t-1}$	.48	.52	.51	2.54	.01
Pop. × Nat. Inc.	.0001	.42	.38	1.74	.05
Mil. Expend.$_{t-1}$	1.27	1.11	.79	7.99	.001
Pop. × (Iron and Steel)[a]	−.00008	−.45	−.52	−3.78	.001
Mil. Ex. Nonallies	.03	.37	.67	5.53	.001
Intersections	861.41	.26	.50	3.54	.001
Constant	−20420.70	.00	−.42	−2.81	.005
Colonial Area	−1112.55	−.16	−.28	−1.83	.05
Mil. Expend.$_{t-1}$	1.70	1.44	.61	4.32	.001
Mil. Ex. Nonallies	.03	.40	.54	3.58	.001
Intersections	745.21	.20	.32	1.91	.05
Pop. × (Iron and Steel)[a]	−0.00017	−.97	−.36	−2.16	.025

expenditures, and the constant term. The influence of other nations is statistically insignificant in the second subperiod; Italian colonial-area and the constant are enough to account for 55 percent of the variance. On the whole, Italy's national growth (including that of the military sector) appears to have propelled the country into conflict with others.

The dynamics of Austro-Hungarian expenditures is a mix of factors: the significant variables are military-expenditures$_{t-1}$, military-expenditures-of-nonallies, intensity-of-intersections, population-times-iron-and-steel production, colonial area, and the constant term.[32]

From Chapter 11 it will be recalled that Austro-Hungarian colonial area (what little there was) could be accounted for primarily by population density and the constant, although other variables were important for subperiods. And in Chapter 12 we reported that Austria-Hungary's intensity-of-intersections was best-accounted for by colonial area, violence-behavior, and violence-of-others, although the empire's military expenditures had some impact for the subperiod 1878–1914. Taken together, these findings might be interpreted as demonstrating that the impact of domestic growth was counter-balanced by pressures from stronger states.[33]

Historical evidence shows that Kaiser Wilhelm II, Tirpitz, Moltke, and other German leaders watched British naval budgets and French army budgets very closely.[34] Various quantitative studies by Richardson and others strongly support the competition model. Our own analysis, however, highlights the importance of domestic factors. How then do we account for the difference between the two findings? We believe that the difference only underscores the intense interdependency of competition and expansion; growth and expansion invite international competition, while competition invites further growth and expansion.[35] We should therefore not be surprised if (as is the case here) one model better captures the expansion process whereas another (the Richardson equations, for example) yields equally persuasive evidence for international competition. In the final analysis, however, it is a matter of empirical evidence. If the growth and

---

[32]All of these variables except the constant ($p = .005$) and colonial area ($p = .05$) are significant at the .001 level. Population-times-iron-and-steel-production, the constant, and colonial area are all related inversely to military expenditures – all other variables are related positively. Ninety-four percent of the variance is accounted for by the six variables. For the period beginning 1878 (when Austro-Hungarian colonial expansion began), 87 percent of the variance is explained by military-expenditures$_{t-1}$ and military-expenditures-of-nonallies (both at .001 level), intensity-of-intersections (.05 level), and population-times-iron-and-steel production ($p = .025$, beta $= -.97$).

[33]Austro-Hungarian expansion (and political and economic influence) was in effect blocked as much by her ally Germany as by any other major power. Austro-Hungarian naval power was inadequate to compete for overseas colonial territory and there was no possibility for expansion into adjacent German-held territory.

[34]Similar comparisons were made by German leaders in terms of tonnage and numbers and classes of ships, number of men under arms, and so forth.

[35]We are referring here to contributions at the national level. It must be kept in mind that the dynamics of national growth and expansion are also likely to include competition among groups *within the nation* (i.e., at another level of analysis).

Table 13-2. Naval arms race, Britain and Germany, 1871–1914.*

Country	R^2	F ratio	Durbin-Watson statistic	Time-dependent correction	Variable	Parameter Estimate Unstandardized	Standardized (beta)	Partial correlation	t statistic	Significance level
BRITAIN	.98	326.62 df = 5,38 p = .001	1.83	None	Naval Expend.$_{t-1}$	0.89	0.86	0.78	7.70	.001
					German Nav. Ex.	0.004	0.002	0.007	0.04	n.s.
					Intersections	308.03	0.05	0.22	1.39	n.s.
					Colonial Area	−27936.20	−0.07	−0.09	−0.54	n.s.
					Pop. × Nat. Inc.	0.00009	0.18	0.21	1.32	n.s.
					Constant	244,727.0	0.00	0.09	0.53	n.s.
GERMANY	.81	32.67 df = 5,38 p = .001	2.53	AUTO2	Naval Expend.$_{t-1}$	0.01	0.01	0.01	0.07	n.s.
					Brit. Nav. Ex.	−0.19	−0.35	−0.27	−1.71	.10
					Intersections	−1516.43	−0.34	−0.53	−3.87	.001
					Colonial Area	−850.02	−0.15	−0.20	−1.25	n.s.
					Pop. × Nat. Inc.	0.00027	1.51	0.77	7.75	.001
					Constant	−20977.10	0.00	−0.41	−2.76	.01

*All statistics refer to the simultaneous-system estimates using both two-stage least squares and, where indicated in the time-dependent correction column, generalized least squares.

expansion variables were "in reality" much stronger than the competition variables, one might then wonder whether the rhetoric of competition were only that—a rationalization for what leaders feel compelled to do for *other* reasons (which may or may not be conscious). For example, although the German military budgets were partly the result of Germany's growth and expansion, the Kaiser, Tirpitz, Moltke, and others regularly justified military budget increases by comparing Germany's capability with that of the British and French. In their public statements these leaders regarded Germany's expansion as "blocked," rather than admitting that Germany might be encroaching on the expansion of others. The resulting arms race was also explained as the result of other nation's actions.

Because of widespread interest among historians and political analysts in the Anglo-German naval race and the Franco-German armaments competition, we made separate analyses of these two phenomena (the results are reported in Tables 13-2 and 13-3).[36] In each case the statistical findings only marginally alter our inferences. With some exceptions, growth and expansion factors again seem to be more influential than competition factors. British naval expenditures are overwhelmingly accounted for by Britain's naval-expenditures$_{t-1}$, with virtually no impact from German naval expenditures or intensity of British intersections. German naval expenditures, on the other hand, although fairly well-explained by the effect of population-times-national-income and the constant, also show an effect from British naval expenditures and intensity of German intersections.[37] From Tables 13-1 to 13-3 we might infer that the behavior of a challenging power may result more from domestic factors than from self-comparisons with the dominant power. The latter, although

---

[36]The regression equations for these two competitions were almost identical to the equation presented at the beginning of this chapter—only the expenditures-of-nonallies term is different. British naval expenditures, for example, were treated analogously to British military expenditures—as a function of naval-expenditures$_{t-1}$, intensity-of-intersections, colonial area, and population-times-national-income. However, the (naval) expenditures-of-nonallies term is specified here as *German* naval expenditures, and no dummy variables are needed. German naval expenditures and French and German army expenditures are treated similarly.

[37]Ninety-eight percent of the variance in British naval expenditures is explained primarily by naval-expenditures$_{t-1}$ (beta = .86, p = .001). In the case of Germany population-times-national-income (beta = 1.51, p = .001), the constant (p = .01), intensity-of-intersections (beta = −.34, p = .001), and the naval expenditures of Britain (beta = −.35, p = .10) account for 81 percent of the variance in German naval expenditures. Thus, unlike the naval expenditures of Britain, those of Germany are somewhat affected by foreign factors. Since the foreign factors have negative coefficients, however, the nature of that impact is uncertain. Certainly, this is contradictory to the expectations of a pure Richardson process. One explanation for the negative relationship might be that the effect of population-times-national-income is so strong as to overpower any other possible relationships, and may generate statistical artifacts of which this set of negative relationships is but one example.

Table 13-3. Arms race, France and Germany, 1871–1914.*

Country	R^2	F ratio	Durbin-Watson statistic	Time-dependent correction	Variable	Parameter Estimate Unstandardized	Standardized (beta)	Partial correlation	t statistic	Significance level
FRANCE	.40	5.03 df = 5,38 p = .01	1.36	None	Army Expend.$_{t,t-1}$	2.18	0.55	0.29	1.86	.05
					Ger. Army Ex.	0.99	0.37	0.22	1.41	.10
					Intersections	−2718.88	−0.15	−0.15	−0.95	n.s.
					Colonial Area	−123,010.0	−0.73	−0.31	−2.00	.05
					Pop. × Nat. Inc.	0.001	0.45	0.19	1.18	n.s.
					Constant	496,219.0	0.00	0.24	1.54	.10
GERMANY	.84	39.82 df = 5,38 p = .001	2.17	None	Army Expend.$_{t,t-1}$	0.31	0.30	0.35	2.29	.05
					Fr. Army Ex.	0.04	0.11	0.20	1.28	n.s.
					Intersections	−97.64	−0.01	−0.02	−0.12	n.s.
					Colonial Area	1463.86	0.15	0.25	1.61	.10
					Pop. × Nat. Inc.	0.00015	0.50	0.54	3.99	.001
					Constant	37319.50	0.00	0.44	3.06	.005

*All statistics refer to the simultaneous-system estimates using both two-stage least squares and, where indicated in the time-dependent correction column, generalized least squares.

increasingly aware of the challenge, may nonetheless also be responding more to domestic demands than to self-comparisons with a challenging power. But the relative statistical weakness of competition
variables in our analysis should not obscure the fact that increases in
military spending were frequently, even regularly, rationalized by both
British and German leaders as an "arms race."

From our analysis of Franco-German arms competition, France's
army expenditures do not appear to be reactive to those of Germany;
they are best-explained by previous expenditures and by colonial
area (the latter relationship is negative, reflecting the fact that French
military expenditures increased as French territorial expansion declined or tapered off). The variance in Germany's military expenditures
is explained wholly by domestic variables, namely, previous expenditures, population-times-national-income, colonial area, and the
constant. The influence of France's army expenditures is not significant. These results again confirm the overwhelming importance of
domestic factors in determining the level of military spending.

The primary importance of domestic factors – the major finding in
this chapter – does not preclude the reality of arms competition. Two
countries whose military establishments are expanding largely for
domestic reasons can, and indeed almost certainly will, become
acutely aware of each other's spending.[38] Thereafter, although spending may continue to be powerfully influenced by domestic factors,
deliberate military competition may increase and even take the form
of an arms race (although the race may be over specific military
features and may be a very small portion of total military spending).

In sum, our analysis of the six great powers prior to WWI shows
that each country's military-expenditures$_{t-1}$ were a primary factor in
the dynamics of military spending. The effect of population-times-
national-income was also important in all cases. Military expenditures-
of-nonallies and intensity-of-intersections were generally less
significant than domestic factors, and in some cases were not significant at all.

---

[38]Gray, 1971, pp. 39–79.

Alliances

14

An alliance is one way whereby a country can increase its capabilities. A land power, for example, may indirectly acquire naval capability by concluding an alliance with a naval power; a sea power may indirectly acquire some of the military capability of a land power. This is essentially what Britain and France achieved through a long series of staff negotiations during several years prior to WWI.

In Part I we noted that to the extent that an alliance is perceived by national leaders as a capability, it may be employed in ways that could increase the probability of war. Clearly, it is the overall interrelationship among the variables in the international system that is likely to determine whether an alliance or system of alliances is negatively associated with the outbreak of war (as Singer and Small found was true during the nineteenth century) or positively associated with it (as they found for the twentieth century).

Alliance-formation is a complex process. The purpose of this chapter is quite limited, however. We do not propose to test existing theories of international alliance or to predict what particular alliance arrangement any particular country is likely to enter into. In Part II we described the history of the consolidation of pre-WWI European alliances. In Chapters 12 and 13 we touched on the interdependence of alliances and intensity-of intersections and military capability. In this chapter we shall investigate quantitively some of the factors that influence the shaping of alliances.

Alliance-formation often carries the connotation of a peaceful activity—in contrast to the development of military or naval capabilities. In fact, however, the conclusion of a military alliance, or defense or "security" pact, implies the existence of a rival (or enemy) country or bloc. Thus, the enhancement of cooperation and even integration "within" an alliance may very well exacerbate conflict "without."

In Chapter 13 we considered military expenditures a measure of a country's military capability. We shall treat alliances somewhat comparably, as another capability, and ascertain how much of the variance in the "alliance capability" for each of the six major powers during the period 1871–1914 can be accounted for.[1]

In Part II we refered to Singer and Small's finding that ". . . both alliance aggregation and bipolarity covary strongly with the amount of war that follows (within a three-year period) during the twentieth century, and correlate *inversely* to almost the same degree during the nineteenth century."[2] How is this difference to be explained? Among the possibilities put forward by Singer and Small is the suggestion that the structural variable "alliance-aggregation" may itself be responsive to other aspects of the international system and that "its predictive power is a function of the interaction with such variables." This appears to be a reasonable explanation. Indeed, when alliances are examined in relation to other phenomena, it becomes easier to understand why the findings were different for different periods.

Singer and Small dealt with "alliance-aggregation" only as an independent variable, and used it as a predictor of the outbreak of war. In our statistical analysis we treat alliances as a *dependent* variable as well, and are concerned with how far a country's total alliances are determined by its military capability, the military capabilities of non-allies, the intensity of collisions with the interests of other nations, and domestic growth.

Despite the concern of recent studies on alliance with the *number* of actors (nations) in the international system,[3] we are inclined to suspect that this factor may be less important for predicting large-scale violence than (a) the levels (and rates) of growth of the different countries on critical dimensions of national power (b) the differences in access to resources and markets or (c) the consequent distribution of political, economic, and military capabilities among them. These factors affect both alliance-formation itself and whether alliances increase propensities for war or peace. Admittedly, there is a little overlap between this viewpoint and theories of the importance of the number of nations involved. In the long run, we believe an analysis of national growth, access to markets and resources, and the resultant distribution of power may yield more precision in predicting violence.

Both the relative weakness of France after the Franco-Prussian War

---

[1]Although The Triple Entente was not a formal alliance, it was included in our data set because through staff level negotiations France concluded military arrangements with both Russia and Britain that made alliance-type responses to a major crisis highly probable.

[2]Singer and Small, 1970, p. 283. Of the 56 correlations run between commitments and different measures of "bipolarity-structure" and "war-magnitude," 17 show the expected strong positive correlation ($r > .01$).

[3]See Deutsch and Singer, 1964; Singer and Small, 1970.

and the Reinsurance Treaty between Russia and Germany may have contributed considerably to international stability during the Bismarckian era. If thereafter the Reinsurance Treaty had been maintained along with the Franco-Russian entente, and if Germany and Britain had been able to achieve some kind of arrangement, a measure of stability might have been preserved in Europe over a considerably longer period of time. Moreover, had treaties been signed regulating conflicts of interests in Africa, Asia, and especially the Balkans, the probability of a major war among the great powers might have been further reduced.[4] But we should not be surprised if anything short of a *universal* alliance system—in which every power has some type of alliance or other conflict-regulating arrangement with every other power—fails to provide an adequate foundation for long-lasting, relatively nonviolent stability. And, in view of differences between nations on critical dimensions (such as population, technology, access to resources) and in the nature and strength of national capabilities, we would expect even a universal system to be subject in the long-run to strains, leading eventually to conflicts and crises.

Our hypothesized dynamics of alliance-formation are shown in the box on page 222. The interaction between population and national income gives us some indication of domestic demands; through the two military-expenditures variables (one domestic and the other foreign) we obtain some indication of the influence of the military on alliances; and we have included intensity-of-intersections in order to get some idea of the impact of conflicts of interests on alliance.

It is important to make explicit the relationship of this equation to previous ones, and to the notions of 'shifts' and 'breakpoints.' In the alliance equation we seek to identify the extent to which the independent variables contribute to changes in the international system between 1870 and 1914 (described in Part II). The measure for the dependent variable in this equation is the *number of alliances in effect for a given power in a given year*. Alliances (or the absence thereof) were indirectly employed in the analysis of intensity-of-intersections (Chapter 12) and military expenditures.[5] Here we test for the extent to which total alliances are directly affected by intensity-of-intersections and other variables. In effect we are searching for feedback relations that will be employed later to link colonial area, alliances, intensity-of-intersections, military expenditures, and violence-behavior.

---

[4] Such arrangements would not necessarily have affected the possibility of wars of colonial liberation.

[5] In the equation for intensity-of-intersections an independent variable was made up from the expansion of *nonallied* powers only. For example, only when Russia is *not* allied to Britain could Russian colonial area influence the intensity of British intersections. Similarly, in the military-expenditures equation (Chapter 13) an independent variable was made up from the military expenditures of *nonallied* powers.

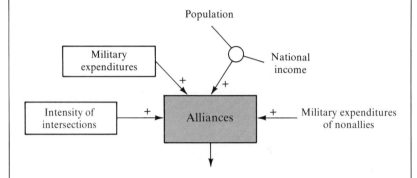

Hypothesized Dynamics of Alliance-Formation

This is represented by the following equation:

total alliances $= \alpha_4 + \beta_{15}$ (military expenditures) $+$
β_{16} (intensity-of-intersections) $+$
β_{17} (military-expenditures-of-
nonallies) $+ \beta_{18}$ (population-times-
national-income) $+ \mu_4$.

The arrow *from* the alliance variable indicates that total-alliances is an explanatory (independent) variable in one other equation.

For our analysis of the dynamics of alliance-formation we have used data from the Singer and Small study.[6] Since 1900 served as a breakpoint for the 130-year period of their analysis (1815–1945), the data we have taken for the period 1870–1914 samples the two sub-periods that yielded Singer and Small quite opposed findings. We shall use breakpoints, as we have in previous chapters; but inasmuch as ours have been derived from an analysis of the residuals or from the guidelines in our theory or from known historical events, they will not necessarily coincide with the 1900 breakpoint used by Singer and Small.

The major European powers can be divided, albeit in an over-simplified way, into three groups: (1) those that increased the number of their alliances as their military expenditures declined (relative to

---

[6] Singer, 1968, Table 3, pp. 268–270.

those of nonallies); (2) those that decreased the number of their alliances as their military expenditures increased (relative to those of nonallies); and (3) those that increased both.[7]

Prior to 1898, as befitted her "splendid isolation," Britain had few alliances with major powers — never more than two per year for the entire period between 1870 and 1900. Between 1900 and 1914, on the other hand, the number of British alliances increased from one to four per year.

The 1902 Anglo-Japanese alliance marked the end of Britain's years of isolation. According to this arrangement, if one party became involved in a war with another party, the other was bound to maintain neutrality, but if another power (or powers) were to enter the conflict, the ally was committed to join. Neither party was to enter into any agreements with another power (Russia particularly) without consulting the other. This arrangement greatly increased British diplomatic and military (especially naval) interests in the Far East and provided a partial counterbalance in the Pacific to any Russian threat to British interests in Europe and overseas.

The lapse of the Russo-German Reinsurance Treaty, on the other hand, and the rapid rise in German naval capabilities were good reasons for Britain and Russia to review their relations, despite the Anglo-Japanese treaty. In 1903 the two countries initiated conversations aimed at an understanding; the attempt failed because Russia was unwilling to agree upon a partition of Persia into spheres of influence. (It was not until October, 1905 that Britain and Russia again discussed entente, and not until 1907 that an arrangement was finally achieved.)

In the meantime, Britain's fear of Russian encroachment along the frontier of India, the inability of the two countries to reach an agreement on Persia, and other outstanding issues prompted Britain to open discussions with Russia's ally France. The Anglo-French Accords of 1904 eliminated a wide range of potential conflicts and thus was a first step in the direction of closer relations between the two countries. In effect, Anglo-French alignment began in January, 1906 with the opening of military and naval discussions, and the stipulation of British "moral obligations" to France (that were not made known to the full British cabinet until 1911).

In the context of this briefly sketched background, how well are total British alliances accounted for by our model? For the full period, 82 percent of the variance in Britain's alliances is accounted for by the variables in the alliance equation, particularly by population-times-national-income, military-expenditure-of-nonallies, Britain's military

---

[7]A fourth possibility, the *reduction of both*, is not applicable to the nations included in our study. However, the Scandinavian countries have often approximated this pattern.

expenditures, and the constant term. All of these terms are significant at or above the .01 level.[8]

Findings for subperiods are quite similar. The same variables remain important throughout (although the constant term loses significance at times). Military-expenditures-of-nonallies in particular are significant, but inversely related to alliances, throughout all periods tested. Population-times-national income has a consistently strong positive relationship to total alliances.

The impact of Britain's military expenditures is weak and negative for the period 1870–1890 (corresponding to the years of her "isolation"), but positive between 1891–1914. In the latter subperiod Britain's military expenditures decreased relative to those of the Triple Alliance. We might conclude that in later years Britain relied more heavily on alliances than her own military for security.

Germany had no alliances with any major power in 1870. By 1890 she had six; thereafter she dropped to five per year, then four, and remained at that level through 1914. It will be recalled from Part II that during the 1880s Germany considered the power of the Triple Alliance equal to the power of France and Russia combined.[9] The alignment of Britain was therefore of critical importance to Germany. A fundamental aspect of Bismarck's policy was to prevent the establishment of a Franco-Russian combination directed against Germany.[10] In this connection, he encouraged Britain to play a more aggressive role against Russia, and in 1886 secured British support against France in North Africa.[11] Meanwhile, by allying other European naval powers with Germany, Bismarck hoped to counterbalance the threat posed to Germany by British seapower.[12] During the 1880s France began to threaten British naval predominance in the Mediterranean. If Bismarck had been successful in creating a European naval combination, Britain would have been faced with a serious threat. But French leaders were wary of the German chancellor's intentions, and Britain was able to retain her role as the fulcrum of power.[13]

Although Germany considered Italy her weakest partner in the Triple Alliance, Italy played a critical role in German diplomacy. For example, the Triple Alliance stipulated that any French attack on Italy would automatically involve Germany and Austria-Hungary. After the potentially strong alliance among the Three Emperors had been

---

[8]Population-times-national-income (beta $= .89$, $p = .001$); military-expenditures-of-nonallies (beta $= -.84$, $p = .001$); British military-expenditures (beta $= .47$, $p = .005$), and the constant ($p = .01$). Table 14-1 gives actual coefficient estimates, plus the results for subperiods.

[9]Rich, 1965, p. 193.

[10]Langer, 1962, p. 429.

[11]Rich, 1965, p. 202.

[12]Langer, 1962, pp. 301–302; also see Chapter 3 here.

[13]Nichols, 1958, p. 115.

severed and Russia drew closer to France, Italy (like Austria-Hungary) demanded more of Germany in return for adherence to the alliance.[14]

During the Bosnian Crisis of 1908–1909 Germany bound herself to Austria-Hungary in what amounted to an offensive (rather than the previous defensive) alliance. Germany's increasing concern for the preservation of the Austro-German alliance encouraged Austria to pursue her Balkan interests — interests that were not systematically regulated or constrained by existing treaty arrangements, and which contributed to crisis in that area more than once before June, 1914. All of the above developments not only further intensified Germany's concern for her allies, but also gave new importance to the configuration of power in the Mediterranean. German concern for British naval power in the Mediterranean, or for any events that brought Britain closer to France (and thence in greater harmony with Russia), was enhanced.

When the Reinsurance Treaty was allowed to lapse, the administration in Berlin hoped that Britain would replace Russia as an alliance partner. By the turn of the century, German leaders calculated that the security of their country would be assured if Britain (and possibly also Japan) could be brought into the Triple Alliance.[15] But, as we saw in Part II, efforts to bring the two countries into a formal alliance persistently failed. The obstacles to an Anglo-German coalition were discussed in Chapter 3. Germany wanted a defensive arrangement that would apply to the *entire* British Empire and the *entire* Triple Alliance — the terms to come into effect in the event that *any* nation of either side were attacked by two or more great powers. What appears to have inhibited Salisbury and other British leaders was an unwillingness to be drawn into a conflict in support of Italy or Austria-Hungary. Although Britain regarded an alliance with Germany alone as desirable, it appeared to the Germans that such an arrangement would give Britain great flexibility while requiring German assistance should any part of the far-flung British Empire come under attack.

If Germany felt "encircled" by the Entente, she also doubted its cohesiveness. Even during the July, 1914 crisis, after Russia had ordered mobilization, German leaders persuaded themselves that France would not enter the conflict. And if France did become involved, Germany believed that Britain probably would not. The first Moroccan crisis of 1905 was in large part the outcome of a German attempt to test the strength of the Anglo-French Entente.

Germany is yet another case in our analysis where a shift in dynamics appears to occur midway through the period. For the entire

[14]Rich, 1965, I: 323; Nichols, 1958, p. 115.
[15]Rich, 1965, II: 641.

period 1871–1914 only 16 percent of the variance in German alliances can be accounted for (the equation is not statistically significant). Two subperiods, however, yield results significant at the .001 level. Between 1871–1900, 57 percent of the variance is accounted for by population-times-national-income, intensity-of-intersections, and military-expenditures-of nonallies, all highly statistically significant. Thus, both domestic and foreign factors had an effect on German alliances. From 1884–1914, however, 85 percent of the variance is accounted for primarily by the constant, although there is some impact from military-expenditures-of-nonallies. It thus appears that once the dynamics of German alliances was set, an inertial effect became predominant, i.e., the process was no longer susceptible to much alteration. Germany, we might infer, was "locked into" a somewhat rigid position.[16]

The efforts of Bismarck to isolate France from the European alliance system were touched upon in Part II. Because of this effort (but also for other reasons), France had no formal alliances with any major power during the 1870s and 1880s. Then, during the 1890s she developed her entente with Russia.

In the wake of the Anglo-Japanese alliance of 1902, France and Russia, declaring themselves in favor of the principles enumerated in the Anglo-Japanese document, reserved the right to consult each other in order to safeguard their interests. (This latter stipulation was generally viewed as a countermove to the Anglo-Japanese arrangement and perhaps as an extension of the earlier Franco-Russian alignment into the Far East.) Nevertheless, Anglo-French relations remained potentially volatile. The Anglo-French Accords of 1904 amounted to a "diplomatic revolution of the first magnitude."[17]

For the full period only 44 percent of the variance in French alliances can be accounted for, and this primarily by military-expenditures-of-nonallies (see Table 14-1 for full results).[18] After 1895 the number of French (and British) alliances increased, whereas the number of German alliances decreased. This trend, noted earlier, was perceived by German leaders as "encirclement," and was one reason given by

---

[16]For the subperiod 1871–1900, population-times-national-income (beta = 1.54, $p = .001$), intensity-of-intersections (beta = .48, $p = .005$), and military-expenditures-of nonallies (beta = −1.18, $p = .001$) are all very important. For the period 1891–1914, the constant is at the .001 level, population-times-national-income is at the .005 level, and intensity-of-intersections and German military expenditures are at the .05 and .10 levels, respectively (with smaller beta values). The decreasing importance of external realities as an influence on German alliances is evident. It is also interesting to note the lack of significance of Germany's own military expenditures.

[17]Rich, 1965, 2: 681; also see Chapter 3 here.

[18]The coefficient for military-expenditures-of-nonallies for the full period is −.24 ($p = .001$). The Chow test indicates an absence of statistically significant differences for three subperiods, although the results are intuitively quite different.

German leaders for strengthening the army and building an even more powerful navy.

Another attempt by Germany to avoid "encirclement" occurred late in 1904 when Russia and Germany, responding to a deterioration in Anglo-Russian relations, negotiated for an alliance. At that time the tsar accepted a treaty drafted by Germany that provided for mutual assistance in the event of attack by another European power. The treaty was never concluded, however, because of Russia's unwillingness to sign without first consulting France. Russia agreed to mutual assistance only in the specific event that complications arose while Russian warships were being coaled by a German company.

Forty-three percent of the variance in Russian alliances for the full period can be accounted for by the variables in the equation. Two variables are statistically significant: military-expenditures and military-expenditures-of-nonallies.[19] We introduced several breakpoints in the analysis of Russian alliances; the most important of these was 1896. For the subperiod 1896–1914, Russia's own military-expenditures are the single most important determinant of total Russian alliances (40 percent of the variance can be accounted for in this subperiod).[20] Since Russia increased her military expenditures (relative to those of her rivals) while simultaneously increasing her alliances, it seems that the tsarist government relied on both means to improve national capabilities.

Italy had no alliances during the early years of the 44-year period under study. As pointed out in Part II, Italy's search for alliances can be explained in part as an effort to increase her international status.[21] Ever since her unification in 1861 she had been "beating about on the fringes of great-power status." From 1880 through 1887 Italy had two alliances per year. By 1890 she rose to nine per year, dropping to three by 1896, and then increasing her commitments again. By 1914 she had a total of six. During much of the period 1870–1914 Italy's expansion in North Africa pitted her against France, and at times against Britain. These collisions prompted Italy to stick with the Triple Alliance. However, her expansionist drive, especially the extension of her interests in Albania during the Balkan wars, tended to push Italy away from Austria-Hungary and thus also from Germany, and toward the Entente. Accordingly, Italy promised neutrality in the event of a war between Russia and Austria-Hungary and negotiated secret treaties with France on the partitioning of Morocco. At the same time, Italy hoped to secure support from both Germany and Austria-Hungary and

---

[19]The beta coefficient for Russia's military expenditures is .84 ($p = .025$); for military-expenditures-of-nonallies the coefficient is $-.32$ ($p = .025$).

[20]The beta coefficient for Russian military expenditures is .53 ($p = .01$); no other coefficients are significant for this period.

[21]*Cambridge Modern History*, 12: 553.

Table 14-1. Alliances — results of estimation from a simultaneous equation system.*

Country	Period	R^2	F ratio	Durbin-Watson statistic	Time-dependent correction	Chow test
BRITAIN	1871–1914	.82	44.33 $df = 4,39$ $p = .001$	1.75	MAV1	
	1871–1890	.65	7.11 $df = 4,15$ $p = .005$	2.67	AUTO2	$F_{24,15} = 1.5$ $p = $ n.s
	1896–1914	.89	27.32 $df = 4,14$ $p = .001$	2.05	AUTO2	
	1891–1914	.84	24.54 $df = 4,19$ $p = .001$	1.93	MAV1	$F_{20,19} = 1.4$ $p = $ n.s
FRANCE	1871–1914	.44	7.52 $df = 4,39$ $p = .001$	1.53	AUTO1	
	1871–1900	.49	5.98 $df = 4,25$ $p = .005$	1.58	MAV1	$F_{14.25} = 0.$ $p = $ n.s
	1880–1914	.43	5.76 $df = 4,30$ $p = .005$	1.52	AUTO2	$F_{9,30} = 0.$ $p = $ n.
	1896–1914	.55	2.82 $df = 4,14$ $p = .10$	1.44	AUTO2	
GERMANY	1871–1914	.16	1.83 $df = 4,39$ $p = $ n.s.	.31	None	
	1884–1914	.85	37.32 $df = 4,26$ $p = .001$	.175	MAV2	$F_{13.26} = 42$ $p = .00$
	1871–1900	.57	8.43 $df = 4,25$ $p = .001$	1.70	MAV1	
	1891–1914	.84	24.39 $df = 4,19$ $p = .001$	1.78	MAV1	

| Variable | Parameter Estimate | | Partial correlation | t statistic | Significance level |
	Unstandardized	Standardized (beta)			
Pop. × Nat. Inc.	.0126[a]	.89	.76	7.3	.001
Mil. Ex. Nonallies	−7.70[a]	−.84	−.80	−8.2	.001
Mil. Expend.	5.45[a]	.47	.43	3.0	.005
Constant	1.14	.00	.39	2.7	.01
Pop. × Nat. Inc.	.028[a]	1.56	.62	3.0	.005
Mil. Ex. Nonallies	−8.90[a]	−.59	−.70	−3.8	.001
Mil. Expend.	−16.8[a]	−.60	−.32	−1.3	.10
Mil. Ex. Nonallies	−5.89[a]	−.64	−.76	−4.4	.001
Pop. × Nat. Inc.	0.27[a]	.47	.67	3.4	.005
Mil. Expend.	4.57[a]	.35	.54	2.4	.025
Mil. Expend.	3.23[a]	.28	.45	2.20	.025
Mil. Ex. Nonallies	−7.82[a]	−.89	−.88	−8.16	.001
Pop. × Nat. Inc.	.00796[a]	.30	.56	2.92	.005
Constant	3.75	.00	.60	3.23	.001
Mil. Ex. Nonallies	−2.66[a]	−.24	−.68	−5.8	.001
Mil. Expend.	16.0[a]	1.22	.58	3.54	.001
Intersections	−.03	−.48	−.43	−2.37	.025
Pop. × Nat. Inc.	−.00788[a]	−.67	−.32	−1.67	.10
Constant	−1.77	.00	−.57	−3.43	.005
Mil. Ex. Nonallies	−2.639[a]	−.24	−.68	−5.11	.001
Mil. Ex. Nonallies	−2.54[a]	−.39	−.70	−3.68	.001
Pop. × Nat. Inc.	.0114[a]	1.14	.25	1.6	.10
Intersections	.10	.39	.26	1.7	.05
Constant	3.43	.00	.59	4.6	.001
Mil. Ex. Nonallies	−1.00[a]	−.31	−.35	−1.9	.05
Mil. Expend.	−3.66[a]	−.25	−.23	−1.19	n.s.
Constant	6.65	.00	.94	14.6	.001
Pop. × Nat. Inc.	.0375[a]	1.54	.75	5.6	.001
Intersections	.18	.48	.51	3.0	.005
Mil. Ex. Nonallies	−13.9[a]	−1.18	−.66	−4.4	.001
Pop. × Nat. Inc.	−.00355[a]	−1.2	−.57	−2.9	.005
Mil. Expend.	3.43[a]	.51	.33	1.5	.10
Intersections	.02	.36	.39	1.9	.05
Constant	4.87	.00	.97	18.26	.001

Table continued

Table 14-1. Continued

Country	Period	R^2	F ratio	Durbin-Watson statistic	Time-dependent correction	Chow test
ITALY	1871–1914	.29	3.98 $df = 4,39$ $p = .01$	2.02	AUTO2	
	1871–1888	.88	24.3 $df = 4,13$ $p = .001$	2.06	AUTO2	
	1889–1914	.73	13.93 $df = 4,21$ $p = .001$	1.82	None	$F_{18.21} = 0.3$ $p = $ n.s.
RUSSIA	1871–1914	.43	7.50 $df = 4,39$ $p = .001$	1.89	AUTO2	
	1896–1914	.40	2.38 $df = 4,14$ $p = .10$	1.55	AUTO2	$F_{25.14} = 3.9$ $p = .01$
	1871–1890	.65	6.92 $df = 4,15$ $p = .005$	2.18	AUTO2	$F_{24.15} = 1.8$ $p = $ n.s.
	1891–1914	.33	2.29 $df = 4,19$ $p = .10$	1.87	AUTO2	$F_{20.19} = 1.3$ $p = $ n.s.
AUSTRIA-HUNGARY	1871–1914	.25	3.18 $df = 4,39$ $p = .025$	1.15	MAV2	
	1878–1914	.21	2.19 $df = 4,32$ $p = .10$	1.51	AUTO2	$F_{7.32} = 2.5$ $p = .05$

*All statistics refer to the simultaneous-system estimates using both two-stage least squares and, where indicated in the time-dependent correction column, generalized least squares.
^aActual value of unstandardized parameter estimate is multiplied by 10^{-6} for scale purposes.

protection against France in her attempt to build a colonial empire.[22] In 1890 (separately influenced by Britain and Germany) Italy refused France's offer of a partition of Tripoli in return for abandonment of Italian claims in Tunis. Subsequent French efforts to completely detach

---

[22]Brunschwig, 1966, p. 97; also see Chapter 4 here.

Variable	Parameter Estimate		Partial correlation	*t* statistic	Significance level
	Unstandardized	Standardized (beta)			
Mil. Expend.	88.3[a]	.75	.42	2.9	.005
Mil. Ex. Nonallies	−3.21[a]	−.16	−.27	−1.7	.05
Intersections	.23	.59	.85	5.80	.001
Constant	−2.61	.00	−.41	−1.64	.10
Intersections	.16	.68	.52	2.8	.005
Mil. Expend.	−82.4[a]	−.34	−.41	−2.07	.025
Constant	12.58	.00	.69	4.4	.001
Mil. Expend.	13.2[a]	.84	.31	2.0	.025
Mil. Ex. Nonallies	−2.54[a]	−.32	−.32	−2.1	.025
Mil. Expend.	12.0[a]	.53	.58	2.7	.01
Mil. Ex. Nonallies	−1.04[a]	.90	−.75	−4.45	.001
Pop. × Nat. Inc.	.0098[a]	.60	.45	1.96	.05
Constant	2.07	.00	.49	2.21	.025
Mil. Expend.	17.9[a]	.82	.61	3.38	.005
Mil. Expend.	108.0[a]	.70	.46	3.2	.005
Mil. Ex. Nonallies	−6.78[a]	−.63	−.57	−4.3	.001
Constant	2.41	.00	.31	2.1	.025
Mil. Expend.	9.90[a]	.65	.44	2.78	.005
Mil. Ex. Nonallies	−5.99[a]	−.63	−.41	−3.21	.001
Constant	4.74	.00	.36	2.20	.025

Italy from the Triple Alliance failed.[23]

For the full period we have been able to account for only 29 percent of the variance in Italian alliances, primarily by Italy's own military-

---

[23]Nichols, 1958, pp. 115–116; also see Chapter 5 here. Italy could not afford to compromise British goodwill because of her vulnerability to naval attack as well as her dependence on British consent to expand holdings in North Africa.

expenditures.[24] For the subperiod 1889–1914, however, intensity-of-intersections and the constant term also become important and together with the other variables in the equation account for 73 percent of the variance.[25] Italy appears to have relied on both alliances and her own military capability for protection against clashes with other powers. Since intensity-of-intersections and the (negative) constant term help account for 88 percent of the variance in the period 1871–1888, and since these terms are not significant for the full period, some shift in dynamics that is not explicitly identified by our model occurred around 1888.

In 1870 Austria-Hungary had no alliances; by 1887 she had eleven. The number dropped to ten in 1890 and to four in 1896. In 1898 she gained one, having five per year through 1908. Thereafter, until 1914, she had four. Austria-Hungary did not respond with any great enthusiasm in 1881 when Italy, stung by the French establishment of a protectorate over Tunis, turned toward Germany and Austria-Hungary. But Bismarck, skeptical of Russia's intentions within the League of the Three Emperors, encouraged negotiations that led to the conclusion, a year later, of the Triple Alliance.[26] Because of her location and relative position among the great powers, Austria-Hungary remained sensitive to shifts in the configuration of power, especially as they might relate to Balkan affairs. In 1909 Bulgaria, which Austro-Hungarian foreign minister Aehrenthal had hoped to harness to the Dual Monarchy, passed over into the Russian camp. The contradictions in relations between Austria-Hungary and Italy became increasingly acute, and Austria-Hungary became more and more dependent on Germany for security.

We were able to account for only 25 percent of the variance of Austro-Hungarian alliances for the full period; the most significant variables are the empire's own military expenditures and military-expenditures-of-nonallies.[27] Analysis of the subperiod 1878–1914 yielded almost identical results.

Although the rate of increase in Austro-Hungarian army expenditures was the highest of any of the major powers, the *level* of military spending remained low relative to that of the other five powers (see Table 7-1). As in the cases of Russia and Italy, Austria-Hungary seems to have used alliances to supplement her military strength. In spite of

---

[24]The beta coefficient for Italy's military expenditures is .75 ($p = .005$); for expenditures-of-nonallies −.16 ($p = .05$).

[25]The beta coefficients are: intensity-of-intersections, .68 ($p = .005$), and military expenditures, −.34 ($p = .025$). The constant, with an absolute value of 12.58, is significant at the .001 level.

[26]Langer, 1962, pp. 244–247.

[27]The beta coefficient for Austria-Hungary's own military expenditures is .70 ($p = .005$), for military-expenditures-of-nonallies −.63 ($p = .001$). The constant term is also significant, at the .025 level, with an estimated value of 2.41.

increases in alliances and military expenditures, Austria-Hungary remained essentially hemmed in politically, militarily, and economically, and unable to expand as other major powers did through acquisition of colonies.

Our analysis reveals that alliances are explained for the most part by military-expenditures-of-nonallies and intensity-of-intersections. Alliances thus appear to be largely a function of foreign events, despite the fact that domestic growth is also important (sometimes extremely so). To treat alliances as a national capability is admittedly an oversimplification, and no doubt many subtleties are lost.[28] On the other hand, we believe this is preferable to the search for an elusive magic number that will indicate whether the international system is stable or unstable. If alliances are treated as one variable within a complex international system, it becomes possible to understand how alliances and war are related, and specify the nature of the linkage. In the next chapter we will discuss how alliances, along with other variables, contribute to violence-behavior.

---

[28]The idea that alliances constitute a national capability is generally recognized, as in the following: ". . . states enter into alliances with one another in order to supplement each other's capability" (Liska, 1970, p. 109); "Governments which seek to construct permanent diplomatic coalitions or military alliances assume that they cannot achieve their objectives, defend their interests, or deter perceived threats by mobilizing [only] their own capabilities" (Kalevi Holsti, 1970, p. 93).

15 Violence-Behavior

It has often been said that the greater part of the nineteenth century and the early twentieth century was a period of relative peace and tranquility, one in which the great powers acted according to some broad consensus of principles. Yet in this same period there was intense competition, expansion, and conflict among these same nations, with alliances and counter-alliances continually being formed. How are these two views of the period to be reconciled?

One's view of the period depends very much on one's perspective. The long era of political stability under the moderating influence of the Concert of Berlin was also a period of rapid national and imperial growth. The great powers did indeed operate within a consensus, but above the vast field of collaboration were hills, peaks, and plateaus of conflict—many of them outside Europe in the relatively low-capability regions of Africa, Asia, and the Middle East, but some within Europe itself.

From our propositions in Chapter 1 one might have inferred that with each successive international crisis the probability increases of any one crisis erupting into large-scale war. History itself might seem to support this inference. But we have already seen (in Chapter 12) that the intensity of intersections among the great powers did not increase continually between 1870 and 1914. In this chapter we shall present additional evidence that raises doubts about the hypothesis that successive international crises cumulate and create the immediate likelihood of major war. There is no simple incremental process.

During the "tranquil" phase of the nineteenth century there was more international violence, especially in connection with the maintenance of colonies, than is commonly assumed. Also, there was less violence immediately prior to WWI than one might believe, particularly between countries that were to be wartime enemies, such as Germany and Britain or France. In fact, it is remarkable how much of the violence among the major powers between 1871–1914 occurred between countries that became allies during WWI – between Britain and Russia, or Italy and France.

Of all the national actions in the data set used to measure violence-behavior, most were relatively low in violence.[1] More important, even though our data show increases in the level of violence among the six great powers between 1870–1914, *they do not show any exceptional increases in violence between nations of the Triple Alliance and those of the Entente or between key rivals.* Interactions between Russia and Austria-Hungary were something of an exception, but for the most part even these were not very high in violence.

Prior to 1890 only two interactions between Germany and Britain were rated above 15 on the 30-point intensity scale: the German acquisition of Angra Pequeña in 1883 (17) and a conference called by Germany in 1884 as an anti-British gesture (18).[2] Even after 1890 very few Anglo-German interactions were ranked high on the scale, including the Kruger telegram (17, surprisingly low in view of the furor it raised at the time); the British halting in 1900 of the German ship *Bundesrath* (17); the 1905 speech of the British first lord of the admiralty directed against the German arms build-up (18); Germany's refusal in 1908 to collaborate with Britain in an arms-reduction program (16); Lloyd George's speech in 1911 at the Mansion House (16); the British decision in 1912 to withdraw her battleships from the Mediterranean and concentrate them in the North Sea (19); the publication in 1912 of a new German Naval Bill (19); and the British order during the summer of 1914 against dispersal of the fleet (19).

The numerical values assigned these events are of course controversial; others may rate this one or that higher or lower.[3] Yet the fact remains that strictly on the basis of the scaled values, from 1870 to 1914 there was not a single truly serious crisis between Britain and Germany that threatened war. With a few modifications, one can say

---

[1]The data set is a list of actions by the nations in our study, collected from historical sources. Each action was assigned a numerical value, representing the "level" of violence of the action, on a scale from 1 (low) to 30 (high). This metricizing procedure is described in Appendix A.

[2]A value of 30 represents organized armed violence. Figures in parentheses are the scaled values.

[3]The charge might also be leveled that by relying on published chronologies our procedure risks eliminating an important event merely because it does not appear in any of our sources. We can only share responsibility with those scholars who made the original selections, and question how important an event was if no scholar thought it important enough to list. In any case, for our purposes such bias is not so important. It is generally recognized that selectivity tends to omit *low*-violence events, not high ones. It is very unlikely that an important provocation has been missed, since we are concentrating on interactions with high levels of violence.

much the same sort of thing about Germany and France after the Franco-Prussian War.[4]

In spite of the relatively low violence between Germany and Britain, the two countries became leaders in opposing blocs, and enemies during WWI. By contrast, two wartime allies, Britain and Russia, had a considerable number of interactions rated above 15.[5]

Even Austria-Hungary, which was deeply involved in a number of Balkan conflicts, took part in only a few actions rated above 15 on the scale.[6] In general, Austro-Russian interactions were not as violent as one might expect—although, compared with interactions in other parts of Europe, those involving Austria-Hungary and Russia in the Balkan region ranked relatively high on the scale. It should be noted, however, that Austria-Hungary interacted comparatively infrequently with other powers, especially compared to such diplomatically active nations as Britain and Germany.

Any attempt to establish a clear and direct link between a high level at one time and a subsequent higher level is less than convincing. Although the level of violence was rising just prior to WWI, previous high levels had already "died down." Our data do not show any "snowballing" in the level of violence. Even if the actions in our data set had been assigned somewhat different values by another panel of judges—and despite the fact that the scaling technique undoubtedly fails to capture a certain amount of violence—nevertheless, we are persuaded that the outbreak of war in 1914 was not directly the outcome of a steadily rising level of violence.

The box on p. 237 shows our hypothesized dynamics of violence-behavior. Three of the variables in this equation are endogenous in the model and have been treated in other equations as *dependent* variables.

---

[4]In 1875 an article in the Berlin *Post* referred to a new French Army Law and concluded that war was "in sight" (18). In 1887 Germany arrested a French official who was accused of espionage, but released him a week later (18). Franco-German interactions after the turn of the century with high ratings of violence were: the first Moroccan Crisis in 1905 (16); the crisis in 1908 at Casablanca (16); and the second Moroccan Crisis in 1911 (24).

[5]These include: the British warning in 1877 against an attempted Russian blockade of the Suez Canal or the occupation of Egypt (26); dispatch of British troops in 1877 to reinforce the garrisons at Gibraltar and Malta (24); the British decision in 1878 to send her fleet into the Black Sea (17) and its passing through the Dardanelles (17); the Anglo-Turkish agreement of 1898 to halt Russia's advance in Asia Minor (14); the clash in 1885 between Russian troops and Anglo-Afghan forces at Panjdeh (30) and the British occupation of Fort Hamilton (19); the seizure in 1904 of a British steamer by the Russian Vladivostok Fleet (18); and the Dogger Bank incident of that same year (21). The British war of 1897 on the northwest frontier of India (30) might also have been included as an Anglo-Russian provocation, as well as Britain's 1904 war with Tibet (30).

[6]These include: the Austro-German Alliance of 1888, considered a diplomatic warning to Russia (19); the 1908 Austro-Hungarian proposal for a railway through the *sanjak* of Novibazar (16); interaction with Russia during the autumn of 1908 in the Bosnian Crisis (16); activities in the same crisis during the spring of 1909 (28); actions in 1911 during the breakdown of mediation in the Tripolitan War (27); and interaction with Russia in the autumn of 1912 (24).

Hypothesized Dynamics of Violence-Behavior

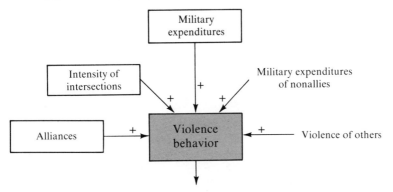

This is represented by the following equation:

$$\text{violence-behavior} = \alpha_5 + \beta_{19} \text{ (intensity of intersections)} + \beta_{20} \text{ (military expenditures)} + \beta_{21} \text{ (military-expenditures-of-nonallies)} + \beta_{22} \text{ (alliances)} + \beta_{23} \text{ (violence-of-others)} + \mu_5.$$

The arrow *from* the violence-behavior variable indicates that violence-behavior is an explanatory variable in one other equation.

In this chapter we examine their effects as *independent* variables in order to isolate their effects on violence-behavior. The variable military-expenditures-of-nonallies is defined as the expenditures of those powers with which a state is *not* allied. It is thus related to the alliance variable in that it refers to the implications of alliances by identifying rivals. By including this variable, we seek to capture the impact of *changes* in alliances.[7] So far as changes in alliances are reflected by the variable, some important breakpoints in the international relations of the time are included in the model.

The variance in violence-behavior is explained quite well by a small number of variables. At first glance this statement may seem to contradict our position that a multiplicity of values, goals, and events contributes to large-scale violence. Yet it should not be overlooked

---

[7]It is also used in explaining military expenditures (Ch. 13) and alliances (Ch. 14).

Table 15-1. Violence-behavior — results of estimation from a simultaneous equation system.*

Country	Period	R^2	F ratio	Durbin-Watson statistic	Time-dependent correction	Chow test
BRITAIN	1871–1914	.32	3.57 $df = 5,38$ $p = .01$	1.92	None	
	1871–1890	.91	26.91 $df = 5,14$ $p = .001$	2.31	AUTO2	$F_{24.14} = 1.64$ $p = $ n.s.
	1891–1914	.49	3.52 $df = 5,18$ $p = .025$	2.00	AUTO2	$F_{20.18} = 2.84$ $p = .025$
FRANCE	1871–1914	.99	9846.21 $df = 5,38$ $p = .001$	1.78	MAV2	
	1871–1900	.38	2.98 $df = 5,24$ $p = .05$	2.03	None	$F_{14.24} = 2.02$ $p = .10$
	1880–1914	.99	114,000 $df = 5,29$ $p = .001$	2.03	MAV2	$F_{9.29} = 2.83$ $p = .025$
GERMANY	1871–1914	.31	3.43 $df = 5,38$ $p = .025$	2.10	None	
	1884–1914	.51	5.20 $df = 5,25$ $p = .005$	2.10	AUTO2	$F_{13.25} = 1.56$ $p = $ n.s.

that many other factors affect the few variables found to contribute most to violence-behavior. It is the dynamics of this *larger system* of factors that accounts for the prevailing level of violence in 1914.

The violence-behavior of Britain in the full period is poorly accounted for; only military-expenditures-of-nonallies and violence-of-others are statistically significant.[8] However, if we take 1890 as a breakpoint, 91 percent of the variance in the country's violence-

---

[8] Military-expenditures-of-nonallies is significant at the .05 level (beta = .62), and violence-of-others is significant at the .001 level (beta = .64).

| Variable | Parameter Estimate | | Partial correlation | t statistic | Significance level |
	Unstandardized	Standardized (beta)			
Intersections	−.43	−.35	−.24	−1.53	.10
Mil. Ex. Nonallies	−19.9[a]	.62	.28	1.77	.05
Violence of Others	.96	.64	.50	3.52	.001
Mil. Expend.	−.0003	−.90	−.67	−3.4	.005
Alliances	5.99	.45	.52	2.3	.025
Violence of Others	1.67	1.06	.54	2.4	.025
Constant	49.32	.00	.72	3.9	.001
Mil. Ex. Nonallies	60.2[a]	1.18	.47	2.26	.01
Violence of Others	.72	.52	.54	2.73	.01
Violence of Others	.75	.62	.60	4.6	.001
Mil. Ex. Nonallies	.00002	.37	.68	5.7	.001
Alliances	1.18	.20	.37	2.5	.01
Intersections	.25	.19	.28	1.8	.05
Constant	−4.84	.00	−.37	−2.5	.01
Mil. Ex. Nonallies	80.49[a]	.78	.41	2.21	.025
Violence of Others	−.46	−.38	−.35	−1.81	.05
Violence of Others	.47	.39	.48	2.97	.005
Constant	10.40	.00	.52	3.31	.005
Violence of Others	.68	.48	.44	3.0	.005
Constant	6.75	.00	.28	1.8	.05
Violence of Others	.96	.66	.60	3.7	.001

Table continued

behavior in the *first* subperiod can be accounted for by the constant term, by Britain's own military expenditures, by violence-of-others, and by Britain's alliances, in that order of statistical significance. The amount of variance accounted for decreases dramatically for the period 1891–1914 (once Britain moved out of her "splendid isolation"). Only 49 percent of the variance is accounted for; again, only military-expenditures-of-nonallies and violence-of-others are statistically significant. Domestic factors that are powerful in the first subperiod, such as military expenditures, totally lose significance. After 1891 the violence-behavior of Britain seems to have been largely reactive,

Table 15-1. Continued

Country	Period	R^2	F ratio	Durbin-Watson statistic	Time-dependent correction	Chow test
ITALY	1871–1914	.36	4.19 $df = 5,38$ $p = .005$	1.97	MAV1	
	1871–1888	.87	16.67 $df = 5,12$ $p = .001$	1.85	AUTO2	$F_{26,12} = 1.45$ $p = $ n.s.
	1889–1914	.44	3.09 $df = 5,20$ $p = .05$	1.63	AUTO2	$F_{18,20} = 1.65$ $p = $ n.s.
RUSSIA	1871–1914	.38	4.66 $df = 5,38$ $p = .005$	1.88	MAV2	
	1871–1890	.48	2.58 $df = 5,14$ $p = .10$	2.29	None	$F_{24,14} = 1.14$ $p = $ n.s.
	1891–1914	.99	57,500.00 $df = 5,18$ $p = .001$	2.01	MAV2	$F_{20,18} = 1.79$ $p = $ n.s.
AUSTRIA-HUNGARY	1871–1914	.44	5.95 $df = 5,38$ $p = .001$	2.02	None	
	1878–1914	.39	3.92 $df = 5,31$ $p = .01$	1.88	None	$F_{7,31} = 0.14$ $p = $ n.s.
	1891–1914	.56	4.58 $df = 5,19$ $p = .005$	2.27	None	$F_{20,18} = .859$ $p = $ n.s.

*All statistics refer to the simultaneous-system estimates using both two-stage least squares and, where indicated in the time-dependent correction column, generalized least squares.

[a] Actual value of unstandardized parameter estimate is multiplied by 10^{-6} for scale purposes.

quite unlike her military expenditures, which were determined largely by domestic factors. (It should be noted that British military expenditures do not contribute significantly to British violence-behavior in this subperiod—although the variable military-expenditures-of-non-allies does.)[9]

---

[9] For the subperiod 1871–1890, the beta coefficient for Britain's military expenditures

Variable	Parameter Estimate		Partial correlation	t statistic	Significance level
	Unstandardized	Standardized (beta)			
Mil. Expend.	−.0002	−.70	−.32	−2.1	.025
Alliances	3.35	1.15	.45	3.14	.005
Violence of Others	.92	.67	.50	3.6	.001
Constant	12.57	.00	.26	1.6	.05
Alliances	−3.76	−.67	−.48	−1.88	.05
Violence of Others	1.78	1.22	.48	1.90	.05
Alliances	2.47	.65	.47	2.37	.025
Alliances	4.95	.72	.45	3.09	.005
Violence of Others	.45	.37	.40	2.71	.005
Mil. Expend.	−.00005	−.46	−.33	−2.14	.025
Violence of Others	.75	.64	.62	2.995	.005
Violence of Others	.75	.60	.62	3.3	.005
Alliances	3.11	.41	.43	2.0	.05
Mil. Ex. Nonallies	.00002	.30	.45	2.1	.025
Intersections	−.32	−.19	−.51	−2.5	.01
Intersections	1.24	.89	.49	3.5	.001
Alliances	−1.27	−.46	−.33	−2.15	.025
Intersections	1.32	.76	.43	2.64	.01
Alliances	−1.28	−.41	−.34	−2.00	.05
Intersections	1.03	.67	.37	1.69	.05
Alliances	−1.88	−.47	−.35	−1.58	.10
Constant	27.11	.00	.40	1.86	.05

A modified Richardson process appears to have been operating: increases in one mode of behavior (military expenditures) stimulated increases by rivals, but in a different mode (violence-of-others), which

is −.90 ($p = .005$), for Britain's alliances .45 ($p = .025$), and for violence-of-others 1.06 ($p = .025$). The constant is the most statistically significant, above the .001 level. For the subperiod 1891–1914, the beta coefficient for military-expenditures-of-nonallies is 1.18 ($p = .01$) and for violence-of-others 0.52 ($p = .01$).

in turn stimulated violence-behavior by Britain. Contrary to deterrence theory, the building of a powerful military establishment (principally naval) and increases in total alliances did not enable Britain to avoid WWI. Indeed, the size of her military force and her obligations to alliance partners may have helped make the escalation of the 1914 crisis highly probable, particularly by awakening fears in rival powers.

The violence-behavior of France, which was also quite reactive, can be accounted for primarily by military-expenditures-of-nonallies, violence-of-others, and intensity-of-intersections, with France's alliances and the constant term playing some role.[10] Results for subperiods also indicate the preeminence of foreign factors.[11]

Only 31 percent of the variance in Germany's violence-behavior in the full period can be accounted for. The most significant variables are violence-of-others and, to a very minor extent, the constant term.[12] Similar results were obtained for the period 1884–1914, although the amount of variance accounted for in the dependent variable increased to 51 percent.[13] Germany's violence-behavior can thus be explained partially as a reaction to the violence directed toward her by other countries.

For Italy, 36 percent of the variance in violence-behavior can be explained, primarily by violence-of-others, although Italy's own military expenditures, alliances, and the constant also have an effect.[14] Italy's violence-behavior is thus explained by both domestic and nondomestic factors. Setting a breakpoint at 1889, only alliances and violence-of-others are statistically significant in the first subperiod, and alliances alone in the second subperiod. (Recall, however, that Italy's alliances are themselves accounted for in large part by military-expenditures-of-nonallies, intensity-of-intersections, and military expenditures.)

Our model accounts for 38 percent of the variance in Russia's violence-behavior in the full period, with most of this attributable to

---

[10]Violence-of-others and military-expenditures-of-nonallies are both significant at the .001 level, with beta coefficients of .62 and .37, respectively. Alliances and the constant term are both significant at the .01 level; intensity-of-intersections is significant only at the .05 level.

[11]In the first subperiod only military-expenditures-of-nonallies and violence-of-others are significant, both at or above the .05 level. In the second subperiod, on the other hand, the R^2 is improved to 99, with violence-of-others and the constant both highly significant; thus, there seems to be a mild "lock-in" effect (signified by the importance of the constant). Nevertheless, we must conclude that the violence-behavior of France was primarily influenced by the actions of other powers throughout the full period.

[12]For violence-of-others the beta coefficient is .48 (significant at the .005 level); the constant term is significant at the .05 level.

[13]The Chow test indicates no significant differences when comparing the coefficients for the full period with those for the second subperiod, although violence-of-others has a higher value (beta = .66, $p = .001$) and the constant is no longer significant.

[14]The significant coefficients are: military expenditures (beta = −.70, $p = .025$), Italy's alliances (beta = 1.15, $p = .005$), violence-of-others (beta = .67, $p = .001$), and the constant term ($p = .05$).

violence-of-others, Russian alliances, and Russian military expenditures.[15] Setting a breakpoint at 1890, violence-behavior in the first subperiod is (poorly) accounted for only by violence-of-others. In the second subperiod intersections, military-expenditures-of-nonallies, violence-of-others, and alliances are important, and account for nearly all of the variance. Clearly, a shift occurred in the dynamics of Russian violence-behavior, which our model does not capture.

Some of the same uncertainties pertain in the case of Austria-Hungary; 44 percent of the variance can be accounted for, primarily by intensity-of-intersections and (negatively) by alliances.[16] Austria-Hungary's violence-behavior increased as her alliances decreased. For the period 1891–1914, the statistical significance of Austria-Hungary's alliances and intensity-of-intersections is less, leaving the constant (representing certain carry-over effects from earlier years) as the only term statistically significant at or about the .05 level.[17]

There are serious limitations to the types of inferences that can be drawn from the analysis presented in this chapter. For example, for statistical reasons it is not possible to identify with confidence the nations to which a given power was reacting in any given period. Consequently, we cannot test all historical hypotheses through our statistical analysis.

Overall, our findings reveal that the violence-behavior of a nation, unlike several other variables (notably military expenditures), tends rather strongly to be a response to the actions of other countries, particularly to military-expenditures-of-nonallies and violence-of-others. In the next chapter we will summarize the dynamics uncovered by our analysis.

---

[15]The significant coefficients are: alliances (beta $= .72, p = .005$), military expenditures (beta $= -.46, p = .025$), and violence-of-others (beta $= .37, p = .005$).

[16]The coefficient for intensity-of-intersections is .89 ($p = .001$), for alliances $-.46$ ($p = .025$).

[17]According to a Chow test comparing the second subperiod with the full period, there appears to be no significant differences between the sets of coefficients; the same is true when comparing the first subperiod with the full period. All periods have comparably poor R^2, indicating that some aspects of the dynamics of Austria-Hungary's violence-behavior have not been captured by our model.

16 A Synthesis

The many links identified so far indicate in general that rather strong paths exist from domestic growth to expansion and military expenditures, from there to alliances, and then to violence-behavior. However, our analysis reveals that international violence can be reached from different initial conditions and along different paths. The processes we have studied are far more complex than was suggested by the propositions in Chapter 1.

In this chapter we shall attempt to pull the pieces together by summarizing the links discussed in Chapters 11–15 and demonstrating their interdependence. We shall examine the relative importance of several factors — domestic growth, expansion, intensity-of-intersections, alliances, military expenditures, etc. — affecting the violence-behavior of the nations in our study, and note which paths to violence are statistically significant.

So far in Part III we have reported the findings for individual equations in the system of simultaneous equations. In this chapter we will summarize our overall findings, both for individual nations and for crucial variables. Full details on the links *for each variable* are found in Chapters 11–15; the links among the variables *for each nation* in our study are diagrammed here in Figures 16-2 to 16-7 (see "Interpreting the Diagrams," page 247).

Our statistical findings generally confirm the links hypothesized in our model (Figure 16-1). Only a few findings were difficult to interpret.[1] Certain relationships proved much stronger than others, depending on the period and the country examined. In addition, the paths to

---

[1]Possible explanations for weak or dubious findings are insensitive indicators or faulty measurement.

violence-behavior are somewhat different for each of the six nations, and even the paths for a single nation vary according to which period (the full period or a subperiod) was analyzed.[2] Despite this multiplicity of paths, *the explanatory power of the variables remains strong.* Our findings therefore sustain the usefulness of the model in the study of international systems.

The case of Britain (Figure 16-2) illustrates the extent to which violence-behavior can be traced to domestic factors of growth and expansion. The population and national-income variables, in various combinations, proved to be important determinants of colonial area (expansion) and military expenditures. Expansion (colonial area) led to increased conflict with other nations over colonial matters (intersections) and thus, at least during the early years of the period studied, to increased military expenditures. These increases contributed to violence-behavior primarily through the intervening link of alliances.

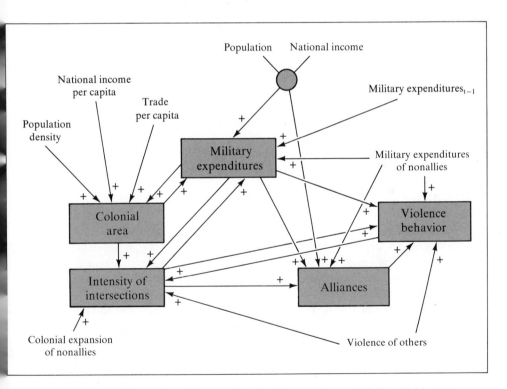

Figure 16-1. Dynamics of international violence: the model. See Table 1-1 for an explanation of the conceptual model.

---

[2]If every link in the model were statistically significant for each nation and for each period analyzed, Figures 16-2 to 16-7 would be identical to Figure 16-1.

This brief sketch leaves out many important relationships in the case of Britain. Figure 16-2 clearly illustrates the extent to which other factors were operative. For example, it is important to note that Britain's violence-behavior was influenced by foreign factors such as violence-of-others and military-expenditures-of-nonallies. On balance, however, at least one distinct path to violence-behavior emerges from expansion through intensity-of-intersections, military expenditures, and alliances, a path that originates in the dynamics of domestic growth.

In the case of France (Figure 16-3) only one path to violence-behavior is demonstrated, although there are many contributing factors. Expansion (colonial area) appears strongly determined by domestic factors; unlike the case of Britain, however, expansion is not significantly related to intensity-of-intersections. A clear path can be traced from domestic growth (including population growth) to expansion (colonial area), through military expenditures and alliances, to violence-behavior.

For Germany (Figure 16-4) the situation is quite different. Germany's violence-behavior can be attributed only to violence-of-others. German expansion (colonial area), although generated primarily by growth factors, is not linked to intensity-of-intersections or military expenditures. This is a unique case; all the other powers show a link from expansion to the rest of the model. Figure 16-4 shows three processes *not* linked: (a) the process of expansion, (b) the interconnection of military expenditures, intensity-of-intersections, and alliances, and (c) the factors contributing directly to violence-behavior. Thus, the hypothesized linkage of these three processes was not substantiated in the case of Germany.

In the case of Italy (Figure 16-5) the variables are highly interconnected, as shown by the four distinct paths between violence-behavior and expansion (colonial area), and thus between violence-behavior and population density. Two of these paths pass through intensity-of-intersections, and two through military expenditures. Despite this complexity, the importance of intersections and military expenditures is clear.

In the case of Russia (Figure 16-6) only one distinct path to violence appears; again, however, there are many contributing factors. Domestic factors lead to expansion (colonial area), and this to intensity-of-intersections. There is a direct (but negative) path from intersections to violence. Probably more important are the further positive links with military expenditures, alliances, and particularly violence-of-others.

Finally, for Austria-Hungary (Figure 16-7) three distinct paths to violence emerge, but with many contributing factors. The most direct can be traced from expansion (colonial area) through intensity-

Interpreting the Diagrams

Figures 16-2 through 16-7 summarize the results for the simultaneous system (the individual equations were reported on in Chapters 11 to 15). Each of the five dependent variables—colonial area, military expenditures, intensity-of-intersections, alliances, and violence-behavior—is enclosed in a box. An arrow from a variable indicates that the variable has a statistically significant effect on the variable at the head of the arrow at or above the .05 level of significance for the periods noted. For example, in Figure 16-1 the following diagram appears:

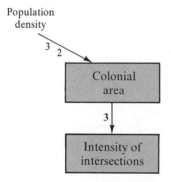

The diagram shows that population density has a statistically significant effect on colonial area for Periods 3 and 2, but not for Period 1 (the periods are identified in each figure). Colonial area is statistically linked to intensity-of-intersections only for Period 3. Thus, the diagram illustrates a *path* (for Period 3) from population density to intersections through colonial area.

of-intersections to violence-behavior.[3] A second path leads from expansion to military expenditures, then to intersections, and then to violence-behavior. A third passes through expansion, military expenditures, and alliances (negative) to violence-behavior. In short, intensity-of-intersections, military expenditures, and alliances are the most important contributors to the violence-behavior of Austria-Hungary.

---

[3]In view of Austria-Hungary's minimal colonial holdings (Bosnia and Herzegovina), the influence of the expansion variable should be interpreted with caution.

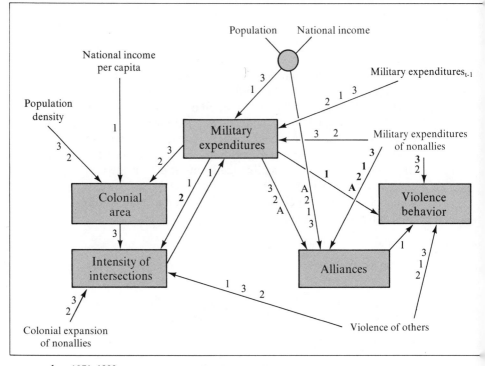

1 = 1871–1890
2 = 1891–1914
3 = 1871–1914
A = 1896–1914 (alliance equation only)
Bold numbers are negative coefficients

Figure 16-2. Britain: statistically significant links in the model.

This is the only case in which violence-of-others is not a determinant of violence-behavior.

Despite the different paths described above, a fairly clear pattern in the causes of violence-behavior emerges. Expansion (colonial area), stimulated by population growth (density) and technological advance (national income per capita), generally leads to increased intensity-of-intersections.[4] The relationship of expansion to military capability is more complex. In our analysis the link between colonial area and military expenditures is occasionally negative, particularly for those nations whose colonial expansion was blocked or otherwise frustrated. (Only the findings for Germany show no statistically significant rela-

---

[4]Military-expenditures and trade-per-capita, although significant in some instances, were not as universally important.

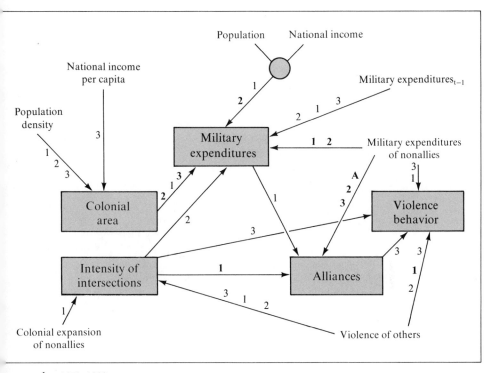

Figure 16-3.   France: statistically significant links in the model.

1 = 1871–1900
2 = 1880–1914
3 = 1871–1914
A = 1896–1914 (alliance equation only)
Bold numbers are negative coefficients

tions between colonial area and the other endogenous variables of the model.) Intensity-of-intersections is also related to the nondomestic factors of violence-of-others and colonial-area-of-nonallies, although a nation's own violence-behavior occasionally had some impact. (Again, Germany is a unique case; intensity-of-intersections is generated almost entirely by domestic factors.) The variables military expenditures, intensity-of-intersections, alliances, and violence-behavior are quite highly interconnected, that is, several paths join them. Although violence-behavior is generated by both domestic factors (alliances, military expenditures, and intensity-of-intersections) and foreign factors (military-expenditures-of-nonallies, violence-of-others), the foreign factors generally predominate.

Our analysis thus substantiates our hypothesis that a nation's defense-related capabilities (the military, and sometimes alliances)

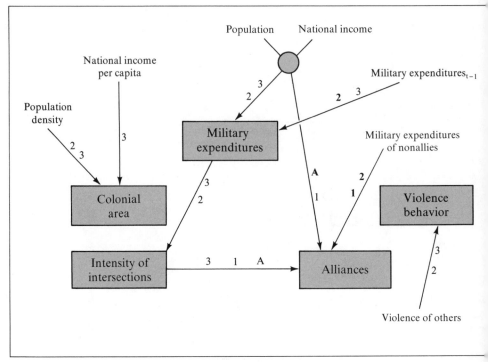

1 = 1871–1900 (alliance equation only)
2 = 1884–1914
3 = 1871–1914
A = 1891–1914 (alliance equation only)
Bold numbers are negative coefficients

Figure 16-4.   Germany: statistically significant links in the model.

are largely generated by domestic growth. But this growth may evoke
violence-behavior from other powers and, in return, the violence (as
well as growth) of others evokes even further violence-behavior. In
short, the violence-behavior of one power appears to be related to the
violence-behavior of other powers — partially validating and partially
modifying Richardson's model (our findings on military expenditures
do not entirely fit Richardson's model).

The intersection variable is not as consistently significant as we had
postulated. This is surprising in view of the powerful colonial thrusts
of Britain, France, and Germany, and the numerous collisions among
them. The relative weakness of the intersection variable may be due
to vulnerability in our procedure for obtaining quantified data (including measurement error), a possible redundancy between intensity-of-
intersections and violence-behavior, or to some other failures of
analysis. Of course, it is also possible that compared with all inter-

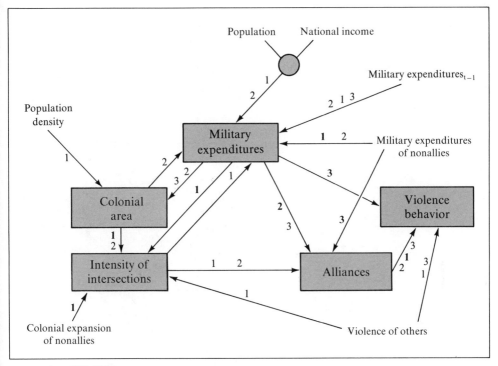

1 = 1871–1888
2 = 1889–1914
3 = 1871–1914
Bold numbers are negative coefficients

Figure 16-5. Italy: statistically significant links in the model.

actions among the major powers, intersections (conflicts over colonial interests) did not in fact exert as direct and powerful an influence on either military capabilities or violence-behavior as we had postulated. As our analysis reveals, it is likely that intersections were only one element in a large network of interdependent factors.

Although reaction to the spending of nonallies appears to have had an effect on growth in military expenditures, the trends uncovered by our analysis seem to support the idea (put forward by, for example, Graham T. Allison and Morton Halperin) that a country's behavior and its interaction with other countries is in great part influenced by bureaucratic politics.[5] Except for periods immediately following a war, bureaucratic demands are for increases, not reductions, in allocations. Thus, the influence of the previous year's allocations is considerable.

---

[5]Allison and Halperin, 1972.

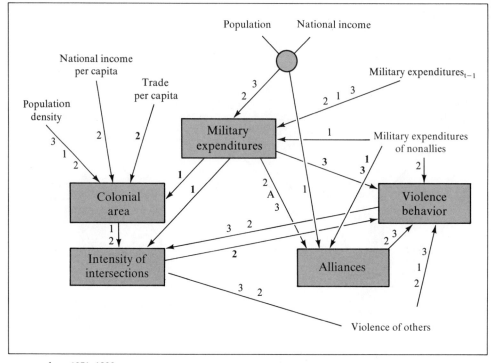

1 = 1871–1890
2 = 1891–1914
3 = 1871–1914
A = 1896–1914 (alliance equation only)
Bold numbers are negative coefficients

Figure 16-6. Russia: statistically significant links in the model.

The significance of bureaucratic politics, of growth in population and technology, and other domestic considerations in accounting for military expenditures does not mean that the notion of competition (or arms race) is useless in explaining military spending levels. It does mean that domestic growth is an important determinant of these levels. In addition, competition may be a powerful *rationalization* for increasing military spending.

The approval of a country's military budget, like the acquisition of colonial territory, is likely to be the outcome of several public and private interests, some of which may have little to do directly with any specific foreign threat. During the period 1870–1914 there was a considerable convergence of colonial and military interests—in some instances they were almost inseparable. Military interests thus con-

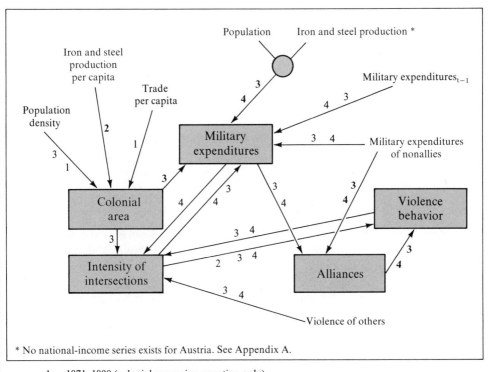

* No national-income series exists for Austria. See Appendix A.

1 = 1871–1890 (colonial expansion equation only)
2 = 1891–1914 (colonial expansion and violence equations only)
3 = 1871–1914
4 = 1878–1914

Bold numbers are negative coefficients

Figure 16-7. Austria-Hungary: statistically significant links in the model.

verged with industrial, commercial, and bureaucratic interests. It would not be surprising, therefore, to find pressure in many parts of government and society for yearly increases in defense spending. In addition, it is far easier for decision-makers to act by only tinkering with previous budgets (incrementalism) rather than constantly rethinking priorities, and there is strong evidence that they usually do act in that fashion.[6]

The strong influence of military expenditures on intensity-of-intersections should not be surprising in view of the part played by the armies and navies of the major powers during 1870–1914 in acquiring, protecting, policing, and often administering colonial territories,

---

[6]Wildavsky, 1964.

and in securing sea and overland trade routes.[7] That is, if a power deploys its troops and warships to serve its colonies, and another power behaves similarly, one would expect their interests to collide. The notable findings of our analysis of intersections is that the intensity of a nation's intersections is best explained by that nation's own military expenditures and, secondly, by violence-of-others. Once again, internal socio-economic dynamics seem to generate activities with strong external consequences.

The number of alliances, which is generally related to the degree of violence-behavior, tends to be influenced by military-expenditures and population-times-national-income (both domestic variables), as well as by intensity-of-intersections.

Violence-behavior generally is a reactive process. The level of violence is not as strongly linked to conflicts of national interests (intersections), military capability, or alliances as we had hypothesized. Nevertheless, increases in these dimensions often provoke some response by a rival power, which in turn stimulates violence-behavior — clearly an action-reaction process. Thus, our hypothesized links throughout the model still appear to be extremely important, but in an indirect and always complex form.

Although the narrow time frame and limited measures in our study make it impossible to provide anything like conclusive evidence, it is safe to conclude that hereafter, as a consequence of our findings, theories of war will have to take into account domestic socio-economic processes as well as foreign relations. It is all the more important, therefore, that much research remains to be done on the ways in which economic factors influence the expansion of national activities and conflicts of national interests. Particularly, much work needs to be done on incorporating more sensitive measures of trade in a political model, and including other economic measures, such as foreign investment and flow of resources. The linkage of population, technology, expansion, and violence uncovered in our analysis might have been stronger if the economic variables had been more refined.

In the next chapter the coefficient estimates from our equations are subjected to vigorous tests by simulation. This undertaking provides further quantitative evidence for our interpretation of the dynamics of international violence.

---

[7]The relationship is often reciprocal; increasing violence in international conflicts of interest may require increases in military expenditures. Indeed, there are statistically significant links in both directions.

Simulating International Processes

17

Although the equations in Chapters 11 through 15 are part of an integrated model (see Figures 16-2 to 16-7 for the specific interconnections among endogenous variables for each nation), *how these variables interact dynamically within the system* is not obvious from the findings. In this chapter we shall report on further analysis used to test the reliability of the equations in representing historical processes. First, we conducted a dynamic simulation of the model that takes into account the mutual dependencies among the variables and processes described in Chapter 10 (and in detail in Chapters 11–15). We employed simulation techniques and quantitative data to see how accurately the model could predict known data on colonial area, intensity-of-intersections, military expenditures, alliances, and violence-behavior. The methods used in this simulation are described in Appendix B.[1] We then exercised the simulation by raising questions of an "if . . . then . . ." nature — systematically changing coefficients and observing the outcomes. Our findings will, in some part, show the fit of theory and data and the extent to which we have been successful in representing the dynamics of international behavior for this period.

Successful simulation is based on having already obtained coefficient estimates that are robust and valid. These parameter estimates (the

---

[1]A distinction must be made between a *forecast* and a *simulation*. In a forecast each dependent variable of each single equation is treated as a discrete "process," independent of the effects of other equations (although the coefficient estimates may still be derived from a simultaneous system). In a dynamic simulation all the dependent variables are simulated simultaneously. A *forecast* of colonial area, for example, would use the historical or known values for all the independent variables in the colonial-area equation along with the coefficient estimates from the equation. On the other hand, a *simulation* of colonial area (the equation for which includes the endogenous variable military expenditures as an independent variable) would not take the actual value for military-expenditures, but rather would use the value estimated from the military-expenditures equation — necessitating the use of iterative techniques until convergence is obtained. Both simulation and forecasting, as understood here, are constrained by the number of time points in the data. Forecasting as "predicting beyond existing data"

coefficients) are then combined with historical or known data for the exogenous variables at the starting date so that the initial values of the endogenous variables can be predicted. Thereafter, the procedure continues by using *simulated* values for all endogenous variables. Simulation can be performed as often as there are time points in the data for the exogenous variables. When it proved impossible to simulate the system, we fell back on single-equation forecasts (which employ only known, not estimated, data for both exogenous and endogenous variables).[2]

Although we could not successfully simulate the system for certain countries in certain periods, our attempts at simulation have been quite successful. In general, we were able to replicate rather closely the dynamics of colonial expansion, military expenditures, and to a lesser extent alliance, all of which involved "hard" measures. Those variables that involved "soft" (metricized) measures — violence-behavior and intensity-of-intersections — presented more severe difficulties.[3]

The results for each variable are presented in Tables 17-1 through 17-5. For each dependent variable we have noted the mean values of the known data, the simulated series, and the forecasted series, as well as the percentage-errors and the root-mean-square errors of the forecasted and simulated series. Each of these values provides important information for evaluating the performance of the simulation or forecast.[4] Plots of the results for colonial area (for those nations that simulated successfully) are presented in Figures 17-1 to 17-6, and for military expenditures in Figures 17-7 to 17-10.

---

is not the meaning intended by us. (See Appendix B for a more complete description of these approaches.) Invariably — one might say almost by definition — successful simulation entails successful forecasts of the constituent equations; however, a successful forecast by no means entails a successful simulation. It is generally much more difficult to simulate a dynamic system than to forecast a single equation. Errors may accumulate across equations when jointly dependent (i.e., endogenous) variables are simulated, causing iteration values to oscillate and even diverge. Thus, single-equation forecasts are only a crude test. Since single-equation forecasting specifies that in each equation the dependent variable is a function solely of the estimated coefficients and the historical values of the independent variables, any accumulated errors are localized, their effects being confined to a single equation. It is possible to combine simulation and forecasting by periodically retrieving historical (as opposed to calculated) values for the endogenous variables within a simulation. This tends to reduce, but not eliminate, cumulative error (although we did not find this technique useful). Results from both simulated for forecasted runs are reported in Tables 17-1 through 17-5.

[2]There are two common reasons for failure to simulate. First, the system may have diverged because (a) parameter coefficients were weak; (b) the theoretical specification of the functional form of the equation was incomplete; and/or (c) the structural form of the equation was erroneous. Second, the use of a logarithmic transformation on colonial area generated error whenever the calculated value of colonial area was zero or negative; under these circumstances, the system could not simulate.

[3]One reason for the variability in success may have been the discontinuity of the data series for violence-behavior and intensity-of-intersections (compared with the generally monotonic series for the "hard" variables). As regression generally captures "trends" rather than points, a trendless series would be expected to yield a much greater degree of error.

[4]See "Interpreting the Tables," p. 258.

Colonial Area

British colonial area was remarkably well-simulated and forecasted, for both the full period and subperiods. Occasional outlying points were not captured (such as sharp gains in Africa in 1890), but the trend was captured with astonishing success, as is evident in Figure 17-1.

The simulation was not nearly as successful for German colonial area; a gentle trend was derived, whereas actual expansion was discontinuous (Figure 17-2). Beginning the simulation at 1884, after Germany's initial acquisition of colonial territory, led to far more successful results (Figure 17-3).[5]

Simulation for France's colonial area did not work for either the full period or the second subperiod, 1880–1914. But simulation for the period 1871–1900 and the forecasts for all periods were extremely successful (see Figure 17-4). The failure in this case sprang not from the colonial-area equation itself, but from the tendency in the case of France for the military-expenditures equation to yield diverging results. Here the nature of a simulation is clear—failure in one part of the model means failure for the entire model.

In the case of Russia the simulation of colonial area was also extremely successful. Nonetheless, only the general trend was captured, without indicating specific acquisitions (Figure 17-5). (The tendency of simulation is to smooth step-increases into a curve. Before and after the acquisition of territory, the dynamics of expansion can be fairly well captured.)

In the case of Italy simulation of colonial area for the full period was only moderately successful (Figure 17-6); however, simulations for the two subperiods and all forecasts were very successful. (Again, it is difficult to represent a step function by means of continuous variables.)

Austria-Hungary was the least successful case. Both the simulation and forecasts of colonial area for the full period and for 1871–1890 failed. For the period 1878–1914, that is, starting with the first territorial acquisition, a single-equation forecast produced excellent results (with a percentage-error of −3.3), although simulation was again unsuccessful. Only the period 1891–1914 could be simulated, but with very poor results; a single-equation forecast for this period was extremely successful. Clearly, this model does not capture the dynamics of Austro-Hungarian colonial area once the effects of the jointly dependent (endogenous) variables are included. (No statistical explanation of the disinclination of Austria-Hungary to compete in overseas territorial acquisition was included in the model.) In view of the limited

---

[5]Again, this makes clear how unsuccessful this methodology is for predicting discrete events, such as *when* colonial territory will be acquired. Assuming that lateral pressure builds up to a certain "critical point" at which expansion takes place, regression analysis would generally provide poor prediction of such a step function.

extent of Austro-Hungarian territorial expansion, these failures are understandable.

Overall, however, we obtained an excellent fit between historical and simulated values of colonial area (and an even better one between the historical values and the single-equation forecasts).

Military Expenditures

Simulated values of military expenditures for the six powers were quite similar to actual values (see Table 17-2). The simulation produced excellent results for British military expenditures, with only minor deviations (Figure 17-7). For the 1870s simulated values ran slightly lower than actual levels. (In the early years of this decade Britain fought the Ashanti Wars and was involved in other colonial conflicts. The equation focuses only on European rivals and domestic growth as

---

Interpreting the Tables

Tables 17-1 through 17-5 summarize the results of the simulations and single-equation forecasts. NA means that the simulation or forecast was unsuccessful, and hence that the appropriate statistics do not exist. RMS (root-mean-square error, defined in Appendix B) is computed on the percentage error for the sake of comparability of units.

The mean values of the simulation or forecast should be compared to the mean value of the historical data. Discrepancies between the historical and simulated (or forecasted) series are summarized in the columns "mean percentage-error." Note that it is possible to obtain a high *percentage* error even though the *numerical* error is fairly small; the reverse is also possible. (For example, when historical values are small, such as the number of alliances, a small discrepancy may result in considerable percentage error. On the other hand, discrepancies for colonial area and military expenditures, although considerable in themselves, are very small in relation to the total values of the series.)

All summary statistics note only the mean values, over the period specified. Such statistics by necessity provide only brief indications of overall trends. More detailed information could be obtained by comparing values with those simulated or forecasted on a year-by-year basis. Although we have not reported the results in such detail, an indication of the relative trends for the colonial-area and military-expenditures variables can be determined from Figures 17-1 through 17-10. These figures plot the historical, simulated (where successful), and forecasted values for all but the most unstable examples.

Table 17-1. Colonial area – simulation and forecast results.

Country	Period	Historical mean[a]	Simulation Mean[a]	Simulation Mean of % error	Simulation RMS of % error	Forecast Mean[a]	Forecast Mean of % error	Forecast RMS of % error
Britain	1871–1914	10,968.4	10,919.9	−.206	3.354	10,920.4	−.204	3.308
	1871–1890	9,612.33	9,612.8	.018	1.034	9,611.69	.006	1.072
	1891–1914	12,098.6	12,095.6	.029	2.124	12,100.0	.045	1.708
France	1871–1914	2,557.13	NA	NA	NA	2,484.14	2.343	24.534
	1871–1900	1,782.34	1,741.03	4.552	19.544	1,741.04	4.555	19.548
	1880–1914	3,072.87	NA	NA	NA	2,916.08	−.904	22.659
Germany	1871–1914	743.92	2,481.92	446.545	861.511	2,471.2	447.914	865.291
	1884–1914	1,055.87	1,038.27	−.326	15.183	1,037.49	−.397	14.963
Italy	1871–1914	263.569	912.912	204.134	443.475	243.067	34.6995	130.089
	1871–1888	5.978	7.354	19.154	76.396	7.357	19.689	77.016
	1889–1914	441.902	373.43	30.897	120.931	380.308	12.951	55.550
Russia	1871–1914	6,779.8	6,701.1	−1.130	2.222	6,703.7	−1.09	2.196
	1871–1890	6,649.6	6,638.6	−.148	1.174	6,648.3	−.01	.911
	1891–1914	6,888.3	6,888.8	.010	.509	6,888.7	.008	.509
Austria-Hungary	1871–1914	18.149	NA	NA	NA	NA	NA	NA
	1871–1890	14.249	NA	NA	NA	NA	NA	NA
	1891–1914	21.40	1,748.17	8,762.87	35,677.7	21.221	−.719	3.208
	1878–1914	21.581	NA	NA	NA	20.830	−3.301	5.242

RMS = Root Mean Square
NA = Not Available
[a] In thousand square miles.

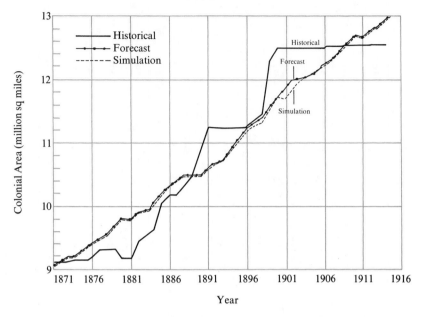

Figure 17-1. Total British colonial area, 1871–1914. The diagram compares the actual total territory acquired by Britain and the totals generated by forecasting and simulation.

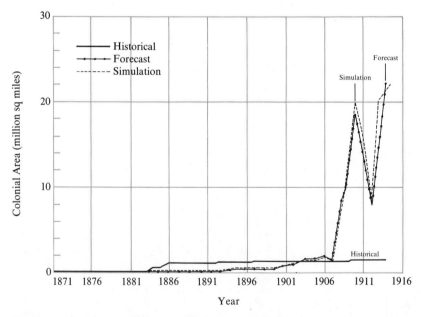

Figure 17-2. Total German colonial area, 1871–1914. The diagram compares the actual total territory acquired by Germany and the totals generated by forecasting and simulation (cf. Figure 17-3 for a diagram of the period 1884–1914).

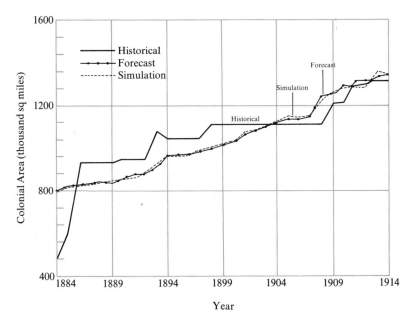

Figure 17-3. Total German colonial area, 1884–1914. The diagram compares the actual total territory acquired by Germany and the totals generated by forecasting and simulation (cf. Figure 17-2 for a diagram of the full period, 1871–1914).

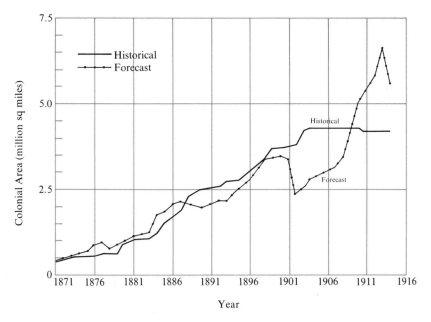

Figure 17-4. Total French colonial area, 1871–1914. The diagram compares the actual total territory acquired by France and the totals generated by forecasting.

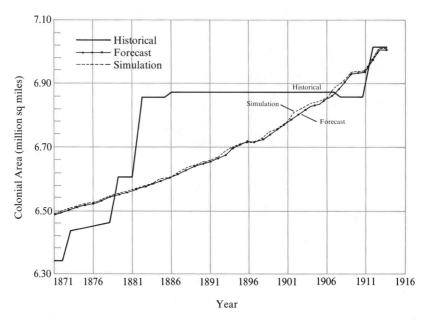

Figure 17-5. Total Russian colonial area, 1871–1914. The diagram compares the actual total territory acquired by Russia and the totals generated by forecasting and simulation.

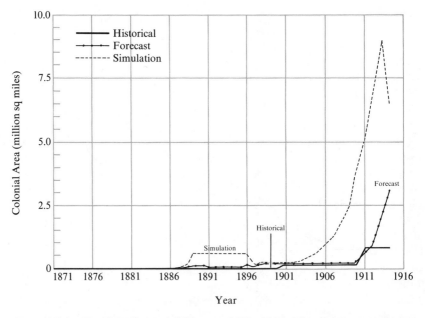

Figure 17-6. Total Italian colonial area, 1871–1914. The diagram compares the actual total territory acquired by Italy and the totals generated by forecasting and simulation.

determinants of expenditures.) Another peak, 1903 (post-Boer War expenditures), was also not captured.

French military expenditures were captured less successfully. The results for 1871–1900 were excellent, but some processes were occurring during the later part of the period that were not captured by our model—the simulation caused the values of French military expenditures to increase explosively. As a result, the full period and second subperiod simulations were unsuccessful, and even the single-equation forecasts showed enormous percentage-errors. The historical upward trend of French expenditures in later years was somehow tremendously overestimated by our equation.

We obtained excellent results for German military expenditures for both the full period (Figure 17-8) and the subperiod. There was no step-function problem with these data; our model captured to within one-percent error the trend of German military expenditures, and even most of the short-term fluctuations.

We also obtained excellent prediction for Russian military expenditures (Figure 17-9). Although the simulation of the full period had a moderate percentage error (11 percent, understating the actual value), the two subperiod simulations and all forecasts were within two-percent mean percentage-error. The simulated values for Italian military expenditures were also surprisingly close to actual data for both the full period and subperiods (Figure 17-10).

The simulation was much less successful in generating Austro-Hungarian military expenditures. Forecasts for the period 1871–1900 yielded excellent results, although we were unable to achieve successful simulation of the system for the same period. The one period for which simulation was successful, 1891–1914, yielded enormous percentage-errors, as did all forecasts. As with colonial area, the processes generating Austro-Hungarian military expenditures do not appear to be successfully captured by this model.

Results from the simulation and forecasts of military expenditures, like those of colonial area, were generally encouraging. Overall, the discrepancy between historical and simulated or forecasted values was so small that confidence in our initial hypotheses, the military-expenditure equation, and our conclusions in Chapter 13 was considerably increased. Notwithstanding that some factors (for France after 1900 and for Austria-Hungary) have not been captured by the model, the enormous success of the model in predicting the military expenditures of four of the nations in our study tends to build our confidence.[6] In any case, the importance of domestic factors in explaining the growth of military spending is clear. Richardson-type processes, although undoubtedly a powerful consideration, do not explain all of the increases in military expenditures.

---

[6]We did not plot results for France or Austria-Hungary because the simulation was unsuccessful.

Table 17-2. Military expenditures — simulation and forecast results.

Country	Period	Historical mean[a]	Simulation			Forecast		
			Mean[a]	Mean of % error	RMS of % error	Mean[a]	Mean of % error	RMS of % error
Britain	1871–1914	212,392.0	211,742.0	1.563	24.396	211,856.0	.934	27.762
	1871–1890	112,673.0	112,972.0	.642	5.806	112,864.0	.498	6.229
	1891–1914	295,490.0	293,918.0	5.876	24.697	293,495.0	6.304	26.177
France	1871–1914	198,165.0	NA	NA	NA	1.680×10^{31}	2.528×10^{27}	1.039×10^{28}
	1871–1900	155,248.0	157,771.0	2.708	9.970	115,798.0	.872	9.178
	1880–1914	221,969.0	NA	NA	NA	3.804×10^{28}	5.109×10^{24}	2.016×10^{25}
Germany	1871–1914	177,648.0	177,243.0	.914	10.001	177,618.0	1.088	9.984
	1884–1914	209,159.0	210,683.0	.587	10.909	210,630.0	.549	10.611
Italy	1871–1914	69,701.1	69,817.8	1.247	18.655	70,165.2	2.016	10.906
	1871–1888	44,953.4	44,571.8	−1.272	6.249	44,692.9	−.399	4.911
	1889–1914	86,834.3	81,178.0	−6.472	32.463	86,851.4	.278	5.815
Russia	1871–1914	183,755.0	168,037.0	−11.069	18.225	182,542.0	1.441	13.653
	1871–1890	103,738.0	105,682.0	1.882	6.540	105,564.0	1.910	6.045
	1891–1914	250,436.0	249,536.0	1.870	16.713	249,922.0	2.016	17.779
Austria-Hungary	1871–1914	63,307.7	NA	NA	NA	6,940,357.0	7,992.38	17,361.2
	1871–1890	45,091.9	NA	NA	NA	45,031.8	.168	5.952
	1891–1914	78,487.0	−1,544,483.0	−1,851.91	3,226.63	−364,189.0	−504.273	885.08
	1878–1914	67,936.2	NA	NA	NA	1.486×10^{11}	1.574×10^{8}	4.422×10^{8}

RMS = Root Mean Square
NA = Not Available
[a]In thousand 1906 US dollars.

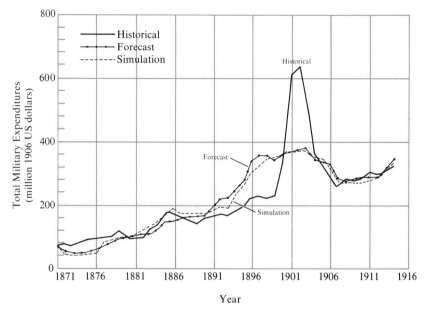

Figure 17-7. Total British military expenditures, 1871–1914. The diagram compares the actual total and totals generated by forecasting and simulation.

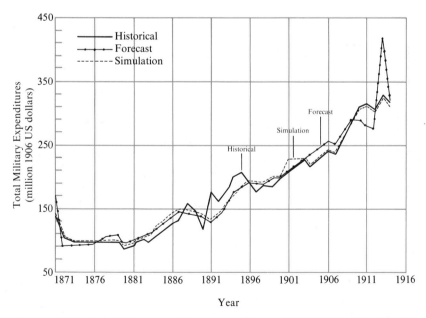

Figure 17-8. Total German military expenditures, 1871–1914. The diagram compares the actual total and totals generated by forecasting and simulation.

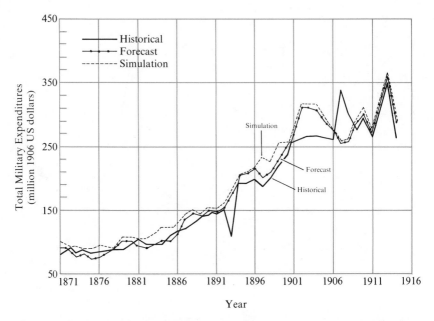

Figure 17-9. Total Russian military expenditures, 1871–1914. The diagram compares the actual total and totals generated by forecasting and simulation.

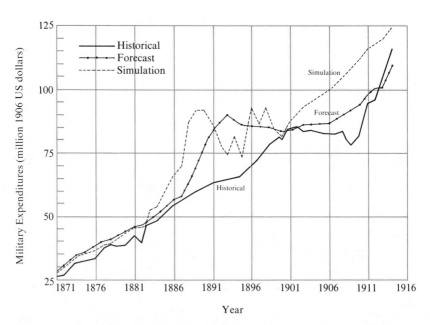

Figure 17-10. Total Italian military expenditures, 1871–1914. The diagram compares the actual total and totals generated by forecasting and simulation.

The Other Variables

Although the mean values for the simulated and forecasted values of violence-behavior were extremely close to the mean historical values, the percentage errors, calculated over the entire period, were considerable (Table 17-3). Only the predictions for Germany, with superior results and *smaller* errors, and France and Austria-Hungary, with poor results from simulation, were exceptions to this general finding. (Acceptable results for France and Austria-Hungary were obtained from single-equation forecasts.)

Similarly, in the case of intensity-of-intersections (Table 17-4) all simulated and forecasted values were quite close to the values in the data set, with the sole exception of the results for France for the full period and the simulated values for Austria-Hungary (again, however, the forecasts were very successful). Percentage-errors were considerable for Britain, France, and Russia, but both percentage and absolute errors were small for Germany, in the period 1884–1914, and for Italy.

In the case of alliances (Table 17-5) both deviations and percentage-errors were relatively small when simulation was successful, except for those for Italy during the period 1871–1888.[7] For Austria-Hungary, only the forecasts of total alliances were successful; the simulations were not.

Our long and often discouraging efforts at estimating and reestimating the equations, specifying and respecifying the functional and structural forms, and searching and testing for breakpoints seem at last to have paid off: *simulation has yielded results that appear to validate many of the inferences drawn in Chapters 11–16.* However, much more work needs to be done in areas where the simulation and forecasts were less successful.[8]

Exercising the Simulation

A successful model should do more than enhance our understanding of the dynamics of a system. Once a model of political interaction is developed and its parameters estimated from empirical data—the

---

[7]The actual discrepancy between the historical and simulated (or forecasted) values was small for violence-behavior, intensity-of-intersections, and alliances. However, because the measures used were also small, minor discrepancies in absolute values became major in percentage values. In such cases we can only observe the close correspondence between the values and draw appropriate inferences. We find it reasonable to conclude that our simulation captured most of the determining factors.

[8]Our inability to satisfactorily simulate or forecast French military-expenditures is a clear indicator of misspecification of the equation and/or weakness in the parameter estimates. We were also unable to obtain a successful simulation of the simultaneous system for Austria-Hungary. At best, we obtained a rough approximation of a simulation by all of the single-equation forecasts. There are other weaknesses in the system, which may be identified by a close examination of the statistics in the accompanying tables.

Table 17-3. Intensity-of-intersections—simulation and forecast results.

Country	Period	Historical mean[a]	Simulation Mean[a]	Simulation Mean of % error	Simulation RMS of % error	Forecast Mean[a]	Forecast Mean of % error	Forecast RMS of % error
Britain	1871–1914	12.989	12.896	73.917	211.261	12.988	72.705	264.524
	1871–1890	9.05	9.118	53.746	202.062	9.050	44.611	174.553
	1891–1914	16.271	16.276	54.685	233.819	16.242	61.374	287.72
France	1871–1914	12.295	NA	NA	NA	12.545	66.735	204.889
	1871–1900	12.367	13.040	91.313	287.131	12.856	79.363	271.335
	1880–1914	13.571	NA	NA	NA	13.677	63.790	215.657
Germany	1871–1914	10.591	10.785	86.633	213.618	10.825	77.961	189.014
	1884–1914	12.548	12.677	13.247	42.377	12.608	12.548	40.565
Italy	1871–1914	13.955	14.990	29.058	73.309	14.893	26.358	65.590
	1871–1888	12.889	12.751	−.412	13.946	12.619	−1.513	15.335
	1889–1914	14.692	13.528	22.413	71.564	14.692	11.908	42.997
Russia	1871–1914	13.273	14.262	207.82	562.277	13.892	190.956	525.402
	1871–1890	11.971	10.671	104.293	360.663	11.960	70.725	198.389
	1891–1914	14.357	14.324	12.004	49.675	14.358	5.810	30.864
Austria-Hungary	1871–1914	10.989	NA	NA	NA	10.989	22.974	70.864
	1871–1890	9.492	NA	NA	NA	9.492	29.147	74.816
	1891–1914	12.236	−.341	−97.733	170.658	12.236	9.451	35.991
	1878–1914	12.581	NA	NA	NA	13.148	17.278	53.529

RMS = Root Mean Square
NA = Not Available
[a]On a 30-point scale.

Table 17-4. Alliances – simulation and forecast results.

Country	Period	Historical mean	Simulation			Forecast		
			Mean	Mean of % error	RMS of % error	Mean	Mean of % error	RMS of % error
Britain	1871–1914	1.568	1.578	−15.627	27.270	1.581	−11.645	34.829
	1871–1890	.55	.574	−33.782	46.099	.579	−36.089	50.519
	1891–1914	2.417	2.433	−6.113	19.332	2.438	−1.631	18.230
France	1871–1914	1.386	NA	NA	NA	2.367	29.058	81.450
	1871–1900	.367	.383	−31.135	34.351	.372	−18.679	35.723
	1880–1914	1.743	NA	NA	NA	1.910	4.105	62.076
Germany	1871–1914	3.886	3.913	16.605	65.074	3.886	13.574	61.211
	1884–1914	4.645	4.701	2.776	12.714	4.705	2.951	12.767
Italy	1871–1914	3.864	3.837	9.711	39.611	3.812	9.863	41.349
	1871–1888	1.333	.652	−60.985	65.360	.668	−66.325	68.134
	1889–1914	5.615	5.890	18.224	63.229	5.615	3.206	19.047
Russia	1871–1914	2.432	2.263	.407	43.394	2.447	9.215	28.934
	1871–1890	1.65	1.650	3.299	26.429	1.668	4.060	26.453
	1891–1914	3.083	3.093	20.575	59.632	3.109	15.177	49.705
Austria-Hungary	1871–1914	5.227	NA	NA	NA	5.337	33.029	96.372
	1871–1890	4.6	NA	NA	NA	4.6	15.810	38.080
	1891–1914	5.75	−54.780	−1,455.55	2,807.94	5.984	8.033	30.019
	1878–1914	5.919	NA	NA	NA	6.067	35.505	125.031

RMS = Root Mean Square
NA = Not Available

Table 17-5. Violence-behavior – simulation and forecast results.

Country	Period	Historical mean[a]	Simulation			Forecast		
			Mean[a]	Mean of % error	RMS of % error	Mean[a]	Mean of % error	RMS of % error
Britain	1871–1914	20.364	20.419	67.101	276.158	20.364	70.664	307.747
	1871–1890	17.6	18.054	102.113	396.343	17.974	96.940	338.412
	1891–1914	22.667	22.726	12.757	44.280	22.628	10.340	37.339
France	1871–1914	17.909	NA	NA	NA	17.918	59.278	171.732
	1871–1900	17.533	17.554	77.528	255.034	17.533	79.397	265.302
	1880–1914	20.257	NA	NA	NA	20.253	45.51	143.21
Germany	1871–1914	16.875	16.908	31.010	114.112	16.875	29.232	106.016
	1884–1914	18.339	18.471	15.886	44.726	18.452	15.123	42.623
Italy	1871–1914	14.102	13.477	72.996	266.935	14.021	48.005	172.828
	1871–1888	12.306	14.307	103.406	273.859	12.165	79.827	250.115
	1889–1914	15.346	17.357	34.171	104.667	15.446	25.983	80.056
Russia	1871–1914	15.852	15.736	57.115	224.276	15.828	50.849	200.571
	1871–1890	16.225	15.968	23.387	59.893	16.225	24.524	69.207
	1891–1914	15.542	15.325	69.661	268.618	15.303	64.087	252.914
Austria-Hungary	1871–1914	13.875	NA	NA	NA	13.875	45.758	210.86
	1871–1890	13.25	NA	NA	NA	13.25	24.546	96.970
	1891–1914	14.396	467.903	3,712.71	7,198.23	14.396	68.550	279.285
	1878–1914	15.041	NA	NA	NA	15.041	51.995	219.608

RMS = Root Mean Square
NA = Not Available
[a]On a 30-point scale.

values being robust and the coefficients statistically significant – the model should allow us to identify critical intervention points at which particular policy changes would yield specific outcomes. For our study, such policy questions have been examined by carefully changing key coefficients – setting these at "high" or "low" values – and then looking at the differences these changes make in the output of the model. This procedure is known as "binding the values of coefficients" or "exercising the simulation."[9] The objective in any exercise of this kind is not to make a single change and observe the consequences, but to experiment with many different alternatives and note the implications of different sets of coefficients. Thus, simulation should enable us to inquire into the *consequences* of changes in any of the coefficients, that is, into the impact of such changes on the behavior of the system and its components. It should also reveal the extent to which the model is sensitive to modifications in the parameters, and how changes in the coefficients in one equation affect the output of another equation. It is important to stress that when components of a system are highly interdependent, changes in any one coefficient will also affect the output in other equations. Conversely, changing independent (or weakly dependent) coefficients amounts in effect to a mere displacement of the dependent variable.[10] Some systems are so robust that the same overall behavior emerges regardless of the changes made; others are so sensitive that slight changes may result in great effects. A model may display sensitivity because the real-world processes have been imperfectly captured or are themselves unstable, or, as is most common, because of strong interdependencies.

A good indicator of the plausibility of a model is the degree of significance of the parameters estimated from empirical data (through multivariate regression analysis) and, by extension, the degree to which the simulation approximates the real world. When a satisfactory degree of correspondence is obtained – there is never any hard and fast rule concerning the precise extent of convergence – it is then possible to bind the coefficient values and test the implications of alternative coefficients.

---

[9]This method is closely related to a possible alternative procedure: changing the values of the data. Multiplying the coefficient estimate by two, for example, is equivalent to dividing each data point by two. Of course, in value-changing experiments it might be desirable to transform instead with a nonconstant function. Transforming values requires that a series be transformed wherever it appears in the model; changing coefficients alters it at only one location, although the effects may have an impact elsewhere in the system. Although closely related, these two procedures have different assumptions. Transforming data assumes no change in relationships in the model: "If the population density were half of what it is today, what would happen?" Changing parameter (coefficient) values, on the other hand, assumes a change in relationships: "If the same population density had only one-half the impact on expansion that it does now, what would happen?"

[10]This result follows mathematically: if $y = a + b_1x_1 + b_2x_2 + \ldots + u$, then changing b_1 to $b_1 + \Delta$ will only change y to $y + \Delta x_1$. Only when there are dependencies, so that changes reverberate throughout the system, will results occur that are not merely linear displacements (additive effects).

In the course of experimenting with our model we provided "high" and "low" values for some key coefficients. In most cases, we obtained the unexciting result of two equivalent bands surrounding the original simulation.[11] Only when a mechanism is specified by which changes can reverberate elsewhere in the model should we expect any other effect. Thus, changing coefficients for endogenous variables when they appear as explanatory variables would be most likely to produce nontrivial outcomes. Those changes yielded some substantively intriguing results, which may have important implications for our assessment of the real world of 1870–1914 and for our understanding of the dynamics of international behavior. The inferences drawn in the following pages are based only on the limited number of computer runs to date. Clearly, experimentation with a given system cannot continue ad infinitum. In addition, most of our effort and resources so far have been spent on development of the methodology and the techniques appropriate to it, rather than on the policy experiments themselves. Consequently, the following analysis—far from being adequate or sufficient—must be viewed as an initial step.

Of the six major powers, we selected only Britain—the still expanding, more or less dominating, empire—for our experiment. The endogenous variables in the model for Germany, which would have been an interesting contrast, were so weakly interdependent as to limit the possibilities for nontrivial changes.

Table 17-6 shows the values of some key coefficients in the model and the changes we made (setting these coefficients alternatively at "high" and "low" values). Specifically, we bound (assigned new values to) the following coefficient values, which were both endogenous and statistically significant: military-expenditures$_{t-1}$ in the military-expenditures equation, colonial area in the intensity-of-intersections equation, intensity-of-intersections in the violence-behavior equation, and military expenditures in the alliance equation.[12] By comparing these alternative simulations with the original simulations, inferences can be drawn that may be relevant to policy analysis.

In evaluating the results it is important to note *feedback effects*. Changes in the coefficients in one equation invariably influence, to some extent, the outcomes in other equations. In this sense, the processes in question are highly interdependent. In some instances we are dealing with *direct* effects, the impact of change in one coefficient on another variable in the *same equation* (such as the effects of military-expenditures$_{t-1}$ on military expenditures). In other circumstances we are concerned with *indirect* effects, the impact of change in one coefficient on variables in *other equations*. These interdependencies are

---

[11]In the example in footnote 10, where a change of Δ was made to b_1, the coefficient associated with the variable x_1, the bands will be at a distance of $+\Delta x_1$ and $-\Delta x_1$.

[12]We did not modify the coefficient for military expenditures in the equation for colonial area because it was not statistically significant and little impact could therefore be expected.

Table 17-6. Parameter values used for "high" and "low" simulations of the model, using the data on Britain.

Equation	Variable Altered	Coefficient estimate	High value	Low value
Military Expenditures	Military Expend.$_{t-1}$	0.46	0.96	−0.04
Violence-behavior	Intersections	−0.427	0.573	−1.427
Intersections	Colonial Area	34.1625	39.1625	29.1625
Alliances	Military Expenditures	0.000005	0.000006	0.000004

sometimes difficult to untangle. The complications stem from the fact that we are dealing with a system of simultaneous equations where feedback effects and mutual dependencies, expressed algebraically and analytically, are difficult to express verbally. It must be emphasized that *only one coefficient is changed at a time*. When the implications of the change have been examined, that coefficient is restored to its original value, and another change is then made. In other words, this analysis involves changing coefficients one at a time. The percentage changes from the original simulated results are reported in Table 17-7.

In most cases, changes in one coefficient have only additive effects on other variables, so that no change is made in the way the system operates. Such linear change is the result when the coefficient for colonial area is changed in the equation for intensity-of-intersections (see Figure 17-11). In other cases, however, altering a parameter has a marked effect, illustrating the interdependence of the system and a potential vulnerability to manipulation at that point. Altering the coefficient for intensity-of-intersections in the violence-behavior equation, either up or down, leads to a *decrease* in the values predicted for colonial area, military expenditures, and alliances (see Figure 17-12).[13] In addition, increases in the coefficient for intensity-of-intersections have a greater impact on violence-behavior and intensity-of-intersections than do equivalent decreases. Interactive effects are clearly operative, resulting in either slightly explosive upward or unidimensional tendencies.

Even more striking, however, is the result of changing the coefficient for military-expenditures$_{t-1}$ (see Figure 17-13). An increase in that coefficient, so that its value is near one, causes an explosive tendency in military expenditures, alliances, and colonial area, while disproportionately decreasing violence-behavior and intensity-of-intersections. A corresponding decrease in the coefficient, so that previous expenditures have virtually no effect on current spending, has far less

---

[13]Possibly, the relationships are curvilinear—a positive impact from one path balancing a negative one from another. In such a case, any changes whatsoever might result in a move away from the point of inflection, and hence a net decrease in value.

Table 17-7. Exercising the simulation—percentage error of deviations from simulated results.*

Coefficient Altered	Colonial Area		Military Expenditures		Violence		Intersections		Alliances	
	High	Low	High	Low	High	Low	High	Low	High	Low
Mil. Expend.$_{t-1}$	5.01	−0.53	365.09	−45.78	−36.08	3.99	73.92	−148.45	328.07	−44.02
Intersections	−0.47	−0.56	−39.41	−48.83	−128.32	67.30	48.17	−29.13	−39.52	−46.17
Colonial Area	0.76	−0.76	95.05	−94.81	−130.61	130.27	−785.17	784.02	78.87	−78.66
Mil. Expend.	−0.00	+0.00	−0.04	0.04	0.51	−0.51	0.02	−0.03	17.81	−17.84

*The entries in this table are percentage errors of the difference between the original simulated values of the endogenous variables and those obtained when the coefficient estimates are set alternatively at the "high" and "low" values shown in Table 17-6.

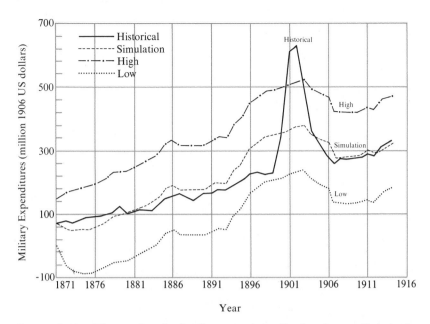

Figure 17-11. The results of a "policy experiment" using data on Britain, in which the coefficient for colonial area in the equation for intensity-of-intersections was altered. The resulting impact on British military expenditures illustrates *linear change*.

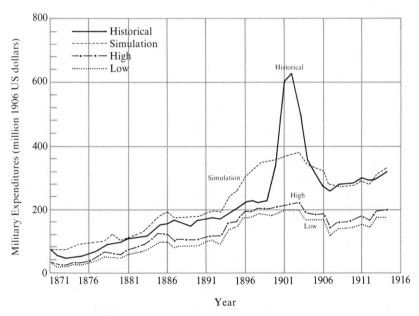

Figure 17-12. The results of a "policy experiment" using data on Britain, in which the coefficient for intensity-of-intersections in the equation for violence-behavior was altered. The resulting impact on British military expenditures illustrates *unidimensional change*.

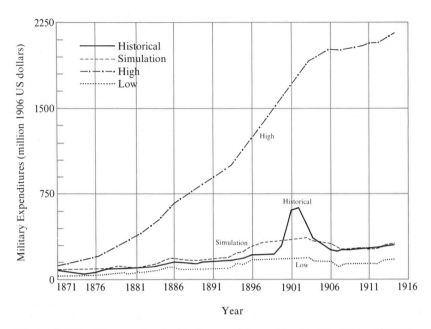

Figure 17-13. The results of a "policy experiment" using the data on Britain, in which the coefficient for military-expenditures$_{t-1}$ in the equation for military expenditures was altered. The resulting impact on British military expenditures illustrates *explosive change*.

impact — military expenditures and colonial area do not decline proportionately. If the *ceteris paribus* assumption holds, and other coefficients do indeed remain unaffected, it is clear that increases in the inertial effect have explosive potential for future spending, whereas decreases have much poorer "payoffs." The lack of a direct link between military spending and violence-behavior is also clear from Figure 16-2 (although they are linked indirectly through the behavior of nonallies, particularly violence-of-others). (The reaction processes prior to 1914 appear to have been primarily in response to violence-behavior, rather than to armament competitions per se.) In any case, we do not obtain any simple one-to-one relationship: the upward swings are substantially more marked than the downward trends.

These outcomes are not only another test of our theory and model, they also illustrate the complexities facing policy analysts and what has been referred to as the "counterintuitive" behavior of large social systems.[14] Simulation, and exercising the simulation, can be a means of assessing the outcomes of regression analysis (and hence the theory on which it is based). It can also be the basis for experimenting with alternative policies.

---

[14]See Forrester, 1971, p. 66.

Epilog

18 A Critical Assessment

This book is essentially a progress report on the initial phases of our research. Here we shall give a brief assessment of what we have accomplished, indicate what aspects of the work still need to be refined, and what might be undertaken in the future.

The narrow limits of our study—encompassing forty-five years and focusing on only six countries—make it impossible to provide anything like conclusive evidence. Nonetheless, our dynamic simulations of the process leading to war have provided us with a partial test of both our specific coefficient estimates and the equations and theory from which the coefficients were derived.

Our most important finding is that domestic growth (as measured by population density and national income per capita) is generally a strong determinant of national expansion. Our investigations have identified strong linkages from domestic growth and national expansion to military expenditures, to alliances, and to international interactions with a relatively high potential for violence.

Our analysis has substantiated our hypothesis that military expenditures and alliances (both generated by national growth) often evoke a violent response from rival powers (although not necessarily an increase in military spending). This response, in turn, evokes violence-behavior by the first country. This action-reaction process, so characteristic of major-power interaction, partially validates and partially modifies Richardson's hypothesis. Our finding that military expenditures have a strong influence on conflicts of interest and possibilities for violence among great powers emphasizes the role armies and navies have in acquiring and protecting national interests.

We have also noted how alliances can serve as a national capability —supplementing more sovereign capabilities. Alliances are related both to domestic growth and to conflicts of interest and violence among nations. They therefore play an important role in the linkage between national growth and international violence. We have also come upon a striking consideration in the course of experimenting with various simulations using different (predetermined) coefficients: the coefficients for certain of the international processes in our model exhibit markedly greater sensitivity to upward than to downward swings. The general trend is toward higher levels of violence and increasing allocations to the military. If further investigations using our model confirm this trend, the finding may have serious implications for the effectiveness of arms limitations policies.

These findings, however suggestive, are not a definitive test of our exploratory theory. Indeed, we are acutely aware of numerous theoretical and methodological problems with our analysis. Clearly, there are problems with any attempt to capture complex social dynamics in an empirical model. Our results bear *only on the variables and measures employed:* it is with great caution that we interpret them as bearing directly on the processes we seek to elucidate. This lack of "fit" among theory, hypotheses, equations, measures, and functional form may account for our biggest failures. Specific dilemmas and failures, such as those caused by degrees of freedom and measurement error, have been dealt with in Part III (especially Chapter 10) and Appendix B. Here, we would like to focus on broader problems implicit in our approach. Many of these revolve around serious difficulties in obtaining data, selecting measures, and applying appropriate methodology for testing theory.

The hypothesized relationships presented in Chapter 1 were not stated in a form that was amenable to empirical testing; our theory was often nonspecific and too general. Nevertheless, we tried to develop a system of simultaneous equations that would decompose some of the more falsifiable and measurable aspects of this conceptual framework and submit them to empirical test. At best we have a first-order (and rough) approximation of the linkage between domestic growth and international violence; we are not at all satisfied with either the model specification or the theoretical guidelines. The theory does not adequately specify the linkages in a manner in which they can be tested, and the equations often do not capture specific links. The methodology employed is constrained by data requirements, and the data base is not as robust as we would wish. The trade-offs among empirical fit, parsimony, and falsifiability are especially difficult.

Nevertheless, although our theory is still too general to be optimally falsifiable, specific links can be, and have been, tested empirically. Some of these links are well represented by the specification of the equations in the simultaneous system; others are not. Taken together, the equations have yielded some empirical evidence regarding the extent to which the hypothesized relationships do or do not "fit" the data. The purpose of our self-criticism here is to identify areas of improvement—we do not feel that in doing so our results are vitiated. However, greater specification, precision, and falsifiability must be achieved before our general theory can be adequately verified. We need to focus attention next on ways in which the negative evidence can be used to refine the model.

We have also searched for, and tried to model, the *transformations* of the dynamic processes leading to international crises and war. The poor empirical fit of some equations for some periods is clear evidence that the real-world dynamics change over time. Although our theory provides some guidelines for modeling transformations, we need a more specific theoretical statement of when and how changes are expected and what forms they may take. Nevertheless, our methodology has to some extent allowed us to model phase shifts. The analysis of residuals has been of critical importance in verifying, and in some cases identifying, transformations of the real-world processes.

Objections can easily be raised with respect to our choice of variables and their measures, and even the sources from which the data were drawn. It is possible that a different choice of variables, indicators, or data might have yielded somewhat different results. Colonial area is clearly only a crude approximation of the manifestation of national expansion, despite the fact that colonial expansion was the principal mode of expansion by the great powers in 1870–1914. The interactive effect of population and national income, designed to represent the combined effects of numbers of people in conjunction with their level of technology, is also clearly inadequate, although no better measure was readily apparent. Similarly, our inclusion of trade per capita as a measure of alternate ways in which needs can be met other than by expansion, is grossly inappropriate.[1] Also, the use of metricized data for intensity-of-intersections and violence-behavior is less than ideal. The accumulation of error resulting from reliance on metricized data tends to confuse the analysis. Moreover, our concepts 'intersection' and 'violence-behavior' are not as independent of each other as we would like. A major task for the future is the identification of a better variety of metric indicators and the development of a "metatheory" to guide their formulation and operationalization.

The colonial-area equation illustrates many of the problems associated with tentative theory, weak specification, and measurement. Despite our ability to account for a large proportion of the variance in colonial area, we are not entirely satisfied with our specification of the theory. In particular, much of the variance is accounted for by the constant term, that is, by preexisting dynamics not incorporated in the

---

[1]A major difficulty stemmed from the fact that while trade can satisfy many demands and thus possibly reduce lateral pressure, trade is itself a major manifestation of lateral pressure. Neither our hypotheses nor the equations captured this vitally important link. Some of our more recent research, not reported in this book, may alleviate this difficulty and provide a better test, as well as a better statement, of the theory.

model. The resulting statistics may not be an accurate indication of what actually took place. In any case, like all statistics, the results must be interpreted with care.

Despite the limitations imposed by the use of regression analysis and its extensions in estimating parameters and then simulating a system of simultaneous equations, we are generally satisfied with the methodology we used for our first cut into the problem. In order to capture the dynamics more fully, however, the regression algorithm may not be adequate.

In view of the nonlinear characteristics of states, it is unfortunate that the conventional wisdom in social-scientific inquiry draws heavily from the regression algorithm, to the exclusion of alternative ways of modeling social processes. The social sciences are dominated by the statistical paradigm, and although this paradigm undoubtedly has an important place, it is constrained by rigid data requirements. But because we seek to understand systemic processes, our concerns must also be with functional relationships. For this reason we feel that greater attention should be paid to system dynamics as a procedure, philosophy, and methodology for modeling social systems, and to experimenting with simulation, forecasting, and policy analysis.

System dynamics is both a theory of system structure and a set of tools for identifying, representing, and analyzing multiloop, nonlinear feedback relationships. As a methodology, the procedure is predicated on the analysis of *functional* relationships in a feedback system (that is, deterministic relations) and not, as is common in the social sciences, on the analysis of the proportion of variance explained (that is, *stochastic* relationships). But there are no methodological reasons why statistical analysis of a system-dynamics model cannot be undertaken. Indeed, if empirical data are available and if future changes in the structural relationships and the exogenous factors can be fully described (in theoretical terms), very effective predictions of single points are possible. On the other hand, where the processes modeled are not fully understood and data are poor in quality, only general statements about the behavior of the system can be made. The behavior of international systems falls into this latter category. Although point predictions are not possible, system-dynamics analyses may still provide a better understanding of international behavior than purely probabilistic models, or models based on linear and additive assumptions. A system-dynamics approach can be extremely useful, particularly when the interaction over time of the elements in a complex process is the focus of concern.[2]

Unfortunately, the gains and losses attached to the two alternative simulation procedures — the statistical and the functional — have not

---

[2]See Choucri, Laird, and Meadows, 1972, for an application of system dynamics to the analysis of international behavior.

been compared to date in any comprehensive study. Nor has a particular problem been investigated using both system-dynamics and econometric analysis, and the outcomes compared. We strongly believe that such investigations are necessary, that they would enhance systematic inquiry into social systems, and that they would provide us with a better understanding of the assumptions underlying alternative methodologies. More important, they should assist us in achieving greater convergence among theory, methodology, measurement, and functional specification in individual equations. To date, studies using system dynamics have not drawn as heavily on real-world data (for estimating coefficients, for example) as would be desirable. (Regression methodologies, by their very nature, are bound and shaped by the data base.) Our experience so far with the use of system-dynamics analysis (not reported on in this book) is limited and inconclusive, but we believe that the efforts will prove worthwhile.

Many issues of methodology involve difficult tradeoffs. Costs and benefits are involved in almost every major choice made in the development and testing of theory. Clearly, it would have been desirable to be able to specify and correct the errors in the analysis so far, and thus be able to present a complete, consistent, and fully tested theory. However, the lesser job that we *did* accomplish took nearly ten years of slow and often discouraging trial and error—with the major returns occurring only in the last year or so. A progress report was long overdue. We owe it to our financial supporters, our families, friends, and colleagues—to say nothing of ourselves. On a long journey one needs to put up at least a rough milestone now and then, or risk losing one's sense of movement and direction.

But there is a further consideration. By publicizing what we have done, by explaining how we did it, and by identifying the uncertainties, pitfalls, and blind alleys, we share our mistakes as well as our gains, and thus hope to facilitate the work of other investigators. In this way, the modification, refinement, and testing of the ideas presented in this book will be greatly accelerated.

The Future

The analysis in Part III revealed a strong interactive relationship between domestic growth, competition among nations, and international violence behavior. This three-way interaction pattern not only characterizes military competition but may also characterize competition for resources, markets, prestige, and strategic advantage.

Embedded in this three-way interactive pattern are some difficult dilemmas. A certain amount of growth is considered desirable, even necessary, for a vigorous society. Historically, many societies that have ceased to grow economically and technologically have declined. Some degree of competition not only seems to facilitate growth (and may even be necessary for it), but also is a likely result of collisions among expanding nations. And yet strong growth combined with strong competition often contributes to violence.

Processes of national growth and competition are complicated by the fact that national leaders, like all people, act on their *perception* of events. It is well known that perceptions may or may not correspond with a "full picture" of reality and that different people often perceive the same phenomenon quite differently. This uncertainty lies at the source of the classic Richardsonian spiral: the leader of country A, fearing that country B may increase its military budget, increases his own country's military budget. Meanwhile, the leader of country B, anxious lest country A increase its military budget, increases *his* own budget. Each thus validates the fears of the other (the pursuit of security often enhancing each country's sense of insecurity). On each side of an arms competition, the initial disposition to increase military budgets may be generated by bureaucratic and other domestic processes.

Similarly, the competition between states for resources and markets may be characterized by a confounding of domestic and international processes. In seeking to strengthen their own position, each country tends to validate the anxieties of its rivals. Although the demand for resources or markets in each country is likely to be generated fundamentally by domestic growth, as world resources are depleted or international markets flooded, each country is likely to increase its efforts, thus exacerbating the spiral. Like military competition, economic competition may contribute to international violence, particularly when the gains of one nation are regarded as a loss to another.

Until WWI, and to some extent thereafter, the industrialized countries of the world were able to secure protected access to resources and markets through colonial expansion. This is no longer the case. Of course, the world is still dominated in important ways by a few powerful industrialized countries, but former colonies are now sovereign states. Penetration of these so-called underdeveloped countries has become both more complex (with modern techniques of credit and investment, multinational corporations, international political movements, commerce in weaponry, and networks of espionage and subversion) and more crucial, with the need for secure access to resources in a world of scarcities. Among the rich and the powerful—such as Britain and Germany prior to 1914—even relatively moderate differences of wealth, capabilities and power can contribute to conflict and large-scale violence. A far more serious gap has always existed between the strong, rich nations and the poor, weak nations. For a long time there was a widely shared assumption that by narrowing this gap through technological and economic growth, the probability of conflict and war would be lessened. This assumption now seems dubious.

During recent decades rival powers have developed ingenious mechanisms for pursuing their interests in foreign countries. This is true of Soviet assistance to the People's Republic of China in the 1950s and to present-day Middle Eastern, African, Latin American, and Southeast Asian countries, as well as American or western European economic, technical, and military aid and "peace corps" operations throughout the Third World. Such aid has undoubtedly served the donor power well, even while contributing to peace, economic security, and political stability within recipient countries (and perhaps in the world at large). But there have also been some unanticipated consequences that policymakers would have preferred to avoid—as the United States discovered in Vietnam, and the Soviet Union in China.

What criteria do we have for policy-making in an increasingly complex world society? In an era of critical shortages, what can we expect of relations between powerful industrialized countries, with spiraling demands for resources and markets, and Third World countries, with low levels of technology, underdeveloped natural resources, and high rates of disease and starvation? How will powerful industrialized countries react to scarcity of critical resources? What are the likely effects of foreign aid programs for countries that are rich in resources but poor in technology? And what of those who are poor in both technology and resources? Can foreign aid programs be used to narrow economic and technological gaps between rich and poor countries, or are they only new and subtler devices for domination and exploitation? What are the short, middle-range and long-range effects of technology transfers, such as the "green revolution" or nuclear proliferation?

Indeed, we must push our inquiry beyond the nation-state. Where is a multinational corporation rooted, and in what ways does it serve to link the processes of growth in an industrialized country with developments in a Third World country and with the general configuration of power? Is it a useful instrument for technological transfer? Who benefits and who loses by its existence? Does it widen or narrow economic gaps between industrialized and developing countries? Do the operations of multinational corporations influence conflict and violence throughout the world?

In a world increasingly armed with weapons of mass destruction, and increasingly plagued with political, social, economic, technological, demographic, and environmental dilemmas, it is quite possible that maximum public information—to the extent where each society as a whole, and each member of that society, knows as much as possible about what every other society is up to—might have a stabilizing effect. Such wide, unrestricted dissemination of accurate information—both from country to country and between leaders and populaces—might in the long run enhance the probability of human survival through reducing uncertainties in decision-making.

Today, far more than in 1914, it is crucial to consider the world as a whole, to assess the comparative advantages and costs associated with different actions, to find ways in which quality may substitute for quantity, to consider whether certain types of growth may be less conducive to antagonistic competition and violence than others, and to design and perhaps find agreement on new ways of allocating technology, resources, and markets for all the world.

These issues raise challenging questions about the most fundamental human values and about the ability of large numbers of people armed with massive weapons to live together in a limited space. As long as there were ample resources for growth—beyond the horizon, if not immediately at hand—and as long as there were outlets for the pressures of growth, human societies could afford to grow and to compete, even though the price they paid was sometimes quite high. During the greater part of mankind's history, the planet offered vast, sparsely inhabited territories for exploration and development, and human societies were to some extent buffered from each other.

The interactive processes inherent in population growth, technological advancement, and rapidly increasing demands for resources have always had implications for conflict and violence. To the extent that the processes identified in this book do indeed operate, people everywhere now confront the enhanced risk that continuing growth and competition, unless channeled in some new ways, may lead to massive self-annihilation.[1] Indeed, it has been widely noted that no society on earth today is more than thirty minutes from potential destruction. And, in an era of scarcities, the dangerous implications of growth have become accentuated. For if the powerful, industrialized countries continue to compete for resources, markets, military superiority, and strategic advantage, their activities and the accompanying dangers are likely to escalate as resource limits (even if short-term) are approached.

On the other hand, if societies are accustomed to growing and competing — if, indeed, the prosperity and welfare of nations depend on growth and competition — what would happen to them if growth and aggressive competition were severely curtailed? Might not such an eventuality lead as surely to disaster as the path of growth and competition? And what about Third World countries? What would happen to them if the possibilities for economic and technological growth were thwarted just as they were in a position to grow? The idea of limited growth is foreign and even threatening to most contemporary societies, and in fact it seems certain that limited growth cannot be achieved without serious economic and some social costs.

Should we therefore try to alter human nature? Cease being acquisitive? Cease being competitive? Should we change our values — bring our operational values more closely in line with those we profess? Share resources with friends, even enemies? Forego the exhilarations of advancement, power, influence, winning the race? Share benefits and bear costs more or less equally? Are there sufficient benefits to share? Will population growth merely cause the entire world to live at the brink of starvation, and equalize the misery? Or should we start with our governments — drastically reform them, overthrow them, redesign our institutions, create whole new societies?

Who will keep order in the brave new world? Who will regulate the fair distribution of resources and technology? Who will make certain that justice is served? Who will govern the weapons of destruction? Who will be given these powers, how will they be bestowed, and how do we ascertain that these powers will not be used — again — to the advantage of power? The international institutions that have been developed to date, however indispensable many of them may be, are scarcely adequate for regulating matters of life and death.

Realistic solutions are difficult to identify. There seem to be no easy answers to the dilemmas of human governance. Inquiries should be pursued on all fronts with all the means at our disposal. The tools

---

[1]See Choucri, 1974, for an analysis of population, resources, technology, and conflict in developing areas.

employed in this study, albeit in a rudimentary fashion, may be extremely valuable for identifying the elusive causes of social events, for exposing hidden feedbacks (and feedbacks within feedbacks) in our social systems, for clarifying some of the complex processes that often transform well-meant intentions into unanticipated, sometimes disastrous outcomes.

An immediate difficulty is the fact that the dynamic processes of national and international systems are not yet fully understood. In the United States, the Soviet Union, Japan, the People's Republic of China, and other countries of the world people find themselves enmeshed in social, economic, and political systems that they and their forebears have helped to create, but never really learned to control — or even comprehend. This is more or less true not only for the ordinary citizen, but also for national leaders and even scholars, whose discipline (whether history, political science, economics, or sociology, etc.) normally focuses on only very limited aspects of the whole system. Actions that citizens (or their leaders) take in one part of a system in order to relieve one kind of distress all too frequently produce an unexpected consequence in some other part of the system. If the links and interdependencies are not sufficiently understood, the outcome of change can be as bad or worse than before. Our immediate problem is to identify these interdependencies so that we may avoid serious mistakes.

We frequently think of public decisions as meeting a community need or responding to some general interest of the citizenry, or as steps directed toward widely shared and publicly identified goals, such as social welfare, cultural survival, national security, the enhancement of trade, the maintenance of political freedom or world peace. When national goals are thus stated, national policies for their achievement give an appearance of having resulted from careful thought, rational calculation, and balancing of alternatives.

When a head of state, or other high official, "pushes a pedal" or "pulls a lever" of power, there is likely to be some effect on another country, on some sector of the nation, or on both. A policy designed to yield positive, highly desirable short-term outcomes may affect another country or the international system in such a way that a grievous price is paid later. This is true not only of the actions of high officials, but also of laws passed by legislative bodies. Similarly, a policy aimed at avoiding future catastrophe may be put aside because the immediate costs are considered too high.

Decisions made by heads of state are rarely entirely independent. They emerge from decisions made by predecessors, from the policies of other states, from bureaucratic decisions made at least in part in pursuit of bureaucratic survival, and from millions of private decisions made by individual citizens. To some extent, national leaders cannot avoid being seriously constrained. For example, they may not be able to escape the limitations created by decisions of their predecessors. But national leaders may also be able to avoid some constraints, or at least minimize them, by widening their perspectives. Although much policy must be shaped incrementally, through day-by-day decisions, to the extent that leaders develop a feel for long-term processes, they may be able to avoid some decisions that purchase short-term benefits at exorbitant long-range costs.

Large bureaucracies are characterized by a fragmented anonymous decision-making process that originates in small decisions and "accumulates" in policy. This tendency is similar to disjointed incrementalism — the breaking down of a large problem into several smaller ones while neglecting the fact that the solution of one small problem may give rise to another. A solution to the new problem creates a third problem, and so on. Often, these problems snowball, giving rise to another "large" problem, possibly a catastrophe. What at first seemed to be a solution "may end as a trap." [2]

If societies are to alter historical trends in growth and expansion, a special effort will be required to correct for the hidden interactions and interdependencies that may propel whole societies along unanticipated courses. This is perhaps another way of asserting that a policy-maker should act in such a way as to maximize his range of choices with the understanding that under some conditions his actions will amount to little more than reaction to the actions of others. This does not mean, of course, that a conscious effort should not be made to break out of reaction behavior and establish independence of choice.

We recognize that national policy-makers cannot easily escape from day-to-day concerns. Yet the findings of our research so far suggest that long-range considerations — the cumulative effects of a growing population, rapidly advancing technologies, and scarcities of resources — can nullify the intended effects of short-term decisions and bring about unintended consequences. The prospect that a people and its leaders may be swept along by national and international process over which no one seems to have adequate control, is somewhat chilling in a nuclear world.

We believe that such processes ought to be systematically monitored to find out how the international system has been operating over the last two or three decades; to project what the world is likely to look like if recent and current trends continue; to assess the domestic and foreign perceptions of national leaders' policies and decisions; to identify alternate courses of action, especially variables that can and should be altered; and to specify the means for changing these variables and the probable benefits and costs associated with such means.

With such monitoring, heads of state and their advisers would have more systematic information with which to balance immediate or short-

---

[2]Deutsch, 1957, p. 202; see also Platt, 1973, p. 641.

term benefits against probable medium- and long-range costs. He would be in a better position to see how each policy alternative reverberates through the international system, and through component nations, including his own. With some reasonable assessments of both costs and benefits, he might perceive more clearly what trade-offs were involved with each alternative—including trade-offs between short-term and long-term interests. It is important to recognize, however, that tools are merely tools. They cannot resolve questions of values, preferences, or priorities. They can in theory, however, ascertain what the consequences of a given course of action are likely to be, and hence how best to reach a desired outcome.

Some variables, such as population and technology, are less amenable to control than others. More easily manipulable variables include diplomatic negotiations of various sorts, the administration of trade, technical assistance, military aid programs, military expenditures, investments in various sectors of the domestic economy, new alliances, troop movements, mobilizations, and various threats to employ military force or other sanctions. The task of the national leader is to use the more easily manipulable variables as levers to control the effects of less readily manipulable variables and maximize net benefits to the system.

The idea of using more manipulable variables, such as budget allocations, as leverage for altering less manipulable long-range variables is not new—the Marshall Plan after World War II is a well-known example. What the evidence of this study suggests is that the network of interdependent variables may be far more intricate and extensive, and yet potentially more susceptible to analysis and planning, than is sometimes assumed.

If human society is to avoid serious dislocations, wars, or other thoroughgoing upheavals, the gathering, transmission, and accurate evaluation of information—as well as the capacity for acting on it (sometimes in new, unprecedented ways)—must be built into the day-to-day operation of societies worldwide. Such a continuing process requires a methodology of some sort for ongoing cost/benefit analyses of alternatives—not just in monetary terms but, more importantly, in environmental and societal terms, and not just in terms of individual societies, but for mankind as a whole. The challenge will be to modify or replace old institutions *before* their malfunctioning or other inadequacy does too much damage, to try out new methods and institutions on a tentative, carefully monitored basis, to assess the benefits against the costs, and to effect the appropriate adjustments.

Decisions and outcomes need to be monitored and analyzed in each capital on a systematic basis—not in terms of the usual intelligence operations—but in terms of (a) how the international system has been operating over the previous two or three decades; (b) how past decisions in one's own country have in fact either improved or exacerbated the situation from various perspectives (those of the country itself, those of other countries, those of mankind as a whole, and so forth); (c) projections of what the world is likely to look like if recent current impulsions and drifts continue; (d) alternative courses of action and the identification of variables that need to be altered; and (e) specification of the means for changing such variables and the probable benefits and costs associated with such means.

After a "pedal is pushed" or a "lever is pulled," a number of critical questions remain to be asked. To what extent are the desired consequences being achieved? To what extent are unanticipated and perhaps undesired outcomes being brought about? To what extent are foreign policies and operations at odds with domestic programs and welfare? Which, in the medium or long run, must override the other? Unless the tell-tale signals and clues are being monitored and analyzed, the whole nation may find itself caught up in a "run-away" situation—an arms race, monetary crisis, inflation, depression, crime wave, environmental crisis, trade war, or even revolution. In each instance, trade-offs must be made. Are the desired outcomes sufficient to render the undesired outcomes worth tolerating? Or is the overall situation being made worse by the action taken?

The questions raised here can be answered to some extent, even if only tentatively, through computer modeling, simulation, and forecasting, along the lines of the analysis reported in Chapter 17. Such techniques have been put forward in the last few years as tools for achieving a better understanding of how social, political, and economic systems work. In general, such methods are still in the early stages of development. And far too little work has been done so far toward integrating social, political, economic, demographic, technological and other variables within systems models.

Computer simulations allow us to alter various coefficients and observe the changes that then take place throughout the whole system. We can imagine thus carrying out policy changes and even bloodless revolutions (all quite reversible or discardable) at no cost other than human labor and computer time. For example, one possible world might involve, first, an equal division—via the computer—of the total existing world product among all human beings; and second, the raising of all mankind to the current per capita consumption level of the United States. By observing the "consequences," one would have some theoretical insights and a rough demonstration of the magnitude of the problems created by vast differences among nations in levels of technology and access to basic resources. These possibilities are limited primarily by our fundamental ignorance of how complex political, economic, and social systems work.

Modeling, simulation, and forecasting can be used to generate a great variety of alternatives with probable benefits and costs made explicit. A number of difficult questions can be addressed in a disciplined fashion. For what purposes and within what limitations should growth be encouraged? How is it to be furthered? What are the expected benefits? What are the possible damaging side effects? Who will reap the rewards and who will bear the costs? Under what conditions do benign activities such as trade, economic aid, and transfers of technology contribute to conflict, violence or other undesirable outcomes? In what ways does domestic development affect foreign relations, and how do international transactions affect domestic programs? What is the relationship between the interests of a nation and the interests of mankind as a whole? To the extent that answers to these questions are available, value choices concerning future policy can be made more rationally, in that policies will be available that are likely to achieve desired ends. In order to make wise decisions now, a fuller understanding of the consequences of making, or *not* making, those choices is essential.

Appendixes

A. The Data: Sources and Problems
B. Methodology
C. Alternative Estimation Procedures
D. Biographies
E. Treaties

Appendix A
The Data:
Sources and Problems

Aggregate annual data on Britain, France, Germany, Russia, Italy and Austria-Hungary for the period 1870 to 1914 were compiled in the following categories:*

1. National (home) size:
    a. Population
    b. Area

2. Colonial size:
    a. Population
    b. Area

3. Economic and Productivity profile:
    a. National income
    b. National income per capita
    c. Steel production
    d. Coal production
    e. Iron-ore production
    f. Pig-iron production
    g. Wholesale-price indexes
    h. Currency conversion indexes (1906 only)
    i. Petroleum production
    j. Wheat production

4. Commercial activity:
    a. Imports (in standardized currency value)
    b. Exports (in standardized currency value)
    c. Merchant marine (in tonnage and number of ships)

*This appendix was written with the collaboration of Raisa B. Deber. The assistance of Linda C. Fields and John Wesley Martin is gratefully acknowledged.

5. Government budget (in standardized currency values):
    a. Revenue
    b. Expenditures
    c. Army expenditures
    d. Navy expenditures
6. Alliances
    a. Number of commitments
    b. Rival powers
7. Violence:
    a. Violence-behavior (metricized measure of violence by one nation toward others; highest level per year).
    b. Violence-of-others (metricized measure of violence toward one nation by others; highest level per year).
    c. Dyadic violence (metricized measure of violence by one state toward another, e.g., Britain against Germany or Germany against Britain; highest level per year).
8. Conflicts of interests (metricized data of intensity of conflicts of national interests, specifically with respect to colonial issues; explained below).

The data in categories 1 through 6a are standard metric data compiled from yearbooks and other statistical sources. The data in category 6b were contrived by the authors as a dummy measure: zero if two powers were aligned, and one if they were not. The data in Categories 7 and 8 were metricized, that is, derived from subjective scaling procedures (explained below).

Sources consulted for each variable are listed in Table A-1 (p. 300). As a general rule we sought to compile at least two series for each variable to allow for some assessment of measurement error or error due to differences in recording practices as employed by different sources. Our major sources were: the *Annuaire Statistique de la France*, the *Statesman's Yearbook*, the *Almanach de Gotha*, the *British Sessional Papers*, and specific national sources. Other sources listed in Table A-1 were used primarily to check the reliability of these major sources.

Several difficulties arose in collecting annual data. Through the years, the data reported for a given country were often selected or compiled according to quite different criteria. For example, all Algerian territorial and population data might be identified as French *colonial* data for some years. For other years the territory and population of northern Algeria might be aggregated as a part of France's *home* territory and *home* population, whereas data for southern Algeria would be under the colonial rubric. For some years a country's gross military expenditures might include expenditures for reserves, or for colonial troops, which might be recorded separately for other years. The Russian data caused problems because some sources separated the data concerning Asian Russia from data concerning European Russia, while others did not. Our own definition of "home territory" was restricted to European Russia; the remainder (including Finland) was considered to be colonial territory. Apart from the problem of definition, the Russian data also appear to contain considerable measurement error.

Certain data series, such as colonial population, were not used in the analyses because of serious inconsistencies in the sources. For such series the degree of probable error was judged to be so substantial as to invalidate any inferences made from these measures.

Data on national and per capita income were perhaps the most difficult to compile, largely because of discrepancies in computational procedures and incompleteness of information. In some instances, the data were not regularly reported on an annual basis. Data on Britain were obtained from *Abstracts of British Historical Statistics* and from the series, *Income and Wealth*; figures on France were derived from *Conditions of Economic Progress* and the series, *Income and Wealth* (see Table A-1). We are not confident of the accuracy of the data on France, in part because the error range is unknown, in part because of the spotty nature of data in the original sources. Data on Germany were compiled from *Income and Wealth* and from *Das Deutsche Volkeinkommen*. National income figures for Italy are based on *Sommario di Statistiche Storicche Italiani, 1861–1955*. Figures on Russia were computed by Paul Bernstein from information covering various sectors of the economy: agriculture, large industry, small industry (handicraft), forestry, fishing and hunting, construction, transportation, communication, and trade. Because our definition of national income included the sectors of personal and government services, Bernstein adjusted the Russian figures to ensure comparability.[1]

We did not use Austro-Hungarian national income in the analysis. Estimates were available for a few scattered years, but in view of the paucity of data, the construction of a series of annual approximations from 1870 to 1914 opened the possibilities of serious error. Because of this difficulty, we used statistics of iron and steel production as a rough indicator of Austro-Hungarian technology.[2]

Wholesale-price indexes, which were used to standardize or deflate individual currencies, were gathered from the 1954 *Annuaire Sta-*

---

[1]The basic source for these computations is Raymond W. Goldsmith, 1961, pp. 446–462. A detailed description of the procedures used to calculate Russian national income is presented in Bernstein, 1969.

[2]The better estimates are provided in Gross, 1967 (for 1865, 1880, 1885, and 1911–1913). See Katzenstein, 1969, for an attempt to develop time-series data for Austrian national income from the gross data.

tistique de la France (the section "Resumé Retrospectif," pp. 439–441). These data have been calculated from publications of individual countries to the base of 1901–1910 = 100, the mean being designated 1906. As with national income, wholesale-price indexes for Russia were calculated on the basis of available information. The index for Austria-Hungary was worked out from figures given in the 1913 Hungarian statistical publication, *Magyar Statisztikai Kozlemenyek*, which was based primarily on information on raw materials and processed commodities and excluded heavy industry.

In order to undertake comparisons across nations, and to construct certain of our measures, it was necessary to standardize all monetary values. This was accomplished by dividing each monetary series by the nation's own wholesale-price index, and converting to 1906 US dollar units. The choice of dollars, rather than British pounds, was based on the desire to render the 1870–1914 data consistent with other data for the years after 1918.

Data on iron and steel and coal output were compiled from the series in the *Annuaire Statistique de la France* (the section "Resumé Retrospectif"). All data in the *Annuaire* were from government sources of the individual nations. We are reasonably confident of the consistency and reliability of the production data because of the high correspondence between the different series that we compiled.

For import and export data we used special rather than general trade measures, since the former were reported more consistently.[3] Sources consulted included the *Annuaire Statistique de la France*, individual national publications, the *Statesman's Yearbook*, and the *Almanach de Gotha*.

Merchant marine tonnage figures were gathered directly from the *Annuaire Statistique de la France* and corroborated with data from individual government publications.

Consistent data on government budgets were difficult to obtain. National publications were employed, as well as the *Almanach de Gotha* and the *Statesman's Yearbook*. Often, only estimates rather than the actual values were presented; this was particularly a problem with military expenditures. When actual figures were available, they often differed from the estimates, although the direction of deviance varied with each country and time period. National-revenue figures were especially unreliable because of inconsistent bookkeeping practices

---

[3]Special imports are total imports directly acquired for domestic consumption plus any *withdrawals* of previously imported goods from bonded warehouses or free zones for domestic consumption. General imports are total imports directly acquired for domestic consumption plus *imports into* bonded warehouses and free zones. Analogously, special exports are exports of national merchandise (goods wholly or partly produced or manufactured in the country) plus exports of nationalized goods (goods included under special imports but exported without transformation). General exports are total national exports plus reexports.

among nations, which often made comparisons impossible. (This problem was particularly acute with Austria-Hungary.)

The alliance data are based on the Singer and Small compilations, although unlike Singer and Small we use total alliances as a measure without differentiating types of alliances, such as defense pacts, neutrality pacts, nonaggression pacts, and ententes. We also developed dummy variables to indicate whether or not two states were allied. This enabled us to calculate the effects of rival powers on intensity-of-intersections, military expenditures, and violence-behavior.

The data for violence-behavior are metricized (subjectively scaled) actions based on historical activities of the nations studied. In the analysis reported in this book approximately 1,000 historical actions were assigned numbers indicating their relative potential for violence. This was done from a 30-point scale, using a set of 30 "marker cards." The marker cards contain statements such as "Nation A concludes an alliance with Nation B," "Nation A executes prisoners of Nation B," and "Nation A invades Nation B." The cards were numbered from 1 (low) to 30 (high), following the consensus of judges working independently.[4]

A marker deck must have certain properties. It must have a sufficiently wide *range of evaluation* so that none of the actions to be scaled will clearly lie outside the range of the cards. It must be applicable to a wide *range of situations*. The set must also be *reliable* in the sense that different judges would independently put them in almost precisely the same order.

The deck of marker cards is the *metric* (or "measuring instrument") against which the data (historical actions) are "measured." The data have been recorded earlier in the form of statements about events or actions and entered on individual cards. Each statement consists of at least two (but sometimes three) elements: an actor, an action, and often a target, e.g., "Germany invaded Belgium."[5] The action may be expressed as a verb, a participle, or a gerund. Qualitative considerations, i.e., adjectives and adverbs, are eliminated: "~~Treacherous~~ Germany ~~brutally~~ invaded ~~helpless~~ Belgium."

"Measurement" of the data is done independently by several judges (not the same as those who arranged the marker cards). The judge places each data card behind the marker card that carries a statement most closely approximating the level of violence suggested by the statement on the data card. For example, if the data card read "Russia called up recent classes of reserves in response to Austria's threat,"

---

[4]See Moses *et al.*, 1967, pp. 1054–1059, for a fuller explanation of the scaling procedures used by us. For refinements in this type of scaling, see Azar, 1970; also Goodman, Hart and Rosecrance. For related approaches, see Coombs, 1964.

[5]Sometimes an action has no specific target (or no targets are explicit in reports of the action). For example, "Nation A dispatched its fleet."

a judge might place it between marker card 20 ("Nation A puts its reserve troops on notice") and marker card 21 ("Nation A warns foreign ships to be ready to leave its ports"). The score awarded would be the lesser, 20.

In cases where two or more judges disagree on the number to be awarded to a particular action, the average of the different scores becomes the measure. In the example cited above, four judges might award the following scores to Russia's call-up of reserves: 20, 20, 19, and 21. The measure would then be 20, the average.[6]

The scale is relatively flexible in that it can be used to measure changes in a number of different variables in addition to the potential for violence-behavior — for example, conflict or cooperation, and so on. Also, variations are possible in the technical procedures. For example, the 30-point scale can be collapsed into a 15-point scale (composed of every other card in the marker deck) with comparable reliability.

In practice, we found that the procedure for scaling the marker cards and the data was more reliable (there was closer agreement among judges) in the *upper* ("more violent") half than in the lower half.[7] This was fortunate for us, since only the highest points for each year were used in our analysis.

The measure for intersections was obtained by identifying all those actions (in the violence-behavior data file) that involved at least two major powers *specifically over matters of colonial (territorial) control or influence*. We then selected the "most violent" actions of this type for each power for each year to make up the intensity-of-intersection file.

The data set used for this study is deposited at the Inter-University Consortium for Political Research at the University of Michigan.

---

[6]This scale is not, strictly speaking, an equal-interval scale like a yardstick or thermometer. However, the metricized data can be used *as if* the scale had equal-interval properties. This convention makes possible the use of numerous modes of analysis that assume an equal-interval scale. We are grateful to Joseph Kadane for clarifying this point.

[7]Procedures for handling missing data and their consequences are noted in Deber, 1974.

Table A-1. Major sources of data.

Country	Home population, area	Colonial population, area	National income	Budgetary data	Inter-sections	Alliance commitments
Great Britain	2,3,7,14, 19,26,35	2,14,19, 22,35	8,18,20,26, 27,36,37	2,3,26, 31,35	1,7,14, 21,30,35	32
France	2,3,7,14, 19,35	2,3,14, 22,35	5,18,20, 29,36	2,3,31, 35	1,7,14, 21,30,35	32
Russia	2,3,7,14,23, 28,33,35	2,14,22,23, 28,33,35	4,10,20, 36	2,3,31, 35	1,7,14, 21,30,35	32
Italy	2,3,7,14, 34,35	2,14,22, 35	20,34,36	2,3,31, 35	1,7,14, 21,30,35	32
Germany	2,3,7,14, 35	2,14,22, 35	12,13,15 20,36	2,3,31, 35	1,7,14, 21,30,35	32
Austria-Hungary	2,3,7,14, 16,19,35	2,14,16, 22,35	6,9,11, 17,24,36	2,3,35	1,7,14, 21,30,35	32

1. Albertini, Luigi. *The Origins of the War of 1914*, 3 vols. London and New York: Oxford University Press, 1952–1957.
2. *Almanach de Gotha, Annuaire, Geneologique Diplomatique et Statistique*, Gotha: Engelhard-Reyhes (volumes for 1870–1920).
3. *Annuaire Statistique de la France.* Paris: Imprimerie Nationale, 1878–1964. Institut National de la Statistique et des Etudes Economique (1931, also 1914–15 volumes).
4. Bernstein, Paul. *National Income of Russia 1870–1914.* March 8, 1969, mimeographed.
5. Clark, Colin. *The Conditions of Economic Progress*, 3d ed. London: MacMillan and Co., 1957.
6. Eckstein, Alexander, "National Income and Capital Formation in Hungary in 1900–1950," in *Income and Wealth*, V (1955).
7. *Encyclopedia Britannica.* Chicago: Encyclopedia Britannica. (various editions used).
8. Feinstein, C. H. *National Income Expenditure and Output of the United Kingdom 1855–1965.* Cambridge University Press, 1972.
9. Fellner, Fredrich von, "Die Schätzung des Volkseinkommens," *Bulletin de l'Institut de Statistique*, 1905, 14(3): 109–151.
10. Goldsmith, Raymond V. "The Economic Growth of Russia: 1860–

1913." Unpublished paper presented at 1955 meeting of the International Association for Research in Income and Wealth.
11. Gross, Nachum Theodor. *Industrialization in Austria in the Nineteenth Century.* University of California Press, 1967.
12. Helfferich, Karl J. *Germany's Economic Progress and National Wealth 1888–1913.* New York: Germanistic Society of America, 1914.
13. Hoffman, W. G. and Mueller, W. G. *Das Deutsche Volkseinkommen 1851–1957.* Tuebingen: J. C. B. Mohr (P. Siebeck), 1959.
14. *International Yearbook.* Frank Moore Colby, ed. New York: Dodd, Mead and Company (volumes for 1907 to 1920).
15. Jostock, Paul. "Long Term Growth of National Income in Germany," *Income and Wealth*, V (1955).
16. Kann, Robert A. *The Multinational Empire: Nationalism and National Reform in the Habsburg Monarchy 1848–1918.* Columbia University Press, 1950.
17. Katzenstein, Peter J. "Political Integration and Participation in 19th Century Germany," unpublished ms. June, 1969.
18. Kindleberger, Charles P. *Economic Growth in France and Britain 1851–*

Violence behavior	Trade	Merchant marine	Iron and steel	Coal	Wheat	Pig iron	Wholesale price index
1,17,14, 21,30,35	2,3	2,3,19, 26,27	3,26	3,19,26	3	3,12,26	3
1,7,14, 21,30,35	2,3	2,3,27	3	3	3	3,12	3
1,7,14, 21,30,35	2,3,25	2,3,27, 35	3,35	3,35	3,25	3,35	3
1,7,14, 21,30,35	2,3	2,3,14, 34	3,34	3,34	3,34	3,34	3
1,7,14, 21,30,35	2,3	2,3	3,12	3,35	3	3,35	3
1,7,14, 21,30,35	2,3	2,3,19, 27	3	3,7	3	3	3,6,9,11

1950. Harvard University Press, 1964.

19. Kolb, Georg Friedrich. *The Conditions of Nations, Social and Political with Complete Comparative Tables of Universal Statistics*, trans. by Mrs. Brewster. London: G. Belt and Sons, 1880.

20. Kuznets, Simon. *Modern Economic Growth: Rate, Structure and Spread*. Yale University Press, 1966.

21. Langer, William L. *Encyclopedia of World History*. Boston: Houghton-Mifflin, 1963.

22. Leibling, David. "Colonial Empires of Major Powers, 1870–1914: A Statistical Survey." Unpublished paper, M.I.T.: Department of Political Science, 1970.

23. Lorimer, Frank. *The Population of the Soviet Union: History and Prospects*. Geneva: League of Nations, 1946.

24. *Magyar Statisztikai Kozlemenyek* [Hungarian Statistical Publications] Uj Sorozit [New Series], Volume 44: "Arstatistika" [Price Statistics]. Budapest: Posti Konyvnyomda, 1913.

25. Miller, Margaret Stevenson. *The Economic Development of Russia 1905–1914, with Special Reference to Trade, Industry, and Finance*, 2d ed. London: Cass, 1967.

26. Mitchell, Brian R. *Abstract of British Historical Statistics*. Cambridge University Press, 1962.

27. Mulhall, Michael. *Balance Sheet of the World 1870–1880*. London: Stanford, 1881.

28. Parker, William Henry. *An Historical Geography of Russia*. Chicago: Aldine, 1969.

29. Perroux, Francois. "Prises de Vues sur la Croissance de l'Economie Francaise, 1780–1950," in *Income and Wealth*, V, 1954.

30. Richardson, Lewis F. *Statistics of Deadly Quarrels*. Pittsburgh: Boxwood Press, 1960.

31. (Great Britain, Parliament.) *Sessional Papers*: Accounts and Papers. London: Wyman and Sons, Ltd., 1839–1920.

32. Singer, J. David and Melvin Small. *The Wages of War, 1816–1965: A Statistical Handbook*. New York: Wiley, 1972.

33. Skrine, Francis Henry Bennet. *The Expansion of Russia*. Cambridge University Press, 1903.

34. *Sommario di Statistiche Storiche Italiane 1861–1955*, Roma: Istituto Centrale di Statistica, 1958.

35. *The Statesman's Yearbook*. London: Macmillan (volumes for 1864–1920).

36. Studensky, Paul. *Income of Nations*. New York University Press, 1958.

37. Walters, Dorothy and James B. Jeffreys. "National Income and Expenditure of the United Kingdom, 1870–1952," in *Income and Wealth*, V, 1954.

Appendix B
Methodology

This appendix describes the statistical procedures used in our investigations, the assumptions underlying our analysis, and the ways by which departures from these assumptions (largely dictated by the properties of time-series data) have been resolved.[*]

A major purpose of our study is, given an underlying theoretical structure, to predict the values of certain key variables from the values of other variables. We have employed multivariate regression analysis and drawn our inferences from the resulting beta (or path) coefficients, rather than (as is more customary in the social sciences) focus on correlations. Correlation provides little additional information and constitutes a weaker method of inference.[1]

The general approach we have employed is one familiar to any econometrician concerned with the analysis of time-series data, or any statistician examining the properties of small samples.[2] But our

---

[*]This appendix was written with the collaboration of Raisa B. Deber. An earlier version appeared as "Applications of Econometric Analysis to Forecasting in International Relations," Nazli Choucri, *Peace Science Society (International) Papers,* 1974.

[1]See Wonnacott and Wonnacott, 1969, Chapter 14, especially p. 305, for a treatment of the relative strengths and weaknesses of correlational and regression analysis. Basically, however, "since regression answers a broader and more interesting set of questions (and some correlation questions as well) it becomes the preferred technique: correlation is useful primarily as an aid to understanding regression and as an auxiliary tool" (p. 305). Specifically, correlation gives no indications concerning cause and effect; it gives only *one* number as an aid towards understanding a complex relationship, rather than the estimation of a mathematical function yielded by regression techniques; it demands more restrictive assumptions concerning the distribution of the data than does regression; and unlike regression, it does not tell us *how* two variables move together. For those interested in correlations, however, the partial correlations between the statistically significant independent variables and the dependent variables are reported in the tables in Chapters 11 to 15.

[2]See, for example, Deusenberry *et al.*, 1965 and 1969.

applications of these methods are not common in political analysis.[3] We have found that applied econometrics is not always consonant with econometric theory. We have also found that many of the problems confronting us (such as the coincidence of lagged endogenous variables and serial correlation in the disturbances) are raised in econometric texts as critical issues, but rarely are sufficient guidelines or practical assistance in resolving such issues provided. For this reason, our approach has been highly exploratory. Since there are as yet no clear-cut solutions to many of these problems, much of what we have done is both controversial and experimental.

Our objective is not to argue the question of causality or to dispute the assumptions underlying the social and behavioral sciences.[4] Nor is it our intent to discuss the algorithms on which elementary statistical methods are based. Rather, we wish to make explicit the critical problems that have confronted us in the course of our investigation and the decisions we have made in seeking to resolve them.

Toward this end we shall discuss (1) the general linear model in regression analysis, taking cognizance of basic assumptions and departures thereof (occasioned by the intricacies of time-series analysis), and then focus more extensively on (2) methodological implications of alternative perspectives on causality (3) some key statistics and common problems in causal inference (4) simultaneous estimation and the problem of identifiability (5) serial correlation and time-dependent corrections (6) the use of instrumental variables together with generalized least squares (7) system-change and break-point analysis, and, finally (8) procedures employed for simulation, forecasting, and policy analysis.

I. An Operational Framework: the General Linear Model

The first step in the transition from a general theoretical statement to an operational model is to identify the variables to be explained (the set of *endogenous* variables).[5] The second is to specify those

---

[3]For a survey of the development of econometrics as a field of inquiry see Klein, 1971. For an instructive application of econometric analysis to political inquiry see Kramer, 1971.

[4]These issues have been addressed by others. See for example, Blalock and Blalock, 1968.

[5]A *dependent* variable is a variable to be explained by the *independent* variables in a single equation. (By convention, dependent variables are written on the left of the equation, independent on the right.) In a system of simultaneous equations all of the dependent variables are termed *endogenous* to the system, i.e., they are predicted by it. All remaining variables are *exogenous*, i.e., they are not predicted by the system. (An endogenous variable may of course be used as an independent variable in some equations of the system.) In this book we use the terms "jointly dependent" and "endogenous" interchangeably. In our system of equations, the endogenous variables are colonial area, military-expenditures, intensity-of-intersections, alliances, and violence-behavior.

effects that contribute to these variables by developing a set of equations designed to account for the behavior of each.

The explanatory variables that are thought to affect the endogenous variables can be other endogenous variables (lagged or unlagged) or *exogenous* variables, that is, variables not to be explained by the model. For policy purposes it is important to select at least some explanatory variables that are manipulable by the policy-maker. For obvious reasons it would not be useful to select variables that are all "givens" or that are manipulable only at very high costs, unless of course one's objectives were to test for the extent to which non-manipulables dominate system behavior.

The problem confronting empirical investigations is how to derive an orderly abstraction from reality and achieve mathematical or statistical rigor and objectivity. Only a priori knowledge can determine which independent variables will be selected as promising areas of investigation and which basic form the relationships are believed to assume.[6] The most elaborate statistical techniques are no substitute for good theory.

In order to predict the value of a dependent variable given only the values of a set of independent variables and a functional relationship (or equation) between the dependent and independent variables, it is necessary to derive some estimates for the coefficients (parameters) of the independent variables. Regression analysis is a statistical method of obtaining parameter estimates. This procedure assumes both that the value of a dependent variable Y is related to the value of another variable X:

$$Y = f(X) \tag{1}$$

and that stochastic (or random) factors also are operative. An explicit disturbance term is therefore added, which represents the error between the actual (real) value of Y and that which would be predicted from Equation 1. The general linear model, the simplest form of Equation 1, assumes that Y is a *linear* function of X, although X itself can be a nonlinear combination of other variables. Equation 1 can thus be written:

$$Y = \alpha + \beta X + u. \tag{2}$$

In the absence of a good reason for specifying a particular nonlinear functional relationship, the linear assumption is probably not only the simplest but also the most justifiable to make. Indeed, nonlinear estimation techniques are still in the developmental stage.

The objective is then to find good estimates for α and β. Ideally,

---

[6]See Fisher, 1966.

these estimates are *unbiased, consistent,* and *precise.*[7] Equation 2 can be readily extended to the case where there are n independent variables as follows (in matrix notation):

$$Y = XB + U, \tag{3}$$

where **Y** is a $T \times 1$ vector of observations of the dependent or endogenous variable over time;

  X is a $T \times (1 + k)$ matrix of the values of the k independent variables in the equation, plus the intercept;

  B is the $(1 + k) \times 1$ vector of coefficients (β) that must be estimated; and,

  U is a $T \times 1$ vector of the error or disturbance term, which has three error components: (1) error due to a linear approximation of the "true" functional form; (2) error resulting from misspecification (erroneously left-out or included variables), and (3) random noise.

An estimate of **B** can be obtained by using the method of ordinary least squares (OLS), if certain assumptions can be justified.[8] The OLS estimate of **B** is the following:[9]

$$\hat{\mathbf{B}} = (\mathbf{X'X})^{-1}\mathbf{X'Y}. \tag{4}$$

The model presented in Chapter 10 is more complex than the general linear case and, by extension, requires other modes of solution. Some

---

[7]Much of the statistics of estimators is based on the assumption that repeated samples of observations (from the theoretical "universe" of data) would yield a statistical *distribution* of the values obtained for the estimate $\hat{\beta}$ distributed around the unknown, "true" value of the parameter β. An *unbiased* estimate is one that, if repeated observations were made, would yield a mean of β (although there would be a variance about this mean). A *consistent* estimator is one that approaches β as the number of observations becomes infinite (in this case the variance would approach zero and we would have a perfect point estimate). In other words, a consistent estimator is asymptotically unbiased (but not necessarily unbiased for any finite sample). A *precise* estimate is one with a minimal variance (and hence more efficient). Technically, precision is sought by minimizing the sum of squares variance of the error term.

[8]The assumptions of OLS are:
1. The disturbances, **U**, are random variables, with an expected value of zero: $E(u) = 0$.
2. The disturbances have a constant variance (homoscedasticity): $E(uu') = \sigma^2 I$, or the expected value of all of the u_i^2 is identical to σ^2.
3. There is no significant correlation across time for the disturbances: $E(u_i u_{i \pm j}) = 0$ for $j \neq 0$.
4. The exogenous variables are not correlated with the disturbances.
5. **X** is fixed, i.e. the values of the independent variables are fixed in repeated sampling.
6. **X** has rank $(K + 1) < T$, where T is the number of observations, i.e., there are more observations than there are parameters to be estimated.

Note that the derivations in this section are shown for single equations only. A simultaneous system would be analogous, although with greater constraints on the rank of X, so that the system would be identifiable. See Fisher, 1966; Hibbs, 1973, Appendix 3.

[9]Fuller explanations can be found in any good econometrics text, such as Johnston, 1972. Briefly, the estimate $\hat{\mathbf{B}}$ of the parameter **B** can be obtained as follows. Rewrite

of the complexity is due to (a) the nature of the dynamics being modeled; (b) the procedures we have employed to correct for significant departures from the assumptions underlying the general linear model, and (c) the use of simultaneous-equation estimators to obtain unbiased coefficients of feedback systems. Changes in OLS estimation necessary to correct for these deviations are presented further on.[10]

Equation 3 in terms of $\hat{\mathbf{B}}$ rather than $\mathbf{B}$: $\mathbf{Y} = \mathbf{X}\hat{\mathbf{B}} + \mathbf{E}$ where $\mathbf{E} = \mathbf{Y} - \mathbf{X}\hat{\mathbf{B}}$ (as opposed to $\mathbf{U}$, the "true" residual, which is $(\mathbf{Y} - \mathbf{X}\mathbf{B})$ rather than $(\mathbf{Y} - \mathbf{X}\hat{\mathbf{B}})$). Thus, the sum of squares variance

$$\sum_{i=1}^{n} (e_i^2)$$

becomes in matrix notation

$$\begin{aligned}\mathbf{e}'\mathbf{e} &= (\mathbf{Y} - \mathbf{X}\hat{\mathbf{B}})'(\mathbf{Y} - \mathbf{X}\hat{\mathbf{B}})\\ &= \mathbf{Y}'\mathbf{Y} - (\mathbf{X}\hat{\mathbf{B}})'\mathbf{Y} - \mathbf{Y}'(\mathbf{X}\hat{\mathbf{B}}) + (\mathbf{X}\hat{\mathbf{B}})'(\mathbf{X}\hat{\mathbf{B}}).\end{aligned}$$

Note that in matrix algebra, $(\mathbf{A}')' = \mathbf{A}$ and $(\mathbf{AB})' = \mathbf{B}'\mathbf{A}'$. Thus,

$$\begin{aligned}\mathbf{Y}'(\mathbf{X}\hat{\mathbf{B}}) &= (\mathbf{X}\hat{\mathbf{B}})'\mathbf{Y}'', \text{ since } (\mathbf{AB})' = \mathbf{B}'\mathbf{A}'\\ &= (\mathbf{X}\hat{\mathbf{B}})'\mathbf{Y}, \text{ since } \mathbf{A}'' = \mathbf{A},\end{aligned}$$

and $\mathbf{e}'\mathbf{e}$ reduces to $\mathbf{e}'\mathbf{e} = \mathbf{Y}'\mathbf{Y} - 2\hat{\mathbf{B}}'\mathbf{X}'\mathbf{Y} + \hat{\mathbf{B}}'\mathbf{X}'\mathbf{X}\hat{\mathbf{B}}$. Since we want a value of $\hat{\mathbf{B}}$ that will minimize $\mathbf{e}'\mathbf{e}$, we differentiate:

$$\frac{\delta}{\delta\mathbf{B}}(\mathbf{e}'\mathbf{e}) = -2\mathbf{X}'\mathbf{Y} + 2\mathbf{X}'\mathbf{X}\hat{\mathbf{B}}$$

(see Johnston, 1972, p. 87). The minimum occurs when $\delta/\delta\mathbf{B}$ equals 0, or $\mathbf{X}'\mathbf{Y} = \mathbf{X}'\mathbf{X}\hat{\mathbf{B}}$. Therefore $\hat{\mathbf{B}} = (\mathbf{X}'\mathbf{X})^{-1}\mathbf{X}'\mathbf{Y}$.

Note that $\hat{\mathbf{B}}$ may not be the "true" value of $\mathbf{B}$. The "goodness of fit" depends upon how reasonable our estimation assumptions and our regression equation are. Consequences of certain violations of these assumptions are explored further in this appendix. In particular, let us relate $\hat{\mathbf{B}}$ and $\mathbf{B}$. Since $\mathbf{Y} = \mathbf{X}\mathbf{B} + \mathbf{U}$ in the original, we can substitue this for $\mathbf{Y}$ in the equation for $\hat{\mathbf{B}}$, obtaining,

$$\begin{aligned}\hat{\mathbf{B}} &= (\mathbf{X}'\mathbf{X})^{-1}\mathbf{X}'(\mathbf{X}\mathbf{B} + \mathbf{U})\\ &= (\mathbf{X}'\mathbf{X})^{-1}\mathbf{X}'\mathbf{X}\mathbf{B} + (\mathbf{X}'\mathbf{X})^{-1}\mathbf{X}'\mathbf{U}.\end{aligned}$$

Since $\mathbf{A}\mathbf{A}^{-1} = \mathbf{I}$ by definition, this reduces to $\hat{\mathbf{B}} = \mathbf{B} + (\mathbf{X}'\mathbf{X})^{-1}\mathbf{X}'\mathbf{U}$. Thus, $\hat{\mathbf{B}}$ is a function both of the true value $\mathbf{B}$ and of the disturbance $\mathbf{U}$.

But if we use the fifth regression assumption, that $\mathbf{X}$ is fixed, and take expected values, we find $E(\hat{\mathbf{B}}) = E(\mathbf{B}) + (\mathbf{X}'\mathbf{X})^{-1}\mathbf{X}'E(\mathbf{U})$ (since we can take the constant $(\mathbf{X}'\mathbf{X})^{-1}\mathbf{X}'$ out of the expected value brackets.) But the first regression assumption is that $E(\mathbf{U}) = 0$. If this is indeed the case, $E(\hat{\mathbf{B}}) = E(\mathbf{B})$, and our OLS estimate is unbiased. Johnston also shows that this OLS estimator has a smaller variance than any other linear unbiased estimator (see pp. 109–113). An alternative notation yields the result:

$$\beta = \frac{\mathrm{Cov_{XY}}}{\mathrm{Var_X}} + \frac{\mathrm{Cov_{XU}}}{\mathrm{Var_X}},$$

while $\hat{\beta} = \mathrm{Cov_{XY}}/\mathrm{Var_X}$. Again, $\hat{\mathbf{B}}$ is unbiased only if $\mathbf{X}$ and $\mathbf{U}$ are uncorrelated, i.e., $\mathrm{Cov_{XU}} = 0$. This formulation will be used later in this appendix (Sec. V) for the discussion of jointly dependent variables.

[10] Useful references include Johnston, 1972, especially pp. 1–8 and 121–176, and Christ, 1966, especially pp. 1–15 and 243–298. For related considerations see Fennessey, 1968; Rao and Miller, 1971; and Wonnacott and Wonnacott, 1970.

The analysis reported in Part III was undertaken on TROLL/1, a set of interactive computer programs developed at the Massachusetts Institute of Technology for the analysis of econometric models and complex systems.[11] We have employed (a) a logarithmic transformation on one of the endogenous variables (colonial area) in order to approximate the underlying theoretical relationship more closely, and (b) a term combining the effects of population and technology (defined as population-times-national-income) in order to obtain some measure of their multiplicative impact. In addition, we have used generalized least squares (GLS), transforming the independent variables according to the structure of the serial correlation in the disturbances, in conjunction with two-stage least squares (2SLS, a limited-information maximum-likelihood estimator), so as to incorporate a time-dependent correction as well as simultaneous effects in the final estimates of the parameters.[12]

The parameters of an equation cannot be estimated purely on the basis of empirical data, no matter how complete, reliable, or extensive these may be.[13] The role of data is as follows: information is useful for model specification only if it can serve to select the most applicable structural equations from among many proposed or allowable sets of such equations. But observational data alone *cannot* perform this

---

[11]See *TROLL/1 User's Guide,* National Bureau of Economic Research.

[12]The dynamic elements in a model are usually generated by lagged relationships, by first (or higher-order) derivatives, the use of endogenous variables as independent variables, and the introduction of random-shock variables. These considerations are important in drawing inferences about the structure of the system of equations and about the ability of the system to predict behavior of both the model and the endogenous variables. In the course of our investigation we used each of these procedures for representing dynamic systems. Here we note only the most effective approaches. See, for example, Fisher, 1965.

[13]The necessity of a priori specification of what are (and are not) expected to be important determinants of particular variables is predicated on two considerations. First, these specifications must allow the investigator to develop a particular system of equations, and to identify the dependent and independent variables and the nature of their relationships. This initial specification in itself constitutes an operational statement of theory, however vague, inarticulated, or implicit. Second, a priori information is necessary for the distinction of one equation from another. Information of this nature generally constitutes restrictions on both the coefficients of the variables (where some are set at zero) and the nature of the random or disturbance term. Without the specification of zero coefficients for *some* variables in *each* equation, there is no way to distinguish one equation from another.

Thus, in our model, we assume that violence-behavior is not directly an important determinant of colonial area, and do not include this potential link in our equation. If we had postulated and tested for every possible link, our model could not have been estimated — it would have been under-identified. It is important to realize that links that have been excluded for a priori reasons can *never* be found statistically significant (or insignificant) by the analysis. Only those variables and their relationships that were *stipulated in the model and which failed to be statistically significant* can be considered "not causally related" for empirical reasons — excluded variables may or may not be related. (Thus, only those links diagrammed in Figure 10-1 could be found statistically significant or insignificant in our model, and our findings concern only these postulated links.) See Fisher, 1962, Chapters 1 and 2.

necessary step in model-building, although analysis of one set of data can provide clues for specification of the next set. Only with a priori restrictions and specifications can empirical data be put to good use.[14] But the most basic issue of all in making the transition from a theoretical statement to an operational model is specification of causal ordering.

II. Directional Relations and Causal Inference

In its most general sense "causation" refers to hierarchies of influences or effects. Although a particular sequence of events is a necessary condition for causation, it is not *sufficient* — a consideration that is commonly overlooked in systematic social and political inquiry. Because of this simple but almost self-evident point, it is important to adopt alternative criteria for the specification of causal relations. Herbert Simon argues persuasively (in *Essays on the Structure of Social Science*, 1963) that causal hierarchies are determined by the appearance of nonzero coefficients in a system of equations.

As mentioned above, a priori specification of zero coefficients is also required so that the equations may be identifiable.[15] "For complete identifiability of a structure those restraints must preclude the existence in the same model of a different equivalent structure, that is (in linear models) a different set of equations whose members are linear combinations of the original equations."[16] Causation is therefore closely related to identifiability, while the requirements of identifiability, by necessity, impose certain constraints on the process of model-building and possible causal links.

The question of causation gives rise to a related set of philosophical and empirical problems.[17] The long-standing debate among social scientists regarding the nature of causal relationships in the "real" world — whether the world is essentially hierarchical, or recursive; or essentially nonrecursive, or simultaneous — is one that can be resolved through a combination of these two positions. In the "block-recursive" approach the overall framework or system of relations (or equations) for the phenomena under consideration is considered basically recursive (thus negating simultaneous relations among the component blocks), although some of the phenomena are considered nonrecursive (thus allowing for feedback relations within each block). For applied analysis the approach one takes has one important effect. How one perceives the phenomena one seeks to model (whether they are considered basically recursive or nonrecursive) will dictate the kind of

---

[14]For a theoretical treatment of data see Coombs, 1964.
[15]For conditions of identifiability, see Fisher, 1966.
[16]Ando *et al.*, 1963, p. 23.
[17]Ibid. Also see Orcutt, 1952.

estimation procedure employed and the ways in which the phenomena are represented in a system of equations. We have adopted the non-recursive view of causality while recognizing that in the long run greater understanding of the dynamics in question may be obtained through expansion of our model and use of a block-recursive approach.

III. Causal Inference: Some Key Statistics and Common Problems

Two of the more common criteria for evaluating the performance of a model are (1) how well the specified equations can predict known data, and (2) where and why findings differ from known data. Examining the patterns of errors (or residuals) therefore becomes an important aspect of model-building.[18]

The variance (or standard error) of the coefficient indicates the precision of the coefficient as derived from empirical data. The statistical significance of a parameter is inferred from the magnitude of the t statistic, and the significance of several parameters is inferred from the F ratio. In a regression equation the value of F measures the joint significance of the parameter estimates. The summary statistic, R^2, refers to the amount of variance in the dependent variable accounted for by the independent variables (and the associated stochastic mechanism). A very high R^2 may imply an identity or a trivial regression equation, whereas a low R^2 does not necessarily indicate an invalid equation.[19] Other summary statistics, such as the standard errors around the parameters, are needed before an educated judgment can be drawn. In practical applications, however, these statistics are often subject to bias in the parameters.[20] When the disturbances are serially correlated, the variances and standard errors will be deflated, producing inflated t, F, and R^2 statistics, leading to possible erroneous inferences. Correcting for serial correlation is a crucial aspect of

---

[18]The formulas for the statistics discussed in this section can be found in any standard econometric text. Here we are concerned primarily with problems of inference—see, for example, Johnston, 1972; Christ, 1966; and Rao and Miller, 1971.

[19]The smaller the variance of a parameter estimate, the less sensitive the estimate will be to errors in the independent variables. Furthermore, the smaller the correlation among the independent variables, the higher will be the precision of the regression estimates. However, computational precision does not necessarily guarantee that the most theoretically precise estimation procedure has been used (see Rao and Miller, 1971, p. 24). For a definition of variance see Chapter 10, n. 10.

[20]The "bias" of a parameter estimate is the difference between the mean value of the distribution of the estimate and its "true" parameter value. Bias may result from the omission of relevant variables in the equation. But this will not increase the variance of the estimates of the coefficients. A "precise" (or efficient) estimate is one of minimum variance, regardless of bias. As a summary statistic, the mean square error provides importance to bias and to precision: $\text{MSE}(\beta) = V(\beta) + (\text{bias }(\beta))^2$. When the estimated equation is the "true" equation, ordinary least squares provides the minimum variance unbiased estimate. See also Kendall, 1954.

causal modeling, and highlights the importance of the Durbin-Watson statistic.

The Durbin-Watson statistic, otherwise known as the d statistic, is a test of the statistical significance of the parameters in a regressive process.[21] The statistic is no longer valid when there is a coincidence of lagged endogenous variables and autocorrelated disturbances. In that case the statistic is asymptotically biased upward toward 2.0 and no longer tests for autocorrelation. Thus, a nonsignificant d statistic does not preclude the possibility that OLS estimates are inconsistent when there are lagged endogenous variables in the equation. In the case of simultaneous equations the same problem exists for the endogenous variables. The endogenous (including lagged endogenous) variables must be replaced by instrumental variables (see Sec. VI).

A common difficulty in statistical analysis is high collinearity among the explanatory variables. But we cannot rule out the use of a particular variable or the estimation of a particular equation simply because of multicollinearity. Other problems might arise.[22] High intercorrelations result in the loss of precision, but the exclusion of a theoretically relevant variable on those grounds might exacerbate serial correlation in the disturbances.[23] Further, multicollinearity affects the precision of

---

[21]The Durbin-Watson statistic is computed as follows:

$$d = \frac{\sum_{t=2}^{n} (u_t - u_{t-1})^2}{\sum_{t=1}^{n} u_t^2}$$

where u represents the error values (which are both positive and negative, with an assume mean of zero.) The d statistic tends to be small for positively autocorrelated error terms and large for errors that are negatively autocorrelated. Durbin and Watson have worked out upper and lower bounds of the statistic, with an area of uncertainty in between. As a rule of thumb, a d statistic of 2.0 (± 0.2) indicates the absence of serial correlation in the disturbances. It is also important to note that the statistic is not applicable in cases with lagged endogenous variables — since the test was developed for non-stochastic vectors of independent variables. In addition, as it only tests for first-order autoregressive processes, correlogram analysis of the residuals is a more appropriate technique for the detection of other forms of serial correlation. See Durbin and Watson, 1950, and 1951. Also see Johnston, 1972, pp. 250–254, and Section V below.

[22]See Rao and Miller, 1971, p. 48.

[23]The precision of the parameter estimate depends on the serial-correlation parameter as well as the process generating the independent variables. OLS is still unbiased in the presence of serial correlation, but it does not have minimum variance. If we can identify the structure and value of the autocorrelation parameter, then by an appropriate transformation of the variables we can use OLS to provide minimum variance estimates. This is appropriate only for single equations where simultaneous effects are not thought to operate. When the *dependent* variables in the equation are serially correlated, the bias depends also on the parameters that generated their serial correlation. And when the variance in the error term is not constant OLS does not produce the best linear unbiased estimates. See Schink and Chieu, 1966. We have attempted to attain high precision by seeking sharp and robust parameter estimates, and minimize bias by respecifying each equation to account explicitly for the effects of separate independent variables.

coefficient estimates rather than their values.[24]

By far the most serious problem in data analysis and parameter estimation is measurement error. It is customary to equate measurement error with faulty data or erroneous quantitative measures. While such problems are undoubtedly the source of much distortion in both analysis and results, it is important to broaden the conventional definition in at least two ways. First, specific estimates of the error in quantitative measures may be obtained from the measures themselves and incorporated as confidence intervals around the basic data for purposes of modifying the results according to the degree, magnitude, and direction of cumulated error.[25] Second, the concept of measurement error may be extended to include problems with the structure of the underlying equation itself. Those cases where the magnitude of the disturbance of the error term raises serious questions concerning the validity of the equation and the viability of the resulting specification may be described as examples of measurement error. Ideally, the most desirable situation is one in which (1) errors in the quantitative measures are known to be negligible, and (2) the disturbance term is small and exhibits no discernible trend of either positive or negative serial correlation. In practice, however, neither of these conditions may hold: the extent of fault in the data is often not known, and the disturbance term often exhibits significant serial correlation, especially in trend analysis of time-series data.[26] The methods used to minimize the effects of serial correlation will be discussed below.

IV. Simultaneous Inference and the Problem of Identifiability

When there is mutual dependence among the endogenous variables, simultaneous estimation of the parameters is called for.[27] This set of procedures is more complex than standard regression analysis.[28]

---

[24]In cases where independent variables X_1 and X_2 are correlated, we can still obtain a good estimate of the total contribution of **X** toward understanding **Y**, but it is difficult to untangle how much of that influence is from X_1 and how much from the correlated X_2, i.e., in the extreme case where X_1 and X_2 are connected by an exact linear relationship, the fourth regression assumption is violated and it is not possible to form $(\mathbf{X'X})^{-1}$, since the determinant $\mathbf{X'X} = 0$. Multicollinearity has the effect of increasing the variance, thus decreasing the t statistic for the coefficients in question and yielding a low precision estimate.

[25]Measurement error may thus be viewed as the consequence of the absence of vital information, i.e. of confidence intervals, rather than as the presence of known error in the quantitative measures.

[26]For related considerations see Blalock, 1965.

[27]See Christ, 1960.

[28]The reason that OLS must be abandoned is clear when the definitions of β and $\hat{\beta}$ are recalled (see n. 9). The OLS estimator is equivalent to $\text{Cov}_{XY}/\text{Var}_X$. This quantity is generally nonzero, as it is assumed that the dependent variable should be correlated with significant independent variables (including any endogenous variables that are independent) and with the disturbance. But it is also assumed that the independent variables

Estimation in the classic regression mode involves one dependent variable and several independent ones. In a simultaneous system there are several jointly dependent variables, which creates an identification problem. That is, even if infinite data were available from which the reduced form of the parameters could be exactly derived, the values of the coefficients could not be estimated without some a priori theoretical restriction on the number of exogenous and endogenous variables in each equation.[29]

---

and the disturbances must *not* be correlated, because the actual parameter value, β, is equivalent to

$$\beta = \frac{\text{Cov}_{XY}}{\text{Var}_X} + \frac{\text{Cov}_{XU}}{\text{Var}_X}.$$

Thus, unless $\text{Cov}_{XU} = 0$, our estimator of β would be biased. In simultaneous equation systems, however, if any of the independent variables in the equation are also *endogenous* variables in other equations in the system, the following situation obtains: Suppose

$$Y_1 = \sum a_1 x_1 + b_1 Y_2 + e_1 \tag{1}$$
$$Y_2 = \sum a_2 x_2 + b_2 Y_1 + e_2 \tag{2}$$

substituting the value of Y_2 in Equation 2 into Equation 1

$$Y_1 = \sum a_1 x_1 + b_1 \left(\sum a_2 x_2 + b_2 Y_1 + e_2 \right) + e_1 \tag{3}$$

We thus see that Y_1 is very likely to be correlated with $b_1 e_2$ (i.e., one of the dependent variables in Equation 3.) But that means that one of the "independent variables" (Y_1) is probably correlated with the disturbance term (e_2) in Equation 2. This violates the assumption $\text{Cov}_{XU} = 0$. Unfortunately, the estimation procedure continues to assume that Cov_{XU} is zero. It therefore assigns some of the explained variance that should belong to the residual term to the correlated X. This results in overstated statistical significance for X, and understated values and significances for the residual, thus leading to erroneous inferences. Since the residual is seriously underestimated, the Durbin-Watson statistic may indicate the absence of serial correlation (as will any correlogram of the residuals) that exists but is masked by the correlation. Thus, in addition to introducing inaccuracy in its own coefficient estimate (overestimation), the endogenous term can prevent us from finding serial correlation in the equation, and thus from purging its distortions (the consequences of serial correlation are treated in Section V of this appendix). Lagged endogenous variables present analogous problems. It is often difficult to postulate that the value of a variable at time t is not somehow related to the value of the same variable at time $t - 1$, i.e., that X_t and X_{t-1} will not be correlated. In particular, the military expenditures of a nation are probably quite highly correlated with previous expenditures. But this means that, for the military-expenditures equation in Chapter 13, Y_{t-1} (one of the X terms) and Y are generally highly correlated. It is thus very likely that $\text{Cov}_{Y_{t-1}U} \neq 0$, and, therefore, that our estimates are biased, with consequences similar to those described above for endogenous variables. A solution for this, and related problems, is suggested in Section VI of this appendix.

[29] The two necessary conditions for identifiability are the order and rank conditions. For the order condition to hold, there must be at least $M - 1$ independent restrictions in an equation where M is the number of endogenous variables—this is clearly an exclusion restriction. The rank condition stipulates that at least one nonvanishing determinant of the order $M - 1$ can be formed from the OLS structure of an equation, corresponding to the variables excluded by a priori specification from that equation. See Fisher, 1966, pp. 39–42 and 60–62, and Fisher, 1959. For an excellent exposition of the identification problem in simultaneous equations, see Hibbs, 1973, Appendix III.

Additional a priori restrictions are useful for identifying an equation only if the same restrictions are not employed to identify other equations as well. However, such additional restrictions generally occur in the form of linear inequalities for the coefficients to be estimated. Linear inequalities add to the efficiency of the estimates but do not assist in the identification of a particular equation. Furthermore, if a model is not identifiable, manipulating the equations or the order of constituent variables will not assure identification—either a model is identifiable or it is not.

The problem of identifiability is thus closely related to the requirements of theory and methods in any model-building effort. An equation is identifiable when a priori constraints and observations allow for a distinction between the parameters of that and other equations. By extension, a model is identifiable if each equation represents a distinct set of relationships. The problem is one of having sufficient a priori restrictions to distinguish among equations—a certain minimum is necessary. Beyond the minimum, any added information may be put to use. In *just-identified* equations there is exactly one way to obtain the "true" equation from the reduced form. In *overidentified* equations there is more than one way. In *underidentified* equations, where a priori restrictions are insufficient to allow us to discriminate among possible forms, there is no way in which the "true" equation may be recovered or distinguished from others with the same functional form. The model we have developed through experimentation and alternative specification is an overidentified set of equations—there is more than one way of retrieving the reduced form of each original equation. In practice, the problem is generally one of choosing among the various alternative formulations in an overidentified equation or model.

Standard statistical theorems developed for the case in which the explanatory variables are treated as if they were fixed in repeated sampling cannot be used when there are lagged endogenous variables, as explained in Note 28. Furthermore, the coincidence of lagged endogenous variables *and* autocorrelated disturbances inflate the *t* statistic and may lead to erroneous inferences. Marked departures from the assumptions underlying the general linear model produce biased parameter estimates, often necessitating equally marked departures from standard regression procedures. The practical implications of serial correlation in simultaneous systems for parameter estimation are sometimes overwhelming.

V. Serial Correlation and Time-Dependent Correction

Serial correlation in the disturbances is a major problem in time-series analysis, and lies at the core of many of our estimation problems.

It will be remembered that one of the assumptions for the OLS estimation was that

$$E(\mathbf{UU'}) = \sigma^2 \mathbf{I},$$

which also implied that successive disturbances are *independent* of previous values (i.e., $E(u_t u_{t \pm j}) = 0$ when $j \neq 0$). Of course, finite samples might show nonzero correlations between successive residuals, but this should be only "noise" and have an expected value of zero. It is more difficult, however, to believe that the value of a variable at time t is not somehow related to the value of the same variable at time $t-1$ than to assume the value of a variable in Country A is unrelated to that observed in Country B. Therefore, the assumption of serially independent disturbance terms in time-series data may be implausible. If a key variable that happens to move in phase with the dependent variable is omitted, serial correlation is virtually assured.

Furthermore, if it is difficult to distinguish between a current endogenous variable and the same variable with a short time lag (e.g., the population of Britain in 1870 and 1872), it may also be difficult to distinguish between the disturbance (that is, the error term) and the same disturbance with a small time lag.[30] Again, the assumption of independent disturbance terms is violated.[31]

Because the nature of the serial correlation in the disturbances is often unclear — if it were known then the solution to the problem would be simply to adjust the parameter estimates accordingly — we are confronted with the necessity of estimating the nature of the autocorrela-

---

[30]Fisher, 1970a.

[31]In this section we assume the absence of simultaneities and/or lagged endogenous terms. These complexities are discussed in Section VI. Recall that our estimate of **B** was derived as follows: $\hat{\mathbf{B}} = (\mathbf{X'X})^{-1}\mathbf{X'Y}$. Fortunately, this estimate is not biased by *correlation* among the disturbances. If we can still assume $E(\mathbf{U}) = 0$, we can substitute $\mathbf{XB+U}$ for **Y** in the estimating equation, take expected values, and find that $E(\hat{\mathbf{B}}) = E(\mathbf{B}) + (\mathbf{X'X})^{-1}\mathbf{X'}E(\mathbf{U})$, which reduces to $E(\hat{\mathbf{B}}) = E(\mathbf{B})$. However, in the case of autocorrelated disturbances the estimate of the variance is likely to be understated, for the variance of **E**, the *estimated* disturbance, is calculated as equivalent to $n\sigma_u{}^2$ the variance of the *actual* disturbance term **U**. However, $E(\mathbf{E'E}) = E(\mathbf{U'U}) - E[\mathbf{U'X(X'X)}^{-1}\mathbf{X'U}]$. In the case of serially correlated disturbances, the second term does *not* have an expected value of zero. Therefore, when we merely use $n\sigma_u{}^2$ as our estimate for the variance of **E**, we are seriously underestimating the variance of the residuals by the value of the second term. It can be shown (although it will not be derived here) that the second term is a function of the relationship among the residuals, and therefore that the degree of underestimation increases as serial correlation increases (see Johnston, 1972, for detailed calculations). Moreover, the formulae for the t and F statistics depend on the variance; if variance is underestimated, t and F are no longer accurate. Not only will our actual variance be too high, but the t statistics will be artificially inflated. We might therefore tend to accept coefficients that are in fact statistically insignificant. The Durbin-Watson statistic can be quite useful in this case, offering strong hints as to the presence of serial correlation and thus enabling the appropriate corrections to be made. However, this statistic measures only one particular form of serial correlation and, is not accurate if either endogenous or lagged endogenous terms are present.

tion parameter empirically and identifying the underlying stochastic process. This involves (a) isolating the systematic component of the disturbances, and (b) adjusting the independent variables in order to develop consistent estimates of the parameters.

Basically, all autocorrelation processes assume that the disturbance U can be broken up into two parts: a "genuine" random disturbance part, which meets the OLS assumptions, and a systematic or correlated part, which does not. Of course, in the real world the disturbance may not fit the most commonly used models for disturbance structures — first- and second-order autoregressive or first- and second-order moving average. Nevertheless, it is usually close enough to one of these four models that a correction based on it will have much validity (although in some cases the pattern of disturbances is so ambiguous as to create serious problems in choosing the proper model).

Aitken has demonstrated that the GLS estimator will produce an unbiased estimate of the error variance (σ^2) when disturbances are autocorrelated, and thus, in theory, provide the optimum solution to the problems created by autocorrelated disturbances.[32] Thus, if the theoretical structure of the time-dependent parameter can be identified, the equation can be estimated.

The four disturbance structures mentioned above have properties that are tractable and well-known: (1) in first-order autoregressive structures each error term (u_t) depends only on its previous value (u_{t-1}) plus a random component (ϵ_t); (2) in second-order autoregressive structures u_t depends on u_{t-1} and u_{t-2}, plus a random component (ϵ_t); (3) in first-order moving averages the disturbances depend only on a series of temporally adjacent, independently distributed random variables, so that all the disturbances prior to u_{t-1} do not contribute to generating u_t; and (4) in second-order moving averages, for the same reason, the autocorrelation of u_t is effectively zero with all terms beyond u_{t-2}.[33] In the "real" world higher-order structures are probably operative; however, their statistical tractability is a major com-

---

[32]Aitken, 1935. Basically, this procedure involves premultiplying by a symbolic transformation matrix **A**, which corrects for the nature of the disturbance and yields proper residuals meeting the OLS assumptions. See Hibbs, 1974, for a derivation of the residuals in the generalized model, and Goldberger, 1964, Chapter 5, for a derivation of the disturbance variance. See also Fisher, 1970a, and Rao and Miller, 1971, especially pp. 70–74. For a comprehensive treatment of issues in time-series analysis see Hannan, 1960, and Anderson, 1942.

[33]These four structures can be written mathematically as follows:

$$(1) \quad u_t = \rho_1 u_{t-1} + \epsilon_t$$
$$(2) \quad u_t = \rho_1 u_{t-1} + \rho_2 u_{t-2} + \epsilon_t$$
$$(3) \quad u_t = \epsilon_t - \rho_1 \epsilon_{t-1}$$
$$(4) \quad u_t = \epsilon_t - \rho_1 \epsilon_{t-1} - \rho_2 \epsilon_{t-2}$$

where u_t represents the disturbance and ϵ_t represents the random component.

putational problem, and it is not always true that the benefits accrued by complex computation are greater than the costs incurred.[34]

Obtaining unbiased GLS estimates of the parameter values and their statistical variance and other attributes involves a careful analysis of the residuals to determine which, if any, of these four disturbance structures approximates that of the residuals. There are at least two ways in which this can be done. The first, correlogram analysis, involves retrieving the residuals from regression analysis and then correlating the initial value of the residual with its subsequent values, up to but not exceeding the $t/5$ term. (Clearly, t must be fairly large — at least more than 15.) These empirical values are then compared to the "theoretical" values that would be expected from a particular disturbance structure. The second way, applicable only to autoregressive processes, involves regressing the residuals (u_t) on their previous values $(u_{t-1}$ for AUTO1, u_{t-1} and u_{t-2} for AUTO2) and observing the statistical significance of the two equations and the values of the Durbin-Watson statistic.[35]

These two procedures are not as clear-cut as they might appear. In applied analysis, for example, it is often difficult to distinguish moving-average processes from autoregressive processes that dampen off sharply.[36] There are also difficulties in determining whether the discrepancy between the theoretical autocorrelation parameter and its empirical counterpart is significant, or can be attributable to chance. Conventional statistics of goodness-of-fit are generally used to distinguish significance from noise. To avoid erroneous inferences, we

---

[34]Econometricians have focused primarily upon first-order autoregressive structures (due to the ease of computation). As a result, the assumption that the world is of a first-order autoregressive nature pervades much of the econometric literature. In our investigations, however, we have rarely encountered an AUTO1 structure. An AUTO2 often appears to be a suitable trade-off between complexity and accuracy. For empirical analyses, see Rao and Griliches, 1969, and Orcutt and Winokur, 1969.

[35]The nature of the autocorrelation process can be determined from the correlogram as follows: If only the first term (the correlation of the residual with its own previous value) is significant, the process is probably a first-order moving average (MAV1). If only the first and/or the second terms are significant, the process is probably a second-order moving average (MAV2). If the nth term is equal to the first-term^n, the process is probably a first order autocorrelation process (AUTO1).

As a practical measure, other significant correlations may tentatively be viewed as a reflection of a second-order autocorrelation process (AUTO2), in the absence of evidence indicating otherwise. An AUTO2 process should also be tested to indicate how well the theoretical process fits empirical data by running a regression of the following equation

$$\text{residual}_t = \rho_1 \text{residual}_{t-1} + \rho_2 \text{residual}_{t-2}.$$

If both coefficients (or at least ρ_2) and the F ratio are significant, and if the Durbin-Watson statistic is close to 2.00, an AUTO2 process may be considered justified. For purposes of correlogram analysis, however, correlations less than $|0.2|$ can be considered insignificant.

[36]See Hibbs, 1974, p. 51, and Hannan, 1960.

identified the structure of serial correlation and made appropriate adjustments when necessary (reported in tables in Chapters 11 through 15).

VI. Instrumental Variables and Generalized Least Squares

As noted earlier, OLS yields inconsistent parameter estimates in models with lagged endogenous variables and serial correlation in the error term. The OLS residuals are no longer the "true" underlying disturbances.[37] This results in an upward bias for the coefficient of Y_{t-1} variable and a downward bias for the other variables (frequently leading to erroneous inferences). In addition, underestimation of the residuals may lead to masking of serial correlation. This is a particularly serious problem in our investigation since determining the effects of one year's military allocations on the next is an important problem in our research. We face the real problem, on the one hand, of being unable to detect serial correlation of the disturbances, and on the other, of seriously overestimating the effects of lagged variables. For this reason, we have had to find ways of compensating for expected distortions.

One important assumption of OLS is that errors are uncorrelated both with the independent variables and with each other. When this assumption is violated, *instrumental variables* may be created to replace the independent variables. However, it is easier to envision than to find such variables.[38] They are designed to be uncorrelated with the error but highly correlated with the independent variables to be replaced. We made up a list of 17 variables (see Table 10-1) that appeared to be related to the variables to be replaced. We then employed these variables to create instrumental variables, or *instruments*, to

---

[37]See Rao and Miller, 1971, Chapter 7. The *true* error does not depend on the value of the independent variables, but the residuals do. Residuals, therefore, reflect the properties of the independent variables as well as the errors and the effects of omitted variables. If errors are homoscedastic and random, the residual corresponding to a particular value of the independent variables (X_n) has a statistical distribution with zero mean and small variance. See Christ, 1966, pp. 394–395; Goldberger, 1964; and Johnston, 1972, pp. 208–242.

[38]Although the choice of variables for an instrument list is intuitive, the list can be refined in two ways. First, by the use of principal components: this method reduces multicollinearity, since the components are mutually orthogonal and principal components summarize the information in the list of instruments. Second, through structurally ordered instrumental variables: the variables related to the term to be replaced are first listed in order of preference, then regressions on each variable are performed successively, in different combinations, to determine whether the variable has an effect or whether its contribution is simply using up a degree of freedom. The constructed elements of Y_t together with the elements of Z_t can then be employed as instrumental variables in constructing Y. See Rao and Miller, 1971; and Eisner and Pindyck, 1972.

replace the endogenous variables and the lagged endogenous variable wherever they appeared as independent variables.[39]

An instrument consists of the weighted sum of certain variables selected from the instrument list. It is in effect the result of regressing the variables on the list against the independent variable to be replaced. The intention of this procedure is to discover a set of instruments Z_j such that the correlation of the Zs and the Xs to be replaced will be quite high, and the correlation of the Zs and the residual will be near zero.[40]

Good instruments must have the following properties: (a) they must be truly exogenous and thus, in theory, uncorrelated with the disturbances, as a lagged endogenous variable usually is not; (b) there must be no simultaneous feedback loops connecting the equations to be estimated with any other equations that would explain the potential instrument; (c) the disturbances in the equation to be estimated must not in fact be correlated with the explanatory variable.[41]

One question remains to be dealt with: should the time-dependent correction be made before or after the IV substitution? In the analysis reported in Part III we followed the algorithms implemented in TROLL/1 by undertaking GLS first, then the IV substitution.[42] Never-

---

[39]In cases where collinearity is high among the variables *in the instrument list*, principal-component transformation produces a new list of variables that are orthogonal linear combinations of the original variables. The new variables are so ordered that each variable explains as much as possible of the remaining variance of the original variables. In this way it is possible to use a smaller number of variables while still accounting for a major fraction of the variance explained by the original equation. We used principal-component transformation only when, because of excess collinearity among the variables in the instrument list, it was not possible to create instruments in any other way.

[40]The *original* data, and not the constructed terms, will be used to calculate the residuals. Instruments can be thought of as two-stage least squares (2SLS) estimators in which not all the predetermined variables need be used. Rules for a good instrument include (a) those which must be observed to yield a consistent estimator, and (b) those designed to improve efficiency while maintaining consistency. To estimate an equation $Y_t = Y_{t-1} + \Sigma X_t + u_t$, 2SLS replaces Y_{t-1} with a Z_t having the properties of a consistent estimator. These are: (a) Z_t is a linear combination of the predetermined variables; this is necessary so that Z_t will, in the probability limit, be uncorrelated with the disturbances, $u_{1...n}$; (b) X_t and Z_t are linearly independent; this occurs if enough predetermined variables are used in the first stage to assure that the matrix inverted at the second stage will be nonsingular; (c) Z_t includes, as part of its instrument list, all of the predetermined variables in the system; and (d) the same instrument *list* is used in both the first and second stages of the regression, otherwise, there is no assurance that all the elements of Z_t will be independent of the error term. Lagged endogenous variables must *not* be treated as exogenous, particularly since the number of predetermined variables (i.e., those truly exogenous to the system) cannot exceed the sample size (this is an absolute limit). For purposes of quantitative analysis, the number of degrees of freedom lost is a critical consideration, as is meeting the order and rank conditions of identifiability, the latter being restrictions upon the specifications of the equation. The 2SLS equation can thus be written $Y_t = Z_t + \Sigma X_t + u_t$, where Z_t replaces the lagged endogenous variable Y_{t-1} and ΣX_t still represents the remaining exogenous variables. All endogenous variables appearing as independent variables are treated in the same way as the lagged term Y_{t-1}.

[41]See Eisner and Pindyck, 1972, for an explanation of the algorithms implemented.

[42]There is a difference of views on the order, and hence, on the residuals to be employed when undertaking an IV substitution. When combining time-dependent correc-

theless, we tested empirically to see how different the results of several alternate procedures would be (the results of this experiment, using the data for Britain, are reported in Appendix C). As several rounds of GLS rarely produce theoretically meaningful results, if an initial use of GLS does not appear to adequately correct for serial correlation, re-specification is definitely called for.[43]

In sum, one possible correction for the coincidence of lagged endogenous variables and serial correlation is IV substitution and the use of GLS. If we treat lagged endogenous variables as endogenous, then a consistent estimate of the equation can be obtained using an IV estimator with current and lagged endogenous variables as instruments, provided the system has a sufficient number of exogenous variables. This estimator is robust against all forms of autocorrelation in the disturbances but not against serial correlation in the explanatory variables. In the latter case it becomes necessary to estimate the structure of the disturbance and then confront the problem of determining the sequence of GLS and IV substitution.

VII. System-Change and Breakpoint Analysis

Breakpoints and problems relating to the estimation of system-change and prediction beyond the break are central issues in model-building and forecasting. Sharp changes in dynamics may signify discontinuities

---

tions (GLS) and instrumental variables, it is not intuitively obvious which residuals should be used, or at what stage, in calculating the relevant statistics for evaluating the parameters at the final stage. Some argue that when GLS and IV are combined, the transformed residuals should be calculated without the substitution. Others argue that substitution should take place before the time-dependent corrections. In the latter case the proper asymptotic variance-covariance matrix must contain the IV substitution; in the former it does not. For the case of single equations see Hibbs, 1974; Wallis, 1967; and Eisner and Pindyck, 1972. For other ways of dealing with this problem, see Fair, 1970.

[43]Technically, 2SLS "purges" the correlation between the independent variables and the error term so that a least-squares estimate can be performed from the reduced-form equation. (See Hibbs, 1974, p. 82, and Rao and Miller, 1971). The procedure is (a) to regress Y_{t-1} on the instrumental variables, and (b) replace Y_{t-1} by the created counterpart (Z_t). If the choice of variables for the instrument list was good, all independent variables will be uncorrelated with the disturbance term. This method yields consistent estimates of the parameters for both the endogenous and lagged endogenous independent variables and the other exogenous variables. The residuals obtained are the "true" residuals and can be used for the next step (c) correlogram analysis (these disturbances are consistent since they are deduced from consistent parameter estimates). The next steps are (d) to analyze the residuals for time-dependent structure, then (e) to generate the GLS estimates. (This is only one method for generating parameter estimates in the presence of significant serial correlation.) Two-stage least squares is thus an IV substitution technique, since it generates Z_t that are independent of the errors. When employed in conjunction with GLS, 2SLS allows one to correct for serial correlation and take into account the simultaneities and interdependencies in the dynamics modeled (although with the problems mentioned above). Appendix C illustrates many of the issues and problems raised here by presenting nine alternative methods of parameter estimation and observing the effect of these methods on the results obtained, and hence on the inferences that might be drawn.

in the nature of the real-world processes being modeled, but they may also arise from quite natural regularities of some other real-world processes. Breakpoints often indicate incompleteness of theoretical specification.

We can think of breakpoints either as sharp changes in slope or as nonlinearities. Some discontinuities can be directly included in the model as dummy variables (as we have done in defining changes in the identity of rival powers).[44] The incorporation of a break directly into the analysis increases the fit between historical and predicted data and between historical and simulated dynamics.

In some instances breaks result from quantitative changes, in others from qualitative changes. There are as yet no known methods for identifying precisely the particular points at which a significant shift has occurred (other than costly and complicated iterative procedures). For this reason, the best alternative is to plot the data, then, on the basis of empirical observation, hypothesize the occurrence of a break and test for its statistical significance. The Chow test is still the most appropriate significance test for breakpoints. Quasi-experimental techniques for coping with such problems provide additional perspectives on these issues, but they are cumbersome and complicated.[45]

We have inquired into the statistical significance of differences between two sets of regressions, one for the full period of the study, the other for a particular subperiod. Cases in which there is a significant difference provide important clues into system-change. Phase shifts are often indicators of breakpoints. Breaks that are more in the nature of nonlinearities may not always be recognized as such. The result is simply a "bad" fit that cannot be attributed to an underlying break, but rather to nonlinearities that are not specified in the functional form of the equation. A search for breakpoints also assists in identifying poor specification or areas of misspecification.

---

[44]For other illustrations see Theil, 1970.

[45]The Chow test, recently modified by Fisher, compares one set of coefficients with a subset, as follows: The least-squares regression for an equation with k variables is applied to the first set of observations (subperiod of m observations) and the residual sum of squares $(u'u)$ computed. A least-squares regression is fitted again to the entire sample (n observations) and the new residual sum of squares $(u_i'u_i)$ computed. The test of the null hypothesis that the m observations obey the same relations as the n observations is provided by an F statistic with $(m, n-k)$ degrees of freedom:

$$F = \frac{(u'u - u_i'u_i)/m}{(u_i'u_i)/(n-k)}.$$

See Chow, 1960, and Campbell and Stanley, 1966. In our analysis we compare the residuals generated by the regression of the n observations with those of the m observations (given k number of variables). In instances where the deviations are great the F test picks these and registers as statistically significant, thereby rejecting the null hypothesis. See Fisher, 1970b, and Johnston, 1972, pp. 206–207.

In sum, the analysis of residuals and identification of breakpoints, like sensitivity analysis, are critical aspects of the research.[46]

VIII. Forecasting, Simulation, and Policy Analysis

The next stage of our analysis was to develop viable simulations of the system as a whole in order to observe the behavior of the system under various conditions.[47] This was done in two stages: the five equations were forecasted one-by-one (by employing historical values at each iteration in place of calculated endogenous variables), and then the entire system was simulated simultaneously (by employing calculated values for all endogenous variables). A successful forecast (of a single equation) increases the probability of a successful simulation; a successful simulation almost certainly implies a successful forecast.[48] The forecast of an equation is conducted independently of the other equations, and depends primarily on the existence of historical or known values for both endogenous and exogenous variables for each year to be forecasted. A simulation involves all equations, and solves for the jointly dependent variables without recourse to their historical or known values. A simulation is thus self-contained, allowing for a fairly controlled method of varying parameters and observing the implications for the system as a whole.[49]

The TROLL/1 system, which we used for simulation, calculates values of the jointly dependent variables in the model over a period for which data for the exogenous variables are available, or for any sub-period therein. Simulation requires four types of information: the structure of the model itself, initial historical or known values for the

---

[46]For purposes of experimentation, and to increase our understanding of our model, we chose to identify and test for breakpoints (using the Chow test) both when the co-efficients were estimated with and without the use of instrumental variables. Generally, we found no significant differences. The tables in Part III report the results of Chow tests on coefficients estimated with the same list of instrumental variables.

[47]Dynamics-modeling, which is current in econometric analysis, can be used in political studies as (a) an aid to understanding political dynamics; (b) a tool for simulating and forecasting political behavior and outcomes; and (c) a guide to the choice of public policy. The primary *use* of any systems model is to allow us to make forecasts and compare the forecasts with actual events or values as a means of understanding how real phenomena are related.

[48]Generally, econometricians talk of "forecasting" when the independent variables in each equation are replaced by historical or known values at each point, and "simulation" when the coefficients, the independent variables, and the error terms together with the dependent variables are employed to generate an artificial replication of the entire system of equations. In looser parlance we often talk of forecasting as a simulation beyond the data used to estimate the coefficients. Clearly, that is not the usage intended by us. Note that although the forecasts take each equation independently, they nonetheless employ the coefficient estimates derived from the entire system of equations.

[49]See Naylor *et al.*, 1968, for an informative study.

endogenous variables, data for the exogenous variables, and constant files (coefficients and parameters that have been estimated earlier). To simulate the model in our study, initial values are required also for the exogenous variables, all inclusive of lags and leads.[50] Values for the constants must be supplied; however, if their numerical values are specified in the model, they are taken as such and incorporated with the other pertinent information.[51]

The solution for a variable for any given period is a function of a series of iterations in which all the equations in the block are solved and iteration values of the endogenous variables produced. Convergence criteria are established by default (or changed by the investigator), and identify the point at which the iteration has reached a solution. Sometimes it is necessary to relax the convergence criteria in order to obtain a solution. A common procedure for checking the performance of the simulation, once convergence is attained, is to examine the summary statistics, particularly percent error, and compare the simulated values of the endogenous variables with historical or known values.[52]

---

[50]For the following model,

$$Y_t = a_1 + b_{11}A_t + b_{12}Z_{t-1} + u_1$$
$$Z_t = a_2 + b_{21}X_t + b_{22}B_t + u_2$$

where Y and Z are endogenous variables, A, B, and X are exogenous variables, and a_1, a_2, b_{11}, b_{12}, and b_{22} are the coefficients (estimated from the previous regressions on the simultaneous system), simulation would proceed as follows. For the first time point (year) Y_t and Z_t are calculated using exogenous values for A_t, B_t, and X_t and an exogenous starting value for the endogenous variable Z_{t-1}. For the second year ($t+1$), Y_{t+1}, and Z_{t+1} are computed using exogenous values for A_{t+1}, B_{t+1}, and X_{t+1} and the simulated endogenous value for Z_t from the previous period. Historical values for the endogenous variables are then no longer employed. This procedure is repeated for each succeeding year, calculating the endogenous variables from their simulated values for the previous period and the current values of the exogenous variables. At each time point subsequent to the initial t, known values for the exogenous variables must be provided.

[51]Three tasks are automatically performed by TROLL/1 prior to the simulation exercise: (1) establishing normalization rules (by linearizing each equation so that only one endogenous variable appears on the left side); (2) structuring the system into blocks (so that each block is organized in terms of an individual simultaneous system); and (3) minimizing the number of simultaneous systems to be solved at the same time. The necessary code is then generated, producing a machine-language representation of the normalized, block-structured model. The use of a machine-language and block-structured model makes the simulation task very efficient. In our analysis, the equations were initially linearized and the system consisted of one nonrecursive block. (These observations are based on Chapter 8 of the *TROLL/1 User's Guide*.)

[52]If the object is short-term forecasts, multicollinearity need not be a necessary drawback. If some of the independent variables are multicollinear, the prediction interval obtained will be large. By eliminating some collinear variables, one can reduce the prediction interval for any given value of the independent variables included while altering the actual outcome only minimally. Pragmatic forecasts and simulation are indifferent to the extent of collinearity, whereas sophisticated ones are not. But both will make similar forecasts and the errors will be very similar. See Kuh and Meyer, 1957.

There are several sources of error in a simulation. First, the disturbance in period *t* may not be accurately forecasted. Second, there may be errors when estimating the parameters from observed samples (errors arising during the sampling period or measurement error). Third, there may be errors in forecasting the endogenous and lagged endogenous variables for the period *t*.[53]

The basic procedure for undertaking policy analysis by simulation is to resimulate the model with different inputs (or sets of information) from those used in the base simulation. Changes in parameters and/or values, estimated coefficients, endogenous variables, or exogenous files may be made. To compare the results, we note any discrepancies between the outputs (the predicted values for the endogenous variables) of the initial and the modified simulations. For purposes of policy analysis it is necessary to modify the coefficients of crucial variables and then observe the effects on the output. This is done by changing coefficients one-by-one and obtaining the output after *each* modification. Only in this way is it possible to identify the effects of artificially introduced policy changes on the simulated system.[54]

In Chapter 17 we reported on our experiment with alternative coefficients and noted the implications for the system as a whole. With such experiments it is possible to begin identifying the consequences of manipulating certain relationships, and ask the question, "What would have happened if . . . ?" In the last analysis, systematic and empirical answers to questions of this kind are the real goal of our research.

---

[53]The root mean square (RMS) of the error is the most important summary statistic in indicating how well the simulated model tracks empirical observations:

$$\text{RMS error} = \sqrt{\frac{\sum_{i=1}^{n} (A_i - P_i)^2}{n}}$$

where n = number of periods simulated, A_i = historical (known empirical) values for an endogenous variable, P_i = simulated values for the endogenous variable. Other important summary statistics include the mean of the forecast and the mean of the simulation and the percentage error for each. See *Troll/1 User's Guide* (June 1972), Section 8:8.

[54]This procedure assumes that changes in one coefficient will not lead to counterbalancing changes in others.

Appendix C
Alternative Estimation Procedures

Raisa B. Deber

The theoretical reasons why ordinary least squares (OLS) is not appropriate for the analysis reported in Part III have already been noted in Appendix B. Since the literature is often vague about the specific consequences of deviations from OLS assumptions, in this appendix we shall report on the implications of alternative assumptions. As an experiment, we used nine different methods to estimate the military-expenditures equation for the data on Britain.[1] The results of our experiment are presented in Table C-1.

As demonstrated in Appendix B (notes 28, 31), the presence of endogenous and lagged endogenous variables in an equation can lead to a masking of autocorrelation, and thereby to false inferences. Although this masking problem was not acute in the case of Britain,[2] another adverse effect of correlated endogenous terms was evident: both the size and statistical significance of the coefficient for the lagged endogenous term were overstated.[3] Although the lagged variable was still statistically significant, it was not quite as significant as would have been assumed with OLS.[4]

Econometricians rarely confront directly the problems of estimation raised by the coincidence of serial correlation and endogenous and/or

---

[1] See Appendix B for the OLS assumptions (n. 8) and a discussion of the consequences of, and possible corrections for, several deviations from these.

[2] The Durbin-Watson statistic (d) was 1.17 under OLS, which would clearly indicate the presence of serial correlation. Although some masking of the serial correlation existed, it was of only minor proportions—purging the effect of the correlated endogenous terms by means of an instrument-variable (IV) substitution dropped the d statistic only slightly, to 1.13. However, this masking effect was more pronounced with several of the other nations—the serial correlation being evident only *after* the IV correction was made.

[3] See Table C-1 for the values of the coefficient estimate and corresponding t statistics of military-expenditures$_{t-1}$ under Method 1 (OLS only, with no corrections) and Method 4 (which measures only the impact of an IV substitution).

[4] Since the endogenous variables were not statistically significant in the military-expenditures equation for Britain, the effect of replacing them with instrumental

lagged endogenous variables. Usually, they either ignore the problem or assume that all processes are first-order autoregressive (AUTO1), and develop corrections accordingly. Many econometric textbook writers avoid the problem entirely by simply noting that the combination of these two conditions creates great difficulties.[5] Even if one chooses to use generalized least squares (GLS) to correct for serial correlation, plus an instrumental-variable substitution (2SLS) to replace the correlated independent terms, the question of which procedure to apply first is one that to date has no definitive answer.[6]

Some scholars argue that it is preferable to perform the 2SLS substitution first, in order to create the proper residuals, and then apply GLS. TROLL/1 reverses this ordering, and applies the GLS matrix to the entire equation, including the residuals, before performing any substitutions. The designers of TROLL/1 claim that their procedure avoids the problem of introducing heteroscedasity (or unequal variances), and thus generates consistent and efficient estimators.[7]

To examine the practical implications of the foregoing considerations, we estimated the military-expenditures equation, with data on Britain, using nine methods:

1   Simple OLS regression with no corrections of any kind.

2   Correcting for serial correlation only, using GLS. A second-order autoregressive (AUTO2) process was employed, established by examining the residuals from the OLS solution and the correlations among them. TROLL/1 was allowed to set the values for the GLS parameters ρ_1 and ρ_2 by an iterative search.

3   Correcting for serial correlation only, using GLS with an AUTO2 correction. Unlike Method 2, the values for ρ_1 and ρ_2 were set from the results of the following regression equation:

$$\text{residual}_t = \rho_1 \, \text{residual}_{t-1} + \rho_2 \, \text{residual}_{t-2}$$

rather than allowing TROLL/1 to search for them iteratively.

4   Correcting for the endogenous and lagged endogenous variables only, using 2SLS. TROLL/1 performed this automatically, re-

---

variables was only minor. In other equations such a replacement had a far more dramatic effect. In fact, one of the notable characteristics of the military-expenditure equation is how little difference the varying regression assumptions made to the values of the coefficient estimates. Given the current uncertainty in this area of estimation, such robustness is most reassuring.

[5]See, for example, Johnston, 1972; Rao and Miller, 1971; Wonnacott and Wonnacott, 1970.

[6]Some authors suggest still other techniques, such as three-stage least squares or maximum-likelihood estimation. Our use of 2SLS and GLS is largely conditioned by the law of the instrument, as that is the way TROLL/1 was equipped to handle the problem. See Ray C. Fair (1970) for an alternative method.

[7]See Wallis (1967) for the first of these methods, and Eisner and Pindyck (1972) for an explanation of the TROLL/1 rationale.

Table C-1. The results of an experiment with alternative estimation methods.[a]

Statistic	(1) OLS	(2) GLS (AUTO 2) TROLL-searched ρ	(3) GLS (AUTO 2) Forced ρ	(4) 2SLS TROLL Method	(5) 2SLS Preceded by GLS (AUTO 2) TROLL-searched ρ	(6) 2SLS Preceded by GLS (AUTO 2) Forced ρ	(7) 2SLS Manual Method	(8) 2SLS (man) Followed by GLS (AUTO 2) TROLL-searched ρ	(9) 2SLS (man) Followed by GLS (AUTO 2) Forced ρ
R^2	0.87	0.85	0.88	0.87	0.74	0.86	0.85	0.69	0.85
$F_{(5/38)}$	52.91	45.62	57.28	51.24	21.52	46.97	43.09	17.12	44.79
DW(0)	1.17	2.03	1.92	1.13	2.07	1.87	1.17	1.89	1.74
ρ_1	None	0.71	0.61	None	0.85	0.63	None	1.00	0.59
ρ_2	None	−0.48	−0.47	None	−0.43	−0.45	None	−0.52	−0.43
Mil. Expend,$_{t-1}$									
Value	0.62	0.54	0.58	0.53	0.46	0.60	0.53	0.32	0.56
t	5.85	4.43	5.09	4.68	3.09	5.18	4.34	2.11	4.27
Beta	0.62	0.54	0.58	0.54	0.47	0.60	0.53	0.32	0.55
Mil. Exp. Nonallies									
Value	0.16	0.16	0.15	0.18	0.18	0.17	0.18	0.16	0.17
t	2.61	2.59	2.74	2.77	2.36	2.85	2.57	2.21	2.69
Beta	0.21	0.20	0.19	0.22	0.22	0.22	0.22	0.20	0.21
Intersections									
Value	−424.34	−168.12	−310.15	−510.59	1492.72	1097.82	−510.41	1285.18	612.86
t	−0.40	−0.22	−0.39	−0.40	1.63	1.14	−0.37	1.44	0.60
Beta	−0.03	−0.01	−0.02	−0.03	0.09	0.07	−0.03	0.07	0.03

Colonial Area									
Value[b]	0.40	0.24	0.26	0.64	0.01	0.01	0.64	-0.05	0.19
t	1.46	0.82	0.91	1.99	0.48	0.27	1.85	-0.13	0.52
Beta	0.39	0.24	0.25	0.62	0.01	0.01	0.62	-0.05	0.18
Pop. × *Nat. Inc.*									
Value	-0.00	0.00	-0.00	-0.00	0.00	0.00	-0.00	0.00	0.00
t	-0.82	0.08	-0.10	-1.31	1.69	1.37	-1.22	1.32	0.10
Beta	-0.21	0.02	-0.03	-0.37	0.24	0.15	-0.37	0.43	0.03
Constant									
Value[b]	-3.69	-2.23	-2.38	-5.78	-0.16	-0.12	-0.58	0.36	-1.75
t	-1.48	-0.84	-0.93	-2.01	-0.90	-0.65	-1.87	0.11	-0.54
Beta	0.00	0.00	0.00	0.00	0.00	0.00	0.00	0.00	0.00

[a]All results are reported to two decimal points only. The figure -0.00 indicates that the value is actually *slightly less* than zero; 0.00 indicates that the value is actually *slightly greater* than zero.

[b]Actual value of unstandardized parameter estimate is multiplied by 10^{-6} for scale purposes.

placing military-expenditures$_{t-1}$, intensity-of-intersections, and colonial area by the prechosen instrument (detailed in Table 10-1).

5   Correcting for both serial correlation and the presence of endogenous and lagged endogenous variables. This is the method used by TROLL/1 and the method used to estimate our model. GLS, with the ρ_1 and ρ_2 values iteratively searched for by TROLL/1, was followed by 2SLS.

6   Correcting for both serial correlation and for the presence of endogenous and lagged endogenous variables. This is identical to Method 5 except that the ρ_1 and ρ_2 values were preset rather than searched for through the TROLL/1 algorithm. Values for the ρs were determined by the same equation used in Method 3 except that the residuals used were retrieved from the 2SLS rather than the OLS solution. Again, GLS was followed by 2SLS.

7   Correcting for endogenous and lagged endogenous terms only. This method is identical to Method 4 except that the 2SLS was performed manually by regressing all of the prechosen instruments on the variables to be replaced, storing the "fitted" values, and then using these "fitted" values as variables to replace the endogenous and lagged endogenous terms. Note that the resulting coefficient estimates were identical to those generated by the 2SLS performed by TROLL/1 (in Method 4).

8   Correcting for both serial correlation and the presence of endogenous and lagged endogenous terms. This method reverses the order of Method 5. The manual 2SLS in Method 7 is followed by GLS (with an AUTO2 correction), allowing TROLL/1 to search for the ρs. This method yielded the only estimate seriously out of line with the others—TROLL/1 appears to have found some sort of local minimum. Even here, however, the general shape of the equation does not change. The value of the coefficient for the lagged endogenous term, as well as its statistical significance and the R^2 for the entire equation, are all reduced; nevertheless, this coefficient remains the most significant.

9   Correcting for both serial correlation and the presence of endogenous and lagged endogenous variables. The order is identical to Method 8 (and the reverse of Method 6). The manual 2SLS in Method 7 is applied, followed by GLS (with an AUTO2 correction), but using ρs forced from the residuals equation (as in Method 3), using the residuals retrieved from the manual 2SLS of Method 7.[8]

---

[8]This is the procedure recommended by Hibbs (1974) and Wallis (1967). It is more cumbersome than the TROLL/1-supported method (since 2SLS must be performed independently) and, according to Eisner and Pindyck (1972), may introduce bias into the estimates. Nonetheless, it is certainly the most intuitive solution to the problem.

The most important result of this experiment is that, although the assumptions for an OLS solution are grossly violated, there is not a great difference in the coefficient estimates obtained from these alternative estimation procedures — with the one exception of the results from Method 8. The Durbin-Watson statistic indicated the presence of serial correlation throughout, which was then minimized by the application of GLS. Generally, the TROLL/1-searched ρs were very close to the values obtained when they were preset. Coefficient estimates and t statistics remained within quite narrow boundaries, and R^2 and F statistics remained statistically significant throughout. Nonetheless, the appropriate corrections reduced the purported significance of the lagged term. Although the results of this equation confirm the incrementalist theory of growth in military expenditures, the impact of incrementalism (as represented by the coefficient for military-expenditures$_{t-1}$) was indeed reduced. This finding reemphasizes the need to evaluate all incrementalist effects more carefully than has generally been done to date — otherwise the effects may be merely statistical artifacts of a correlation between the lagged term and the error term.

The particular equation (military expenditures) and data (Britain) chosen for this experiment were for purposes of illustration only, and did not reflect methodological concerns. Different results might have been obtained with another equation and another set of data. Although in this particular experiment no significant differences resulted from varying the regression assumptions, this may not always be the case. Still, it is reassuring to know that an equation can be estimated with vastly different assumptions and give generally similar results. Counterexamples indicating the precarious state of any assumptions regarding the nature of disturbances, the presence or absence of correlations, and the adequacy of equation specification or the correctness of measurement of the variables are available from the authors.

In addition, we must emphasize that the proper choice of a 2SLS substitution is crucial. If a set of instruments is more highly correlated with the disturbance term than were the variables that have been replaced, the problem that one is supposed to be correcting will only be aggravated. The use of lagged or unlagged total government expenditures in the instrument list for the military-expenditures equation led to great differences: the unlagged variable proved to be highly correlated with the disturbances, resulting in an *increased* significance for the military-expenditures$_{t-1}$ coefficient. We must therefore stress that indiscriminate use of instruments without consideration of their theoretical and empirical properties is a dangerous undertaking.

Regression analysis, far from being an exact science, depends on the expertise, intuition, judgment, and sophistication of the analyst. Clearly, art and good fortune play a large part in the analysis.

Appendix D
Biographies

Aehrenthal, (Count) Alois Lexa von
1854–1912
Austro-Hungarian foreign minister, 1906–1912.

Asquith, (Earl) Herbert Henry
1852–1928
Home secretary, 1892–1895; chancellor of the exchequer, 1905–1908; prime minister, 1908–1916.

Balfour, (Earl) Arthur James
1848–1930
Conservative MP, 1874–1885, 1886–1905 and 1906–1911; Chief secretary for Ireland, 1887–1891; First lord of the treasury, 1892, 1895, and 1900; Prime minister, 1902–1905; First lord of the admiralty, 1915; Foreign minister, 1916–1919

Berchtold, (Count) Leopold von
1863–1942
Austro-Hungarian ambassador to Russia, 1907–1911; foreign minister, 1912–1915; signed Austrian ultimatum to Serbia beginning WWI.

Bethmann-Hollweg, Theobald von
1856–1921
German Chancellor, 1909–1917

Bismarck, Otto von
1815–1898
President and foreign minister of Prussian cabinet, 1862; became chancellor of German Empire, 1871; resigned 1890.

Bülow, Bernhard von
1849–1929
German foreign secretary, 1897–1900; chancellor, 1900–1909.

Campbell-Bannerman, Sir Henry
1836–1908
Chief secretary for Ireland, 1884–1885; secretary for war, 1886, 1892–1895; leader of liberal party, 1895; prime minister, 1905–1908.

Cambon, Pierre Paul
1843–1924
French ambassador to Madrid, 1886 (–1890?). ambassador to constantinople, 1890 (–1898?); ambassador to London, 1898–1920.

Caprivi, (Count) Leo von
1831–1899
Chief of staff of Prussian 10th Army Corps, 1870–1871; chief of admiralty, 1883; succeeded Bismarck as chancellor, 1890–1894.

Chamberlain, Joseph
1836–1914
Member 2nd and 3rd Gladstone cabinets; leader of Liberal-Unionists in parliament; negotiated treaties for semi-home-rule for Ireland; colonial secretary, 1895–1902.

Churchill, Sir Winston Leonard Spencer
1874–1965
Undersecretary for colonies, 1905–1908; president of board of trade,

1908–1910; home secretary, 1910–1911; first lord of admiralty, 1911–1915.

Clemenceau, Georges
1841–1929
Senator, 1902–1906; minister of interior, 1906; French premier, 1906–1909, 1917–1919.

Conrad, (Prince) George
1869–1957
Greek high commissioner of Crete, 1898–1906.

Conrad von Hötzendorf, (Count) Franz
1852–1925
Austro-Hungarian field marshal; chief of staff, 1906–1911, 1912–1917; commander of Italian front 1917–1918.

Delcassé, Théophile
1852–1923
Minister of colonies, 1893–1895; minister of foreign affairs, 1898–1905, 1914–1915.

Edward VII
1841–1910
King of Great Britain and Ireland, 1901–1910.

Franz Ferdinand (Archduke)
1863–1914
Inherited title of Archduke of Austria, 1875; became heir apparent to Austrian crown 1896.

Franz Josef
1830–1916
Emperor of Austria, 1848–1916.

Frederick II (Frederick the Great)
1712–1786
King of Prussia, 1740–1786.

Ferry, Jules François Camille
1832–1893
Premier of France, 1880–1881, 1883–1885.

Gladstone, William Ewart
1809–1898
Member of Parliament, 1832–1905; president of board of trade, 1843–1845; colonial secretary, 1845–1846; chancellor of exchequer, 1852–1855, 1859–1866; prime minister, 1868–1874; 1880–1885, 1886, 1892–1894.

Goschen, (Viscount) George J.
1831–1907
First lord of the admiralty, 1895–1900.

Goschen, Sir William Edward
1847–1924
British Minister to Belgrade, 1889–1900; ambassador to Copenhagen, 1900–1905; ambassador to Vienna, 1905–1908; ambassador to Germany, 1914.

Granville, Earl (George Leveson-Gower)
1815–1891
Leader of Liberals in House of Lords from 1855; colonial secretary, 1868–1870, 1886; foreign secretary, 1870–1874, 1880–1885.

Grey, Sir Edward (Viscount Grey of Fallodon)
1862–1933
English foreign undersecretary, 1892–1895; foreign secretary, 1905–1916.

Haldane, (Viscount) Richard Burdon
1856–1928
Member of parliament, 1885–1911; secretary of state for war, 1905–1911; lord chancellor, 1912–1915, 1924; led Labour opposition in House of Lords, 1925–1928.

Hardinge, (Baron) Charles
1858–1944
British ambassador to Russia, 1904–1906; viceroy of India, 1910–1916; Ambassador to France, 1920–1923.

Hohenlohe-Schillingsfürst, (Prince) Chlodwig Karl Victor
1819–1901
German Ambassador to Paris, 1874–1878; secretary for foreign affairs, 1880–1885; governor of Alsace-Lorraine, 1885–1894; chancellor of Germany, 1894–1900.

Holstein, Friedrich von
1837–1909
"Mystery man" of the German foreign office (known as the "Gray Eminence"). Shaped German foreign policy in his tenure (1878–1906) in the foreign office as counselor in the political department.

Humbert I (Umberto Humbert I)
1844–1900
King of Italy, 1878–1900.

Izvolsky, Aleksandr Petrovich
1856-1919
Russian foreign minister, 1906-1910;
ambassador to Paris, 1910-1917.

Kiderlen-Waechter, Alfred von
1852-1912
German deputy foreign secretary,
1908-1910; foreign secretary, 1910-
1912.

Kitchener, (Earl) Horatio Herbert
1850-1916
Governor of Eastern Sudan, 1886; led
Khartoum expedition, 1898; governor-
general of Sudan, 1899; chief of staff
in South Africa, 1899; organized
guerrillas in Boer War, 1900-1902;
commander in chief in India, 1902-
1909; secretary of state for war, 1914;
organized British forces for WWI,
1914-1916.

Lansdowne, (Marquess) Henry Charles
Keith Petty-Maurice
1845-1927
Viceroy of India, 1888-1893; secretary for war, 1895-1900; foreign
secretary, 1900-1905; minister without portfolio, 1915-1916.

Lesseps, (Vicomte) Ferdinand Marie de
1805-1894
Engineer organizing construction of
the Suez Canal, 1859-1869; began
construction of Panama Canal, 1881-
1888.

Liman von Sanders, Otto
1885-1929
German general; liaison with, later
commander of, Turkish forces, 1913-
1918.

Lloyd George, (Earl) David
1863-1945
President of board of trade, 1905-
1908; chancellor of exchequer, 1908-
1915; minister of munitions, 1915-
1916; secretary of state for war, 1916;
prime minister, 1916-1922.

McKenna, Reginald
1863-1943
Member of parliament, 1895-1918;
financial secretary of the treasury,
1905; president of the board of edu-
cation, 1907-1908; first lord of the

admiralty, 1908-1911; home secretary, 1911-1915.

Metternich, (Prince) Klemens Wenzel
Nepomuk Lothar von
1773-1859
Austrian minister of foreign affairs,
1809-1848.

Millerand, Alexandre
1859-1943
Deputy, 1885-1920; held various
cabinet offices, 1899-1915.

Moltke, (Count) Helmuth Carl
Bernhard von
1800-1891
Aided in organization of Turkish
army, 1835-1839; chief of Prussian
general staff, 1858-1888; created
field marshal, 1871.

Moltke, Helmuth Johannes Ludwig von
1848-1916
German quartermaster general, 1904;
chief of German general staff, 1906-
1914.

Müller, Admiral Georg Alexander von
1854-1940
Head of German Naval Secretariat
1909-1918

Nicolson, Sir Arthur
1849-1928
English ambassador to Madrid, 1904-
1906; ambassador to Russia, 1906-
1910.

Poincaré, Raymond
1860-1934
French deputy, 1887-1902; held
several cabinet positions, 1893-1903;
senator, 1903-1912, 1920-1922;
prime minister, 1912-1913; president
1913-1920.

Rosebery, Earl of (Archibald Philip
Primrose)
1847-1925
Undersecretary in Home Office,
1881-1883; foreign secretary, 1886,
1892-1894; prime minister, 1894-
1895.

Salisbury, Marquess of (Robert Arthur
Talbot Gascoyne-Cecil)
1830-1903
Secretary for India, 1866-1867, 1874-
1878; foreign secretary, 1878; prime

minister and foreign secretary, 1885–1886, 1886–1892, 1895–1902.

Sazonov, Sergei Dmitrievich
1866–1927
Russian foreign minister, 1910–1916; became Minister of Foreign Affairs for Kolchuk; "White" leader during Russian civil war.

Schlieffen, (Count) Alfred von
1833–1913
Chief of German general staff, 1891–1905; became field marshal, 1911.

Tirpitz, Admiral Alfred von
1849–1930
German state secretary of navy, 1898–1916; Prussian minister of state, 1898–1916.

Tsars during 1850–1917:
Nicholas I, 1825–1855; Alexander II, 1855–1881; Alexander III, 1881–1894; Nicholas II, 1894–1917.

Tweedmouth, Baron (Edward Marjoribanks)
1849–1909
First lord of the admiralty, 1905–1908.

Tittoni, Tommaso
1885–1931
Italian foreign minister, 1903–1905, 1906–1909, 1919; ambassador to London, 1905–1906; ambassador to Paris, 1910–1916.

Tschirschky und Bögendorff, Heinrich von
1858–1914
German foreign minister, 1906–1907; ambassador to Vienna, 1907–1916.

Wilhelm I (Wilhelm Friedrich Ludwig)
1797–1888
King of Prussia, 1861–1888; Emperor of Germany, 1871–1888.

Wilhelm II (Friedrich Wilhelm Viktor Albert)
1859–1941
Emperor of Germany and King of Prussia, 1888–1918.

Zimmerman, Arthur
1864–1940
German undersecretary for foreign affairs, 1911–1916; foreign minister, 1916–1917.

Appendix E
Treaties

The following list is selective and is not the basis for the alliance data used in the analysis. The purpose of this list is to assist the reader in identifying treaties mentioned in the text.

20 November 1815, Paris

Great Britain, Austria, Russia, Prussia

Treaty of alliance between the courts of Austria, Britain, Prussia, and Russia.

8 October 1818, Aix la Chapelle

Britain, France, Russia, Prussia, Austria

Convention between his majesty the King of France on one part and each of the courts of Austria, Great Britain, Prussia and Russia on the other part.

6 May 1873

Germany, Russia

Treaty of Alliance (with next entry, formed first League of Three Emperors).

6 June 1873

Russia, Austria-Hungary

Treaty of Alliance.

8 March 1878, San Stefano

Russia, Turkey

Preliminaries to Peace (signed at San Stefano 3 March 1878).

13 July 1878, Berlin

Germany, Austria-Hungary, France, Britain, Italy, Russia, Turkey

Treaty of Berlin (see next entry for Protocols).

13 June to 13 July 1878, Berlin

Germany, Austria-Hungary, France, Britain, Italy, Russia, Turkey

Protocols of the Congress of Berlin (see next entry for Serbian independence).

19 August 1879

Germany, Austria-Hungary, France, Italy, Britain, Russia, Serbia, Turkey

Protocols of the European Commission to set the limits of Serbia (followed by annexes, maps and descriptions).

19 May to 3 July 1880, Madrid

Germany, Austria-Hungary, Belgium, Denmark, Spain, United States of America, France, Britain, Italy, Morocco, Netherlands, Portugal, Sweden and Norway

Protocols of conferences to regulate the exercise of the right of protection to Morocco and related questions

18 June 1881, Berlin

Austria-Hungary, Germany, Russia

Convention between Austria-Hungary, the German Empire, and Russia (ratified June 1882, and followed by two protocols). Extended for 3 years 15 April 1884, Berlin.

18 June 1881, Berlin

Austria-Hungary, Germany, Russia

Treaty to assure, by an entente, the defensive positions of the respective states. Followed by a protocol, 18 June 1881, Berlin, and an explanatory protocol, 27 June 1881, Berlin.

28 June 1881, Belgrade

Austria-Hungary, Serbia

Treaty of Friendship and Alliance, followed by a letter of 12 October 1881, and an explaining Declaration 30 October 1881.

20 May 1882, Vienna

Austria-Hungary, Germany, Italy

Treaty of Alliance (signed in Vienna 20 May 1882, followed by several Declarations signed 22 and 28 May 1882, and ratified 30 May 1882).

20 February 1887, Berlin

Austria-Hungary, Germany, Italy

Treaty in view of confirming and extending the treaty of Alliance concluded 20 May 1882.

24 March 1887

Italy, Britain, Austria-Hungary

Correspondence concerning the question of the Mediterranean and adjacent seas (see also next entry).

21 May 1887

Spain, Italy, Austria-Hungary

Exchange of notes concerning the Mediterranean. Germany agreed to this Accord 4 May 1891.

22 May 1887, Constantinople

Turkey, Britain

Convention concerning Egypt

22 May 1887, Constantinople

Britain, Turkey, Egypt

Convention concerning the Egyptian question

18 June 1887, Berlin

Germany, Russia

Treaty to assure, by an entente, the defensive position of the two states

(followed by an additional and very secret protocol). Otherwise known as the "Reinsurance Treaty."

7 October 1887

Austria-Hungary, Germany

Treaty of Alliance.

16 November 1887, Paris

Britain, France

Convention relating to the New Hebrides and the islands to the leeward of Tahiti (see also next entry).

26 January 1888, Paris

Britain, France

Declaration agreed upon pursuant to Article III of the convention of 16 November 1887 relative to the New Hebrides (see also next entry).

2 to 9 February 1888, London, Paris*

Britain, France

Agreement concerning the coast of Somali. (*Exchange of letters.)

30 May 1888, Paris

Britain, France

Declaration on the subject of the abrogation of the Declaration of 19 June 1847 concerning the islands to the leeward of Tahiti.

10 August 1889, Paris

Britain, France

Two agreements concerning the respective possessions on the West Coast of Africa.

1 July 1890, Berlin

Britain, Germany

Agreement concerning the respective possessions in East Africa and the island of Heligoland.

6 May 1891, Berlin

Austria-Hungary, Germany, Italy

Treaty to renew the Triple Alliance, followed by a protocol.

27 August 1891, Paris, St. Petersburg*

France, Russia

Understanding with respect to mutual defense and common interests. (*Exchange of letters.)

17 August 1892, St. Petersburg

France, Russia

Military Convention.

17 April 1895, Shimonoseki

China, Japan

Treaty of Peace.

14 October 1896, St. Petersburg

France, Russia, Tunisia

Declaration concerning the reports between France and Russia on Tunisia.

30 August 1898, London

Germany, Britain

Convention between Britain and Germany regarding Angola, Mozambique, and Portuguese Timor (followed by secret convention and note).

18 May–29 July 1899, The Hague

Germany, Austria-Hungary, Belgium, China, Denmark, Spain, United States of America, France, Britain, and Ireland, United States of Mexico, Greece, Italy, Japan, Luxemburg, Montenegro, Netherlands, Persia, Portugal, Rumania, Russia, Serbia, Siam, Sweden and Norway, Switzerland, Turkey, Bulgaria

Diplomatic Documents and Official Proceedings, Final Act, Conventions, and Declarations of the International Peace Conference.

14 November 1899, London

Germany, Britain

Convention and Declaration to settle the differences arising from the dispute over the islands of Samoa (ratified February 1900).

16 October 1900, London

Britain, Germany

Agreement concerning the Maintenance of the Territorial Integrity of China.

30 January 1902, London

Britain, Japan

Agreement concerning the situation of China and Korea (see next entry for further agreements).

30 January 1902, London

Britain, Japan, China, Korea

Agreement concluded by Britain and Japan to assure the territorial integrity of China and Korea.

28 June 1902, Berlin

Austria-Hungary, Germany, Italy

Treaty to renew the Triple Alliance, and a closing protocol.

30 March 1904, Belgrade

Serbia, Bulgaria

Convention of Friendship and Commerce.

8 April 1904, London

Britain, France

Diplomatic Arrangement concluded on the subjects of Morocco, Egypt, Newfoundland, Siam, Madagascar, and the New Hebrides, with related correspondence.

3 October 1904, Paris

Spain, France

Declaration about the adherence by Spain to the French-English Declaration of 8 April 1904 concerning the Maintenance of the Integrity of Morocco. A separate, secret agreement established French and Spanish "zones of influence" in Morocco.

[?] 1905

Spain, France

Secret North African Accord.

24 July 1905, Björkö

Germany, Russia

Treaty, not ratified.

16 January to 7 April 1906, Algeciras

Germany, Austria-Hungary, Belgium, Spain, United States of America, France, Britain, Italy, Morocco, Netherlands, Portugal, Russia, Sweden

Official Report and Documents of the Conference of Algeciras. General Act of the International Conference of Algeciras ratified 7 April 1906.

July 1907

Austria-Hungary, Italy, Germany

Renewal of the Triple Alliance.

18 to 31 August 1907, St. Petersburg

Russia, Britain

Convention concerning Persia, Afghanistan and Tibet (ratifications exchanged 23 September 1907).

18 October 1907, The Hague

Germany, United States of America, Argentina, Austria-Hungary, Belgium, Bolivia, Brazil, Bulgaria, Chile, China, Colombia, Cuba, Denmark, Dominican Republic, Ecuador, Spain, France, Britain, Greece, Guatemala, Haiti, Italy, Japan, Luxemburg, Mexico, Montenegro, Nicaragua, Norway, Panama, Netherlands, Peru, Persia, Portugal, Roumania, Russia, El Salvador, Serbia, Siam, Sweden, Switzerland, Turkey, Uruguay, Venezuela

Final Act of the Second International Peace Conference.

9 February 1909, Berlin

Germany, France

Declaration concerning Morocco.

29 February 1912, Sofia

Bulgaria, Serbia

Treaty of Friendship and Alliance (followed by a Military Convention and an Agreement by the great powers).

16 May 1912, Sofia

Bulgaria, Greece

Treaty of Alliance (Military Convention signed 22 September 1912).

16 July 1912, Paris

Russia, France

Naval Convention.

12 September 1912

Serbia, Montenegro

Alliance (Political and Military Conventions).

5 December 1912, Vienna

Austria-Hungary, Germany, Italy

Treaty to prolong the duration of the Triple Alliance, followed by two protocols.

30 May 1913, London

Greece, Bulgaria, Montenegro, Serbia, Turkey

Treaty of Peace.

10 August 1913, Bucharest

Rumania, Greece, Montenegro, Serbia, Bulgaria

Treaty of Peace (followed by two official records of the exchange of ratifications). See next entry.

10 August 1913, Bucharest

Bulgaria, Greece, Montenegro, Serbia, Rumania

Protocols of the above conference.

Bibliography

General

Albertini, Luigi. 1952–1954. *The Origins of the War of 1914*, tr. from Italian by I. Massey, 3 vols., London: Oxford University Press.

Allison, Graham T. 1969. "Conceptual Models and the Cuban Missile Crisis," *American Political Science Review*, 63:689–718.

Allison, Graham T., and Morton H. Halperin. 1972. "Bureaucratic Politics: A Paradigm and Some Policy Implications," in *Theory and Practice in International Relations*, Richard H. Ullman and Raymond Tanter, eds., Princeton University Press.

Andrew, Christopher. 1968. *Théophile Delcassé and the Making of the Entente Cordiale*, New York: St. Martin's Press.

Aron, Raymond. 1967. *Peace and War: A Theory of International Relations*, New York: Praeger.

Art, Robert J. and Kenneth N. Waltz, eds. 1971. *The Use of Force: International Politics and Foreign Policy*, Boston: Little, Brown.

Ash, Maurice A. 1961. "An Analysis of Power with Special Reference to International Politics," in Rosenau, 1961.

Austro-Hungarian Monarchy. Ministerium des K. und K. Hauses und des Äussern. 1878. Aktenstücke in *Orientalischen Angelegenheiten, Prälemenarfriede von San Stefano, Congress-Protokille und Vertrag von Berlin*, Wien: KK Hof- und Staatsdruckerei.

Aydelotte, William Osgood. 1937. *Bismarck and British Colonial Policy*, University of Pennsylvania Press.

Barnett, Correlli. 1966. *The Swordbearers: Studies in Supreme Command in the First World War*, Baltimore: Penguin.

Berkowitz, Morton and P. G. Bock, eds. 1965. *American National Security: A Reader in Theory and Policy*, New York: Free Press.

Bertalanffy, Ludwig von. 1968. *General Systems Theory*, New York: Braziller.

Bethmann-Hollweg, Theobald von. 1920. *Reflections on the World War*, London: Thornton Butterworth.

Bittner, L. and H. Uebersberger, eds. 1930. *Oesterreich-Ungarns Aussenpolitik von der Bosnischen Krise 1908 bis zum Kriegsausbruch 1914*, 9 vols., Vienna and Leipzig; Oesterreichischer Bundesverlag für Unterricht, Wissenschaft und Kunst.

Bloomfield, Arthur I. 1968. *Patterns of Fluctuation in International Investment Before 1914*, Princeton Studies in International Finance, Princeton University, Department of Economics.

Boulding, Kenneth E. 1969. "Economics Imperialism" (review article of David Braybrooke and Charles E. Lindbloom, *A Strategy of Decision*), *Behavioral Science*, 14(6):496–500.

Brandenburg, Erich. 1927. *From Bismarck to the World War*, Oxford University Press.

Braybrooke, David and Charles E. Lindbloom. 1963. *A Strategy of Decision*, Glencoe, Ill.: Free Press.

Bridge, F. R. 1972. *From Sadowa to Sarajevo: The Foreign Policy of Austria-Hungary, 1866–1913*, London: Routledge and Kegan Paul.

Brody, Richard A. 1966. "Cognition and Behavior: A Model of International Relations," in *Experience, Structure and Adaptability*, O. J. Harvey, ed., New York: Springer.

Brunschwig, Henri. 1966. *French Colonialism, 1871–1914*, New York: Praeger.

Bülow, Bernhard H., Prince von. 1931–1932. *Memoirs of Prince von Bülow*, 4 vols., Boston: Little, Brown.

Burns, Arthur Lee. 1961. "From Balance to Deterrence: A Theoretical Analysis," in Rosenau, 1961.

Burton, John W. 1961. *Peace Theory: Preconditions of Disarmament*, New York: Knopf.

Campbell, Donald T. 1969. "Variation and Selective Retention in Socio-Cultural Evolution," *General Systems: Yearbook of the Society for General Systems Research*, 14:69–85.

Carneiro, Robert L. 1970. "A Theory of the Origin of the State," *Science*, 169(3947):733–738.

Chamberlain, Joseph. 1897. *Foreign and Colonial Speeches*, London: Routledge and Sons.

Chamberlin, Waldo. 1939. "The German Navy Law of 1912," dissertation, Stanford University.

Choucri, Nazli. 1974. *Population Dynamics and International Violence: Propositions, Insights, and Evidence*, Lexington, Mass.: D. C. Heath.

Choucri, Nazli, Michael Laird, and Dennis Meadows. 1972. *Resource Scarcity and Foreign Policy: A Simulation Model of International Conflict* M.I.T.: Center for International Studies.

Choucri, Nazli and Robert C. North. 1969. "The Determinants of International Violence," *Peace Science Society (International) Papers*, XII: 34–63.

————. 1972. "In Search of Peace Systems: Scandinavia and the Netherlands, 1870–1970," in *War, Peace and Numbers*, Bruce M. Russett, ed., Beverly Hills, Calif.: Sage Publications.

Churchill, Winston S. 1923–1929. *The World Crisis, 1911–1914*, 3 vols., New York: Scribner's.

Conrad von Hötzendorf, Feldmarschall. 1921–1925. *Aus meiner Dienstzeit, 1906–1918*, 5 vols., Vienna: Rikola Verlag.

Davies, James C. 1962. "Toward a Theory of Revolution," *The American Sociological Review*, 27(1):5–19.

Davis, Otto A. *et al.* 1966. "A Theory of the Budgetary Process," *American Political Science Review*, 60(3):529–547.

Deber, Raisa B. 1971. "International Political Behavior: An Historical Analysis of Scandinavia and the Netherlands," master's thesis, Massachusetts Institute of Technology.

Deutsch, Karl W. 1963. *The Nerves of Government*, New York: Free Press.

Deutsch, Karl W. and J. David Singer. 1964. "Multipolar Power Systems and International Stability," *World Politics*, 16(3):390–406.

Documents Diplomatique Francais. 1901–1911, 2ᵉ Serie. 1911–1914, 3ᵉ Serie. Paris: Imprimerie Nationale.

Dugdale, E. T. S., ed. 1928–1931. *German Diplomatic Documents, 1871–1914*, 4 vols., London: Methuen.

Durkheim, Emile. 1933. *The Division of Labor in Society*, Glencoe, Ill., Free Press.

Easton, David. 1965. *A Systems Analysis of Political Life*, New York: Wiley.

Edmonds, Sir James E. 1937. *History of the Great War: Military Operations*, 3rd ed., London: Macmillan.

Ehrlich, Paul R. and Anne H. Ehrlich. 1970. *Population, Resources, Environment*, San Francisco: Freeman.

Eisenstadt, S. N. 1963. *The Political Systems of Empires*, Glencoe, Ill.: Free Press.

Farb, Peter. 1968. *Man's Rise to Civilization as Shown by the Indians of North America from Primeval Times to the Coming of the Industrial State*, New York: Dutton.

Fay, Sidney Bradshaw. 1966. *The Origins of the World War*, 2nd rev. ed., New York: Macmillan.

Fieldhouse, David K. 1966. *The Colonial Empires*, London: Weidenfeld and Nicolson.

Fischer, Fritz. 1967. *Germany's Aims in the First World War*, New York: Norton.

————. 1969. *Krieg der Illusionen: Die Deutsche Politik von 1911 bis 1914*, Düsseldorf: Droste Verlag.

Fisher, Sir John. See Kemp, 1964.

Fleming, Denna F. 1968. *The Origins and Legacies of World War I*, New York: Doubleday.

Forrester, Jay W. 1971. "Counterintuitive Behavior of Social Systems," *Technology Review*, 73(3):52–68.

———. 1971. *World Dynamics*, Cambridge, Mass.: Wright-Allen.

Friedheim, Robert L. 1971. "The Satisfied' and 'Dissatisfied' States Negotiate International Law: A Case Study," in Quester, 1971.

Friedman, Julian, Christopher Bladen, and Steven Rosen, eds. 1970. *Alliance in International Politics*, Boston: Allyn and Bacon.

Geiss, Immanuel. 1967. *July 1914, the Outbreak of the First World War: Selected Documents*, New York: Scribner's.

George, Alexander L. 1972. "The Case for Multiple Advocacy in Making Foreign Policy," *American Political Science Review*, 66(3):751–785.

Germany, Reichsarchiv. 1930. *Der Weltkrieg 1914 bis 1918: Kriegsrustung und Krigswirtschaft*, Berlin.

Gibbs, J. Willard. 1948. *The Collected Works of J. Willard Gibbs*, 2 vols., New Haven: Yale University Press.

Gladstone, Arthur. 1962. "Relationship Orientation and the Processes Leading toward War," *Background*, 6:13–25.

Goldsmith, Raymond W. 1961. "The Economic Growth of Tsarist Russia, 1860–1913," *Economic Development and Cultural Change*, 9(3):441–475.

Gooch, G. P. and Harold Temperley, eds. 1926–1938. *British Documents on the Origins of the War, 1898–1914,* 11 vols., London: His Majesty's Stationery Office.

Gray, Colin S. 1971. "The Arms Race Phenomenon," *World Politics*, 24 (1):39–79.

Grey, Sir Edward, Viscount of Fallodon. 1925. *Twenty-Five Years, 1892–1916,* 2 vols., New York: Stokes.

Groennings, Sven, E. W. Kelley, and Michael Leiserson, eds. 1970. *The Study of Coalition Behavior: Theoretical Perspectives and Cases from Four Continents*, New York: Holt, Rinehart and Winston.

Gross, Nachum Theodor. 1966. "Industrialization in Austria in the Nineteenth Century," Ph.D. dissertation, University of California, Berkeley.

Gurr, Ted Robert. 1972. *Polimetrics: An Introduction to Quantitative Macropolitics*, Englewood Cliffs, N. J.: Prentice-Hall.

Haas, Ernst B. 1971. "The Balance of Power: Prescription, Concept or Propaganda?" in Quester, 1971.

Haldane, Sir Richard Burdon. 1920. *Before the War*, London: Cassell.

Hale, Oron James. 1931. *Germany and the Diplomatic Revolution*, University of Pennsylvania Press.

———. 1940. *Publicity and Diplomacy with Special Reference to England and Germany, 1890–1914*, New York: Appleton-Century.

Halperin, Morton. 1974. *Bureaucratic Politics and Foreign Policy*, Washington, D.C.: Brookings Institute.

Halperin, Samuel William. 1930. "Anglo-Germany Rivalry Before the World War," Ph.D. dissertation, University of Chicago.

Hawley, Amos H. 1965. "The Ecological Point of View," in *Human Behavior in International Politics*, J. David Singer, ed., Chicago: Rand McNally.

Helfferich, Karl. 1914. *Germany's Economic Progress and National Wealth, 1888–1913*, New York: Germanistic Society of America.

Helmreich, Ernst C. 1936. "The Conflict Between Germany and Austria over Balkan Policy, 1913–1914," in *Essays in the History of Modern Europe*, Donald C. McKay, ed., New York: Harper.

———. 1938. *The Diplomacy of the Balkan Wars, 1912–1913*, Harvard University Press.

Hermann, Charles F. 1963. "Some Consequences of Crisis Which Limit the Viability of Organizations," *Administrative Science Quarterly*, 8:61–82.

———. 1969. *Crises in Foreign Policy: A Simulation Analysis*, Indianapolis: Bobbs-Merrill.

Hinsley, Francis H. 1963. *Power and the Pursuit of Peace*, Cambridge University Press.

Hislam, Percival A. 1908. *The Admiralty of the Atlantic*, London: Longmans, Green.

Hobson, J. A. 1938. *Imperialism*, London: Allen & Unwin.

Hoffman, Ross J. S. 1933. *Great Britain and the German Trade Rivalry, 1875–1914*, University of Pennsylvania Press.

Hoffmann, Stanley. 1971. "International Systems and International Law," in Quester, 1971.

Holsti, Kalevi J. 1970. "Diplomatic Coalitions and Military Alliances," in Friedman *et al.*, 1970.

Holsti, Ole R. 1971. *Crisis, Escalation and War*, McGill-Queens University Press.

Howard, Alan and Robert A. Scott. 1965 "A Proposed Framework for the Analysis of Stress in the Human Organism," *Behavioral Science*, 10(2):141–160.

Huntington, Samuel P. 1971. "Arms Races: Prerequisites and Results," in Quester, 1971.

Hurd, Archibald and Henry Castle. 1913. *German Sea Power*, New York: Scribner's.

Huxley, Sir Julian. 1964. "The Impending Crisis," in *The Population Crisis and the Use of World Resources*, Stuart Mudd, ed., The Hague: W. Junk.

Janis, Irving L. 1972. *Victims of Groupthink*, Boston: Houghton Mifflin.

Kaplan, Morton A. 1957. *System and Process in International Politics*, New York: Wiley.

———, ed. 1968. *New Approaches to International Relations*, New York: St. Martin's Press.

———. 1970. "International Law and the International System," in *Great Issues of International Politics*, Morton A. Kaplan, ed., Chicago: Aldine.

Kautsky, Karl. See Montgelas and Schücking, 1924.

Kelman, Herbert C. 1965. *International Behavior*, New York: Holt, Rinehart & Winston.

Kemmerer, Edwin Walter. 1916. "The Theory of Foreign Investments," *The Annals* [of the American Academy of Political and Social Science], 68:1-9.

Kemp, Lt. Commander P. K., ed. 1964. *The Papers of Admiral Sir John Fisher*, 2 vols., London: The Navy Records Society.

Kindleberger, Charles P. 1962. *Foreign Trade and the National Economy*, Yale University Press.

Kissinger, Henry A. 1971. "Domestic Structure and Foreign Policy," in Quester, 1971.

Knorr, Klaus and James N. Rosenau, eds. 1969. *Contending Approaches to International Politics*, Princeton University Press.

Kohn, Hans. 1968. "Nationalism," in *International Encyclopedia of the Social Sciences*, D. E. Sills, ed., Vol. 2, New York: Macmillan.

Kuznets, Simon. 1966. *Modern Economic Growth: Rate, Structure and Spread*, Yale University Press.

Lafore, Laurence. 1965. *The Long Fuse: An Interpretation of the Origins of World War I*, Philadelphia: Lippincott.

Landes, David S. 1969. *The Unbound Prometheus*, Cambridge University Press.

Langer, William L. 1951. *The Diplomacy of Imperialism*, New York: Knopf.

———, ed. 1952. *An Encyclopedia of World History*, Boston: Houghton Mifflin.

———. 1962. *European Alliances and Alignments, 1871-1890*, 2nd ed., New York: Knopf.

Lenin, V. I. 1939. *Imperialism, The Highest Stage of Capitalism*, New York: International Publishers.

Lepsius, Johannes, Albrecht Mendelssohn Bartholdy, and Friedrich Thimme, eds. 1922-1927. *Grosse Politik der Europäischen Kabinette, 1871-1914* [collected diplomatic papers of the foreign office], 40 vols., Berlin: Deutsche Verlagsgesellschaft für Politik und Geschichte.

Liska, George. 1970. "Alignments and Realignments," in Friedman *et al.*, 1970.

MacIver, R. M. 1947. *The Web of Government*, New York: Macmillan

Marder, Arthur J. 1961. *From the Dreadnought to Scapa Flow*, Oxford University Press.

Martens, Georg Friedrich von. 1920. *Nouveau Recueil General de Traités et Autres Actes Relatifs aux Rapports de Droit International*, Troisième Serie, Vol. 10, Leipsig: Librairie Theodor Weicher.

Marz, Edward. 1953. "Some Economic Aspects of the Nationality Conflict in the Habsburg Empire," *Journal of Central European Affairs*, 13(2):123-135.

Mason, Otis T. 1966. *The Origins of Invention*, M. I. T. Press.

Maurice, Sir Frederick. 1937-1939. *Haldane, 1856-1915: The Life of Viscount Haldane of Cloan*, 2 vols, London: Faber and Faber.

McClelland, Charles A. 1960. "The Function of Theory in International Relations," *Journal of Conflict Resolution*, 4(3):303-336.

_____. 1961. "Applications of General Systems Theory in International Relations," in *Rosenau, 1961*.

_____. 1965. "The Communist Chinese Performance in Crisis and Non-Crisis: Quantitative Studies of the Taiwan Straits Confrontation, 1950–1964," Naval Ordnance Test Station, China Lake, Calif. Report N60530–11207.

McClelland, David C. 1961. *The Achieving Society*, Princeton, N. J.: Van Nostrand.

McEntee, Girard Lindsley. 1937. *Military History of the World War*, New York: Scribner's.

Medlicott, William N. 1956. *Bismarck, Gladstone, and the Concert of Europe*, London: Athlone Press.

_____. 1963. *The Congress of Berlin and After: A Diplomatic History of the Near Eastern Settlement, 1878–1890*, Hamden, Conn.: Anchor Books.

Miller, James G. 1965. "Living Systems: Basic Concepts," *Behavioral Science*, 10(3):193–237.

_____. 1971. "Living Systems: The Group," *Behavioral Science*, 16(4):302–398.

Moll, Kenneth L. 1971. "Politics, Power, and Panic: Britain's 1909 Dreadnought 'Gap'," in Art and Waltz, 1971.

Montgelas, Max and Walther Schücking, eds. 1924. *Outbreak of the World War, German Documents Collected by Karl Kautsky*, Oxford University Press.

Moon, Parker Thomas. 1930. *Imperialism and World Politics*, New York: Macmillan.

Moore, Barrington, Jr. 1967. *Social Origins of Dictatorship and Democracy: Lord and Peasant in the Making of the Modern World*, Boston: Beacon Press.

Morgenthau, Hans J. 1965. "Another 'Great Debate': The National Interest of the United States," in Berkowitz and Bock, 1965.

_____. 1967. *Politics Among Nations: The Struggle for Power and Peace*, 4th ed., New York: Knopf.

Nekludov, A. 1920. *Diplomatic Reminiscences*, New York: Dutton.

Nichols, J. Alden. 1958. *Germany After Bismarck: The Caprivi Era, 1890–1894*, Harvard University Press.

Nomikos, Eugenia V. and Robert C. North. 1975. *International Crisis: The Outbreak of World War I*, McGill-Queens University Press.

North, Robert C. 1970. "Wright on War," *Journal of Conflict Resolution*, 14(4):487–498.

North, Robert C. and Richard Lagerstrom. 1971. *War and Domination: A Theory of Lateral Pressure*, New York: General Learning Press.

Odum, Howard T. 1967. "Energetics of World Food Production," in *The World Food Problem*, A Report of the President's Science Advisory Committee, Vol. III, Report of the Panel on World Food Supply, Washington, D. C.: U. S. Government Printing Office.

Organski, A. F. K. 1968. *World Politics*, 2nd ed., New York: Knopf.

Overlach, T. W. 1919. *Foreign Financial Control in China*, New York: Macmillan.

Paige, Glenn D. 1968. *The Korean Decision*, New York: Free Press.

Parliamentary Debates, Great Britain (Authorized Ed.), Fourth Series, vols. 129–199, 1904–1908; *Parliamentary Debates* (Official Report), Fifth Series, vols 1–57, 1909–1913, London: His Majesty's Stationery Office.

Petrie, Sir Charles. 1949. *Diplomatic History, 1713–1933*, New York: Macmillan.

Pfeiffer, John E. 1969. *The Emergence of Man*, New York: Harper.

Pinson, Koppel S. 1954. *Modern Germany: Its History and Civilization*, New York: Macmillan.

Platt, John. 1973. "Social Traps," *American Psychologist*, 28(8):641–651.

Price, Morgan Philips. 1956. *A History of Turkey: From Empire to Republic*, London: Allen and Unwin.

Prosterman, Roy L. 1972. *Surviving to 3000*, Belmont, Calif.: Duxbury.

Pruitt, Dean G. and Richard C. Snyder, eds. 1969. *Theory and Research on Causes of War*, Englewood Cliffs, N. J.: Prentice-Hall.

Quester, George H., ed. 1971. *Power, Action and Interaction: Readings on International Politics*, Boston: Little, Brown.

Reinsch, Paul S. 1916. *World Politics at the End of the Nineteenth Century*, New York: Macmillan.

Remak, Joachim. 1967. *The Origins of World War I, 1871–1914*, New York: Holt, Rinehart and Winston.

Renouvin, Pierre and Jean-Baptiste Duroselle. 1967. *Introduction to the History of International Relations*, New York: Praeger.

Rich, Norman R. 1965. *Friedrich von Holstein: Politics and Diplomacy in the Era of Bismarck and Wilhelm II*, 2 vols., Cambridge University Press.

Richardson, Lewis F. 1960a. *Arms and Insecurity*, Pittsburgh: Boxwood Press.

———. 1960b. *Statistics of Deadly Quarrels*, Pittsburgh: Boxwood Press.

Richey, Jeffrey E. [1970] "The Role of Disordering Energy in Microcosms," unpublished paper, Department of Environmental Science and Engineering, School of Public Health, University of North Carolina.

Ritter, Gerhard. 1956. *Der Schlieffenplan: Kritic Eines Mythos*, Munich: R. Oldenbourg.

———. 1965. *The German Problem*, Ohio State University Press.

Röhl, J. C. G. 1967. *Germany Without Bismarck*, University of California Press.

Rosecrance, Richard N. 1963. *Action and Reaction in World Politics: International Systems in Perspective*, Boston: Little, Brown.

Rosenau, James N., ed. 1961 (1969). *International Politics and Foreign Policy*, New York: Free Press (rev. ed., 1969).

Rosenberg, Hans. 1943. "Political and Social Consequences of the Great Depression of 1873–1896 in Central Europe," *Economic History Review*, 13:58–73.

Rummel, R. J. 1966a. "Dimensions of Dyadic War, 1820–1952," Research Report prepared in connection with research supported by the National Science Foundation (NSF G-536 and NSF GS-0956), Yale University.

———. 1966b. "Some Dimensions in the Foreign Behavior of Nations," *Journal of Peace Research*, 3:201–224.

Russell, Josiah C. 1958. *Late Ancient and Medieval Population*, Philadelphia: American Philosophical Society.

Sauvy, Alfred. 1969. *General Theory of Population*, New York: Basic Books.

Schelling, Thomas C. 1971. "The Diplomacy of Violence," in Art and Waltz, eds., 1971.

Schmitt, Bernadotte E. 1937. *The Annexation of Bosnia, 1908–1909*, Cambridge University Press.

———. 1918. *England and Germany, 1740–1914*, Princeton University Press.

Schoen, Freiherr Wilhelm Eduard von. 1922. *The Memoirs of an Ambassador*, London: Allen & Unwin.

Schumpeter, Joseph A. 1951. *Imperialism and Social Classes*, New York: Augustus M. Kelley.

Scott, Andrew M. 1961. "Challenge and Response: A Tool for the Analysis of International Affairs," in Rosenau, 1961.

Service, Elman R. 1962. *Primitive Social Organization*, New York: Random House.

Singer, J. David. 1965. "The Political Science of Human Conflict," in Elton B. McNeil, ed., *The Nature of Human Conflict*, Englewood Cliffs, N. J.: Prentice-Hall.

———. 1968. *Quantitative International Politics: Insights and Evidence*, New York: Free Press.

———. 1969a. "The Compleat Theorist: Insight Without Evidence," in Knorr and Rosenau, eds., 1969.

———. 1969b. "The Level-of-Analysis Problem in International Relations," in Rosenau, 1969.

Singer, J. David, and Melvin Small. 1970. "Alliance Aggregation and the Onset of War, 1815–1945," in *Alliances: Latent War Communities in the Contemporary World*, Frances A. Beer, ed., New York: Holt, Rinehart and Winston.

Snyder, Glenn H. 1971. "Balance of Power in the Missile Age," in Quester, 1971.

Sontag, Raymond James. 1933. *European Diplomatic History, 1871–1932*, New York: Appleton-Century.

Sprout, Harold and Margaret Sprout. 1962. *Foundations of International Politics*, Princeton, N. J.: Van Nostrand.

———. 1968a. "The Dilemma of Rising Demands and Insufficient Resources," *World Politics*, 20(4):660–693.

———. 1968b. *An Ecological Paradigm for the Study of International Politics*, Research Monograph 30, Center of International Studies, Princeton University.

Steinberg, Jonathan. 1965. *Yesterday's Deterrent*: *Tirpitz and the Birth of the German Battle Fleet*, New York: Macmillan.

Taylor, A. J. P. 1954. *The Struggle for Mastery in Europe, 1848–1918*, Oxford: Clarendon Press.

Tirpitz, Alfred von. 1919. *My Memoirs*, 2 vols., London: Hurst & Blackett.

―――. 1924–1926. *Politische Dokumente*, 2 vols., Vol. 1, Stuttgart und Berlin: Cotta'sche Buchhandlung Nachfolger; Vol. 2, Berlin: Hanseatische Verlagsanstalt.

Townsend, Mary E. 1921. *Origins of Modern German Colonialism*, dissertation published by the Faculty of Political Science, Columbia University.

―――. 1930. *The Rise and Fall of Germany's Colonial Empire*, New York: Macmillan.

Toynbee, Arnold J. 1935. *A Study of History*, 3 vols., Oxford University Press.

Turner, Henry Ashby, Jr. 1967. "Bismarck's Imperialist Venture: Anti-British in Origin?" in *Britain and Germany in Africa*, Prosser Gifford and William Roger Louis, eds., Yale University Press.

Wainstein, Leonard. 1971. "The Dreadnought Gap," in Art and Waltz, 1971.

Waltz, Kenneth N. 1959. *Man, the State, and War*, Columbia University Press.

Weber, Max. 1968. *Economy and Society*, 3 vols., New York: Bedminster Press.

Wehler, Hans Ulrich. 1969. *Bismarck und der Imperialismus*, Cologne and Berlin: Kiepenheuer and Witsch.

White, Ralph K. 1970. *Nobody Wanted War*, rev. ed., Garden City, N. Y.: Anchor Books.

Wiener, Norbert. 1956. *The Human Use of Human Beings*, Garden City, N. Y.: Doubleday.

Wilhelm II. 1922. *The Kaiser's Memoirs*, New York: Harper.

Williamson, Samuel R., Jr. 1969. *The Politics of Grand Strategy*: *Britain and France Prepare for War, 1904–1914*, Harvard University Press.

Wolfers, Arnold. 1971. "The Pole of Power and the Pole of Indifference," in Quester, 1971.

Woodward, Ernest L. 1935. *Great Britain and the German Navy*, Oxford: Clarendon Press.

Wright, Quincy. 1965. *A Study of War*, 2nd ed., University of Chicago Press.

Methodology

Aitkin, A. C. 1935. "On Least Squares and Linear Combination of Observations," *Proceedings of the Royal Society of Edinburgh*, 55:42–48.

Alker, Hayward R., Jr. 1969. "A Typology of Ecological Fallacies," in *Quantitative Ecological Analysis in the Social Sciences*, Mattei Dogan and Stein Rokkan, eds., M. I. T. Press.

Amemiya, Takeshi and Wayne Fuller. 1967. "A Comparative Study of Alternative Estimators in a Distributed Lag Model," *Econometrica*, 35(3–4):509–529.

Anderson, R. L. 1942. "Distribution of the Serial Correlation Coefficient," *Annals of Mathematical Statistics*, 13:1–13.

Anderson, T. W. and A. Rubin. 1949. "Estimation of the Parameter of a Single Equation in a Complete System of Stochastic Equations," *Annals of Mathematical Statistics*, 20:46–64.

Ando, Albert, Franklin M. Fisher and Herbert A. Simon. 1963. *Essays on the Structure of Social Science*, The M. I. T. Press.

Azar, Edward, 1970a. "Analysis of International Events," *Peace Research Reviews*, 4(1):

_____. 1970b. "The Dimensions of Violent Conflict: A Quantitative Analysis," *Peace Research Society (International), Papers* 15:122–167.

Blalock, Hubert M., Jr. 1960. *Social Statistics*, New York: McGraw-Hill.

_____. 1965. "Some Implications of Random Measurement Error for Causal Inference," American Journal of Sociology, 71(1):37–47.

Blalock, Hubert M., Jr. and Ann B. Blalock. 1968. *Methodology in Social Research*, New York: McGraw-Hill.

Campbell, Donald T. and Julian C. Stanley, eds. 1966. *Experimental and Quasi-Experimental Designs for Research*, Chicago: Rand McNally.

Choucri, Nazli. 1974. "Applications of Economic Analysis to Forecasting in International Relations," *Peace Science Society (International) Papers*, XXI:15–39.

Chow, Gregory C. 1960. "Tests of Inequality Between Sets of Coefficients in Two Linear Regressions," *Econometrica*, 28(3):591–605.

Christ, Carl F. 1960. "A Symposium on Simultaneous-Equation Estimation: Any Verdict Yet?" *Econometrica*, 28(4):835–871.

_____. 1966. *Econometric Models and Methods*, New York: Wiley.

Cochrane, Donald and Guy Orcutt. 1949. "Application of Least Squares Regression to Relationships Containing Auto-Correlated Error Terms," *Journal of the American Statistical Association*, 44(245):32–61.

Coombs, Clyde H. 1964. *A Theory of Data*, New York: Wiley.

Davies, James C. 1962. "Toward a Theory of Revolution," *American Sociological Review*, 27(1):5–18.

Deber, Raisa B. 1974. "Missing Data in Events Analysis: The Problem and Suggested Solutions," in Edward E. Azar and Joseph Ben-Dak, eds., *Theory and Practice of Events Research Studies in Internation Actions and Interactions*, New York: Gordon and Breach.

Deusenberry, James *et al.*, eds, 1965. *The Brookings-SSRC Quarterly Econometric Model of the United States*, Chicago: Rand McNally.

_____. 1969. *The Brookings Model: Some Further Results*, Chicago: Rand McNally.

Durbin, J. and G. S. Watson. 1950. "Testing for serial Correlation in Least-Squares Regression: I," *Biometrika*, 37:409–428.

_____. 1951. "Testing for Serial Correlation in Least-Square Regression:II," *Biometrika*, 38:159–178.

Eisner, Mark and Robert Pindyck. 1972. "A Generalized Approach to Estimation as Implemented in the TROLL/1 System," Computer Research Center for Economics and Management Science, National Bureau of Economic Research, Cambridge, Mass. (unpublished).

Fair, Ray C. 1970. "The Estimation of Simultaneous Equation Models with Lagged Endogenous Variables and First-Order Serially Correlated Errors," *Econometrica*, 38(3):507–516.

Farrar, D. E. and R. R. Glauber. 1967. "Multicollinearity in Regression Analysis: The Problem Recited," *Review of Economics and Statistics*, 49(1):92–107

Fennessey, James. 1968. "The General Linear Model: A New Perspective on Some Familiar Topics," *American Journal of Sociology*, 74(1):1–27.

Fisher, Franklin M. 1959. "Generalization of the Rank and Order Conditions for Identifiability," *Econometrica*, 27(3):431–447.

———. 1960. "On the Analysis of History and the Interdependence of the Social Sciences," *Philosophy of Science*, 27:147–158.

———. 1962. *A Priori Information and Time Series Analysis*, Amsterdam: North Holland Publishing.

———. 1963a. "On the Cost of Approximate Specification in Simultaneous Equation Estimation," in Ando, Fisher and Simon, 1963.

———. 1963b. "Two Theorems on Ceritis Paribus in the Analysis of Dynamics Systems," in Ando, Fisher, and Simon, 1963.

———. 1963c. "Uncorrelated Disturbances and Identifiability Criteria," *International Economic Review*, 4(2):134–152.

———. 1965. "Dynamic Structure and Estimation in Economy-Wide Econometric Models," Deusenberry *et al.*, 1965.

———. 1966. *The Identification Problem in Econometrics*, New York: McGraw-Hill.

———. 1970a. "Simultaneous Estimation: The State of the Art," M. I. T. Working Paper, No. 55, Department of Economics.

———. 1970b. "Tests of Inequality Between Sets of Coefficients in Two Linear Regressions: An Expository Note," *Econometrica*, 38:361–366.

Fishman, George S. 1966. *Problems in the Statistical Analysis of Time Series Generated by Simulation Models*, RAND Corporation, RM-4880-PR, Santa Monica.

Goldberger, Arthur S. 1964. *Econometric Theory*, New York: Wiley.

Goldfeld, Stephen M. and Richard E. Quandt. 1968. "Nonlinear Simultaneous Equations: Estimation and Prediction," *International Economic Review*, 9(1):113–136.

Goodman, Ronald, Jeffrey Hart, and Richard N. Rosecrance. No date. "Testing International Theory: Methods and Data in Situational Analysis of International Politics," Peace Studies Program, Cornell University, Occasional Papers No. 2 (unpublished).

Griliches, Zvi. 1961. "A Note on Serial Correlation Bias in Estimates of Distributed Lags," *Econometrica*, 29(1):65–73.

———. 1967. "Distributed Lags: A Survey," *Econometrica*, 35(1):16–49.

Hannan, E. J. 1960. *Time-Series Analysis*, London: Methuen.

Harberger, A. D. 1953. "On the Estimation of Economic Parameters," Cowles Commission Discussion Paper, Economics No. 2088 (unpublished).

Hibbs, Douglas A. Jr. 1973. *Mass Political Violence: A Cross-National Causal Analysis*, New York: Wiley.

_____. 1974. "Problems of Statistical Estimation and Causal Inference in Dynamic, Time Series Regression Models," in *Sociological Methodology 1973–1974*, H. L. Costner, ed., San Francisco: Jossey-Bass.

Jenkins, G. M. 1961. "General Considerations in the Analysis of Spectra," *Technometrics*, 32(2):133–166.

Johnston, John. 1972. *Econometric Methods*, 2nd ed., New York: McGraw-Hill.

Kendall, M. G. 1954. "Note on Bias in the Estimation of Autocorrelation," *Biometrika*, 41:403–404.

Klein, Lawrence R. 1971. "Whither Econometrics?" *Journal of the American Statistical Association*, 66(334):415–421.

Kramer, Gerald H. 1971. "Short-Term Fluctuations in U. S. Voting Behavior, 1896–1964," Cowles Foundation Paper No. 344, Cowles Foundation for Research in Economics, Yale University.

Kuh, Edwin and John R. Meyer. 1957. "How Extraneous are Extraneous Estimates?" *Review of Economics and Statistics*, 39(4):380–393.

Liviatan, N. 1963. "Consistent Estimation of Distributed Lags," *International Economic Review*, 4(1):44–52.

Marquardt, D. W. 1963. "An Algorithm for Least-Squares Estimation of Nonlinear Parameters," *Journal of the Society of Industrial Applied Mathematics*, 11(2):431–441.

Moses, Lincoln E., Richard A. Brody, Ole R. Holsti, Joseph B. Kadane and Jeffrey S. Milstein. 1967. "Scaling Data on Inter-Nation Action," *Science*, 156(3775):1054–1059.

Naylor, Th. H., K. Wertz, and Thomas Wonnacott. 1968. "Some Methods for Evaluating the Effects of Economic Policies Using Simulation Experiments," *Review of the International Statistical Institute*, 36(2):184–200.

Nerlove, Marc and Kenneth F. Wallis. 1966. "Use of the Durbin-Watson Statistic in Inappropriate Situations," *Econometrica*, 34(1):235–238.

Orcutt, Guy H. 1952. "Actions, Consequences, and Causal Relations," *Review of Economics and Statistics*, 34:305–313.

Orcutt, Guy H. and Donald Cochrane. 1949. "A Sampling Study of the Merits of Auto-regressive and Reduced Form Transformations in Regression Analysis," *Journal of the American Statistical Association*, 44(247):356–372.

Orcutt, Guy H. and Herbert S. Winokur, Jr. 1969. "First-Order Autoregression: Inference, Estimation, and Prediction," *Econometrica*, 37(1):1–14.

Pindyck, Robert S. 1973. "A Small Quarterly Model of the U. S. Economy," in *Optimal Planning for Economic Stabilization*, Amsterdam: North Holland Publishing.

Rao, Potluri and Roger LeRoy Miller. 1971. *Applied Econometrics*, Belmont, Calif.: Wadsworth.

Rao, Potluri and Zvi Griliches. 1969. "Small-Sample Properties of Several Two-Stage Regression Methods in the Context of Autocorrelated Errors," *Journal of the American Statistical Association*, 64(325):253–272.

Sargent, Thomas J. 1968. "Some Evidence on the Small-Sample Properties of Distributed Lag Estimators in the Presence of Autocorrelated Disturbances," *Review of Economics and Statistics*, 50:87–95.

Schink, William A. and John S. Y. Chiu. 1966. "A Simulation Study of Effects of Multicollinearity and Autocorrelation on Estimates of Parameters," *Journal of Financial and Quantitative Analysis*, 1(2):36–67.

Theil, Henri. 1961. *Economic Forecasts and Policy*, Amsterdam: North Holland Publishing.

———. 1963. "On the Use of Incomplete Prior Information in Regression Analysis," *Journal of the American Statistical Association*, 58(302):401–414.

———. 1970. "On the Estimation of Relationships Involving Qualitative Variables," *American Journal of Sociology*, 76(1):103–154.

———. 1971. *Principles of Econometrics*, New York: Wiley.

Theil, Henri and A. S. Goldberger. 1961. "On Pure and Mixed Statistical Estimation in Economics," *International Economic Review*, 2(1):65–78.

TROLL/1 User's Guide. Computer Research Center for Economics and Management Science, National Bureau of Economic Research, Inc., Cambridge, Mass. (prepublication version, 1972).

Wallis, Kenneth. 1967. "Lagged Dependent Variables and Serially Correlated Errors: A Reappraisal of Three-Pass Least Squares," *The Review of Economics and Statistics*, 49(4):555–567.

Wildavsky, Aron B. 1964. *The Politics of the Budgetary Process*, Boston: Little, Brown.

Wise, J. 1955. "The Autocorrelation Function and the Spectral Density Function," *Biometrika*, 42:151–159.

Wonnacott, Roland J. and Thomas H. Wonnacott. 1970. *Econometrics*, New York: Wiley.

Zellner, Arnold. 1962. "An Efficient Method of Estimating Seemingly Unrelated Regressions and Tests for Aggregation Bias," *American Statistical Journal*, 57(298):348–368.

Index

DATE DUE

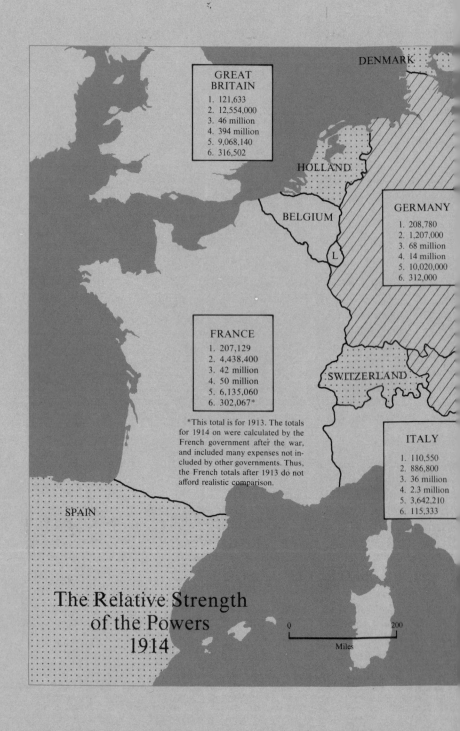

GREAT BRITAIN
1. 121,633
2. 12,554,000
3. 46 million
4. 394 million
5. 9,068,140
6. 316,502

DENMARK

HOLLAND

BELGIUM

L

GERMANY
1. 208,780
2. 1,207,000
3. 68 million
4. 14 million
5. 10,020,000
6. 312,000

FRANCE
1. 207,129
2. 4,438,400
3. 42 million
4. 50 million
5. 6,135,060
6. 302,067*

SWITZERLAND

*This total is for 1913. The totals for 1914 on were calculated by the French government after the war, and included many expenses not included by other governments. Thus, the French totals after 1913 do not afford realistic comparison.

ITALY
1. 110,550
2. 886,800
3. 36 million
4. 2.3 million
5. 3,642,210
6. 115,333

SPAIN

The Relative Strength
of the Powers
1914

0   200
Miles